The Cinema of Michael Powell

The Cinema of Michael Powell

International Perspectives on an English Film-Maker

Edited by
Ian Christie and Andrew Moor

 Publishing

This collection is dedicated to the memory of Raymond Durgnat
(1932–2002), pioneer advocate of taking Powell seriously and one of
the most trenchant critics of his work. We miss his presence in this book
and his lifelong commitment to writing and teaching about British cinema
in an international perspective.

This edition first published in 2005 by the
British Film Institute
21 Stephen Street
London W1T 1LN

The British Film Institute promotes greater understanding and appreciation of, and
access to, film and moving image culture in the UK.

Cover design: ketchup
Cover Illustration: (front) Karlheinz Böhm as Mark Lewis in *Peeping Tom* (1960).

Set by D R Bungay Associates, Burghfield, Berkshire
Printed in the UK by St Edmundsbury Press, Bury St Edmunds, Suffolk

British Library Cataloguing-in-Publication Data

A catalogue record for this book is available from the British Library
ISBN 1-84457-094-0 (pb)
ISBN 1-84457-093-2 (hb)

Contents

Collaborators

Gender Matters

Notes on Contributors

Nannette Aldred teaches at the University of Sussex. Her publications include 'A Short History of the ICA' in Davies and Sinfield, eds, *British Culture of the Postwar: an introduction to literature and society 1945-99* (Routledge, 2000); 'A Canterbury Tale: Powell and Pressburger's Film Fantasies of Britain' in David Mellor, ed., *A Paradise Lost: The Neo-Romantic Imagination in Britain 1935-55* (Barbican/Lund Humphries, 1987) and a forthcoming essay on Herbert Read.

Charles Barr is Professor of Film and Television at the University of East Anglia. His writings on British Cinema include *Ealing Studios* (1977: 3rd edition, 1999), *English Hitchcock* (Cameron and Hollis, 1999), and, as editor, *All Our Yesterdays: 90 Years of British Cinema* (BFI, 1986). He collaborated with Stephen Frears on the BFI/Channel 4 centenary programme, *Typically British* (1995).

Ian Christie is Professor of Film and Media History at Birkbeck, University of London, and co-editor of *Film Studies* (MUP). He has lectured, written and broadcast extensively on Powell and Pressburger, and publications include *Powell, Pressburger and Others* (BFI, 1978); *Arrows of Desire: the Films of Michael Powell and Emeric Pressburger* (Waterstone, 1985; 2nd edn, Faber, 1994); the screenplay of *The Life and Death of Colonel Blimp* (Faber, 1994) and *A Matter of Life and Death* (BFI, 2000)

Tom Gunning is Professor in the Department of Art History at the University of Chicago. His publications include *D. W. Griffith and the Origins of American Narrative Film: The Early Years at Biograph* (University of Illinois Press, 1991), *The Films of Fritz Lang* (BFI, 2000), and numerous essays on early cinema.

Graeme Harper is Professor and Head of the School of Creative Arts, Film and Media at the University of Portsmouth. He is the author of *Swallowing Film* (DVDX, 2000), *Comedy, Fantasy and Colonialism* (Continuum, 2000) and *Dancing on the Moon* (Eclipse, 2003); and co-editor of *Signs of Life: Medicine and Cinema* (Wallflower, 2005) and of the international journals *Studies in European Cinema* (Intellect) and *New Writing* (MLM).

Philip Horne is Professor of English at University College London and a regular writer on film for *Sight and Sound*. In addition to articles on telephones and literature, zombies and consumer culture, Emily Dickinson and Scorsese, his publications include *Henry James and Revision: The New York Edition*, *Henry James: A Life in Letters*, and editions of James's *The Tragic Muse* and Dickens's *Oliver Twist*.

Jean-Louis Leutrat is a former President of Paris III-Sorbonne Nouvelle, where he teaches cinema history and aesthetics in the department of cinema studies. He has published books on Jean-Luc Godard, Alain Resnais, John Ford, and Jean Renoir; and his study of *L'année dernière à Marienbad* appeared in translation in the BFI Film Classics series in 2001.

Andrew Moor lectures in Film at the University of Wales, Bangor. He is the author of *Powell and Pressburger: A Cinema of Magic Spaces* (I.B. Tauris, 2005) and co-editor of *Signs of Life: Medicine and Cinema* (Wallflower Press, 2005). He has published various essays and articles on Derek Jarman, Anton Walbrook, Neil Jordan, Hein Heckroth and Emeric Pressburger.

Laura Mulvey is Professor of Film Studies at Birkbeck, University of London and an independent filmmaker and curator as well as theorist. She has published two collection of essays, *Visual and Other Pleasures* (Macmillan/Indiana, 1989, with a new edition due in 2005) and *Fetishism and Curiosity* (BFI, 1996). Her study of *Citizen Kane* appeared as a BFI Film Classic in 1992 and *Death 24 times a second: stillness in the moving image* will be pubished in 2005.

Thelma Schoonmaker-Powell is a distinguished film editor, who has won the Academy Award twice: in 1980 for *Raging Bull* and in 2005 for *The Aviator*, both directed by Martin Scorsese, with whom she has worked exclusively since 1980. She married Michael Powell in 1984 and worked closely with him on the two volumes of his memoirs, *A Life in Movies* and *Million Dollar Movie*.

Robert Shail is a lecturer in film studies at the University of Wales Lampeter. He has published a number of essays on stardom and masculinity in both British and.American cinema. He is currently working on a study of Stanley Baker for the University of Wales Press and a critical guide to British directors for Edinburgh University Press.

Lesley Stern is Professor of Film in the Department of Visual Arts at the University of California, San Diego. She is the author of *The Scorsese Connection* (BFI, 1995) and *The Smoking Book* (Chicago, 1999) and is co-editor of *Falling For You: Essays on Cinema and Performance* (Power Publications, Sydney, 1999). She writes fiction and has published extensively in the areas of film, performance, photography, cultural history and feminism.

Natacha Thiéry has completed her doctorate on Powell and Pressburger's films of the 1940s and 1950s at Paris III-Sorbonne Nouvelle and is the organiser of a conference 'Michael Powell, la passion iconoclaste du cinéma' in Paris in June 2005. She edited a special issue of *La lettre de la maison française d'Oxford* on British cinema in 1999 and has published a study of Lubitsch's American comedies.

ACKNOWLEGMENTS

Thanks are due to Thelma Schoonmaker-Powell and Marianne Bower for help with illustrations. All quotations from unpublished manuscripts by Powell and Pressburger appear by courtesy of the estates of Michael Powell and Emeric Pressburger. Andrew Moor wishes to acknowledge the help of Janet Moat, Keeper of BFI Special Collections, the Arts and Humanities Research Council for funding research leave, and Greg Thorpe for much else. Ian Christie owes his usual but heartfelt thanks to Patsy for helping see it through. Particular thanks are due to Rob White and Tom Cabot for speeding this long-mooted book to its final wrap.

Introduction

Ian Christie and Andrew Moor

In 1915, a young boy – technically a Man of Kent, as he was born east of the Medway – sat on his pony and prepared to take part in a cavalry charge, having attached himself to a mounted regiment that was waiting to be sent off to war. Michael Powell's account of that exhilarating experience, vividly described in the memoir he wrote in the 1980s, helps to remind us that he belonged to a very different world from the one now contemplating the centenary of his birth.[1] It places him between the pioneers, who mostly moved from the stage into the new business of moving pictures – Griffith, Chaplin, DeMille, Murnau, Eisenstein – and the generation of film-makers born after the First World War, who grew up with sound cinema and would become the stalwarts of the 1940s and 50s, as well as the founders of new national cinemas.

But Powell was different. He was lucky enough to serve an apprenticeship with Rex Ingram's expatriate Hollywood company in Nice; lucky to find a niche in British film-making, just as it was being reinvigorated by quota legislation in the early 1930s; lucky to be noticed by Alexander Korda shortly before the Second World War, in time to find Emeric Pressburger and with him create some of the most enduring British productions of the 1940s. And then – unlucky to stay in Britain while production opportunities dwindled during the 1950s; unlucky to be out of step with the new themes and styles of the 1960s; unlucky in his ventures abroad; and unlucky to have his ideas for television films ignored. Writing his memoirs on a grand scale – engaging, indiscreet, poetic and infuriating in varying measures, as John Ellis notes here – gave his career an unexpected final act: a happy ending, though tinged with the frustration that he had been unable to work as a film-maker for nearly two decades.

The period of this final act coincided with the rise of academic film studies in the UK and North America. But the pioneers of such study were, for the most part, hostile to, or contemptuous of, British cinema. The critics who launched *Movie* in the 1960s had inherited many of the prejudices against the native film-making of their forerunners at Oxford in the late 1940s, the editors of *Sequence*. After the release of *The Red Shoes* in 1948, *Sequence* wrote:

> Few directors have striven so consistently as Michael Powell and Emeric Pressburger to be novel, experimental, surprising; and few have been so consistently unsuccessful. However their subjects vary, the qualities of their films remain the same, their failure constant.[2]

Sequence recommended 'a study of Minnelli's films' to avoid the 'elementary mistake' of *The Red Shoes*, before turning 'with relief' to the achievements of Colonial Office and Board of Trade documentaries. Fourteen years later, *Movie* would continue to prefer American cinema to British, making an exception only for Hitchcock, who was by then regarded as a Hollywood film-maker.[3] When Robin Wood published his pioneering study *Hitchcock's Films* in 1965, he dealt only with films from *Strangers on a Train* to *Marnie*, noting that 'one day perhaps we shall rediscover Hitchcock's British films … they are so overshadowed by his recent development as to seem little more than "prentice work"'.[4]

During the 1970s and 80s, when film studies was preoccupied with theoretical and methodological debates, its canons of taste remained largely unexamined and routinely excluded all British cinema. Discussions of authorship, genre and spectatorship were conducted with examples mostly drawn from films and film-makers validated in the 1960s, by *Cahiers du cinéma*, *Movie* and Andrew Sarris.[5] Later, as British cinema and television moved onto the broadening academic agenda, their acceptance was dominated by a dichotomy between 'realism' and 'anti-realism'. Film-makers who did not fit the mould of realism could be redeemed by being declared 'anti-realists', but in this they ran the risk of seeming insubstantial or – returning to an old objection to Powell and Pressburger – erratic.[6] Ironically, it was the emergence of another critical category, the 'heritage film', that probably did most to legitimise the study of Powell and Pressburger's work in the 1990s. Although the term had first been used to refer to Second World War films that included The Archers' *A Canterbury Tale*, it came to be applied most widely as a critical (in the pejorative sense) position from which to discuss literary adaptations of the 1980s and 90s.[7] In this new academic climate, the growing popularity of the Powell–Pressburger films could be acknowledged and addressed, even if it often meant projecting onto them later concepts of the post-colonial and the commodification of nostalgia.

The films became popular as they were restored and became easier to see, initially in repertory and festival screenings, and later through video and DVD releases. Indeed, it seems likely that their growing reputation owed almost as much to new means of access as it did to the enthusiastic endorsement of such influential figures as Martin Scorsese, Francis Coppola and Bertrand Tavernier. Polls and lists of 'greatest films' became popular in the 1990s, many stimulated by the celebration of the centenary of cinema. In the *Time Out* '100 Best Films' poll of 1995, *A Matter of Life and Death* came surprisingly high in thirteenth place, tying with Carné's *Les Enfants du paradis*, and followed by *The Life and Death of Colonel Blimp* at number

23, with *Black Narcissus* and *The Red Shoes* tying at number 72. A similar exercise conducted by the British Film Institute in 1999 rated the same films high in two 'Top 100' lists of British films, with the addition of *A Canterbury Tale*, *Peeping Tom*, *Blimp* and *I Know Where I'm Going!*.[8] The DVD release in 2004 of Powell's breakthrough film *The Edge of the World* (1937) produced a remarkable number of enthusiastic reviews in America, demonstrating how significant this new format continues to be in furthering filmic reputations.

However familiar and popular at least some of Powell's films have become during the last decade, critical discussion and research have not kept pace. Despite a number of biographically based monographs,[9] this collection represents the first gathering of critical and interpretive essays devoted to its subject since a slim volume produced by the British Film Institute in 1978.[10] The occasion is certainly to celebrate Michael Powell's centenary, but this has also provided an opportunity for us – who have both produced our own monographs and contributions to other collections – to commission new writing from acknowledged experts in the field as well as from, we hope, unexpected commentators. We have not tried to survey the full range of Powell's work, preferring to let our authors follow their own paths, but have sought to create an international view, with American, Australian and French, as well as British, perspectives.[11]

Powell with his future wife Frankie Reidy as the yachting couple whose arrival on Foula introduces *The Edge of the World*.

But should we say 'British', when we actually mean English (and Northern Irish, in the case of Ian Christie)? As the discussion of Powell's work has been so dominated by imputations and questionings of 'Britishness', we have chosen to present him as an English film-maker, to raise the issues of belonging and owning, as well as to indicate our dissatisfaction with the imperious term 'British'. Powell, who enjoyed quoting Kipling's line 'what should they know of England who only England know?', would certainly have approved. If he no longer needs to be defended from the criticism that he failed to measure up to the obligations of a 'British film-maker', this does not mean that film scholars can ignore nationality, as clearly, however much global, regional, continental and virtual spaces figure in our lives, and other allegiances condition our sense of who and where we are, national identity still pervades our consciousness.

Powell was unquestionably produced by a pre-world war English Edwardian culture, but this was immediately coloured by the global parameters of the British Empire, an affinity for and close familiarity with continental Europe, and a fascination, filtered through Hollywood, with the United States. This may explain why the English landscape itself concerned him less than might be expected. Against his two impassioned celebrations of the Scottish Highlands and islands, *Edge of the World* and *I Know Where I'm Going!*, we can set only two English location-based films: *Gone to Earth*, flooded with a Celtic mysticism spilling into Shropshire from Wales, and *A Canterbury Tale*, which certainly drew on his boyhood memories of Kent, but which views this territory through a series of prisms.[12] Otherwise, Powell's landscapes are those of the minds and imaginations of his characters, often figured by a striking topographic feature, which may be 'real', as in the beach of Staunton Sands in *A Matter of Life and Death* and Chesil Beach in *The Small Back Room*, but are more often constructed, like the celebrated 'Himalayan' convent of *Black Narcissus*.

The writers of some of the essays that follow consciously draw on some of the theoretical languages and perspectives that help us think through what troubles our society most. Natacha Thiéry's and Robert Shail's pieces, on the images of women and men in the films, are both clearly influenced by the rise of gender studies, albeit of different varieties, while Graeme Harper's essay on Powell's late Australian films draws on post-colonial ideas to highlight how far both cinema (globally) and its theorisation have developed within a distinctly European frame of reference. Ian Christie considers *A Canterbury Tale* in the light of approaches such as cultural geography, and local and social history, seeking to explicate its many layers of meaning. And Andrew Moor sees Powell and Pressburger's work through the lens of contemporary ideas about sexuality to argue that gay and queer encounters with them experience less resistance than might be expected, precisely because the films are 'open texts' and because they articulate such a range of contrary attitudes.

Just as Powell and Pressburger's films in a sense *disprove* the totalising impetus behind wartime and post-war prescriptions of British cinema, by being both singularly British/English *and* stylistically 'other', it might be argued that by making apparently mainstream commercial films that deploy a gamut of cinematic styles normally associated with 'art-house' modernist cinema, they also challenge universalist theories of 'classical cinema'.[13] Here are films made during the heyday of classical cinema that observe its typical aesthetics as much by breaching as observing them. This is not zero-degree, invisible film-making; neither are its expected audiences the blank receptors that classical cinema implies. The theories of the ideological effects of classical cinema that achieved currency from the late 1960s were motivated by counter-establishment politics and a range of 'liberation' movements; and, polemically, it became important to create a binary opposition between commercial cinema and its obverse, radical (or anti-) cinema. But it would be wrong to put Powell and Pressburger into the latter category just because they do not fit into the former. Powell's 'spectacle' may constantly draw attention to itself, and thereby take on meta-cinematic meanings, but the spectacle is also clearly pleasurable in itself ('How *did* they do that!').

The key dynamic in Powell's work might not, therefore, be voyeurism – despite conspicuous 'eye imagery' from *The Thief of Bagdad* to *Peeping Tom* – but exhibitionism, a parading of cinematic technique that, in its dialogue with its spectators, expects a response from them, somewhere between belief and disbelief. Lesley

Exhibitionism in *The Thief of Bagdad*: the Djinn's giant foot threatens to crush Sabu in a sequence that Powell probably directed.

Stern's essay in this collection, and her work elsewhere on Powell and Pressburger's 'operality', explores the nature of the visual discourse in play in their films and its ability to make time 'visible', in a Deleuzian sense. But Laura Mulvey's detailed textual commentary on *Peeping Tom* also makes clear how profound and complex is that film's exploration of the dialectic of sadism and masochism, voyeurism and exhibitionism; thus providing a strong theoretical underpinning for the film's cult status as a meditation on the nature of cinema itself.

One of the central critical questions about Powell is the nature of his working relationship with Emeric Pressburger, a question that continues to trouble the concept of authorship and, despite its singular title, this collection does not seek to deny Pressburger's contribution to their jointly signed films. However, both Charles Barr and Ian Christie try to distinguish Pressburger's role in their essays, not to diminish it, but to identify his characteristic stylistic peculiarities. They find an author fascinated by patterning, by the mechanics of narrative, by the devices through which stories are told. In showing Pressburger to be a writer who parades both his curiosity and his understanding of narrative *form*, they emphasise interests that meshed ideally with Powell's own self-conscious visual rhetoric. If partnership was at the heart of Powell and Pressburger's production company, The Archers, Nanette Aldred reminds us in her essay on the designer Hein Heckroth that this was governed by an idealised sense of collaboration, and that in its happiest projects, individual authorship merged into a concerted whole. We are acutely conscious that much more work remains to be done on The Archers' other key personnel.

Philip Horne stresses how much *A Matter of Life and Death* belongs to a tradition of narrative that deals with what cannot be shown literally or discussed in 'realist' terms; yet the very precision of its fantasy and 'machinery' indicates how profoundly its makers had engaged with the emotions of those who had survived the Second World War. In a highly personal and equally wide-ranging essay, Tom Gunning follows in the tradition of work by Stanley Cavell and Virginia Wright Wexman that explores how films mirror courtship and marriage rituals, claiming that *I Know Where I'm Going!* 'possesses the secret of every love affair' in its combination of the universal and particular, as well as being a film one falls in love with, and perhaps through. But he also places it in a much wider context of narratology and myth, helping to counteract any parochial tendencies in a purely domestic celebration of Powell and Pressburger's work. So too does Jean-Louis Leutrat, approaching *Black Narcissus* in terms of its sensuous appeal, noting specific affiliations with Pre-Raphaelitism that seem to have eluded most English critics. Leutrat also follows through the premise of the film's title, revealing perfume as 'the horror film subject par excellence', and tracing how its intangible presence here testifies to the 'power of that other kind of visuality at the heart of cinema'.

What unites the different approaches collected here is a belief that The Archers' and many of Powell's other films invite critical analysis on the highest level. Stepping beyond a peculiarly 'British' tradition that persists in regarding them as eccentric or excessive, these essays take the films seriously as works of art, which means –

as Richard Allen recently argued when introducing a Hitchcock centenary collection – as 'objects valued in their uniqueness and specificity for what they are and what they say'.[14] We believe Powell and Pressburger would have wanted to be judged by these standards alone.

NOTES

1. Michael Powell, *A Life in Movies: An Autobiography* (1986), London: Faber & Faber, 1992, p. 63.
2. *Sequence* 5, Autumn 1948.
3. The first issue of *Movie*, in May 1962, published a chart classifying directors in which Michael Powell was placed in the fifth category (of six), labelled 'Competent or Ambitious', along with Carol Reed and David Lean.
4. Robin Wood, *Hitchcock's Films*, London: A. Zwemmer, 1965, p. 29.
5. Andrew Sarris's pithy judgments on directors played an important part in establishing their reputations for the first generation who read his *The American Cinema: Directors and Direction, 1929–68*, New York: Dutton, 1970.
6. See, for instance, Alan Lovell, 'The British Cinema: The Known Cinema?', in Robert Murphy, ed., *The British Cinema Book*, 2nd edn, London: British Film Institute, 2002, p. 203: 'Michael Powell … has been a key figure in the critical attempt to construct a British anti-realist cinema'.
7. See Sheldon Hall, 'The Wrong Sort of Cinema: Refashioning the Heritage Film Debate', in Murphy, ed., *British Cinema Book*, pp. 191–9.
8. BFI Top 100 rating, with BFI Library Users' Poll rank in brackets: *The Red Shoes* 9 (12); *A Matter of Life and Death* 20 (2); *Peeping Tom* 78 (26); *A Canterbury Tale* (21); *Life and Death of Colonel Blimp* (47); *The Thief of Bagdad* (50); *I Know Where I'm Going!* (67).
9. Monographs include: Ian Christie, *Arrows of Desire: The films of Michael Powell and Emeric Pressburger*, London: Waterstone, 1985 (2nd edn, revised, Faber & Faber, 1994); James Howard, *Michael Powell*, London: Batsford, 1996; Scott Salwolke, *The Films of Michael Powell and the Archers*, Lanham, MD: Scarecrow Press, 1997; Llorenç Esteve, *Michael Powell y Emeric Pressburger*, Madrid: Cátedra, 2002; Andrew Moor, *Powell and Pressburger: A Cinema of Magic Spaces*, London: I. B. Tauris, 2005.
10. Ian Christie, ed., *Powell, Pressburger and Others*, London: BFI, 1978. This contained short essays by Raymond Durgnat, Thomas Elsaesser and Jean Paul Török, and a detailed study of *A Matter of Life and Death* by John Ellis that remains indispensable. Other booklet-size studies appeared in the following years, including: Roland Cosandey, ed., *Powell & Pressburger*, Locarno Festival, 1982; Fritz Gottler *et al.*, eds, *Living Cinema: Powell and Pressburger*, Munich: Filmwelt Verleih, 1982; E. Martini, ed., *Powell and Pressburger*, Bergamo Film Meeting, 1986.
11. The most significant omission is any substantial discussion of Powell's career up to *The Spy in Black* and *The Thief of Bagdad*, or after *The Age of Consent*. For a brief account of the 1930s films discovered during the late 1980s and early 90s, see the Postscript to *Arrows of Desire* (1994); and for a preliminary survey of Powell's later projects, including *The Tempest*, see the special dossier in *Film Studies* 2, Spring 2000, pp. 77–104.

12. Several more could certainly be regarded as 'London films': *Contraband, The Life and Death of Colonel Blimp, Peeping Tom, The Queen's Guards* and *The Boy Who Turned Yellow*.

13. We might recall Martin Scorsese's remark: 'I always felt that the most successful experimental film-makers in the world were Michael and Emeric', Foreword to *Arrows of Desire* (1994), p. xix.

14. Richard Allen and Sam Ishi-Gonzáles, eds, *Hitchcock Past and Future*, London: Routledge, 2004, p. 2. This book was based on a 1999 Hitchcock centennial conference.

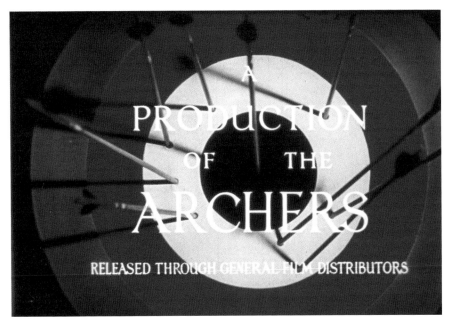

The Archers' trademark target. 'The idea was: we always aim for the centre but we sometimes miss it' (Powell, 1977).

A tale of two studios: Mark Lewis (Carl Boehm) with the model Pamela Green in a Soho glamour studio in *Peeping Tom*.

Jean Simmons as Kanchi in *Black Narcissus*, a reincarnation of the figures depicted on the wall of the former house of women, contrasted with the image of the Virgin in this studio portrait.

Sister Ruth (Kathleen Byron) flaunts her crimson lipstick in *Black Narcissus.*

Mark is fascinated by Lorraine's (Susan Travers) deformed face and wants to film her (*Peeping Tom*).

The seductive Giulietta (Ludmilla Tcherina) seems to rise from the waters of the Venetian lagoon in *The Tales of Hoffmann.*

SUBJECTS OF DESIRE (see chapter 14): **1.** Clodagh amazed by Ruth (*Black Narcissus*); **2.** Dean's virility and Ruth's agitation (*Black Narcissus*); **3.** Flowers (*Gone to Earth*); **4.** Defloration (*Gone to Earth*); **5.** Ruth's blackout, dissolving into red (*Black Narcissus*); **6.** Vicky's fall before her death (*The Red Shoes*); **7.** Crossing the frame: Hazel and the vixen (*Gone to Earth*); **8.** Hounds excited on the edge of the abyss (*Gone to Earth*).

Law in action: the heavenly court visits Peter's operation on earth in *A Matter of Life and Death.*

'A storm from the mountains lashing the sea into great waves… of applause. I can see nothing beyond the footlights except Lermontov on his lonely rock' (*The Red Shoes*, a novel by Michael Powell and Emeric Pressburger).

The poet bemused by the showman's trickery: one of Heckroth's sets for *The Tales of Hoffmann.*

The cartoon figure of 'Blimp' poignantly incarnated by Roger Livesey in *The Life and Death of Colonel Blimp*.

Anton Walbrook as the 'aristo-dandy' Lermontov in *The Red Shoes*: charmingly dismissive, ultra precise, masking his feelings.

Robert Helpmann, in one of his three roles in *The Tales of Hoffmann*, as the sinister, epicene Dr Dapertutto.

Pamela Brown, with whom Powell shared his later life until her death in 1975.
(Photograph by Powell)

Powell with Aki Kaurismäki at Lee Cottage, having given him his own copy of Henri Murger's
Scènes de la vie de bohème, when Kaurismäki told him this would be his next film.

Alfred Junge's design for the celestial staircase in *A Matter of Life and Death*.

One of Hein Heckroth's oil sketches for the phantasmagoric ballet sequence in *The Red Shoes*.

For *The Tales of Hoffmann*, Heckroth created three distinct milieux that mark the three stages of the poet's disenchantment, each evoking a different painterly world.

Beginnings and Endings

1 At the Edge of Our World

John Ellis

Michael Powell was a European film-maker whose misfortune it was to be British. As the last act of his long and fraught career, he wrote his autobiography. The second half, *Million Dollar Movie*, is an entirely un-British confection.[1] At once boastful and self-pitying, it is a last desperate act of remembrance by a much-wronged man. When I first met him, his financial embarrassment was plain to see; yet equally conspicuous was his stubborn, suspicious pride. Pride invites a humbling, perhaps, but little in Powell's conduct would justify the miserable condition in which he found himself in the 1970s.

However badly he was treated by the British cinematic establishment – and undoubtedly he was – the abiding paradox of Powell is his deep love of Britain. As a film-maker he may be European, a dramaturg; but as a citizen he was a British patriot, the son of a Kentish farmer. Or is it such a paradox?

Much of Powell's patriotism seems uncannily like that of Sir Alexander Korda, the patriotism of an outsider trying to get in, rather than of a dyed-in-the-wool Englishman. Powell appreciated Korda (apart from his backstairs business deals), and worked happily in an extraordinary collaboration with another Hungarian who made England his home: Emeric Pressburger. Powell remarks on Pressburger's eagerness to assimilate every nuance of the English language, to be more English than the English. One look at the photographs of Powell in his autobiography would make you think the same about him.

Powell and Pressburger collaborated closely for so long because they were both trying to make sense of the culture where they lived, a culture where they both felt like outsiders. Powell could make much of his authentic Englishness, of course. But even in his paean to the Kent of his childhood that begins *A Life in Movies*, the first volume of his autobiography, there is an almost resentful sense of being left out. In reality, Powell was just as much the son of a Riviera hotelier as he was of a Kentish farmer.

A deep sense of love for Britain and its inhabitants runs through all the Powell–Pressburger films set in Britain. But this love if suffused with a peculiar nervousness. An unease lurks beneath, as though both Pressburger and Powell felt that they were permitted a place in Britain only within certain limits. They could criticise, they could comment, they could even make jokes; but somewhere or other, there were boundaries that they could not cross unpunished. During their collaboration, they held each other just within those limits. Then, when they drifted apart, Pressburger stepped too far back into whimsy, and Powell overstepped with *Peeping Tom*.

Powell and Pressburger were both super-patriots, each for his own reasons. Yet what was it that drove them to make such fundamentally un-British films, to associate with European artists, 'ballet types' and the rest? They certainly shared a full-blooded, rather middlebrow, romantic taste, which marks them out from the mainstream of British opinion. It is a cliché based on fact that the British are uncomfortable with intense emotionality, especially in public; and it is certainly true that all the terms I used ('full-blooded', 'middlebrow' and 'romantic') tend to be used as derogatory terms.

However, all these features are also shared by Gainsborough melodramas, widely regarded as British popular cinema at its best. Powell and Pressburger's films added further ingredients. They dealt with serious issues. They presented intellectually challenging material in popular cinematic forms. They did not pretend to be genre pieces made for the popular audience. This was not the result of any particular snobbery; rather it was a cinephile's blindness to external cultural values being imposed upon the cinema of popular entertainment. Powell's shock at the critical reception of *Peeping Tom* was the shock of finding that critics detested horror films, and thought that he had made a particularly meretricious one.

All of these factors mark out Powell and Pressburger's films from British cinema culture. But crucially, their films had a particularly European feel to them. Three factors give rise to this. The films have a very un-British attitude to artifice. They use *mise en scène* rather than dialogue to convey complex emotions. They are at home with the questions of sexuality with which British cinema was habitually uncomfortable.

ARTIFICE

The question of artifice has often been identified as a key aspect of Powell and Pressburger's films, in that critics have remarked on their 'theatricality'. But this is imprecise. Powell has little regard for the habits of theatre when they are carried over to the screen. He lays into poor Margaret Leighton because 'she was stage through and through. Many actors and actresses don't understand the difference between the audience watching you act and the camera watching you think. … Words! Words! Actors get drunk on words, and so do directors, to their shame'.[2] (He then launches into a delicious denunciation of *The Draughtsman's Contract* for its obsession with words.)

What Powell sought from his actors was not theatricality but an awareness of artifice. Theatricality is easy to find on the British cinema screen; awareness of artifice is outstandingly rare. It belongs to European cinema, the cinema of Max Ophuls or Carné's *Les Enfants du paradis*; of such classics of the inter-war years as *The Cabinet of Dr Caligari*, *Haxan* and *Le Crime de M. Lange*, and later of *La strada*.

Powell found actors who could handle this sense of artifice: Wendy Hiller in *I Know Where I'm Going!*; David Niven, as he gratefully acknowledges; and Max Ophuls's favourite actor, Anton Walbrook. In *La Ronde* and *Lola Montes*, Walbrook's sense of artifice is effortlessly bound up into games of pretence and revelation. In *The Life and Death of Colonel Blimp* it plays against the solid directness of another favourite Powell performer, Roger Livesey. Livesey's importance to Powell was, of course, his ability to project secret doubts and prevarications behind every instance of bluff Englishness.

Other directors are capable of coming up with the occasional flash of this elusive European sensibility. Even Anthony Asquith, the quintessential deferential director of Englishness, could achieve it occasionally. After all, he had studied the German cinema of the 1920s every bit as closely as Powell. But for Asquith, it remains something that he occasionally took a risk to create. For Powell, it was a defining principle. The distance between the two cinemas can be seen in the crucial sequence of *The Life and Death of Colonel Blimp*. Amid all the artifice, Powell and Pressburger turn the film over with a moment of direct sincerity. Anyone else would have used Livesey the phlegmatic for this effect; in Powell and Pressburger, sincerity has to come from Walbrook the mercurial.

Walbrook plays Theo Kretschmar-Schuldorff as, like both Pressburger and Walbrook himself, a refugee from Nazism. He delivers a weary but impassioned speech to the British immigration officer who questions his good faith, a speech that revolves around the question of truth. Does a precise, literally correct answer to the officer's question really tell the truth? Theo had answered correctly, but his correct answer had left out all that was important: his emotions. The speech is filmed in a respectful mid-shot, with the absolute minimum of cuts and cutaways. There are no tricks, no bravura camera moves like the spectacular ascent through the roof at the culmination of the duel scene. Everything is down to the performance of this weary old man.

On the surface, this sequence belongs to the great British tradition of cinematic refusal, of effective understatement. It would not look out of place in Charles Crichton's superb *The Divided Heart*; it is still the style used by the Tony Garnett of *Prostitute*. It is an enduring British style, achieving great emotional intensity precisely by the refusal of sophisticated cinema. It is something that many film-makers have forgotten, to their cost. But what is it doing in the middle of a Powell and Pressburger film?

The sequence provides a sudden glimpse behind the appearances and acceptable forms of behaviour. Powell shot this speech so simply to make it the deliberate antithesis of the style of the rest of the film, which has an ambitious historical structure and

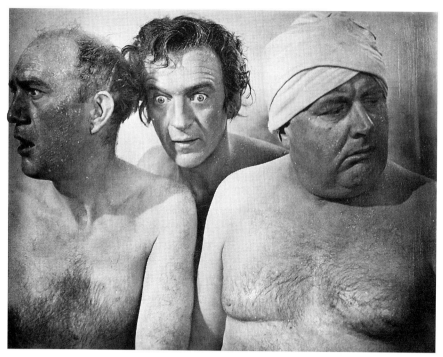

An actor who could handle Powell's sense of artifice: David Niven (c) as Sir Percy in *The Elusive Pimpernel*.

Max Ophuls' favourite actor, Anton Walbrook, was allowed late in his career with Powell and Pressburger to indulge his mercurial quality in *Oh, Rosalinda!!*.

assigns three roles to Deborah Kerr (with whom Powell was having an affair, as he tells us rather often). Indeed, it stands out from the whole of the rest of Powell's work.

This exceptional sequence underlines the sudden emotional nakedness as Theo speaks of his English wife; how he never returned to England with her; how their children – now Nazis – did not even attend her funeral. This is emotional nakedness of a very extreme kind for the cinema of its era. It asks us to sympathise with a most problematic fragment of the inhabitants of Britain at that time: German refugees, most of whom had been interned.

From the handling of this sequence, we can see why Powell and Pressburger's films deployed a European emphasis on artifice so continually. It is to reveal and emphasise the role of conventions that lay at the heart of British society. Powell and Pressburger clearly see conventions as the necessary artifice of social interaction. Yet as film-makers, they are uncomfortable in British culture because they are too acutely aware of the turbulent sea of emotions beneath the surface, a sea whose geography can be revealed only through the foregrounding of artifice rather than its refusal in the name of some kind of 'naturalism'.

MISE EN SCÈNE

It was a risk for a wartime film like *Blimp* to engage sympathies so clearly for an 'enemy alien'. Pressburger himself was just such an alien. The Chief Constable of Kent refused him permission to visit the location shoot of *A Canterbury Tale* for this reason. Powell could tell this as a good story when the film was eventually screened in its uncut version in Canterbury in 1980; for Pressburger, the event still hurt.

The Chief Constable's actions seem ironic at first sight. *A Canterbury Tale* is a film that is constructed explicitly as a hymn to the English countryside. But, after all, it is the hymn of a couple of enemy aliens. Quite apart from its gloriously sticky plot premise, it refuses the British cinema habit of getting characters to tell you how they feel. 'Proper' British films, of the sort that Powell and Pressburger's clearly aspired to be, distrusted the use of *mise en scène* to communicate emotions. That was for the despised melodramas. The disadvantage of the great tradition of cinematic understatement and refusal was the overstatement of dialogue. From off the theatrical stage come those vast speeches, those elaborate forms of words in which characters tell us how they feel.

None of this for Powell and Pressburger. In *A Canterbury Tale*, the difficult emotions of the film arise from the *mise en scène*: from the fog-bound opening sequence, through the glowing location photography of a blitzed Canterbury, to the final narrative synthesis in the studio-constructed cathedral. The encounters between characters matter less than the staging of them: the final train journey into Canterbury, the discovery of the abandoned caravan. The dialogue exchanges between a series of sharply defined social types are the least of the matter.

Compare the climactic moments of revelation for the various characters. Each character finds what they have lost: for three of the characters, it is their moral equilibrium. For the American soldier, it is simply his lost love. The characteristic British

The difficult emotions of *A Canterbury Tale* arise from the *mise en scène*, starting with the fog-bound opening scene which throws the three 'pilgrims' together.

movie would have handled these moments of realisation as dialogue-based scenes, scenes of confession. But not Powell and Pressburger. The American soldier comes across a long-lost companion-in-arms (through the viewfinder of his camera, naturally) and he hands him a bundle of letters from his beloved that have followed him around the world. The *mise en scène* is at a minimum: it takes place in the tearoom at the cathedral gates (later to become Pizzaland): our American hayseed has no spiritual revelation to come, therefore. We have already seen how morally and personally balanced he is: he understands the ways of the country.

Three of the other characters are far more troubled. For them, the emotional *mise en scène* is reserved. Colpeper, the glue man, is forced to realise his errors during a train journey that passes through a totally fictional set of tunnels, throwing shadow, darkness and light across a tense exchange of words that coincide with his own turbulent emotions. At the end of the scene, he slips away: there is no confession from him. The *mise en scène* has made us complicit with his emotions at hearing what he does.

The tank commander Peter Gibbs is finally forced to forego his world-weary cynicism by playing the cathedral organ in a sequence imbued with all the spirituality that Powell could wrest from Junge's sets. And Alison Smith finds her lover and is reconciled with her family in an emotional roller-coaster of a sequence, in which she first discovers the decaying caravan where she spent a brief period of love; and then clearing it out, literally letting in light, when she learns the good news. The idea might be a cliché, but the execution, the emotion, is intense, however often you see the film.

This emphasis on the concrete, upon *mise en scène*, extends even to their definition of nationalism. In the end, the Powell conception of nation – which some find problematic – is a matter of the concrete rather than the ideological: one of place and sounds rather than of people and characteristics. A sense of space, of shape and graphic qualities, of direct sound and empty silence (remember Chesil Beach in *The Small Back Room*): these are the defining characteristics of the Britain of Powell and Pressburger's films. Such is the presence around which the characters orient themselves. The exceedingly odd people in *I Know Where I'm Going!* are sure of one thing, that the landscape of Scotland provides their sense of being alive. The British countryside is Kretschmar-Schuldorff's reason for returning to Britain; it animates *Gone to Earth*; it is offered as the solution to the ills of urban Britain (*Red Ensign*, *A Canterbury Tale*).

In the strongest possible rebuff to Truffaut, Britain and cinema *do* go together in the films of Powell and Pressburger. Cinema is the point of integration of their work, from which everything else radiates. Just as *A Matter of Life and Death*'s Dr Reeves sees the whole of the village through his camera obscura, Powell and Pressburger mounted their affectionate-ironic explorations of Britain from the optic of cinema. They refused the conventional British use of cinema as filmed theatre, and instead – at least in Powell's case – used the voyeurism that *Peeping Tom* explores. The activity of film and spectator provides the emotional content. Around this centre, Pressburger was able to elaborate a series of paradoxical essays about the culture of the British into which he desires integration (at the same time as fearing absorption). Powell was able to indulge his taste for complex games of deception and artifice, together with a predilection for melodrama that was also at once profoundly cinematic and hardly proper in the British sense.

SEXUALITY

Behind all of this lies a third vital ingredient: the nature of the strong collaboration that existed between Powell and Pressburger. Powell without Pressburger is a rather different character, more likely to get lost following a digression. Only with Leo Marks, the scriptwriter of *Peeping Tom*, did he find the same intensity of creative collaboration. The motivating force of each collaboration seems to have been an extraordinary male bonding, perhaps a latent homosexuality. The nature of this relationship often becomes the secret subject of the films themselves, providing their structuring principle.

Both *A Matter of Life and Death* and *The Life and Death of Colonel Blimp* have the same basic structure: two men compete for the love of one woman, but the intensity of the relationship between the two men is such that there is no jealousy between them. Instead, the films produce a magical solution. In *Blimp*, it is three

Hit by the bottle: too much verve and too much style in *A Small Back Room* to convince us of the real tragedy of Sammy?

women of identical appearance, a wife for each and an ideal companion for their old age. In *A Matter of Life and Death*, one of the men dies so that the other can marry the woman, but dies only so that he can save his friend in the Other World. The magic is present to make the reality absent, and the magic is plausible only because the central dilemma is so convincing.

Powell and Pressburger's sensitivity to the deep undercurrents of strong male bonding marks them out from most of their cinematic (or even artistic) contemporaries on the British scene. Such honesty – for this is what it is – means that they have no problems in portraying real passion, real sexuality. *Black Narcissus*, *The Red Shoes* or *Gone to Earth* show how easily they could carry off a kind of film-making that eluded many of their contemporaries.

Seen in this way, many of the strands of Powell and Pressburger's work fall into place. Powell has a romantic insistence of 'I am Cinema'. They share a romantic nationalism; they oscillate between defiance and conformity. Pressburger loves paradox; Powell loves extravagance. Emotion in their films is provided through cinema itself: it comes from looking, from hearing, from being caught up in the spectacle that you are watching.

What tended to elude Powell and Pressburger were tragedy, deprivation, domesticity: the largely unsung strengths of British cinema in general. *The Small Back Room* has too much verve, too much style, to convince us of the real tragedy of Sammy (David Farrar). He seems altogether too big for the cinema of Kenneth More, John Gregson and Jack Hawkins. From Hawkins, however, Powell was able to draw two surprisingly effective and untypical performances, as a smooth bureaucratic operator in *The Small Back Room*, and a deliciously camp Prince Regent in *The Elusive Pimpernel*. Neither were aspects of his personality that Hawkins cared to explore further once he gained a large degree of control over how he was cast. Again, Powell was pushing at the limits of another icon of Britishness, the Hawkins who incarnated the beleaguered yet resourceful commander in Charles Frend's *The Cruel Sea* (1952).

Powell and Pressburger have always existed at the edge of the world of British sensibility. The particular nature of their edginess has been difficult to comprehend, as it is allied with what seems at first sight to be an aggressive, even romantic, assertion of British patriotism. Yet theirs is the clamour of the outsider wanting to be let in, aware that any real acceptance would be a defeat for both sides. They were European film-makers whose misfortune it was to be interested in being British.

NOTES

1. Michael Powell, *Million Dollar Movie*, London: Heinemann, 1992. This article originally appeared in a different version in *Vertigo* 3, Spring 1994 as a review of Powell's 'second volume of his life in movies'.

2. Ibid., p.28.

2 The First Four Minutes

Charles Barr

'This is the universe. Big, isn't it?' In 1946, when they opened *A Matter of Life and Death* with this voiceover line, neither Michael Powell nor Emeric Pressburger may have been aware of the likelihood that it was growing bigger all the time, still expanding in the wake of an initial 'Big Bang'. Three decades later, a book by Steven Weinberg helped to put into popular circulation the phrase, and the concept, of *The First Three Minutes*: a spectacular formative period that succeeded the Big Bang, the explosive inauguration of our universe, creating space and time and the basic laws of nature.[1] Everything follows from that starting point; in a sense, the potential for all that follows is contained in, can be predicted from, that initial explosion.

Powell and Pressburger had first met in 1938, brought together by Alexander Korda to work on a project, *The Spy in Black*, that was giving trouble. The meeting sparked off a lengthy creative partnership. I see the beginning of their first collaboration – the *First Four Minutes* of Powell and Pressburger – as resembling the first period after the Big Bang, a dazzling explosion of energy, which, in retrospect, created a framework for all that would follow. While cosmologists, even through the most powerful of telescopes, cannot reach back directly through space-time to that originating event, *The Spy in Black* remains available to us. Though I would not want to make especially high claims for the film as a whole, in itself or in comparison with the finest of its successors, the opening rewards the most detailed analysis, both on its own exhilarating merits and for what it foreshadows. Indeed, many of the key elements and qualities of the more complex later films are already recognisable.[2]

Both in his autobiography and in television interviews, Powell gave memorably vivid descriptions of the momentous first encounter. On hearing Pressburger, at Korda's round-table meeting, outline his revised script treatment for *The Spy in Black*, he realised at once that he had met 'a marvel: a screenwriter who could really write':

I was not going to let him get away in a hurry. I had always dreamt of this phenomenon: a screen-writer with the heart and mind of a novelist, who would be interested in the medium of film, and who would have wonderful ideas, which I would turn into even more wonderful images, and who only used dialogue to make a joke or to clarify the plot.[3]

The script was an adaptation of a novel by the Scottish author J. Storer Clouston, bought by Korda as a vehicle for his contract artist Conrad Veidt, to be made under a co-production deal between his own London Films and Columbia. The initial adaptation had been completed by Roland Pertwee; according to Powell, this was over-literal and dialogue-bound, and offered no interesting star roles, least of all for Veidt. 'Emeric threw [the plot] out and invented a new one', in line with the principle that 'when you buy the rights to a famous book which turns out to be useless for a screenwriter's purpose, you keep the title and throw away the book'.[4] Korda gave his two junior employees a free hand to go ahead together on the basis of the new outline. Although Pertwee would retain a credit for 'scenario' alongside Pressburger's for 'screenplay', and although it would not be until three films later that the distinctive shared final credit, 'Written, Produced and Directed by Michael Powell and Emeric Pressburger', would actually appear on screen, it is as clear from the evidence of the film as it is from the retrospective literature that the process of forging the partnership was an instant rather than a gradual one.[5] Pressburger in turn had quickly recognised that Powell was different from anyone else he had ever met in films, 'a person who not only understood what I was driving at, but guessed already half of it before I'd said it'.[6]

Clouston's *The Spy in Black* was a story of the First World War, published in 1917. The film declines to update the story in the manner of, to take a celebrated example of free adaptation from 1935, *The 39 Steps*.[7] Produced in early 1939, when the onset of another war was becoming more and more likely, it had been released by the time war was declared in September 1939, and was widely seen in the months of the 'Phoney War'.

The choice of story, of hero and of star made it inevitable that the central figure would be a German engaged in war against Britain. The film thus has to tackle head-on the problem of audience sympathy. It starts by introducing Conrad Veidt as U-boat captain Ernst Hardt, and then establishing his mission of spying and sabotage. In outline, what happens is this: Hardt returns, with a junior officer, from his previous mission in the Atlantic to his bustling hotel in the city of Kiel, base of the German fleet. Hoping for a period of rest, he is intercepted by a sailor, who tells him to report back to headquarters at once. He obediently resumes his duties, and heads for

the British fleet's base at Scapa Flow. This
already overturns the structure of a book
that is set entirely in the Orkneys, a structure that was evidently retained in Pertwee's
initial adaptation.

The credits are followed by a title: 'Kiel,
Base of the German Grand Fleet, 1917'. A
newspaper boy bustles up to the entrance of
a building, and the camera lingers for a
moment on its name: the Kieler Hof Hotel.

At the reception, two German officers pick up one of the newly delivered papers: its
title is the *Kieler Post*. No uncertainty, then, about where we are. As the standard
work on classical Hollywood puts it, 'Any narrative text must repeat important story
information, and in the cinema, repetition takes on a special necessity … Three is in
fact a mystical number for Hollywood dramaturgy. The Hollywood slogan is to state
every fact three times'.[8] The film has crammed its triple statement into the first half-
minute in a manner that is disarmingly emphatic; it does not seem precious or pon-
derous, partly because the tempo is so nicely judged, partly because of the rapid way
the action at once darts forward as people come and go around a busy reception
desk.

Another basic narrative principle is summarised thus by screenwriter-critic
Michael Eaton:

> As Vladimir Propp, the initiator of modern structural analysis of popular narrative, suggested,
> all stories must start with the central character (or indeed characters) being defined as having
> something missing, whether they know it or not, and it is that which propels them on their narra-
> tive journey, their quest. In other words, all stories are predicated on a lack. Every specific story
> genre tends to depend on particular founding lacks that will be overcome by the eventual closure.[9]

Eaton goes on to illustrate this principle in terms of the detective story in general,
and of *Chinatown* in particular. *The Spy in Black* sets up its own series of 'founding
lacks' with the same energetic rapidity that it used in locating us in Kiel. These
attach primarily to the central characters, but we do not meet them quite yet, and
the build-up to their entrance is remarkable.

The *Kieler Post*'s headline reads, 'England Starving'. One officer asks, 'Is it
true?', and the other starts to read out a story about successful attacks on shipping
by U-boats – key narrative information – only to find the bulk of the text blocked
out by black ink and the word 'Censored'. Instead of the humourless 'Achtung!'
that we might expect, the response is a gentle English-style irony: 'so now we
know!'. A double shift, then, inside a few seconds: Germany triumphant/under-
mined/human.

Next, in the bustle around the hotel desk, a young couple push forward and
breathlessly address the male receptionist:

Both in unison: We want a room …
He: I want a room for my wife and
myself.
Receptionist: Sorry, full up.
He: We were only married today.
She: He has to join his ship tomorrow.

At once, the receptionist turns to a hook
marked 'Emergency' and hands them a key,
directing them to 'room 29'. Off they go,
never to be seen again. We switch to a sailor outside the hotel, who asks the two
emerging officers (the ones who were reading the paper) if either of them is Captain
Hardt. They think his submarine is still at sea, but the sailor knows better: 'U.29
came to moorings an hour ago'. He strides into the hotel to look for Hardt. But
before he reaches the desk, we are treated to another brief erotic vignette. Aa a different senior officer moves away from the desk towards the lift, a young woman
passes in the same direction:

> *Receptionist*: Oh Lottie, Captain Richter wants another manicure. Room 46.
> *Lottie* (pausing only briefly): I know.

In the foreground of the same shot, the sailor
smiles knowingly, then delivers his message:
'Captain Hardt to report to headquarters
immediately'.

> *Receptionist*: He hasn't arrived yet.
> *Sailor*: What is his room number?
> *Receptionist*: 54
> *Sailor*: Have you seen him?
> *Receptionist*: Not for sixteen days.

Cut now from a frontal close-up of the receptionist to a reverse shot, his eyeline, of
two more officers coming through the swing doors, behind the back of the enquir-
ing sailor. From their body language, from the way the camera pulls back with
them, from Miklos Rozsa's stirring new musical theme and from the fact that the
imposing one in front is the star of the film, Conrad Veidt, we immediately share
the man's knowledge that this is Hardt, and are then gratified by the success of his
instant stratagem to give him and his junior a breathing space:

> *Receptionist*: Do you know him by sight?
> *Sailor*: No.
> *Receptionist*: Well, try the Turkish baths in the Koenigstrasse.

The sailor obediently exits, saluting the pair as he goes, and we are ready to be introduced to Hardt and to his junior from the submarine crew, Schuster, played by Marius Goring.

It is hard to believe that all of this has taken less than two minutes. In the course of its artful build-up to the entrance of the star, the film has created a bustling environment, with at its hub a memorable minor character in the receptionist, played by Bernard Miles. Resourceful, perceptive, humane, never wasting a second, he is like a surrogate for the film-makers in the way he responds to, and controls, the action.

No fewer than seven other individuals have registered vividly as well, in their few seconds of screen time.[10] And four numbers have been foregrounded: 29, 29, 46, 54. The emergency key is taken off peg 13, a room number that, presumably, is unused for superstitious reasons; Miles instructs them firmly to go to room 29. A few seconds later, Captain Hardt's submarine is identified as U-boat 29; that number will be kept visually prominent during later action scenes, and indeed *U-Boat 29* was the film's title for its American release. Two confined off-screen spaces are thus evoked, linked mysteriously by number: the space of urgent sexual consummation, and the space of all-male war service. Next, two further rooms are evoked: 46, where one captain is rushing off to enjoy his 'manicure', and 54, where the other, Hardt, is

scheduled to go alone to wind down from his sixteen days at sea. As rooms in the same hotel, they could hardly be given the same number, but the film does the next best thing and makes them what are evidently known as *complementary* numbers: 46 + 54 = 100. At some level, arguably, we register this connection, as we surely do the immediate repetition of 29. So a double juxtaposition is lightly sketched in, underscored by the number system: between spaces of immediate gratification and spaces of austerity.

The film then develops the austerity motif by putting its central naval pair through a quick but intense succession of frustrations, made more poignant by the lavishness of the hotel *mise en scène* and of Rozsa's music. In Propp/Eaton terms, it establishes a cluster of 'founding lacks'. Hardt asks the receptionist, by now identified as

Hans, for a cigarette; the hotel is out of them ('again'), but he offers to sell him tobacco and a pipe, which Hardt says he never smokes. After going to their rooms to tidy themselves up – a time-gap covered in a quick dissolve – they prepare to dine. Schuster gets out a cigar, but Hardt insists that he wait till after they have eaten. A young woman greets him warmly, but again Hardt tells him: '*after* dinner!'. In the restaurant, they order lavishly, but everything they have been longing for during the successful pursuit, ironically, of food ships bound for Britain turns out to be unavailable. Rather than accept the only option of boiled fish, carrots and beetroot, they give up. With a paternal tenderness, Hardt draws the curtain around their dining cubicle, and leaves Schuster to sleep, placing beside him a cigar for when he wakes: it looks, for a moment, as though the younger

man at least will achieve the long-deferred gratifications of sleep, a good smoke and then the company of the woman who greeted him. Hardt leaves to go up to his room, and enters the lift. In it is the sailor who was looking for him earlier, now back, we infer, from his fruitless exploration of the Turkish baths. Neither of them knows the other. But Hardt, as he slumps back in exhaustion, is holding his room key. The sailor sees it: close-up, showing the number 54. He snaps to attention and addresses him: 'Captain Hardt – message from Headquarters to report immediately'. Hardt wearily starts to rise. In a transition of thrilling economy, a dissolve takes us to a shot of the submarine, on the surface in daylight, cutting through the waves. Hardt and Schuster are below. Maybe the narrative proper will give them a chance to satisfy the range of appetites that have so far been frustrated – in Propp's terms, to liquidate their lack. Meanwhile, their public mission is soon defined for them, as they open their sealed orders: to head for Scapa Flow and sabotage the British fleet.

There is no room here to go through the rest of the film in detail, nor does it sustain the same level of intensity as the opening; but one can see why Pressburger's outline of his new structure for the overall narrative made an immediate positive impression both on Korda and on Powell. Smoking and food will be recurring motifs in the story as it develops, alongside the major questions of

whether the mission will succeed, and whether the hero will find love. To sum-
marise: when the submarine reaches its destination, Hardt goes ashore alone to meet
an undercover German agent, Frau Teil, who is waiting for him in the schoolhouse.
We have already seen how a young Englishwoman travelling north to take up the
post of teacher has been brutally abducted and replaced. Hardly has the woman
admitted him safely to the house than Hardt is satisfying his longing for proper food
with butter and ham, neither of which he could get in Kiel (two of the waiter's
deflating lines were 'sorry, it's a meatless day' and 'we may have margarine tomorrow'); in gratifying the German hero's appetite, the film takes the incidental opportunity to suggest that Britain, for all the U-boat attacks on food ships, is better off.

From this point, the sharing of an isolated house by Hardt and the woman creates a strong erotic tension, and audiences for a film co-starring Conrad Veidt and
Valerie Hobson are likely to share Hardt's expectation that a romance will develop;
but in the event, this element is displaced onto another, safer and more conventional
'creation of the couple'. We learn, and subsequently Hardt learns, that the Hobson
character is not German after all, but a double agent – the killing of the original
teacher had been detected, and the substitute was in turn killed and replaced. The
British officer who convinced Hardt that he was a traitor, ready to hand over details

Did the audience for a film starring Conrad Veidt and Valerie Hobson expect that a romance
would develop in *The Spy in Black*?

of naval movements, is no more anti-British than Hobson, to whom indeed he is married. So Hardt is foiled, U-boat 29 is destroyed and the narrative lacks are resolved through a successful end to the mission (but the British one not the German) and a successful affirmation of the heterosexual couple, now reunited. Sebastian Shaw as Blacklock has nothing like the appeal, as actor or character, of Conrad Veidt as Hardt, nor is he as worthy an opposite number for Hobson, but this twist undeniably offers a neat conclusion to the narrative, and an equally neat answer to the problems of making a British film with a German star/protagonist in 1939.

In the opening of *The Spy in Black*, and the story that it introduces, we can already recognise four particular factors that, in retrospect, seem typical of Powell and Pressburger, prophetic of their subsequent career.

1. TOPICALITY

It was Alexander Korda, and the chance of their simultaneous availability, that brought the pair together on this project, but they leaped at the opportunity to develop it, handling the shift between German and British viewpoints in ways that were calculated to make it an intriguing attraction for audiences in the autumn of 1939, whether this turned out to be a period of continuing tension, relief of tension or (as obviously happened) the start of a new war. Hitherto, neither the films directed by Powell nor those written by Pressburger had addressed the political tensions of the time in the manner of, say, the thrillers Hitchcock directed between 1934 and 1938; the one partial exception is Powell's 1934 film *Red Ensign*, whose hero fights vigorously in mid-Depression to provide employment for British shipbuilders. Though set in 1917, *The Spy in Black* clearly did touch a contemporary nerve on release,[11] and the new Powell–Pressburger team, as soon as they got the chance to work together again, continued in the same spirit up to 1946 with a series of seven feature films, all of them original screenplays, not even allowing themselves the occasional non-topical subject in the manner of contemporaries like Carol Reed (*Kipps*, 1941) and David Lean (*Blithe Spirit*, 1944).[12]

2. REPRESENTATION OF GERMANS

The start of *The Spy in Black* introduces a set of Germans who are notably, roundedly, human: the newspaper-reading officers with their amused response to press censorship, the romantic couple, Hans the receptionist, the patient waiter in the restaurant, Schuster, and above all Hardt, a figure whose heroic stature will by no means be cancelled out by the later twists of the plot. They have a range of honest human appetites, and possess as strong a sense of ironic humour as any Englishman could lay claim to. Quite early in the war, the Ministry of Information would lay down the rule that all Germans were to be portrayed as equally guilty, lacking in basic humanity, and one of the standard propaganda devices was to mock them as humourless. See, for instance, Leslie Howard's *Pimpernel Smith* (1941), whose hero teases the German official played by Francis L. Sullivan for his inability to detect the humour in the works of P. G. Wodehouse and Lewis Carroll. Not all film-makers accepted the advice to eliminate the figure of the sympathetic German, and Powell and Pressburger famously carried on foregrounding him. A clear line can be traced from Hardt through Anton Walbrook's roles as anti-Nazi Germans in *49th Parallel* (1941) and *The Life and Death of Colonel Blimp* (1943), to Peter Finch as Langsdorff in *The Battle of the River Plate* (1956). As for the actors, Veidt will make only one more film for the partnership, and one for Powell without Pressburger, before leaving for Hollywood,[13] but Marius Goring will remain a strong recurring presence in later films, culminating in his role as the German General Kreipe in the last film of the regular partnership, *Ill Met by Moonlight* (1957).[14] So Veidt and Goring's memorable joint entry into the hotel, two minutes into *The Spy in Black*, is indeed the start of something.

3. THE PLAY WITH NUMBERS

There is more to this than the pointed numbering of off-screen spaces discussed earlier (29, 29, 46, 54). The naval pair have been away for sixteen days, and have sunk four British food ships. Hardt asks for a table for two, and a meal for ten. Throughout their mission, Schuster tells the waiter, they have lived on sardines: forty-eight tins each, adding up to '768 little fishes'. In the submarine, the first thing they will do is to read their sealed orders, which are due to be opened at 11.15. Schuster is impatient, but Hardt points out that it's only 11.14, and insists on waiting for the remaining seconds to tick away. Both men, then, in their different ways, relish numbers. Schuster's calculation skips a step, as if to invite his, and the film's, audience to fill it in by mental arithmetic: they must have eaten three times a day, and each tin contained sixteen sardines. Hardt's punctiliousness about time is like that of Pressburger himself, as recalled by Powell and others, a quality in his daily behaviour that can surely be linked to the precision with which he manages time in his screenplays.[15] Time and date are, of course, measured out by number, and this numerical dimension of his work can in turn be linked to his musicianship, the connections between music and mathematics being very basic.[16] 'The movies aren't drama, they aren't literature, they are pure mathematics': this resonant line from Christopher's Isherwood's *Prater Violet* (1945), a *roman-à-clef* about the film industry, is spoken by a film editor, and has a clear application to the shot-by-shot constructional work of editing, but it can be applied equally to the 'mathematics' of narrative construction.[17] Moreover, Pressburger was much more closely involved than Powell in the editing of their films.[18]

Their two supreme films of wartime, *The Life and Death of Colonel Blimp* and its successor *A Canterbury Tale* (1944), owe much to the beautiful precision and clarity of their respective, contrasting, time-scales. The former takes us through a forty-year flashback narrative, with every date meticulously filled in through visual cues. The latter, in contrast, after its Chaucerian prologue, spans a single weekend, Friday evening to Monday morning; in counterpoint, an exhilarating range of historical dates is laid out, this time, for the most part, not visually but verbally. Highlights include:

The Iron Age, source of the artefacts in which the local squire, Colpeper, and the visiting land girl, Alison, have a passionate interest; the 14th century of the prologue, after which Esmond Knight's voiceover tells us that '600 years have passed'; 1485, the date of Chillingbourne's town charter, which is, as the stationmaster reminds the visiting GI, 'seven years before Columbus discovered America'; and 1888, the date at which the same GI's grandfather built his church in Johnson City.

Dates and numbers are also crucial to *A Matter of Life and Death* (1946; hereafter *AMOLAD*). Where *The Spy in Black* began by giving us a precise date visually (17th March 1917), *AMOLAD* does so verbally: the opening voiceover tells us that this is the night of 2nd May 1945. The pilot, Peter Carter, preparing to jump from his burning plane without a parachute, introduces himself to the American radio operator, June, by saying that he is 'age 27, 27, did you get that? It's very important.' Why? The answer emerges in the conversation he has with Dr Reeves, in June's presence, some 40 minutes of screen time later. As he starts to explore Peter's case, Reeves questions him: are both his parents living? No, he has a mother and two sisters. His father died in 1917. What of? The same reason as him – war. Reeves then asks him: 'You're 29?' Answer: 'No, 27.' The exchange could so easily have been written more simply: 'How old are you?' '27.' The actual dialogue makes more of a point of the precise age, in line with his initial statement to June that it is 'very important' – as well as, whether deliberately or not, repeating the magic number 29 from the start of *The Spy in Black*. Why then *is* it important? If Peter were 29, he would probably have known his father. Since he is 27, it is almost certain that he did not, that the father died without ever seeing him. You can construct, in retrospective calculation, scenarios whereby Peter could (a) be 29 and not have known him, or (b) be 27 and still have known him, at the age of a few months; it depends on precise birth and death dates, and on frequency of leave. But surely the film expects us, as it makes the point and moves on, to do a quick subtraction of 27 from 1945, giving 1918, and to infer that the father's death in 1917 must have happened, as it did to so many war babies (both in the First World War and much more recently), between his conception and his birth. The fact of him being fatherless, as fatherless as one can possibly be, is, on one reading, a key to the film. It is not simply a parable of Anglo-American relations, as per the original commission by the Ministry of Information, but also an intense Oedipal drama happening, as the unscrolling initial title tells us, 'inside the mind of a young airman' – one who has, he tells us, a loving mother and sisters, and who now embarks on a sudden agonising struggle to form a union with a new woman. The father is no more present than he is to Cary Grant as Thornhill in the rather comparable scenario of Hitchcock's *North by Northwest* (1958), and like Thornhill he has, in the course of his Oedipal journey, to (symbolically) kill a father-figure. Why does Peter show no interest in meeting his father in the monochrome world of the dead? Why could he not look for his father to defend him in the heavenly trial? Dr Reeves qualifies for the role of father-figure instead; his death by reckless driving is like a suicide caused by recognition of Peter's *need* for him to die. I believe that an account on these lines could be developed, by someone fully competent in psychoanalytic reading, that would be as persuasive as

Raymond Bellour's celebrated reading of
North by Northwest.[19]

This has taken us a long way from *The
Spy in Black*; the point is that the key themes
and structures are being established at the
beginning of *AMOLAD*, as at the start of the
very first collaboration, by means of an
intense, witty and thoroughly characteristic
play with numbers.

4. OFF-SCREEN ACTION

The first scene of *The Spy in Black* establishes a single locale, the ground floor of
the Kieler Hof Hotel, in vivid detail, while referring us to four other numerically
labelled spaces, only one of which, the interior of U-boat 29, we subsequently get
access to. This strategy, the pointed evocation of spaces that remain off screen, will
also become a characteristic of the Powell–Pressburger narratives at their most
intense.

One function of the strategy is to evade, or even tease, the censor. For a film of
1939, the sexual references at the start are unusually bold. The first woman to
appear in a Powell–Pressburger film is patently eager for sex, and has her wish
granted by Hans's immediate provision of the room key. The fact that she is
(newly) married, that we do not follow her and her husband away from the reception desk, let alone to the bedroom, and that the film quickly moves on, presumably made it acceptable. The vignette of the 'manicurist' going up to room 46,
likewise never seen, to service the senior officer may have flashed by too quickly
for the censor to register its implications, despite the knowing smile of the observing sailor. Together with the glimpse of the young woman who launches herself
lustily at the returned Schuster, these offer a realistic, adult acknowledgment of
sexual urges, made more intense by the pressures of wartime and being fulfilled in
off-screen places that, naturally, we cannot enter.

We can look ahead from this to *A Canterbury Tale*, in many ways such an innocent,
U-certificate film, but with more complex undercurrents. Colpeper's compulsive pouring of glue into young women's hair is kept off screen, though we almost witness it at
the beginning. Alison reveals that she has spent a week's holiday the previous summer
in a caravan with her fiancé, in a wooded section of the Pilgrim's Way close to the village; Powell confirmed that to him, this clearly implied that premarital sex had taken
place.[20] It remains too elusive, too off screen and in the past, to be censored. In Nigel
Balchin's novel of wartime, *The Small Back Room*, published in the same year (1943)
in which *A Canterbury Tale* was shot, the unmarried central couple, Sammy and Susan,
share a flat, but the 1949 Powell–Pressburger film adaptation, foreseeing the unac-
ceptability of this to the censor, gives them separate places. The first time we see
Sammy's flat is when Susan, early in the film, takes the army officer, Captain Stuart,
there to meet him, and makes coffee for them. At the end of the evening, Stuart offers

to take her home. 'You have. I live across the hall.' But we never see her flat, though we will keep seeing her in Sammy's; twice, coming home, they enter it together. The separate flat insures against censorship, while the keeping of it off screen represents a riposte to censorship, suggesting that it is unlived in, or even non-existent – a very neat manoeuvre, and an index of the realistically adult dimension of the film that Lindsay Anderson's contemporary review acknowledged: the main relationship is, in contrast to so much screen artificiality, 'recognisably one between a man and a woman'.[21]

The off-screen strategy is not, however, just about censorship. Partly it is a matter of basic narrative economy. Unlike theatre, cinema has the freedom to take us more or less wherever it wants to, to cut away; film-makers have a continual choice between using this freedom and not using it; not showing is often more effective than showing. We could have cut away to the U-boat at its moorings, or entered room 54 with Hardt when he prepared for dinner, but it makes dramatic sense not to. It leaves things to the imagination, and enables the main narrative, on the ground floor, to proceed in a more focused way. There is nothing special about this, but Powell and Pressburger will extend the narrative strategy of not-showing in distinctive ways. The duel in *Colonel Blimp* is left to the imagination, as the camera withdraws from the action in the gesture that so captivated Martin Scorsese;[22] later, we learn of key events like the respective deaths of Blimp's wife and of his servant Murdoch by the most indirect means. In *A Canterbury Tale* we do not see Alison's fiancé or Bob's girlfriend even in photographs, let alone in crosscut sequences; in *I Know Where I'm Going!* (1945; hereafter *IKWIG*), we never see the rich man whom Joan is due to marry, or the island of Kiloran of which he is temporary master, even though, with her, we see the island on the horizon, view a map of it, learn a lot about it and hear his voice in a long telephone conversation. All of these omissions make good psychological and dramatic sense, and indeed, almost paradoxically, become a positive part of the pleasure the films offer.

In counterpoint to Kiloran, *IKWIG* deploys another off-screen space: the castle of Moy, which Torquil, himself the actual owner of Kiloran, is forbidden by a mysterious family curse to enter. We see it from the outside but, like Torquil, are denied access, until the final scene. This relates to a deep structure that I have pointed to in an earlier article: 'A quintessential Powell–Pressburger title is *The Small Back Room.* Repeatedly, they relate their protagonists to a private space, often a secret or taboo room, which constitutes a retreat, and a source of energy, power, vision, magic.'[23] Among these *charged spaces* are Dr Reeves's camera obscura in *AMOLAD* and the room at the top of the house in *Peeping Tom* (1960, Powell without Pressburger); others are kept off screen until a late stage of the film, when the tension built up by this withholding can be powerfully released. Prime examples are another non-Pressburger film, *Bluebeard's Castle* (1964), and two climactic scenes that have as intense an emotional force as anything in their joint work: the episode in *IKWIG* when Torquil finally enters the taboo space, finds that he is thereby doomed to lose his freedom and is joined by the one he is losing it to, Joan; and the scene in *A Canterbury Tale* when Alison visits the backstreet garage in which the caravan is laid up, learns from the garage owner that her fiancé is not a war casualty after all and, weeping, throws open the caravan's doors and windows.

As with the theme of numbers, this has come a long way from the start of *The Spy in Black*, but again we can detect the seeds in the early film of what is to come, especially in the quick evocation of the *charged off-screen space* of room 29.

Those first four minutes: yes, they unroll like a dazzling trailer for the pleasures to come – the rapid sketching in of a topical context, the deployment of numbers and of off-screen space, the entry of the German hero and loyal supporting player. But go back in imagination to 1939, try to forget what the future holds for this chance teaming of writer and director, and one is struck afresh every time by the sheer life and creativity of the film's opening, by the swift confidence with which everything fits together. It is already a consummate illustration of the principles of classical narrative (as touched on earlier), and of professional teamwork: music and design and editing, acting and writing and directing. I cannot think of a more impressive entrance, in any film, than that of Veidt/Hardt and of Goring/Schuster. First the build-up, then the arrival: each angle, each cut, each movement and expression has to be precisely judged in order for us to follow, and enjoy, Hans's brilliant improvised response in both greeting them and protecting their identity from the messenger. The high-intensity interaction here of image and movement and music affords a glimpse of Powell's ideal of the 'composed film', just as the integration of creative elements bears out the message with which Powell had ended his recent book on the making of *The Edge of the World* (1937), his last film before *The Spy in Black*: 'in the long run it is good team-work that makes a good film'.[24]

I shall end with an item not referred to under any of the previous headings, though it relates to the 'classical narrative' model, according to which every detail fits in. As the pair order their dinner, not yet knowing the limits of the day's menu, Hardt climaxes the notional feast by asking for plum pudding. At once, Schuster, spreading his arms out, asks that it should be as 'big as a depth-charge'. It is a superb line, both for its poetic vividness and for the dramatic irony with which it foreshadows the film's end: U-boat 29, with Schuster on board, will be destroyed by depth-charges. Powell exploits his writer's invention to the full, both by the way he has Goring deliver the line, and by composition. In the reverse shot of the waiter, he is juxtaposed with a pair of spherical lamps that have the shape and size of plum puddings – one for each of them – or, if you like, depth-charges. And in turn, the rhyme, contrived here by writer/director interaction, will be extended by the invention of the film's editor. At the end, we hear the order given by a British naval officer to 'fire depth-charges', and see two of them being lobbed to the spot where U-boat 29 has just submerged; they duly match the shape and size of plum puddings, and of the spherical wall-lights. Then come the explosions, making, in Powell's words, 'a marvellous climax to the film', and he gives generous credit to Hugh Stewart for using his own initiative to locate the depth-charge footage: 'This is the kind of thing that an editor can bring to a film in which he's interested.'[25] Powell's line about teamwork was far from being an empty gesture.

Kevin Macdonald recounts how:

> In 1947, while on a trip to Hollywood, Emeric visited his old friend Anatole Litvak at Paramount. Having lunch in the studio restaurant Emeric was introduced to the head of the script department. Paramount, he said, owned its very own print of *IKWIG*. Whenever his writers were stuck for inspiration, or needed a lesson in screenwriting, he ran them the film, as an example of the perfect screenplay. He had already screened it a dozen times.[26]

Note that they did not just read the script, they screened the film. The first four minutes of *The Spy in Black* can stand, equally, as an example of the perfect beginning – to a script, to a film and to a twenty-year partnership.

NOTES

1. Steven Weinberg, *The First Three Minutes: A Modern View of the Origins of the Universe*, London: Deutsch, 1977.
2. To be pedantic, the Big Bang may have created space and time, and the 'laws of nature' that keep the universe together, but it did not create all the *elements* that are crucial to life on Earth: most of these were generated far later, in the stupendous heat of exploding stars. And, sure enough, we find one of those in the prologue to *A Matter of Life and Death*: the supernova seen and remarked on as the camera pans leftward through the universe towards our solar system.
3. Michael Powell, *A Life in Movies: An Autobiography*, London: Heinemann, 1986, p. 305. Compare his account of the same encounter in, for instance, the 1986 episode of London Weekend Television's *The South Bank Show* (1986), timed to coincide with the book's publication (director David Hinton, interviewer-presenter Melvyn Bragg).
4. Powell, *A Life in Movies*, pp. 302–3.
5. The joint formula first appears on the credits of *The Life and Death of Colonel Blimp* (1943). In the meantime, they had collaborated closely on *Contraband* (1940), *49th Parallel* (1941) and *One of Our Aircraft is Missing* (1942).
6. Pressburger, interviewed for *A Pretty British Affair* (BBC TV, *Arena* series, 1981, presenter-interviewer Gavin Millar).
7. John Buchan's novel, published in 1916, was set during the build-up to the First World War; Charles Bennett's free adaptation of it, for Alfred Hitchcock, updated it to the 1930s.
8. David Bordwell, Janet Staiger and Kristen Thompson, *The Classical Hollywood Cinema*, London: Routledge, 1985, Chapter 3, 'Classical Narration', p. 31.
9. Michael Eaton, *Chinatown*, London: BFI Classics, 1997, p. 40. *Chinatown* (1974) was scripted by Robert Towne and directed by Roman Polanski.
10. Newsboy, two officers, honeymoon couple, sailor, manicurist (her client passes by too quickly to be counted). But it looks as if an eighth ended on the cutting-room floor: another officer at reception is recognisable as Howard Marion Crawford, already an established character actor – he had a supporting role in Hitchcock's *Secret Agent* in 1936 – but just as he begins to speak, we cut to the honeymooners.
11. '*The Spy in Black* was released on 12 August to exceptionally good reviews. With the declaration of war, audiences, hungry for a taste of battle, rushed to see the film .... Then, at

the beginning of October, the film became even more topical when the battleship *Royal Oak*
was indeed sunk in Scapa Flow. … It was a foretaste of the kind of up-to-the-minute
topicality that Emeric and Michael were to strive for in all their wartime films.' Kevin
Macdonald, *Emeric Pressburger: The Life and Death of a Screenwriter*, London: Faber & Faber,
1994, p. 158. It also had an immediate success in New York, as reported by Herman G.
Weinberg: '*U-29* (*The Spy in Black*) was released here almost simultaneously with the
beginning of hostilities abroad and naturally there was a rush to see it. Stevenson's [*sic*]
intelligent direction and Veidt's fine playing elicited enthusiastic comment from the press and
the film was a great financial success.' *Sight and Sound*, vol. 9 no. 33, Spring 1940, p. 40.
Weinberg evidently confuses Powell with Robert Stevenson, an exact contemporary of
Powell's, who was about to move to Hollywood.

12. 'It is sometimes forgotten … that all the Powell–Pressburger wartime films were original
stories, written for the screen, keeping pace with events and trying to put into action what
people were thinking and saying at the time.' Powell, *A Life in Movies*, p. 384.

13. Veidt played the Grand Vizier in *The Thief of Bagdad* (1940), co-directed by Powell, and then a
Dane, Captain Sorensen, in *Contraband*. His last film before his death in 1943 was *Casablanca*.

14. Goring played the Heavenly Messenger in *A Matter of Life and Death*, and the composer
Julian Craster, who marries Moira Shearer in *The Red Shoes* (1948).

15. Pressburger's obsessive punctuality is well attested. On the editing of *Black Narcissus*, Powell
noted that 'Emeric enjoyed the editing of the picture. He loved the cutting room and bristled
over Reggie Mills's unpunctuality. Emeric is never late.' (*A Life in Movies*, p. 621.) Rodney
Ackland, who worked on the dialogue of *49th Parallel*, found that 'With Emmerich, if I
arrived a second more than ten minutes late for a conference I would find him gone,
sometimes leaving a note with the uncompromising statement: "Couldn't wait any longer".'
Macdonald, *Emeric Pressburger*, pp. 174–5.

16. 'His favourite subject at school was mathematics. But outside school it was music that
captured his attention. [He] played the violin. … It is easy to forget that music was Emeric's
first love – even before films.' Macdonald, *Emeric Pressburger*, pp. 9 and 320.

17. *Prater Violet*, 1961 Penguin edn, p. 68. In my essay on Victor Saville in Pam Cook, ed.,
Gainsborough Pictures, London: Cassell, 1997, I apply the Isherwood quotation to the shot-by-
shot construction of key sequences in *The Faithful Heart*, edited by Ian Dalrymple, on whom
Isherwood's editor character is clearly modelled; he also edited *The Little Friend*, the 1934
film, co-scripted by Isherwood, that inspired the novel. It is notable that Powell repeatedly
goes out of his way to mention his admiration for Dalrymple, three of whose scripts he filmed
pre-1940, as if to suggest his *need* for the kind of mathematically-minded, editing-minded
collaborator that he finally found in Pressburger.

18. See note 16 above, and Macdonald, *Emeric Pressburger*, p. 268.

19. Raymond Bellour: 'Le Blocage symbolique', the main essay in his collection *L'Analyse du film*,
Paris: Éditions Albatros, 1979. English version: *The Analysis of Film*, Bloomington: Indiana
University Press, 2000.

20. Powell later recalled, 'I remember also the suggestion that the young girl spent her holiday in
the caravan with her young man shocked some people. … I thought they can't have been
around much. Such ridiculous conventions there were.' Interview with David Badder, *Sight
and Sound*, Winter 1978–9, p. 11. See also Powell, *A Life in Movies*, p. 440.

21. Lindsay Anderson, 'British Cinema: The Descending Spiral', *Sequence* 7, Spring 1949, p. 9. It was evidently Kathleen Byron who made the suggestion that her character should live no further away than across the hall – though the decision never to show her place was presumably that of Powell and Pressburger. See Macdonald, *Emeric Pressburger*, p. 300.

22. Martin Scorsese, 'British Movies: An Introduction', in Raffaele Caputo and Geoff Burton, eds, *Second Take*, St Leonards, Australia: Allen & Unwin, 1999, p. 142.

23. Charles Barr, 'In a Strange Land: The Collaboration of Michael Powell and Emeric Pressburger', *La Lettre de la Maison Française* 11, Oxford 1999, p. 102.

24. Michael Powell, *Edge of the World*, London: Faber & Faber, 1990, p. 327. Originally published by Faber & Faber in 1938 as *200,000 Feet on Foula*.

25. Powell, *A Life in Movies*, pp. 318–19. See also Macdonald, *Emeric Pressburger*, p. 152: '[Stewart] recalls that Michael, unable to come to the cutting room, sent him a 23-page letter, "all written in his own hand", detailing his ideas and suggestions on the editing'.

26. Macdonald, *Emeric Pressburger*, p. 249. See also Powell, *A Life in Movies*, p. 538.

3 From the Other Side of Time

Lesley Stern [1]

There is a pivotal moment in *A Matter of Life and Death* (1946) when everything freezes. It occurs in an operating theatre during an operation. In a tableau, figures are suspended mid-gesture; a scalpel is arrested in its passage from one hand to another. The hero lies unconscious on the operating table, suspended in time, poised between life and death, between this world and The Other. It is a rather hokey and hoary cinematic trick. Yet it is also a moment charged with expectation and pathos. The trope of suspension effects a break in continuity, in the flow of images and in our somatic apprehension of this flow. We hold our breath. Of course, we often hold our breath in the movies, but usually it is at a point of dramatic climax, at the height of suspense rather than in a moment of suspension. Here, rather than being swept up in a narrative orchestration of suspense, fear, expectation, we are presented with a tableau: motion is assaulted by stillness, the cinematic is invaded by a pictorial theatricality. The tableau acts, affecting in us a mimicry of its lack of vitality; breathless, we too are suspended, poised between our own solid three-dimensional world and that other world where nothing moves. In the stillness, sensations flutter – frailty, grief, hope and incredulity (that the movement of the film can be stopped just like that!).

This is the situation: it is during the Second World War and Peter Carter (David Niven), an English fighter pilot, has bailed out of his flaming plane without a parachute, fallen into the ocean and miraculously survived. But he is prone to hallucinations, indicating brain damage, and so now he is being operated on and his life hangs in the balance. Everything freezes. Then movement erupts into the scene with the arrival of two figures from The Other World who walk among the immobile human statues and raise Peter from his unconscious state, literally summoning him from the operating table to rise and walk with them through this ghostly *unheimlich* scene. Peter is hallucinating, it would seem. Yet while there is clearly a hallucinatory quality to the sequence, it is not so clear that the hallucination originates in, or can be attributed to, the consciousness of a character. The film, as indicated by the title, posits the coexistence of two worlds: this world, and what is referred to as The Other World. The drama of *A Matter of Life and Death* (hereafter *AMOLAD*) is generated out of a collision of perceptions. Those in The Other World believe that Peter has already passed over into their domain, but because of some record-keeping error has gone missing, and so an escort (Conductor 71, played by Marius Goring) is sent to retrieve him. Those in this world believe that he is still 'of this world'. Thus, there is no clear distinction between the two worlds in terms of reality and fantasy. As Michael Powell has said, 'everything was to be as real as possible in both worlds'[2] in this script, 'which called for wizardry and trick work on a grand scale.[3]'

Suspense would turn on a hermeneutic inflection: will Peter live or die? The suspension of *AMOLAD* turns rather on an indeterminacy. If we ask where and when is Peter? the film answers: somewhere between past and future, somewhere between here and there. Of course, when the scene freezes, the film in fact keeps on running through the projector, the series of tableaux are sequenced, the sense of stillness is created through movement. We might be tempted to say that the suspension of time is *represented*, that there is a straightforward relation between the narration and the diegesis, that the 'trick' is a device for indicating to the audience (though not to the characters, who have less knowledge) that time is stopped within the world of the story. However, although we might grasp that someone within the diegesis (though it is unclear whether it is Peter or the Conductor) is performing a trick, in fact it is hard not to be, *at the same time*, tricked (by the film-makers) – not into believing, but into feeling. Time, as Deleuze might say, rises to the surface. We experience a sense of suspension, a feeling of duration, of felt time. An intensity is conjured out of the moment. Fantasy and reality commingle in a space charged by imaginative projection. The force of the moment derives not from a signified; it is not that this moment *represents* a suspension, it *is* a suspension. If cinematic stories generally proceed through a putting into place, an acting out of character, a playing out of drama, then Powell and Pressburger rather proceed through disturbing the hierarchical relation between fantasy and reality, and through messing with the time-space continuum.

'Somewhere between past and future, somewhere between here and there': if this phrase gestures towards the hallucinatory, it also gestures towards what it often feels like to be a viewer of a Powell and Pressburger film. It feels like being in a hallucinatory world, immersed in the irreal; though you are caught up in a narrative. it is not narrative time that contours affect so much as cinematic time, registered in sensation, duration.

The phrase 'the other side of time' comes from *The Thief of Bagdad* (1940). The prince awakens the sleeping princess and it is love at first sight. He seems to have materialised out of thin air and she asks him where he has come from. He replies, 'From the other side of time.'

The princess put to sleep by the Vizier in *Thief of Bagdad*, who will awake to the prince telling her that he has come 'from the other side of time'.

The Thief of Bagdad is not a Powell and Pressburger film, but Michael Powell was one of several directors who worked on it, and he has often acknowledged its influence (his first job on the film was to shoot the emergence of the djinni from the bottle).[4] It was his first experience of Technicolor, and moreover it used colour in all its glory to render a fabulous fantasy world. *Thief* messes about with time and space in a marvellous fashion: it is a film in which a giant 40-foot djinni flies through the air, and in which people and things are transformed (a boy turns into a dog, a mechanical horse trots into the air and takes flight). Richly endowed with special effects, it is spectacular and sensational, more concerned with affecting the senses than corralling belief. In of the most exciting sequences, the djinni flies with the tiny figure of the boy Sabu clinging to his pigtail, over and through a kaleidoscopically mutating landscape. It is exhilarating, you feel lifted out of your seat and transported, a bodily sensation of liberation from three-dimensional certainty. There is a comparable flying sequence in *Star Wars*, which is also thrilling and somatic, but there we seem to be moving with the camera, cutting through the landscape as though we are *there*. An effect of the real is achieved through a technique of identification. In *Thief*, by contrast, the camera does not move through space with the impossibly flying figure. The camera shows us the djinni flying through a magically changing landscape, and simultaneously the film exhibits its trickery (the details – matte paintings, traveling mattes, rear projection, foreground miniatures, model work, and so on – do not matter, it is the allusion to trickery). How, then, is the sensation of being moved, of exhilaration, achieved? We might say that this is the *trompe l'oeil* effect. *Trompe l'oeil* can pertain to any sort of visual trickery, but most commonly it is a conceit for creating an illusion of three-dimensionality. For *trompe l'oeil* to succeed, the viewer must be fooled; but – and this is crucial – also amused, and for the amusement to take effect, the trick must be perceived. So it is a momentary deceit rather than a sustained illusion. And the trick shows off, displays itself, is conceited.[5]

Where does Peter come from? He falls from the sky without a parachute and then within a few minutes falls again: after stumbling out of the sea (miraculously alive) onto a beach, where a naked goatherd, a young boy, plays pan pipes, he encounters a girl cycling along the beach. They gaze into each other's eyes and he falls, they both fall, instantly, in love. If she were to ask him, 'where have you come from?', he might well answer, 'From the other side of time.' In fact, Peter and June have encountered one another prior to this, not in the flesh but virtually. The film opens in space, in something like an abstract painting, a blue vortex over which a voice intones, in a documentary manner, initially about the universe and then progressively closing in to the sky, to our planet, to 'a real English fog'. As the narrator muses, 'I hope all our aircraft got home safely', a face emerges out of the fog, like an apparition materialising out of chaos. This is June (Kim Hunter), an American WAC based in England, and she is talking by radio with Peter, who is surrounded by flames, his plane in tatters, the dead body of his radio man lying next to him. Although they are in quite separate places, the sequence is orchestrated in such a way as to suggest spatial continuity and to evoke intimacy. It is as though they are in a world of their own, outside time and place.[6] Kim Hunter plays June as a grounded, everyday sort of a girl, someone familiar whom we can believe in. Yet she is also a sleeping princess, woken from slumber by the force of wish-fulfilment, by the desire of the prince. When they meet on the beach, we watch her face in close up as her expression changes, as emotions flutter over her features. She drops her bicycle, realising that it is him, the voice of the doomed fighter has materialised in the body of David Niven. In a tight two-shot, they embrace. Is it then she who is hallucinating, who wishes Peter back to life, back from the other side of time? All we can say with certainty is that this story has been signalled as a fairy story, a fantasy, just as all love stories are fantasies, that the performative exchange of falling in love involves wish-fulfilment, denial, projection.

Then again, perhaps June and Peter are both hallucinations, characters conjured out of the fog, like all cinematic characters? If the fantasy of love takes flight in a space-time vortex, then it is also grounded in the bodily. This tussle between psychic abstraction and embodiment is what fuels romantic fiction. In Powell and Pressburger, embodiment itself is often inflected fantastically.

Let us return to the frozen moment. June in mid-shot is looking through the glass doors into the room where the operation is taking place. She has just scratched her head and is beginning to lower her hand. Time stops, she freezes in the pose. We are given her view of the operating room where the operation is suspended, and the surgery team is also frozen, in mid-action, handing implements to each other. Two figures from The Other World are here, the conductor and Peter's radio-operator (who we last saw lying dead in the plane). They walk into the room, through the tableau of doctors and nurses holding frozen poses, and raise Peter from the operating table. In The Other World, there is to be a court case to determine whether Peter is alive, and therefore entitled to remain on earth, or dead, in which case he must take his place in The Other World. A defence case is being prepared for Peter, and the two visitants have come to earth in search of evidence. The evidence they need is love: if Peter is in love he is alive. All eyes are on the 'sleeping' June. Peter asks if he may kiss her. 'You may, but she will not know it.' As he kisses her, the Conductor remarks testily, 'Oh, he is English. What is the point of kissing a girl if she does not feel it?' This joke is

The frozen moment: June's tear allows emotion to be transmitted between different worlds in *A Matter of Life and Death*.

actually a pretext for the unravelling of a more serious conceit to do with sensate knowledge (it is characteristic of the film that it frequently and surprisingly shifts register). Peter feels something on his cheek. It is a tear. They look and see a tear on June's cheek even though she is clearly asleep, or unconscious, or not of this world. Conductor 17 takes the rose from his lapel and captures the tear on its petal. This is the evidence of love that they will take back to The Other World. It is at this point that colour is drained from the image, leaving a translucent teardrop in pearly monochrome, and a transition to The Other World is effected. This world is in colour; the Other is rendered in black and white. The more serious conceit concerns the transmission of emotion between different realms, or worlds, between the inanimate (or represented) and the real (or those occupying a living three-dimensional world), and by extension, between the cinema screen and the audience.

The notion of the between is important to *AMOLAD*: Peter is situated between life and death; his hallucinations, comparable to an experience of actual life, occur between times. The category of the between is also fundamental in topology. My body sees in a projective space; it touches, caresses and feels in a topological space. *Trompe l'oeil* pertains primarily to sight, although it entails bodily perception. There is also, in Powell and Pressburger, a kind of trickery that is not simply about visual sleight of hand, about spectacle and the sensations associated with spectacle, but more about sentiment. There is a psycho-logic to the orchestration of their films that is not strictly psychological – often this involves a kind of cinematic trickery, that, for the sake of symmetry with *trompe l'oeil*, we can call a trick of the heart, or tricking the heart. The process and effect is similar to the mechanisms of *trompe l'oeil*, in that in order for it to work, we have to be aware of the trick, to enter into it (the trick of the captured tear on the rose petal, colour fading from the image, transport between realms), to be moved.

In fact, this is not the first, or only, occasion when time has been stopped in the film. The first time the Conductor visits earth in search of the missing Peter, he arrives in a grove of rhododendrons, where he makes the famous Technicolor joke: 'One is starved for Technicolor up there.' Powell tells of how Pressburger had written the line as 'one is starved for colour', but when it came to shooting the scene, Powell was

> Interested in finding out whether you can make an escapist joke like that within conventions of a naturalistic super-film in colour. So I deliberately changed the line from the script, changing 'colour' into 'Technicolor.' To my delight, the whole audience, this huge audience of 3,000 people [at the Royal Performance], gave a roar of laughter right on the joke, which is a professional one, and then without the slightest difficulty, or noticeable transition, they went right back into the film and went on following it in the normal way of involvement.[7]

The camera tracks through the bushes and finds the lovers lying on the ground picnicking. Peter is offering June a drink, but she is asleep. The Conductor says, 'She cannot wake. We are talking in space, not in time.' He continues, 'Look at your

watch. It has not moved since you said so charmingly, "Drink, Darling?" Nor will it
move, nor will anything move until we have finished our little talk. It is only a trick.'

A trick certainly, but not only a trick. This moment, like the exemplary moment
in the operating theatre, has the capacity to tickle, to simultaneously amuse and
move. In diegetic terms, the 'trick' refers to the stopping of time (on earth) by the
Conductor. What takes place, then, while some of the characters are frozen, occurs
in another dimension. The Conductor says, 'We are talking in space, not time,' and
Powell has said, 'The Collector's visits to Earth take place in space but not in time.
So the whole argument between him and Peter has taken place in the fourth dimension, and June has heard nothing.'[8] Powell tosses off this notion of the fourth dimension but let us think about it for a moment, let us take it as an opportunity to ponder
spatio-temporal configurations. This scene is not exactly outside of the space-time
continuum, or the world of the representation. But insofar as it inserts into the *mise
en scène* bodies existing in different spatio-temporal dimensions, it posits the coexistence of different realities, or of fantasy and the designated real, of real people and
apparitions.

It is commonplace to say that before 1915, time and space were fixed. Things happened in them. After the theory of general relativity, space and time became dynamic
quantities. The general theory of relativity posits three dimensions of space and one
of time, though they are articulated together. Although it is straightforward to describe
this mathematically, it is hard to visualise, especially the curvature of space. However,
since the general theory of relativity, other theories have emerged, and now the space-
time continuum is conceived of as only one of many different types of four-dimensional spaces. When the fourth dimension is invoked in discussions of art and
performance, it is usually elaborated in terms of abstraction. One of the most detailed
applications is Linda Henderson's *Duchamp in Context*, in which she discusses the
fourth dimension as a mathematical modelling of a fiction. She focuses on the intersection between science and art in Duchamp, and also discusses ways in which an anti-
representational practice, as epitomised in the Large Glass (1915–23), provokes an
activity of visualisation on the part of the spectator. This activity is not aimed at rendering the four-dimensional bride as material, but rather is a way of entering the fictional space of the conceit via the materiality of the art.[9] Now clearly, any narrative
fiction film is more representational than *The Bride Stripped Bare*, but the
Powell–Pressburger oeuvre is also more dedicated to elaborate cinematic conceits, and
the films employ various tropes and stratagems to entice the viewer to stretch the representational contract and enter the fictional space of the conceit.[10] Not exactly a
mathematical modelling, but nevertheless a modelling of fiction.

This modelling of fiction involves time and space and bodies (bodies on the
screen and in the theatre, more substantial and bodily bodies, on the whole, than
Duchamp's bride). Since Bergson, there has been a move away from mathematical
modelling as the key to understanding time, and a turn towards questions of how
time is experienced, how it is felt, how it is articulated spatially (or, at least, this is
one tendency, of particular pertinence to film study). Early modernist experiments

with time and space in cinema and the other arts are testimony to this, and Eisenstein, the great practitioner and theorist of felt time, who experimented more than most with time and space through the media of body and brain (to borrow terms from Deleuze), stands as an eccentric precursor to Powell and Pressburger. But as cinema developed as a predominantly narrative realist form, so the relation between time and space became more commonly seamless (although, of course, there are exceptions, not only in art cinema/auterist cinema, but also in the high moments of genre cinema (such as the shoot-out) and in non-Hollywood cinemas (think of the irreal speed of Hong Kong action cinema on the one hand, and the equally irreal slowness of Hou Hsiao-hsien on the other).[11]

Let me turn to another 'fourth-dimension' episode – the ping-pong scene. June and Dr Reeves (Frank, played by Roger Livesey), shown in a static long shot, are playing a lively game of ping-pong while Peter, in an adjacent room, has fallen asleep reading. Suddenly Frank and June freeze, caught in animated poses. A close-up of Peter shows him dozing, nostrils twitching (indicating the smell of fried onions, a cue for his hallucinations). He wakes, rushes outside into the ping-pong tableau, throws his arms into the air and holds the gesture. For a moment, all three figures seem to be occupying the same spatio-temporal continuum, but then Peter moves and asymmetry registers. Asymmetry is emphasised in the montage that follows, during which Peter both looks at June and Frank (reverse shots, although, weirdly, their gaze is not directed at him) and tries to enter their space or consciousness (tight

The arrested ping-pong game in *A Matter of Life and Death* conjures an atmosphere of irreality, solicits our complicity, and announces its own trickery.

framing bringing moving, breathing, speaking Peter into close proximity with the macabre, grimacing inanimate versions of Frank and June). The sense of irreality provoked by this sequence is strong, an uncanniness that somehow seems to register bodily in the act of viewing. And at the same time, you feel uneasy, like not quite fitting into your own skin, cognisant of an absurdity. This irreality undoubtedly has to do with the spatio-temporal dynamic in the cinema, some affect circulating between the bodies on the screen and bodies in the theatre. The tableau emphasises pose and gesture, and the gestural inflection has the capacity to move us (viewers) in ways that involve less semantic cognition than a kind of sensory or bodily apprehension. But it is also about the way in which bodily disposition is imbricated with cinematic technology, or, in this case, trickery. As soon as the scene is frozen, ambient sound disappears from the image creating an eeriness. Jack Cardiff, the cinematographer on *AMOLAD*, has explained the trick: 'It's done by a combination of stop-frame and posing by the actors with the ball suspended on an invisible thread' (back projection was not an option, because Niven has to walk around among them).[12] In addition he used a lemon rather than an amber filter to create 'the magical atmosphere the scene was meant to have'.[13]

This scene both conjures an atmosphere of irreality and solicits our complicity with the fiction, but at the same time announces its trickery. Often it is assumed that this degree of reflexivity leads to a distancing of the viewer, a reducing or severing of emotional engagement. But what Powell and Pressburger alert us to is the sensational aspect of cinema, the orchestration of cinematic elements with performing bodies to elicit an emotional and sensory engagement.

Having set the scene, as it were, by teasing out a number of conceptual strands (and flying a few whimsical kites) emanating from the suspended moment in the operating theatre, I will now rein in these strands and focus on braiding something betwixt a meditation and an argument. I have given some attention to the notion of the fourth dimension as deployed in *AMOLAD* not in order to invoke it as an authoritative scientific principle but rather to pose it as a cinematic trope central to Powell and Pressburger's oeuvre and practice. Although the Conductor says, 'we are talking in space, not in time', we have seen that what actually happens in these moments is that time rises to the surface and is experienced as an affective intensity. Though we might be caught up in a narrative, it is not narrative time that contours affect. Emotional duration exceeds diegetic temporality. And this sensation is often produced by the way bodies are configured cinematically in a spatio-temporal dynamic. Although this intensity is frequently achieved through cinematic trickery, it usually involves a performing body. Bodily movement, however, is not necessarily expressive of individualised psychological interiority, but might follow a different psycho-logic that often in Powell and Pressburger is closer to a logic of sentiment, articulated as a trick of the heart. In other words, we (the viewer, although of course I use the royal we heuristically) willingly enter into a fictional regime (an irreality, often) where sensation and sentiment contour affect (whether it means holding our breath or shedding a tear).[14] If *trompe l'oeil* is most commonly a conceit for creating an illusion of three-dimensionality, then a trick of the heart pertains more to the fourth dimension.

In the remainder of this chapter, I will bring the performing body in cinema more to the fore, discussing a few general issues to do with its spatio-temporal configuration, and its place in the circuit of affect. This discussion will be fuelled by a cluster of Powell and Pressburger's films – *The Life and Death of Colonel Blimp*, *AMOLAD*, *Black Narcissus*, *The Red Shoes* and *The Tales of Hoffmann*, made between 1943 and 1951 – though mostly they will smoulder in the background of the discussion.[15] I will, however, explore the ideas raised here in more detail in relation to two scenes from *The Life and Death of Colonel Blimp*.

The argument is sometimes made that in theatre, in live performance, actors are able to generate and transmit energy because the audience occupies the same space-time continuum as the actors, whereas the cinema is struggling always to create and sustain an illusion of presence. In fact the argument can be made that the audience in live theatre needs to fictionalise the solid three-dimensional bodies of the actors in order to enter into the dramatic fiction, to effect a performative exchange. We know that actors in film can and do generate and transmit energy (how else do we account for the star system?) for much the same reasons – a complex act of fictional engagement. But the circumstances are different in film, and so the processes too are different. It might be true that the body in cinema is made up of parts and manipulated like a puppet; but it is also the case that the presence of actors, their bodily presence, disposition, movement can also be a factor in the generation of sensation. The challenge is to understand *how* the body in cinema can produce affects and transmit energy when it is an unreal or fictional body: always figured out, spatialised by the camera, lighting, framing, cutting, and temporalised too – cut up, dispersed, faded in, speeded up, slowed down.

We can approach this conundrum by remembering that even though the cinematic body is insubstantial, ephemeral, it is also indexical of the real, and it is in this tension (between the indexical and the fictional) that mimetic engagement is generated. The affect produced by cinematic bodies arises out of an imbrication of acting techniques and cinematic technologies. Powell and Pressburger's films are highly orchestrated, the *mise en scène* is intricate and elaborate and yet not entirely in the service of verisimilitude (ensured by the imprint of set designers and art directors like Hein Heckroth and Alfred Junge). Within this elaborate performative machine, where and how does the actor figure? Can he/she figure as anything more than an element of the *mise en scène*, a prop, or even perhaps a perverse inflection of the Bressonian 'model' (*Tales of Hoffmann* would be an exemplary instance in its confusion of puppets and people)? Yes, I would say the actor does figure as more than a prop (which is not to say that he/she is not also and at the same time a prop). Powell and Pressburger accord to the actorly performance an important place. The spatio-temporal orchestration of bodies is a significant feature of their films: space is spatialised by motion and bodily dynamics, and temporalised through the 'timing' of the actor's performance and cinematic action upon the body.

Most of Powell and Pressburger's films are distinguished by an air of theatricality. In some cases, this can be attributed to their subject matter (*Tales* being based on an opera, *The Red Shoes* about ballet). They aspire to the condition of opera, ballet, fairy tales. But even the films that do not take the performative as their ostensible subject matter nevertheless are concerned with role-playing and performativity. In the commentary to the Criterion DVD of *The Life and Death of Colonel Blimp*, Martin Scorsese remarks on the relation between the music and the way people move. He observes that when actors move, it is like a 'mini ballet but in a dramatic movie', it is extremely subtle, however, movement registered in 'just a bow of the head'. He also describes how he learned from *Tales* to move the camera to music. 'Michael Powell's Guilty Pleasures' is instructive for identifying the actors and performances that made a strong impression on the young Powell (and which, we may surmise, persisted as an influence in his choice of performers): Menjou in *A Woman of Paris* ('sophisticated, flawless, tactful, tasteful, Gallic to a degree' – could Powell not be describing Anton Walbrook?), Navarro in *Scaramouche* ('this was what romantic acting was all about!') and Alice Terry ('she moved beautifully'), Emil Jannings in *Tartuffe*, Ivan Mozhukhin in *Kean* ('a very theatrical film' with 'one of the most successful dance sequences I have seen filmed').[16] Powell often tended to choose actors whose idiom registered a pronounced theatricality or histrionic disposition, actors distinguished by hyper-emphatic timing, such as Anton Walbrook and Robert Helpmann. Helpmann was a dancer and actor, and there is a discernible dancerly quality to his non-dancing parts. Again, Scorsese describes his

> gestures or ballet moves, I don't know what really to call them, when he's on the gondola [in *Tales*] and during the sword fight when he sort of moves his hand across his face and his eyes go from left to right.[17]

Yann Tobin has called *Tales* a film that renders Minnelli Bressonian.[18]

But despite a penchant for the histrionic, Powell and Pressburger were equally interested in the counterposing of actors and performance styles, particularly in playing off the more theatrically inflected performers against more quotidian styles. This is not to say that the quotidian is simply a foil, for in fact what emerges as distinctive in Powell and Pressburger is precisely a permeability between the histrionic and the quotidian (just as reality and fantasy are intermeshed). In *AMOLAD*, for instance, David Niven and Kim Hunter are thus partnered, as are Livesey and Goring. Roger Livesey can swing between a certain kind of bluff English Tory typicality and a histrionic streak that is always threatening to caricature his own persona (which makes him ideal for *Blimp*). In *The Red Shoes*, the cast freely mixes ballet dancers and actors, just as *Tales* mixes singers, dancers and actors. An apparently more orthodox actor like Deborah Kerr is exploited by

Powell (in *Blimp* and *Black Narcissus*) for a quality of submerged intensity. As David Denby puts it, 'Deborah Kerr was a restrained performer, but what she held in was as vivid as what she let come to the surface.'[19] In *Black Narcissus*, this is instantiated in the mirroring of Deborah Kerr and Kathleen Byron, in the transmission of energy between them, in a dance that takes place between the rhythm (or timing) of the camera, the shots and the performances.

Timing is always an element of acting performance, and is a crucial element in the generation of affect, the production of a mimetic sensation in the viewer. This is easy to grasp in the case of screwball comedy, where the pace and timing of dialogue induces a sense of speedy exhilaration. Yet timing sculpts not only dialogue but also bodily rhythms and gestures. In Powell and Pressburger's cinema, the attention to bodily rhythms and gestures is unusually pronounced; the sense of emotional time exceeding diegetic time is achieved through such attention. And it is executed through a combination of performance (bodily technique) and filmic language (cinematographic technique). Often an affect is generated through something as simple as a camera movement in conjunction with an expression or gesture. But at other times, camera speed is important. We tend to think of slow and fast motion as pertaining to action, but Powell has often stressed that the speed of twenty-four frames per second is just a convention, and 'we're always using different speeds, all the time … Every shot that you take in a film has a speed of its own.'[20] Faces can be filmed at different speeds, overcranking, for instance, producing a sense of focused intensity. Under the influence of Powell, Scorsese achieved this intensity in the close-ups of Robert de Niro's face in *Taxi Driver*. And just as time can be slowed, so it can be speeded up. Powell's gloss on Vicky's flight down the spiral staircase at the end of *The Red Shoes* is instructive:

> Moira did that beautifully … it's a lovely example of movement. Most actors don't grasp that movement tends to slow down in sound film. Twenty-four frames per second is a totally arbitrary speed. I always tried to shoot scenes at different speeds, even dialogue scenes: anything from 10 to 29, although of course, you know it'll be projected at 24 frames per second. But every shot has its own viewpoint, its own pace, its own mood. We didn't shoot Moira at normal speed in her dancing scenes on stage; it was 18 or 19.[21]

In turning now to *The Life and Death of Colonel Blimp*, I want to explore, through two different scenes, how speed (though not necessarily camera speed) can paradoxically elongate time, and conversely, how elongation can produce a sense of focused distillation. *Colonel Blimp* tells a story, in flashback, that spans forty years, but the overarching conceit (partly fuelling the narrative, but also existing as a parallel poetic) is of love that transcends time and space, that is to say, remains constant as the times change. This love is given two inflections, but in each case the romance is centred on the least romantic of the characters, Clive Candy (the 'Colonel Blimp' figure, played by Roger Livesey). On the one hand, there is his one and only 'true love', incarnated by three different women, in three different historical periods – all

played by Deborah Kerr; and on the other, there is his abiding friendship with the
German, Theo Kretschmar-Schuldorff, surviving in defiance of their historically
determined role as enemies.[22] As Olivier Assayas has pointed out, one of the
remarkable things about *Blimp* is that it features a character who does not change,
grow or acquire insight.[23] In temporal terms, there is an unusual – for a narrative of
epic proportions – meshing of the synchronic with the diachronic, more typical of
poetry or fairy tale. I want to look at two sequences that, in a concentrated way, play
out these conceits, each charging a moment with particular intensity so that felt time
exceeds diegetic time. Both deploy the human body in interesting ways, though in
terms of performance they proceed quite differently.

During the First World War, while stationed in France, General Candy takes
refuge one night in a convent where British nurses have been billeted. Having lost
his first great love, Edith, to his friend Theo after the Boer War, he has continued
on, soldiering alone. He enters the refectory, where about a hundred nuns, in grey
and white uniforms, are seated at long trestle tables eating dinner. The large and
ancient space is cavernous with vaulted ceilings, filled with women. The camera dol-
lies behind Candy as he moves down the hall between the tables, led by the matron.
Then, almost imperceptibly, he slows down, turns to his left and pauses. Cut into a
close-up of Deborah Kerr, elbow leaning on the table, head resting on her hand,

Charging a moment with intensity: Clive Candy arrives at a convent where English nurses are
billeted and suddenly pauses at the sight of one.

After Clive's 'recognition' in *The Life and Death of Colonel Blimp*, the nurses move away and wind up the staircase as if in a wave.

asleep. A classic portrait, a still life. The shot lasts only a few seconds. Cut back to the view behind Candy as he moves on and takes his seat. In long shot, he looks over his shoulder, searching. Cut to a mid-shot of the women rising and beginning to move away from the table, the redhead is among them, but part of a *mélange* of movement. He asks the nurse sitting opposite him, with urgency: 'Do you know that girl over there?' A brief glimpse of the girl from behind, her head turned in profile. The nurses move away, towards the stair, like a tidal wave, a mass of uniforms. Candy is aghast. As he asks where the nurses have come from, they wind en masse in the background up the massive stone spiral staircase. Fade.

The effect here, the affect too, is created less through performance and more through a combination of *mise en scène*, camera movement, cutting and music. Although the close-up lasts only a few seconds, it seems to persist much longer, to reverberate through the entire sequence. Indeed, it is partly its very brevity that paradoxically invests the image with an intensity, a sense of dilation. And partly, it is also the way that the static close-up is cut into a sequence of movement. These cinematic devices work together rhetorically both to trigger and mimic the process of

The first of two crucial staircase scenes in *The Red Shoes*: Vicky dressed as a princess arriving at a Riviera villa for her fateful meeting with Lermontov.

memory – both for the character and for us, though in slightly different ways. The image of the young woman – inanimate, cut out, framed – evokes a memory of Edith, of Deborah Kerr animated, talkative, moving in and out of the frame. But for us, unlike for the character Candy, it is clearly the same actress and thus in a sense the same woman. The conceit is displayed for us, though not for him. Even though I see the trick, I am moved by this sequence, by its uncanny reverberations. I fall for this trick of the heart.

Although I have implied that Deborah Kerr is not 'acting' here, there is in fact a performative element in her gestural disposition, in the pose. It is a bodily disposition that contributes to the pathos of the scene. It is also significant because it serves as an example of a more general tendency: the mixing of animate and inanimate. Sometimes this occurs in relation to puppets and people, as in *The Tales of Hoffmann*, or things and people, as in *The Red Shoes*, but often it is manifested in terms of a dynamic of motion and stillness. Generally this tendency, often played out in an uncanny scenario, serves to advertise a regime of stylised fictionality, while at the same time drawing us into an emotional and sensory engagement.

This scene is interesting too for its incorporation of a recurring Powell–Pressburger trope: scale as a measure of emotion. The audacious contrast between the brief close-up of a face and the more lengthy long shot of a large expanse of space

The *trompe l'oeil* staircase of the Olympia sequence in *Tales of Hoffmann*, painted on the floor, allowing dancers to move freely 'up' and 'down'.

filled with a mass of bodies winding up a monumental staircase serves to crystallise the emotive force of the scene. This juxtaposition of the miniature and the gigantic (or close and far, foreground and background) need not be manifested in a close-up montaged with a wide long shot; rather it might be the positioning of a small human body in a huge environment (at once the story and the *mise en scène* of *Black Narcissus*), a spectacular feature of the movie that ghosts this chapter and the Powell–Pressburger oeuvre, *The Thief of Bagdad*. The privileged motif of this trope is the staircase. It is, of course, central to *AMOLAD*, and *The Red Shoes* contains two featuring stairway scenes: Vicky's suicide flight down the spiral staircase, which has already been mentioned; and her ascent, dressed like a princess, up the fairy-tale, romantically overgrown stone steps, to a meeting with Lermontov (from pathos to bathos). In *Tales*, there are several featured stairway scenes: in the Olympia tale, a carpet painted as a staircase is unrolled on the floor, upon which the characters proceed to dance, up and down, in a magnificent demonstration of *trompe l'oeil*; Giulietta walks on a stairway made of the heads of dead men; and Antonia runs up and down the steps of a classical garden. Stairs are the acme of 'in between', denoting not simply the passage between one place and another, but a suspension of time and place, where time rises to the surface, and spatial apprehension escapes from the place of the narrative, from narrative place.

In *The Life and Death of Colonel Blimp*, much of the pathos is generated between the two men. Anton Walbrook and Roger Livesey are perfectly contrasted. Laurence Olivier was originally slated to play Clive, but he was doing military service and could not be released. As Powell told Bertrand Tavernier in a 1968 interview, he opted for Roger Livesey, 'who I knew was another good actor; but being as he was sentimental, the film became sentimental'.[24] Against Walbrook's steely restraint, Livesey plays Blimp as exuberant and bluff; against Walbrook's aloof and elegant European courtesy, Livesey's Clive is impulsive and generously demonstrative. Even as an old man and a general he is, beside Walbrook, an English puppy dog, albeit with a raspy voice. Walbrook exudes a quality of stillness, he concentrates time; Livesey blusters, disperses time. The two men deploy a theatricality as they act out on the stage of history, act out aspects of their national personae. This film takes history as its stage rather than invoking, as do some of the other Powell and Pressburger films, more directly the theatre or ballet or opera. *Blimp*, like all of their films, stretches the conventions as a film, but it is also, maybe more than many, *about* the conventional, about *how to act* (though perhaps it shares the honours in this regard with *Black Narcissus*, which is about being a nun, acting and entering into the part). The range of codified mores is extensive – from the duel that proceeds histrionically and literally according to the rule book, to the quotidian habits, ingrained gestures and small intimate rituals of friendship. The film is thick with gestural detail (a kind of performative 'thick description'), and it is these gestures that tie the two men together in a physical space that is very touching, and rare to see, outside the buddy genre.

The second scene I want to draw attention to does not, however, involve the two men, although it is ghosted by all the gestural traces of their friendship. It is Theo's speech delivered in a makeshift English court (a converted schoolroom) to a judge in mufti during the Second World War. Theo is appealing for asylum, and the president of his tribunal who is listening to his case has decided to intern him after he has bluntly recounted how his two sons have become Nazis. When asked if he has anything to add, Theo says, 'I have not told a lie. But I also have not told the truth. A refugee soon learns that there is a great difference between the two … The truth about me is that I am a tired old man.' And so begins the long speech in which he narrates the rise of Nazism, the loss of both his children to the Nazi party and the death of his wife. He ends: 'And very foolishly I remembered the countryside, the gardens, the green lawns, the weedy rivers and the trees she loved so much. And a great desire came over me to come back to my wife's country. And this, sir, is the truth.' This speech, lasting nearly four minutes, is shot in a single take. It begins on a medium shot of Theo and very gradually moves in to a medium close-up, and then out again to the initial framing. Ambient sound is faded out of the scene as he begins to speak, and is brought back again as he finishes. As he speaks, Theo's eyes glisten with tears. This is a moving speech, but it is also presented as a virtuoso performance. Theo understands that his initial explanation to the judge has been too blunt, and this speech is meant to move and persuade. But it is also, as he avers, not a lie. It is, then, rhetorical, presented like a theatrical soliloquy. As Andrew Moor has written:

Theo (Walbrook) and Clive (Livesey) after the former's great four-minute speech, in which 'time rises to the surface'.

The fact that Pressburger often wrote crucial set-piece speeches for Walbrook indicates the weight his oratory carried … Always eloquent, Walbrook's voice is a subtly modulated and rhythmed tenor, tightening in moments of urgency into a guttural, strangulated rasp – a flicker of the barely submerged hysteria which would break loose in Walbrook's more histrionic moments.[25]

The length of the take (combined with the very formal framing and symmetrical camera movement in and out) declares itself as rhetorical ploy, just as the brevity of the close-up in the previous example declared something of its discursive purview. Although Theo's speech is shot in real time (and so not subject to what we customarily call 'cinematic trickery'), it acquires a kind of irreality, as though occurring in a spatio-temporal dynamic of its own. Time rises to the surface. Once again: a trick of the heart.

In both of these scenes, just as in the suspended moment in the operating theatre, fantasy and reality commingle in a space charged by imaginative projection: somewhere between past and future, somewhere between here and there.

NOTES

1. My thanks to Orly Shevi for research assistance.
2. Michael Powell, *A Life in Movies: An Autobiography*, London: Heinemann, 1986, p. 498.
3. Ibid., p. 499.
4. Powell recounts how his very first day working for Rex Ingram was spent observing the setting up of a shot involving a foreground miniature ceiling. 'I was to do a lot of this foreground miniature work later on, on *The Thief of Bagdad*, for Korda, and the amusing link to me, as I look back to that first day, is that priest-like miniature maker, Walter Pahlman, had done the miniature work on Douglas Fairbank's *Thief of Bagdad* two years before. So my first day in movies was centred on a trick shot as, I have no doubt, my last will be.' Powell, *A Life in Movies*, pp. 122–3.
5. For a more extensive discussion of *trompe l'oeil*, see Lesley Stern, 'The Tales of Hoffmann: An Instance of Operality', in Jeongwon Joe and Rose Theresa, eds, *Between Opera and Cinema*, New York: Routledge, 2001, pp. 39–57.
6. As John Ellis has pointed out, it is edited '*as though* this were a shot/reverse shot set-up'. See Ellis, 'Watching Death at Work: An Analysis of *A Matter of Life and Death*', in Ian Christie, ed., *Powell, Pressburger and Others*, London: BFI, 1978, p. 94.
7. Powell, *A Life in Movies*, pp. 591–2.
8. Ibid., p. 496.
9. Linda Dalrymple Henderson, *Duchamp in Context: Science and Technology in the Large Glass and Related Works*, Princeton: Princeton University Press, 1998.
10. See Ian Christie's discussion of figural strategies of various kinds in *AMOLAD* in Ian Christie, *A Matter of Life and Death*, London: BFI, 2000.
11. Ian Christie notes as a possible antecedent 'Eisenstein's idea of "synaesthesia", or the total mobilization of all elements within the spectacle towards a single expressive end'. See Ian Christie, *Arrows of Desire: The Films of Michael Powell and Emeric Pressburger*, London: Faber & Faber, 1994, p. 6.

12. David Badder, 'Powell and Pressburger: The War Years', *Sight and Sound*, vol. 118 no. 1, Winter 1978–9, p. 12.

13. Jack Cardiff, *Magic Hour: The Life of a Cameraman*, London: Faber & Faber, 1996, p. 86; and Justin Bowyer, *Conversations with Jack Cardiff: Art, Light and Direction in Cinema*, London: Batsford, 2003, p. 63.

14. A number of writers have referred to the romantic sensibility in Powell and Pressburger. Jean-Pierre Coursodon, for instance, identifies a 'romantico-surrealiste' strain in *AMOLAD*. See Coursodon, 'Michael Powell et les Archers, en guerre et en paix 1940–1950', *Positif* 478, December 2000, p. 86. Ian Christie discusses the influence of English Neo-Romanticism in *AMOLAD* in Christie, *A Matter of Life and Death*, pp. 72–3. Raymond Durgnat discusses it in several places, but see particularly Durgnat, 'Michael Powell', in Christie, ed., *Powell, Pressburger and Others*, pp. 65–74. Finally, Andrew Sarris speaks of the 'redemptively romantic' in Powell and Pressburger. See Sarris, 'The Life and Death of Colonel Blimp', *Film Comment* vol. 26 no. 3, May–June 1990, p. 32.

15. I discuss *The Red Shoes* in more detail in Lesley Stern, *The Scorsese Connection*, London and Bloomington: BFI and Indiana University Press, 1995; and *The Tales of Hoffmann* in Stern, 'The Tales of Hoffmann.

16. Michael Powell, 'Michael Powell's Guilty Pleasures', *Film Comment*, vol. 117 no. 4, July–August 1981, pp. 28–31.

17. In discussion with Powell and Pressburger and Ian Christie at the National Film Theatre in July 1985. David Lazar, *Michael Powell: Interviews*, Jackson: University Press of Mississippi, 2003, p. 121.

18. Yann Tobin, 'Post-Scriptum: Le Point du Jour et les horizens perdus', *Positif* 241, April 1981, p. 30.

19. Cited by Celestino Deleyto, 'The Nun's Story', in Bruce Babington, ed., *British Stars and Stardom: From Alma Taylor to Sean Connery*, Manchester: Manchester University Press, 2001, p. 128.

20. Lazar, *Michael Powell: Interviews*, p. 121.

21. Harlan Kennedy, 'A Modest Magician', in Lazar, *Michael Powell: Interviews*, p. 174.

22. Ian Christie has noted, 'In a device which anticipates the theatrical disguises of *The Tales of Hoffmann*, we are seduced into sharing Clive's fantasy of an "eternal recurrence".' Michael Powell, Emeric Pressburger and Ian Christie, *The Life and Death of Colonel Blimp*, London: Faber & Faber, 1994, p. xviii.

23. Olivier Assayas, 'L'Esprit du temps', *Cahiers du Cinéma* 321, March 1981, p. 11.

24. Lazar, *Michael Powell: Interviews*, p 37.

25. Andrew Moor, 'Dangerous Limelight: Anton Walbrook and the Seduction of the English', in Babington, ed., *British Stars and Stardom*, p. 83.

4 A Life in Pictures

Thelma Schoonmaker and Ian Christie

The young author.

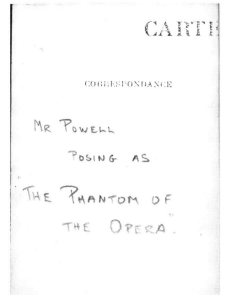
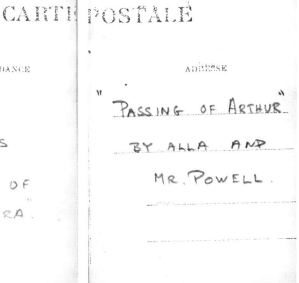

Photographs sent by Powell to his mother while working for Rex Ingram's company at the
Victorine Studios, Nice, *c.* 1926. Parodies of the recent *Phantom of the Opera* and the popular
image from *Morte d'Arthur.*

Portrait dated 1925.

Powell as an English tourist in Ingram's *The
Garden of Allah* (1927), a role he would
recreate in *Riviera Revels*, a series of shorts
made in 1927–8 with Harry Lachmann.

Michael Powell and Frankie Reidy after their marriage in 1943.

On the set of *The Life and Death of Colonel Blimp* at Denham in 1943. Powell directing Anton Walbrook, Roger Livesey, Deborah Kerr and Ursula Jeans. The cinematographer Georges Perinal (with an eyeshade) and chief electrician Bill Wall appear in the second photograph.

Directing local children for the river battle in *A Canterbury Tale*.

Powell queuing for lunch with members of the crew at Staunton Sands for the beach scene in *A Matter of Life and Death*.

Directing Wendy Hiller for the sleeping car sequence in *I Know Where I'm Going!*.

With J. Arthur Rank on the set of *Black Narcissus* at Pinewood.

With Rank and John Davis during the shooting of *The Red Shoes*, which the latter would deplore.

With Moira Shearer in Monte Carlo, preparing the death scene for *The Red Shoes*.

Shooting *The Sorcerer's Apprentice*, a ballet short designed by Hein Heckroth in Stuttgart in 1956.

Powell and Pressburger in 1948, during the production of *The Small Back Room*.

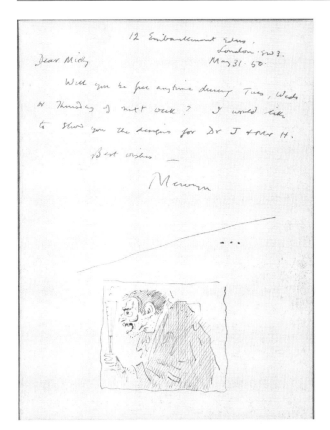

Letter from the writer
and illustrator Mervyn
Peake, with whom Powell
hoped to collaborate.

On an expedition to Israel in 1953, researching *Salt of the Earth*, a proposed Archers' film about
Chaim Weitzmann and the foundation of Israel.

Kevin Powell with his father during the shooting of *Peeping Tom* in 1959.

Kevin and Columba Powell
(r) on the set of *The Queen's
Guards*, with a note to
Alistair Dunnett.

Godard and Powell at Coppola's
Zoetrope Studios.

At Thelma Schoonmaker's house in San
Quentin: with Pat Biernacki, a
sociologist (l), and Peter Scarlet, then
director of the San Francisco Film
Festival. Photo by Powell.

"L.A. to N.Y. 1981
Is that the Mayflower Hotel?"

Photograph by Powell
of him phoning
Schoonmaker in New
York while at Zoetrope.

Portrait of Powell by
Lisa Law.

Photograph of
Thelma Schoonmaker
taken at the Cloisters,
the Metropolitan
Museum's medieval
collection, with
Powell's instructions
to his regular photo
printer in New York.

Powell and Schoonmaker
bringing the manuscript
of *A Life in Movies* to Lee
Cottages to finish it in
1985.

Writing his first book, *200, 000 Feet on Foula*, about the making of *Edge of the World* in 1936. Photo by Powell.

Writing his memoirs in a New York loft. Photo by Powell.

Reassessing the Films

5 'History Is Now and England': *A Canterbury Tale* in its Contexts

Ian Christie

'Tell them all the tale, Sir Richard,' says Puck, 'It concerns their land somewhat.'
Rudyard Kipling, *Puck of Pook's Hill* (1906)

There is such a thing as the English vision, and war, luckily, is only one stimulus that affects it.
John Piper, 1944[1]

A Canterbury Tale reached the late 20th century like a time capsule. Thirty years after its making, the film was virtually unknown and could only be viewed in a shortened and rearranged version, apparently intended for the American market. Then, after being restored to its original length and structure in 1977, it began a rapid ascent to classic status – recognised as a key representation of the Second World War home front, and also as an important expression of Neo-Romanticism or the Romantic Right, within a renewed interest in the history of 'Englishness'. Under these headings, it has already attracted at least five substantial readings, all of which offer different degrees of sympathetic contextualisation.[2] But the question this essay poses is: can we go further in showing how the film draws on certain quite specific contemporary sources and offers its own inflection of these? Is it a film even more rooted in the propaganda and ideological themes of 1943–4 than has already been demonstrated, as well as belonging to the long tradition of the 'Canterbury text', and how do these considerations affect our continued reading of it today?

PROPAGANDA

The most obvious context in which to locate *A Canterbury Tale* is as a propaganda film, which is clearly how it was in large part first conceived and received. In his memoirs, Powell placed it in a logical series that had begun with *49th Parallel*, which 'told the Americans we were fighting their war as well as ours'.[3] After Pearl

Harbor, the issues became more complex and various. Powell describes the propaganda aims of *One of Our Aircraft Is Missing* and *The Life and Death of Colonel Blimp* as telling the world that Europe and Britain respectively 'would never be conquered'. In this vein, *A Canterbury Tale* was to explain 'to the Americans, and to our own people, the spiritual values and traditions we were fighting for'.

However Powell and Pressburger may have interpreted them, the issues canvassed for attention by the Ministry of Information in 1943 were more mundane, and more pressing. After America's entry into the war in 1941, growing numbers of service personnel were stationed in Britain. From fewer than 5,000 at the beginning of 1942, the total rose rapidly to just under a quarter of a million in October, and, after a slight dip in mid-1943, rose again to 1.5 million in Spring 1944.[4] (Shooting began on *A Canterbury Tale* in August 1943 and was trade shown in May 1944, then presumably held over on account of the D-Day landings of June, before being released in August). The problem that had emerged early in 1942 was how to counteract poor relations between the incoming US service personnel and the British civilian population, which is certainly where *A Canterbury Tale* started from.

Popular legend has identified the problem as essentially sexual, with American troops seemingly 'over-sexed' and English women over-impressed by their

Yanks in Britain: American soldiers fraternise with locals, after warnings about how to behave in pubs, during the US 'invasion' of 1943–4.

attentions. In reality, there were a number of factors simultaneously at work, starting with the reality that American troops were considerably better fed and paid than their British counterparts, and so able to afford much more when 'on pass'. Added to this were very different attitudes to dating, and resentment at American personnel being forcibly billeted with British families between late 1943 and D-Day.[5] Relations between GIs and local civilians simmered throughout 1942 to 1944, with many skirmishes remaining unreported under a general newspaper agreement, until the *Daily Mirror* 'invited Britons and American to voice their mutual grievances' at the end of 1943.[6]

Behind the scenes, both British and American authorities were active in trying to understand and improve this largely unforeseen problem. The contributions of many experts were sought, including the poet Louis MacNeice, whose pamphlet *Meet the U.S. Army* was widely distributed in July 1943, and the anthropologist Margaret Mead. Best known for her work on social customs in the South Seas, Mead was commissioned by the US and British armies to distil her first-hand observations during 1943 into an article, 'The Yank in Britain', which analysed differences of attitude towards social interaction. Mead proposed a theory of mismatched 'dating patterns'. According to this, Americans understood dating as a game or social ritual, rather than a prelude to a personal relationship. Successful dates, on this pattern, involved the man asking for everything and getting nothing 'except a lot of skilful, gay witty words'.[7] As British women were unfamiliar with these rules, they were either shocked, or produced shock by their acquiescence. One important underlying factor was the educational, as well as the material, disparity: 79 per cent of Americans reaching Britain had more than eight years of schooling, compared with only 17 per cent of the local population.

Against this background, The Archers' strategy in *A Canterbury Tale* had to be ingenious to avoid cliché, while also relating to contemporary common knowledge. Without some eccentricity, it could easily have 'turned into a self-praising documentary', as Powell later admitted.[8] However, its basic template is clearly that established by many orientation guides for GIs, and dramatised in a contemporary film that was widely shown. *Welcome to Britain* was made by the Ministry of Information in 1943 and featured the American stage and screen actor Burgess Meredith showing Americans what they could expect in Britain, including the usual warnings about behaviour in pubs, and the pitfalls of accepting hospitality from Britons.[9] According to John Sweet, the serving US soldier who eventually played Sgt Bob Johnson in *A Canterbury Tale*, Powell and Pressburger hoped at one stage that Burgess Meredith would play the part, and he reworked the character who had been written as 'something of a wise guy'.[10] In fact, the opening confusion of *A Canterbury Tale*, when blackout and country railway station customs conspire to leave Sgt. Johnson one stop short of Canterbury, recalls the comic-didactic tone of *Welcome to Britain*. And Bob's subsequent adventures recall the three stages of GI acclimatisation identified by a Canadian adviser to the British government in 1943:

[first] the antiquities, old cottage, sight-seeing stage (a period dominated by garrulous guides); [then] the anti-coffee, anti-climate, anti-slowness stage (a longer period punctuated with rude encounters in trains and buses); and finally the adjusted stage when friendships begin to form.[11]

The Archers' GI protagonist, Bob Johnson, is the least brash imaginable: a softly spoken country boy from Oregon with an interest in antiquities, while his friend Sgt Micky Roczinsky, seen only briefly at the end, embodies all the stereotypical attitudes of GI good-time behaviour (like the raucous US aircrew who treat heaven like a hotel in *A Matter of Life and Death*).

But Bob is not the only protagonist of *A Canterbury Tale*, and the 'GI story' is not its only underpinning. Alison Smith, whom he meets at Chillingbourne station, belongs to another 'army', the Women's Land Army, revived in mid-1939 to provide an alternative source of agricultural labour when men were called up for the services.[12] By 1943 there were over 50,000 women filling jobs previously done by men around the country, and a third of these came from London and other large cities. A 'Short Guide' to the proposed film, written by The Archers in April 1943, suggests that telling the story of a 'land girl' who comes to Kent from London may originally have been its main intention, prompted by an acute home labour shortage that led to a freeze on recruitment to the women's forces.[13] Alison had been an assistant in 'a big London department store', where 'she used to sell garden furniture for rich people's gardens and outfits for their picnics'. Much is made in this early synopsis of the poetic irony of the city-bound shop girl ('who had lived all her life in Kensington') who has come to love the country 'with a deep, true love' through her attachment to a geologist who brought her to Kent for a week, where they lived together in a caravan. The synopsis sketches how Alison heard about the WLA build-up on the radio, gave in her notice

and 'went with the first batch of girls to train in Scotland', before requesting a transfer to the area in Kent she already knew. Behind this, there was already considerable anecdotal evidence of how many actual WLA members were badly treated by their farmer employers, becoming the butt of sexist mockery and humiliation. In *A Canterbury Tale*, this is transmuted into Colpeper's brisk refusal to employ any women, balanced by Alison then finding work at an all-female farm.[14] Although this may seem improbable and too schematic, the war provided many opportunities for both lesbian women and others impatient with pre-war restrictions on female 'mobility'. The bisexual Vita Sackville-West became a leading chronicler of the WLA, and Lady Eve Balfour pioneered fertiliser-free organic farming at her Haughley Farm, publishing a manifesto, *The Living Soil*, in 1943.[15]

Both the GI story and the land girl story reflect contemporary priorities, and quite possibly resulted from briefing or direction by the Ministry of Information.[16] Their combination, with the addition of a third 'outsider' character, Peter Gibbs, a British tank officer assigned to training, has the effect of cancelling any straightforward romance plot, as both Bob and Alison are effectively shown as mourning absent loves: he impatiently, because his letters are not answered, and she tragically, believing her fiancé killed in action. Meanwhile, the erotic motive of the film's plot is supplied by an elaborate strategy of displacement in the 'glue man' mystery.[17] Colpeper's scheme to prevent local girls dating soldiers might have been understandable in a GI holding area, where tensions often ran high and spilled into violence; but here in Kent, with only British soldiers in camp, it seems more misogynistic than moral.

Despite Colpeper's clearly signposted homosociality, the film also implies that he and Alison are attracted to each other, in one of its most ambiguous and evocative scenes. The attraction may be sublimated, based on their common interest in the archaeology of the land, but it is shown to be all the more powerful for this, as they meet on Chilman's Downs overlooking the river Stour and Canterbury. Colpeper has already enthralled Alison in the lecture scene, where close-ups of their eyes alternate, suggesting her ready, almost hypnotised response to his speech. Now he startles her by speaking while invisible in the long grass, before rising like a supernatural *genius loci*, his clothes crumpled and eyes bright with a strange intensity. She – and we – have heard the sounds of Chaucer's time in a moment of epiphany. These sounds, he tells her, 'come from inside'. Both admit they were wrong about the other, now recognising a kindred interest in the past, while Alison draws them close in a metaphor – 'you have to dig to find out about people as well as roads' – recalling Freud's parallel between archaeology and psychoanalysis.[18] At the same time, the film also draws them close by perspectival means. In the frontal shot during which their conversation begins, Alison leans sideways on her elbow; then a 70-degree cut reframes the pair, with Colpeper larger in the frame at the right, and Alison appearing to rest her head on his shoulder, while he turns the conversation toward miracles. Here, the film implies what it cannot show: the 'miracle' of Alison and Colpeper consoling each other; and it is this sense of union that Victor Burgin has enlarged and commemorated in a recent video work, *Listen to Britain*.[19]

If GI orientation and the need to direct women to land work provided *A Canterbury Tale* with key parts of its narrative structure, so too did the War Office's determination to boost awareness and morale among British troops. Faced with evidence that four out of five soldiers were not benefiting from any educational activity, a new Adjutant-General, Sir Roland Adam, launched the Army Bureau of Current Affairs in August 1941, with an initial target of one hour per week to be spent in compulsory educational discussion.[20] By the winter of 1942–3, three hours per week

In *A Canterbury Tale*, the framing and editing of the scene on the downs between Alison and Colpeper draws them close as they admit they were wrong about each other.

After the frontal shot, a cut reframes the pair, making Alison appear to rest her head on his shoulder, as they discuss miracles.

Finally, a closer shot implies the 'miracle' of Alison and Colpeper conforting each other.

was allocated, with one of these spent following a course on citizenship, based on a monthly series of booklets entitled 'The British Way and Purpose'.[21] And by late 1943, despite Churchill's continued opposition to the ABCA, some 110,000 courses and lectures were on offer to troops in camps around the UK. Whether or not such activities developed an appetite for political change and paved the way for the 1945 Labour victory – and it seems likely that they did – discussing why the war was being fought and what kind of Britain would emerge from it was clearly in vogue. Typically of the period, Powell recalled taking Wingfield-Stratford's *The History of British Civilisation* to read during the production, while staying in a pub in historic Fordwich outside Canterbury.[22]

How does this context affect our view of Colpeper's voluntary educational activities? Even those not directly exposed to discussion of the 'The British Way and Purpose' could hardly be unaware that such debate was under way in all kinds of situations. But Colpeper's antiquarian theme is hardly the ABCA's repertoire, as reported in *The Times* in 1942, which no doubt explains his continued failure to win a voluntary audience.[23]

Although *A Canterbury Tale* boldly substitutes its own concerns for those of actual army education, the official British effort had been noted and commended to the American authorities on a number of occasions during 1942–3. In a report entitled *The Mobilization of the Home Front: The British Experience and its Significance for the United States*, Eric Biddle applauded the attempt to 'inculcate in every citizen the maximum feeling of responsibility as part of the actual defense of the community', thus avoiding the panic that had gripped France in 1940, and aiming to '[preserve] the vital force' of the nation, rather than its material fabric.[24] In 1943, the popular American theologian Reinhold Niebhur visited Britain and was impressed by what he saw of the educational work being done with troops. He was quoted in *Time* magazine:

> Compared with this British program, the United States Army is culturally and educationally poverty-stricken … The American soldier has Hollywood, in both the literal and symbolic sense, to fill his leisure hours; but he lacks help in finding the spiritual and moral significance of the titanic struggle in which he is engaged.[25]

Niebhur's verdict appeared first in *The Nation* in August 1943, before extracts were published in *Time*, and soon led the American Army to launch its own, unacknowledged, equivalent of 'The British Way', known as 'Army Talks'. Meanwhile, Emeric Pressburger, a devout reader of *Time*, would almost certainly have seen the report just as *A Canterbury Tale* was going into production.

One trace of Niebhur's argument, which was also a more general concern among British and American propagandists of the period, is the powerful influence of Hollywood on shaping attitudes on both sides of the Atlantic. Powell and Pressburger return insistently to the movies and their specious glamour in *A Canterbury Tale*, making film 'a byword for spiritual vacuity', in Peter Conrad's phrase.[26] The GIs see the world in movie terms, as does Peter, the 'fallen' organist;[27] while Colpeper cites screen 'glamour girls' as the main competition with his lantern lectures on natural beauty. Why do The Archers denigrate their own medium? Conrad has an explanation:

> Powell's … aim is the redemption of his art. He wants to change film from a fickly mobile, inattentive substitute for seeing (which is how Roczinsky employs it at the cathedral [with his movie

camera]) to an entranced mediation on images. 'I am', he later declared in his memoirs, 'a high priest of the mysteries.' For him film is not a convenience for documentation but a means of engineering transcendence.[28]

A Canterbury Tale cannot be reduced to its propaganda dimension, but neither can it be divorced from the dominant discourses of the period in which it was conceived. By seeing how it inflects and, in so doing, largely subverts or contradicts these, we can gain a better sense of how The Archers created, not a 'self-praising documentary', but their first utopia of Anglo-American understanding in the form of a pastoral idyll.[29]

THE IDEOLOGY OF ENGLAND

The fact that Biddle could write unselfconsciously about 'the vital force of the nation' in 1942 is an indication of how pervasive the discourse of nationhood had become in wartime. But while much of this discourse looked to a post-war Britain that would be 'planned' and so, by implication, more egalitarian or even socialist, what of the past, the English tradition that Thomas Colpeper believes is more relevant than ever? Kipling had already given several earlier generations a primer in the idea of temporal 'depth' with his two story sequences, *Puck of Pook's Hill* and *Rewards and Fairies* (1910). In a letter, he explained his purpose as

> to give children *not* a notion of history but a notion of the time sense which is at the bottom of all knowledge of history and history rightly understood [*sic*] means love of one's fellow men and the land one lives in.[30]

This could well describe what Colpeper is trying to communicate in his quasi-hypnotic evocation of the Pilgrims' Way, which resonates so strongly with Alison that she can summon her own 'inner sounds', equivalent of the visions from history conjured up by Puck for Dan and Una in Kipling's stories. An important feature of these stories, as Harry Ricketts notes, is that the children do not simply travel back into history, rather 'the past travelled forward to meet them in the present', which is essentially how the Chaucerian past functions in *A Canterbury Tale*.[31]

T. S. Eliot (an admirer of Kipling) had expressed the same idea in more metaphysical terms in the opening lines of 'Burnt Norton':

> Time present and time past
> Are both perhaps present in time future
> And time future contained in time past.

However, as he added, from a Christian standpoint:

> If all time is eternally present
> All time is unredeemable.

Seven years later, in 1942, Eliot took up the same theme in the last of the *Four Quartets*, 'Little Gidding', revealing how immanent history had become in wartime England:

> A people without history
> Is not redeemed from time, for history is a pattern
> Of timeless moments. So, while the light fails
> On a winter's afternoon, in a secluded chapel
> History is now and England.

Here, we are again close to that sense of the past made urgent by the present that Colpeper preaches. On a less theological, though equally mysterious level, Virginia Woolf's last novel, *Between the Acts* (1941), rehearsed a fragmentary, ironic history of England in the form of a village pageant, focusing the idea of the nation in the microcosm of the village, while the war carries on in the air above. It transpires that Woolf was reading *The Canterbury Tales* while writing her novel, and villagers dressed as 'the Canterbury pilgrims' make a brief appearance in the pageant, singing a chorus that combines the sacred and the profane: 'To the shrine of the saint … to the tomb … lovers … believers … we came'.[32]

Before the war, Canterbury had twice served as the focus of a challenge to modernity. In his 1932 book on Chaucer, G. K. Chesterton proposed the idea of an updating of *The Canterbury Tales* in the form of a novel. But as he considered how Chaucer's characters would behave in modern life, he concluded that there was no longer any common goal that would keep the company together. For Chesterton, this was a matter of profound regret, revealing the bankruptcy of modern ideology, devoted to progress rather than to the order of the medieval world. Peter Conrad criticises Chesterton's reading of Chaucer, arguing that disunity is as much a problem for the original Canterbury pilgrims, which helps explain why they never reach their goal; but he suggests that this counterpointing of the medieval and the modern lies behind Powell and Pressburger's conception of a new pilgrimage. Although the film begins with a leap forward from falcon to Spitfire, its deeper movement 'shows the modern world retreating into the medieval, with Order overruling Progress as the ground for values'.[33] Three years after Chesterton's book, T. S. Eliot wrote the verse play *Murder in the Cathedral* at the invitation of the cathedral, for performance in the annual Canterbury festival, and created an unexpected popular success that went on to the West End. The martyrdom of Becket by Henry II's knights had, of course, made Canterbury a prime place of pilgrimage, and led to the creation of the great cathedral. By returning to this primal event, Eliot was seeking to connect himself with a tradition that he had flouted in his breakthrough poem *The Waste Land* (which parodies the opening of Chaucer's poem). His Becket is a proud, isolated figure, haunted by a sense of unease and foreboding. Powell and Pressburger could hardly have been unaware of Eliot's play, which ran for some months in London and toured the country before being broadcast by the BBC in 1936.[34] A speculative reading of their eventual film might identify the proud, troublesome figure of Colpeper with Becket, both of whom believed themselves above the authority that they officially embody, while their assassins appeal for understanding in terms of reason and common sense.

During the war, Canterbury had become a new focus for the idea of affirming 'spiritual values' in the face of the new barbarism represented by Nazi Germany. The city experienced the first of four major bombing raids on 1 June 1942, which destroyed much of the eastern end of the historic city, while leaving the cathedral largely intact. William Temple, who became Archbishop of Canterbury in that same year and published a Penguin Special *The Church and the Social Order*, was a charismatic communicator with trenchant views that alarmed many conservatives. He appeared with Hewlett Johnson, already notorious as the 'Red Dean' of Canterbury for his open support of Soviet Russia, in a short film by George Hoellering, *Message from Canterbury* (1942), delivering a sermon that articulates the ideas of a pilgrimage as a source of inspiration in wartime and of a message going forth from Canterbury to guide the work of rebuilding Britain. Less polished than Humphrey Jennings's contemporary morale-boosters, *Words for Battle*, *The Heart of Britain* and *Listen to Britain*, *Message from Canterbury* nonetheless provides a preliminary sketch of the idea of modern cinematic pilgrimage.[35]

What, then, do the film's three pilgrims find? Somewhat like their near contemporaries, the characters in J. B. Priestley's play *They Came to a City* (1943), they find themselves in an unfamiliar place that invites them to reassess their values.[36] Priestley's

Fordwich's Town Hall is believed to be the oldest and smallest of such buildings in England: an ideal microcosm of the traditional values of *A Canterbury Tale*.

cross-section of society discovers a literal yet schematic utopia, an imaginary city organised along socialist lines, in what is clearly an allegory about the opportunity to remake the post-war world. The Archers' trio, however, find themselves in a traditional English village, 'Chillingbourne', which is in fact a composite of several villages near Canterbury, notably Chilham and Fordwich, although largely recreated in the studio. Two features of this imagined village become more significant after visiting the real Fordwich and Chilham.[37] The first is Fordwich's distinctive town hall, dating from 1544 and believed to be the oldest and smallest such building in England, used as a courtroom until 1886. Although what we see in the film is a larger studio reproduction of the real town hall, it retains the pleading bar, with its motto 'love and honour the truth'. Alison stands before this emblematic prop, her hair still wet from the effects of an attack by, we will learn, the local magistrate. This Tudor town hall, with its trappings of traditional English justice – questioned, only to be reasserted, by the film's moral plot – serves to evoke the pastoral England of wartime patriotism that Stephen Daniels has discussed in relation to Constable's *The Hay Wain* and its real Suffolk landscape.[38] The second significant feature of the film's village is an absence – that of Chilham's imposing seventeenth-century manor house and Norman castle, or indeed any equivalent 'big house'. Instead, we see the more modest home of Thomas Colpeper, gentleman farmer and magistrate – based on a house in the village of Wickhambreaux – which Alison falls in love with at first sight, as we are encouraged to do. Through this absence, I suggest, Chillingbourne becomes less feudal and more democratic: a more fitting location for reasserting 'the spiritual values and traditions we were fighting for'.

Within this house, as built in the studio, the film offers a cluster of visual and graphic clues to Colpeper's values that can take us beyond, or behind, the rhetoric of his various speeches to the pilgrims. When Peter (Dennis Price) calls unannounced, in search of evidence to support the trio's belief that he is the 'glue man', he is shown into the study by Colpeper's mother. What follows is closely modelled on Powell's 1941 film *An Airman's Letter to His Mother*, in which the reading of an inspirational letter that had appeared posthumously in *The Times* is given a richly detailed *mise en scène*.[39] The mother reads the letter, spoken in voiceover by John Gielgud, in her dead son's room, while the camera tracks across the books and images that have shaped the sentiments he expresses. Captain Scott and T. E. Lawrence are immediately recognisable, together with the Second World War flying hero Richard Hillary, amid school photographs and the relics of sports and hobbies. The fact that many of these items can be identified as belonging to, or highly valued by, Powell himself encourages a belief that he shares many of the values expressed by the young airman, although this iconography can also, to a large extent, be seen as that of an inter-war English generation. But it can also be read as the surprisingly precise iconography of a particular English 'type'. In *A Canterbury Tale*, as well as the expected shotgun and heavy boots, skis and mountain-top photographs identify Colpeper as an Alpinist, and a later insert shot of a well-worn handbook, *Climbing in the British Isles*, confirms that he is also a mountaineer at home.

Iconography and self-reference: climbing photographs and a copy of Powell's book *200,000 Feet on Foula* in Colpeper's study.

These are perhaps uncommon pursuits for a Kentish farmer of the 1930s, and Powell spoke of how Colpeper's study was dressed to show that 'he's a loner', suggesting that this explains the fact that he was 'a bit cracked'.[40] Yet two further pieces in the iconographic jigsaw link Colpeper with 'progressive' thinking about agriculture. A carefully arranged overhead shot of the desk shows three clearly legible book jackets: *Island Years* by Frank Darling, a Home Guard pamphlet entitled *Rough Stuff,* and *Soil and Sense.* The Home Guard is mentioned later in Peter's conversation with Colpeper, but the two books are otherwise unremarked upon – silent clues to Colpeper's interests, for those willing or already able to decipher them. Both were recent publications. Frank Fraser Darling (1903–79) was a pioneer ecologist, who had risen from farm-labouring to become an expert on animal conservation in Scotland in the 1930s and would later work with Julian Huxley and UNESCO on global ecological issues arising from human mismanagement.[41] *Island Years* (1940) was based on his own experience of farming in Scotland, and integrated zoology, genetics and the emerging discipline that he named 'human ecology'. *Soil and Sense*, by Michael Graham, was published by Faber & Faber in 1941 and argues for grassland cultivation without recourse to artificial fertilisers or excess mechanisation, appealing to the example of Robert Elliott's turn-of-the-century 'Clifton Park system' of

Evidence that Colpeper is a progressive gentleman farmer from his reading: Graham's book *Soil and Sense* contributed to the post-war organic farming movement.

holistic farming. Graham's book formed part of a movement to reassess farming methods, prompted in large part by wartime food requirements, which would include the republication of Elliott's original book and Balfour's *The Living Soil*, both also published by Faber, in 1943; while Oxford published Sir Albert Howard's *An Agricultural Testament*, 'intended to draw attention to the destruction of the earth's capital, the soil, and to suggest methods by which the lost fertility can be restored and maintained'. This radical farming movement would result in the formation of the Soil Association in 1946 and eventually lead to today's organic farming movement.

Colpeper, then, is intended to be at least a progressive gentleman farmer, up to date with the latest thinking about ecology and fertility – no doubt helped by Powell's interest in the Scottish Highlands and islands ever since his involvement with St Kilda and Foula.[42] Darling's path would lead to the criticism of all human exploitation of flora and fauna for reasons of profit or sport, and to the modern ideology of ecosystem conservation. Graham looked back to an earlier era, before the industrialisation of the countryside, and called for an end to 'land robbery' after the war that has made it necessary, proposing that future subsidy should only go to 'good farmers who feed the land as tradition says it should be fed, and that none should go to those who merely exploit it'.

Do these two advertisements for contemporary thought help us interpret Colpeper beyond what we glean from his speeches and Portman's compelling performance? In the simplest terms, as Aldgate and Richards established, he represents a version of Baldwinite Toryism, which emphasised the *continuity* of English sounds and sights: 'the tinkle of the hammer on the anvil in the country smithy, the corncrake on a dewy morning, the sound of the scythe against the whetstone ... the sight that has been seen in England since England was a land'.[43] The diagnosis of England's espousal of ruralism between the wars, and a concomitant anti-industrialism, was persuasively set out by Martin Weiner,[44] who observed that this ruralism could foster both a proto-fascist ideology of 'blood and soil' and a form of managed capitalism, which the young Harold Macmillan described as the renewal of 'that organic conception of society which was the distinctive contribution of medieval thought'.[45] Extrapolating from this tissue of quotation, we could perhaps even identify Colpeper as a gentry version of Gramsci's 'organic intellectual', working actively to develop as well as preach his ideas about the need for a return to pre-industrial values. And we can understand better why Powell and Pressburger wanted to link the time of Chaucer with the present, as a basis for their repudiation of materialistic capitalism.

There was also the issue of how the course of the war had affected intellectuals. Arthur Koestler, former communist, refugee and friend of Pressburger's, wrote in 1943:

> The nearer victory comes in sight, the clearer the character of the war reveals itself as what the Tories always said it was – a war for national survival, a war in defence of certain conservative nineteenth-century ideals, and not what I and my friends of the left said it was.[46]

In similar vein, among the artists grouped under the banner of Neo-Romanticism, including Michael Ayrton, Henry Moore, John Piper and Graham Sutherland, there was a feeling, articulated by Piper in 1944, that the war had helped British art to 'raise its head and become more perky'.[47] In short, the length and demands of the war had produced a noticeable regression to a simplified, picturesque patriotism of Eliot's 'winter's afternoon, in a secluded chapel'.

By making Colpeper a troublesome radical, willing to break the law that he is supposed to uphold as a magistrate, for the sake of his militant belief in 'English tradition', The Archers seem to have been trying to challenge the blandness that resulted from artists and intellectuals merely serving the 'war effort'. Just as *The Life and Death of Colonel Blimp* had run the risk of exploring Blimpishness when this had been anathematised, so *A Canterbury Tale* probed the very values that underlay the wartime appeal to a timeless England symbolised by the 'garden of Kent', irreverently asking how far these could be impressed on townsfolk. Nor did it condemn the zealous Colpeper – whose name evokes Nicholas Culpeper, a physician and ardent Parliamentarian during the English revolution, author of a pioneering handbook of herbal and astrological medicine[48] – any more than it had Clive Candy.

This Colpeper, as has often been remarked, is also a magical figure, abruptly appearing and disappearing, especially in Alison's presence; and shown twice in 'supernatural' lighting, before the lantern lecture and in the train carriage, which removes him from the merely mortal plane. He is not yet the playful Conductor of *A Matter of Life and Death*, able to move between worlds, or the protean nemesis of the poet in *The Tales of Hoffmann*, Dr Dapertutto. He is perhaps closer to the mysterious figure of the Stranger in Jerome K. Jerome's *The Passing of the Third Floor Back*, who changes lives by simply allowing 'better selves' to get the upper hand;[49] or to the wartime equivalent, *Halfway House*, in which a ghostly hotel proprietor helps a disparate group of visitors overcome their problems.[50] Without being given any explicit powers, he seems to be responsible for the 'blessings' conferred on Alison, Peter and Bob after they reach Canterbury and discover they each have a future. However, this is also a reciprocal relationship. The 'bad' Colpeper of misogyny and

Colpeper as a magical figure, hypnotising Alison by his speech before the lantern lecture.

Bad timing: *A Canterbury Tale* was not released until after D-Day, when its muted tone seemed out of keeping with the new urgency of the war's progress.

resentment has been exorcised, through contact with them, to become a 'good' Colpeper, facing the future with the same optimism as Clive Candy.

Did *A Canterbury Tale* 'fail' in its own time, as has so often been reiterated? The evidence is at best partial, or ambiguous. Although Powell and Pressburger habitually spoke of it as having failed, an objective reading of contemporary reviews shows that these were far from negative, and indeed little different in their balance of praise and criticism from those The Archers normally received.[51] All drew attention to the weakness, strangeness or pathology of the glue-man plot, but most also praised the film's other qualities. The main trade review, in *The Cinema*, praised it unequivocally as 'another of those distinctive British pictures which we have come to expect from The Archers', offering 'a thoughtful story', an 'impressive cast' and 'the scenic charm of the the Kentish countryside, emphasised by many telling touches in by-play and dialogue'.[52] As to whether it fared poorly at the box-office, very little is known about the economic performance of films of this period; and as John Sedgwick's work on film popularity in the 1930s has shown, a properly calibrated account of 'success' involves knowing much more than bare exhibition receipts.[53]

What may have damaged the film's reception was the timing of its release. Trade shown in May 1944, before the D-Day landings that it predicts in the final church parade scenes, it was not released until August, by which time its very specific location in August 1943 would already have seemed dated. And amid the news of Allied advances in France, films such as *This Happy Breed* and *The Way Ahead*, both released in June, would offer more emphatically affirmative pleasures, as would The Archers' own *I Know Where I'm Going!*, with its unashamedly romantic rejection of 'materialism'. The other recurrent allegation has been of 'muddle', starting with Dilys Powell's original *Sunday Times* review and repeated most recently by Robert

Murphy.[54] Compared with the vague benevolence of *Halfway House* and the dia-
grammatic certainty of *They Came to a City*, it is certainly less programmatic. Yet in
a climate of relentless propaganda about war aims and discussion of post-war reconstruction, it may well have appealed to many as a welcome relief from these ringing
certainties. William Whitebait's wholly positive *New Statesman* review expressed
such a reaction:

> The plot, such as it is, points to the Cathedral; round it and inside we go; the camera leads through
> arches, travels up and down pillars, with a real appreciation of its subject. Some sort of decision
> has been reached in the lives of the people there. I carried away from *A Canterbury Tale* an enjoy-
> ment that I was loath to examine too closely.[55]

If it had a message in 1944, it was perhaps that those with a messianic belief in
what is best for others should be resisted – a gentle rebuke to all the propagandists
– but its real achievement, recognised by most reviewers, was clearly that of de-
privileging message and narrative, in favour of evocation and audiovisual counterpoint. Jeffrey Richards's musical metaphor of the film, 'constructed like a
symphony, orchestrating the themes of the three pilgrims' around the 'dominant
theme' of Colpeper, seems truer, linking with Powell's own pride in the 'wonderful
movement' of the last three reels.[56] There was no critical framework to recognise
such aesthetic aims in 1944, which may help explain the puzzlement that hovered
around the film, before it effectively disappeared from view for thirty years – only
to re-emerge in the era of such varied forms of 'new pastoral' as Derek Jarman's
Jubilee, Ermanno Olmi's *Tree of the Wooden Clogs* and Terence Mallick's *Days of
Heaven*, as a film bearing witness to its time, yet seeming remarkably modern in its
handling of landscape, time and the mysteries of the human heart.

NOTES

1. *The Listener*, 21 December 1944, quoted in Robert Hewison, *Under Siege: Literary Life in
    London 1939–45*, London: Weidenfeld & Nicolson, 1977.
2. In date order: Nannette Aldred, '*A Canterbury Tale*: Powell and Pressburger's Film Fantasies of
    Britain', in David Mellor, ed., *A Paradise Lost: The Neo-Romantic Imagination in Britain,
    1935–55*, London: Lund-Humphries/Barbican Art Gallery, 1987, pp. 117–24; Antonia Lant,
    'From Mufti to Civvies: *A Canterbury Tale*', in *Blackout: Reinventing Women for Wartime British
    Cinema*, Princeton, NJ: Princeton University Press, 1991, pp. 197–219; Graham Fuller, '*A
    Canterbury Tale*', *Film Comment* March–April 1995, pp. 33–6; Peter Conrad, 'Arrival at
    Canterbury', in *To Be Continued: Four Stories and Their Survival*, Oxford: Clarendon Press,
    1995, pp. 7–45; Anthony Aldgate and Jeffrey Richards, 'Why We Fight: *A Canterbury Tale*', in
    Best of British: Cinema and Society from 1930 to the Present, London: I. B. Tauris, 1999, pp. 57–78
3. Michael Powell, *A Life in Movies: An Autobiography*, London: Faber & Faber, 2000,
    p. 437.
4. Sources: tables in David Reynolds, *Rich Relations: The American Occupation of Britain
    1942–1945*, London: HarperCollins, 1995, pp. 78, 103.

5. Ibid., p. 183.

6. Ibid., p. 184.

7. Ibid., p. 265.

8. Powell's comment in 1986 is quoted by Fuller, '*A Canterbury Tale*', p. 34.

9. *Welcome to Britain* was directed by Anthony Asquith.

10. Paul Tritton, *A Canterbury Tale: Memories of a Classic Wartime Movie*, Maidstone, Kent: Tritton Publications, p. 28.

11. Graham Spry, quoted in Reynolds, *Rich Relations*, p. 260

12. Originally created during the First World War, the WLA was revived in June 1939. See Angus Calder, *The People's War, Britain 1939–1945*, London: Granada Publishing, 1971, pp. 494ff.

13. The six-page mimeographed 'Short Guide to A Canterbury Tale' is dated 22 April 1943. Powell Papers, BFI Special Collections.

14. Although the woman farmer, Prue, implies that she is not a spinster by choice, her dress and manner might suggest otherwise, and contemporary rumours painted the WLA as a hotbed of lesbianism (Lant, 'From Mufti to Civvies', pp. 108, 204).

15. Vita Sackville-West, *The Women's Land Army*, London: Michael Joseph, 1944. Lady Eve B. Balfour, *The Living Soil and the Haughley Experiment*, London: Faber & Faber, 1943.

16. Early in the war, it was established that 'film propaganda will be most effective when it is least recognisable as such … The influence brought to bear by the Ministry on the producers of feature films … must be kept secret.' 'Programme for Film Propaganda', PRO. INF 1/867 [undated, but likely to be early 1940], reproduced in Ian Christie, ed., *Powell, Pressburger and Others*, London: BFI, 1978, p. 124.

17. See my 'Another Life in Movies: Pressburger and Powell' in this collection, pp. 171–86.

18. See Sigmund Freud, 'Delusions and Dreams in Jensen's *Gradiva*' [vol. 9, *Standard Edition*], *Art and Literature*, Penguin Freud Library, vol. 14, London: Penguin Books, 1985. See especially Freud's comment on the symbolism of the girl in Jensen's archaeological fantasy: 'I told myself I should be able to dig out something interesting here' (p. 76).

19. Victor Burgin's video work *Listen to Britain* (2002), uses the Downs sequence of *A Canterbury Tale* as its basis, reworking the original film with interpolated new material.

20. Calder, *The People's War*, p. 289.

21. Paul Addison, *The Road to 1945*, London: Quartet Books, 1977, p. 146; Calder, *The People's War*, p. 290.

22. Powell, *A Life in Movies*, p. 443. Esme Wingfield-Stratford's *The History of British Civilisation* was a popular narrative, first published by Routledge in 1930. Wingfield-Stratford's other works included *The Foundations of British Patriotism*, first published in 1913 and reissued in 1939. On other patriotic-historical works of the period, see Aldgate and Richards, 'Why We Fight', pp. 68–70.

23. Addison, *Road to 1945*, p. 150.

24. Eric Biddle, *The Mobilization of the Home Front: The British Experience and its Significance for the United States*, Chicago: Public Service Administration Press, 1942, quoted in Lant, *Blackout*, p. 5.

25. Quoted in Reynolds, *Rich Relations*, p. 172.

26. Conrad, 'Arrival at Canterbury', p. 29.

27. Although the cathedral organist tells Peter that he started his career playing in a circus, the film does not seem to dissent from Colpeper's scathing verdict on Peter's vocation as a cinema organist – a position that recalls D. H. Lawrence's portrayal of the heroine of his novel *The Lost Girl* as reaching her nadir when she plays for the moving pictures.

28. Conrad, 'Arrival at Canterbury', p. 30.

29. Their second such utopia, *A Matter of Life and Death*, as I have argued elsewhere, takes the form of a modernised masque. See Ian Christie, *A Matter of Life and Death*, London: BFI, 2000, pp. 14–20.

30. Letter to Edward Bok, July 1905, quoted in Harry Ricketts, *The Unforgiving Minute: A Life of Rudyard Kipling*, London: Chatto & Windus, 1999, p. 289.

31. Ricketts, *The Unforgiving Minute*, p. 291.

32. Virginia Woolf, *Between the Acts* (1941), Harmondsworth: Penguin Books, 1992, p. 50.

33. Conrad, 'Arrival at Canterbury', p. 26.

34. On the play's success, see Peter Ackroyd, *T. S. Eliot: A Life*, New York: Simon & Schuster, 1984, pp. 226–8.

35. Conrad outlines a sequence of works that cite and 'continue' the Canterbury story of pilgrimage, ranging from Chaucer to nineteenth-century poems and twentieth-century works, including *A Canterbury Tale* and Pasolini's film *The Canterbury Tales* (1972), up to William Burroughs's novel *The Wasted Lands* (1987) and Jim Jarmusch's film *Mystery Train* (1989). I have termed this 'the Canterbury text', borrowing the formulation from Julian Graffy's account of 'the Petersburg text' in Russian literature, in *Scottish Slavonic Review*, XXX.

36. Priestley's play was filmed by Ealing Studios in 1945.

37. Thanks are due to Paul Tritton for a first guided tour of Chilham, and for his subsequent pioneering of 'site visiting' in his annual *Canterbury Tale* walks. For details, see the website maintained by Steve Crook, *Michael Powell & Emeric Pressburger – Pure Genius*, www.powell-pressburger.org.

38. Stephen Daniels, *Fields of Vision: Landscape Imagery and National Identity in England and the United States*, Princeton, NJ: Princeton University Press, 1993, p. 213.

39. For more detail on this and its relationship to flying mythology, see my monograph on *A Matter of Life and Death*, pp. 13–14.

40. Tony Williams, Michael Powell interview, *Films and Filming*, November 1981, p. 13. Pressburger had enjoyed mountain walking when living in Germany, and Powell was an avid walker.

41. Information on Darling from the NAHSTE (Navigational Aids for the History of Science, Technology and the Environment) project, University of Edinburgh, www.nahste.ac.uk.

42. One of the photographs in Colpeper's study appears to be of Foula, the location of Powell's *The Edge of the World*; and Powell recalled in *A Life in Movies* (p. 8) that his grandfather had climbed with Edward Whymper, the first conqueror the Matterhorn – which was also the subject of a film co-scripted by Pressburger entitled *The Challenge* (1938).

43. Stanley Baldwin, *On England*, 1926; quoted in Aldgate and Richards, 'Why We Fight', pp. 70–71 and in Martin Wiener, *English Culture and the Decline of the Industrial Spirit, 1850–1980* (1981), Harmondsworth: Penguin Books, 1992, pp. 100–1.

44. Wiener, *English Culture*, Chapter 6.

45. Ibid., p. 109.

46. Arthur Koestler, *Horizon*, January 1943, quoted in Calder, *The People's War*, p. 605.

47. Piper, quoted in Hewison, *Under Siege*, p. 149.

48. Culpeper's *The English Physitian*, published in 1652, was one of the first medical manuals written in English (rather than Latin) and would remain highly popular.

49. Jerome's original 1904 story was turned into a successful play in 1910, and filmed by Berthold Viertel with Conrad Veidt as the Stranger, in 1935.

50. *Halfway House*, directed by Basil Dearden and based on a play by Denis Ogden, was released in April 1944.

51. See, for instance, my survey of reviews of *A Matter of Life and Death* in Christie, *A Matter of Life and Death*, pp. 57–62.

52. *The Cinema* [*Today's Cinema*], 14 May 1944.

53. John Sedgwick, *Popular Filmgoing in 1930s Britain: A Choice of Pleasures*, Exeter: University of Exeter Press, 2000.

54. *Sunday Times* review, 15 April 1944; Robert Murphy, *British Cinema and the Second World War*, London: Continuum, 2000, p. 169.

55. *New Statesman*, 13 May 1944.

56. Aldgate and Richards, 'Why We Fight', p. 67.

6 On Knowing and Not Knowing, Going and Not Going, Loving and Not Loving: *I Know Where I'm Going!* and Falling in Love Again

Tom Gunning

Dedicated to Aelia Laelia
'nec vir nec mulier nec androgyna
nec puella nec juvenis nec anus
nec casta nec meretrix nec pudica
sed omnia sublata'.

Love and Stories
I liked topology: a few years before that I had written a story on a Möbius band, designed to be read from any point in it around to that point again, and to be a complete and sensible story regardless of where you started. It had worked out pretty well – I don't mean perfectly; what story ever does that?

Dashiell Hammett[1]

I first saw Michael Powell and Emeric Pressburger's 1945 film *I Know Where I'm Going!* in 1984 at the Brattle Theater near Harvard Square. Legendary for sparking the Bogart cult that swept US campuses in the 1960s, audiences at the Brattle attached themselves to certain films as acts of devotion. Although the Brattle never sparked a national cult for *I Know Where I'm Going!* (henceforth *IKWIG*, which I will use on the authority of its appearance on the blackboard in the film's credit sequence), it at least originated a local one, leading to regular (I think yearly) screenings of the film with introductions by enthusiasts and maintaining a committed group of returning fans. As Ian Christie, in his nearly definitive voiceover for the Criterion laser disc (and now DVD) edition of the film, and Pam Cook, in her insightful BFI handbook for the film, both claim, *IKWIG* draws a deep personal investment from viewers.[2] It is, quite simply, a film one falls in love with.

It is hardly incidental that *IKWIG* is also a love story. This is a tricky form for cinema, although I would claim that, along with action, love forms the most fundamental narrative gestalt for film viewers. The love story, curiously, does not really work as a genre in a simple sense, if only because any list of films focusing on falling in love would divide almost equally between Hollywood's two primary modes, comedy and melodrama (*IKWIG* uses both modes), and that makes the love story a difficult genre to classify.[3] Film scholars have claimed heterosexual romances regulate and order the classical Hollywood film: the establishment of a romantic couple brings closure to films within many genres, while the 'love interest' plays an essential role in Hollywood's double plots.[4] But these analyses, as a rule, do not privilege films that centre on love affairs; rather than defining the specific nature of love stories in cinema, the stability and consistency of popular narrative cinema more generally has formed their focus.

In *IKWIG*, love brings less order and stability to the film than it invites their opposite. Far from facilitating the establishment of social and narrative order, in *IKWIG* love destabilises and transforms, forcing characters to change their goals and identities. A more dynamic force than many narrative analyses of film would lead us to believe, when not subservient to other narrative demands, love takes on many forms. Rather than simply using the formation of the couple as a predictable convention that can be employed mechanically, love stories in many media offer human beings a means to figure out the power (both individual and social) of love. In this chapter I hope to trace how narrative, rather than using love as ready-made material, engages with its dynamic, protean aspects in order to help us make sense out of falling in love, helping us, to quote William Blake, 'learn to bear the beams of love',[5] which is no easy thing. I will trace recurring patterns *IKWIG* shares with other films and other forms of love stories, but I will also stick closely to the contours of this specific film. *IKWIG* possesses the secret of every love affair: forging a relation to a universal, if not cosmic experience that, at the same time, seems fundamentally unique and individual.

Let me examine the second component of the term 'love story'. As I indicated, most analysts of film narrative approach love affairs as a way to close off stories. In *The Classical Hollywood Cinema*, David Bordwell points out the structural role that the nearly omnipresent romance plot plays in Hollywood films, providing a goal for the classically purposeful protagonists and therefore the most frequent form of resolution and closure.[6] But closure tells only part of any story. Narrative theorists (most explicitly, Viktor Shklovsky and Roland Barthes[7]) claim that storytelling operates primarily by delay. Narrative, Barthes might have said, is a drag; skilful storytellers forestall premature completion by keeping options open and retarding outcomes, until closure ultimately comes by completing principle actions and resolving enigmas. But rather than resolving anything, falling in love in *IKWIG* triggers a devious and labyrinthine process, providing a means of narrative distention, stretching out and slowing down progress towards denouement. Even outside of stories (if there is such a place), delay plays a fundamental role in the 'art of love'. As Ovid put it, 'Crede mihi, non est veneris properanda voluptas, /Sed sensim tarda proficienda mora' ('Believe me, love's bliss must not be hastened, but gradually lured on by slow delay').[8] Thus, during the classical era of Hollywood, love stories fit in well with production codes and relatively repressed morals, as social mores and film conventions combined to delay the final clinch, as marriage and sex took place after the credits, or only briefly before. Love stories deploy a variety of devices, from comic misunderstandings to tragic missed opportunities, to delay either resolution, whether final union or ultimate separation. A love story spends less time on the outcome than on the dalliance, the lingering, during which love builds and becomes inevitable.

IKWIG tells the story of a woman, Joan Webster, who embarks on a journey that has a specific destination, the Isle of Kiloran, and an ultimate purpose, her wedding to Sir Robert Bellinger. A purposeful forward motion dominates the first 16 minutes of this 91-minute film. The opening credit sequence establishes Joan's tenacious character through her ability to move resolutely through space, from an infant's determined crawling ('Going right? Left? No, straight on!' the narrator tells us) to a young woman's confident stride through a fancy nightclub in high heels and stockings. We learn of her expectations and fantasies about her pending wedding, as she embarks on her journey to join her fiancé. An apparently unstoppable momentum builds up throughout the sequence, as Joan's journey proceeds by various modes of transportation (trains, boats and cars), propelled by rhythmic editing and sound.

Everything seems to move in concert and in one direction. But narrative can only be so simple and straightforward at its own peril; storytelling proceeds, as Borges tells us, by forking paths.[9] When Joan reaches the penultimate point in her trajectory, Port Erraig, a halt occurs. After a series of subordinates have conveyed her rapidly from place to place, here the connections break down as fog delays the boat sent by Sir Robert to ferry Joan to Kiloran, and a palpably different pace intervenes in editing and sound. Wrapped in fog, Joan sits on her luggage at the sea's edge, as her itinerary blows out of her hand and slowly sinks in the water. Although the Isle of Kiloran seems so near, Joan cannot complete the last leg of the journey, the boat trip from Port Erraig to Kiloran. The path forks, the journey stalls, creating an interlude that ultimately ends in Joan's transfer of her love from Bellinger to the young Scottish navy officer she meets while waiting for passage, Torquil MacNeil, hereditary Laird of Kiloran, who also hopes to cross to his native island.

After such a hurried opening, time seems to stop in Port Erraig – or, as some would claim from the film's subsequent immersion in archaic Scottish customs and lore, runs backwards. However, time does not really stop (which would be fatal for a temporal form like narrative), but rather becomes transformed, as emotional investments and goals become redefined. Love stories frequently create such subliminal spaces, within lacuna or interruptions, because within these spaces, love appears as something different, a force outside the ordinary. This redefinition of space and time sets the stage for love's own transformations to take place.

Narrative entails transformation. As Todorov and the structuralists put it, a story chronicles a transition from one state to another.[10] In their most classical (or as Bordwell calls it, canonic[11]) form stories pass from an initial stable state into one of disequilibrium, which is then resolved by achieving a new state of equilibrium, one which differs from the initial situation, but resolves the disequilibrium and ends the story. This structural model provides a first step in thinking through the transformations that stories chronicle, but it also potentially short-changes the process of transformation. Structuralists tend to transform temporal progression into atemporal patterns, reducing, as Paul Ricoeur put it, the chronological into the logical.[12] Such treatments of narrative valorise resolution, the re-establishment of balance, making a story into a symmetrically formed classical arc.[13] To quote Ricoeur, this view of story logic 'transformed the structure of the tale into a machinery whose task it is to compensate for the initial mischief or lack by a final restoration of the disturbed order'.[14]

Order and closure always play a role in storytelling, but without disequilibrium there would be no story, whereas, as Scheherazade (or any serial form of fiction including, for example, television soap operas, the Fantômas novels or the serials of Pearl White) demonstrates, a story's ending can appear as an ever-receding limit, more sensed than achieved. Likewise, the opening equilibrium the structuralist model demands not only often tends to be brief, but frequently has to be assumed, even reconstructed – for instance, when tales begin *in medias res*. Thus, rather than an economical arc of completed action, stories – and love stories in particular – frequently tend to be prodigal with time and delay, marking time in some intermediary space. Rather than experiencing delay as simply a frustration of narrative progress, we need to recognise its positive role, its relation to the skilful lover's slow hand in heightening desire. Temporal interruption creates the space of transformation, the place, in love stories, where love is born. Here, purposes and goals change and established senses of self are challenged.

Ricoeur relates this space of transition and transformation to the dark forest that must be crossed in fairy tales and romances. His discussion is worth quoting at length for its uncanny congruence with the plot of *IKWIG*:

> Before projecting the hero forward for the sake of the quest, many tales send the hero or heroine into some dark forest where she or he goes astray or meets some devouring beast … These initial episodes do more than merely introduce the mischief that is to be suppressed; they bring the hero or heroine *back* into a primordial space and time that is more akin to the realm of dreams than to the sphere of action. Thanks to this preliminary disorientation, the linear chain of time is broken and the tale assumes an oneiric dimension that is more or less preserved alongside the heroic dimension of the quest. Two qualities of time are thus intertwined: the circularity of the imaginary journey and the linearity of the quest as such.[15]

Most commentators on *IKWIG* note its echoes of fairy tales and the oneiric. With the aid of Ricoeur's comments, we realise these play a more fundamental role than just creating a 'romantic' atmosphere. The drama of transformation that takes place on the island of Mull, as Joan and Torquil wait for the weather to permit their crossing to Kiloran, depends on invoking and – ultimately – overcoming the primordial force of dreams and myths.

A PURPOSEFUL HEROINE? WISH-FULFILMENTS?

> 'Alas,' said the mouse, 'the world is growing smaller everyday. At the beginning it was so big that I was afraid, I kept running and running, and I was glad when at last I saw walls far away to the right and the left, but these long walls have narrowed so quickly that I am in the last chamber already and there in the corner stands the trap that I must run into.' 'You only need to change your direction,' said the cat, and ate it up.
>
> Franz Kafka[16]

The linear forward thrust of the film's opening focuses on its heroine, Joan Webster. The delightful opening credit sequence (which, on first viewing, had me falling in love with Joan even before she was embodied as an adult by the extraordinary Wendy Hiller) emphasises not only Joan's constant mobility, but her undeviating sense of direction and purpose. The film's title beautifully welds together two essential aspects of her character: Joan not only *goes*, she *knows* where she is going. She consciously

Joan practising her future role as Lady Bellinger when changing trains at Glasgow in *I Know Where I'm Going!*.

propels the momentum of the film's initial journey, calling out to her father as the train pulls out of Manchester station: 'Don't worry about me, I know where I'm going!' Joan's knowledge – of where she is going, of what she wants and of who she is – becomes as deeply questioned as her destination during the extended delay that makes up most of the film. The space of transformation that appears when her journey becomes interrupted not only alters ordinary senses of space and time; it also, as Ricoeur says, disorients the protagonist. In most love stories, including *IKWIG*, love and knowledge become antithetical – or, rather, love possesses and proceeds by a mode of knowing that overturns logic and consistency. In a love story, characters begin to doubt their previous knowledge, especially what they thought they knew about themselves. In place of former patterns of clarity or singleness of purpose, lovers find themselves split and conflicted about what they know and what they want.

If we closely examine what Joan knows and wants, we realise that, even from the beginning, her relationship to dreams and desire is more complex than it might initially seem. Her opening journey seems on the surface to be purposeful and rational, guided by maps and itineraries, managed by a rich man's hirelings and modern modes of transportation. As Cook says, the preparations of the wedding have 'all the attributes of a well-planned business deal'.[17] But as the film's *mise en scène* also reveals, this journey carries hidden freight, what Christie calls the 'irrational side of her journey, the one she can't really acknowledge, until she sleeps and dreams'.[18] Joan's journey, while seemingly calculated and even mercenary, invokes the power of dreams long before she gets to Port Erraig. Powell and Pressburger's understanding that deep desires underlie Joan's materialist longings allows us to sympathise deeply with a woman we might otherwise dismiss as a gold-digger and nothing more. Joan's delight in pretty shiny things, emblems of the world Robert Bellinger offers her – the diamond engagement ring that gleams in close-up as she shows it to her father; the chrome-plated accessories of her private sleeping car; the plastic covering of her wedding dress – reveals a childish drive lurking under her sophisticated adult exterior. But being childish is far from a simple fault; it reveals Joan as yet unshaped and unfulfilled, dreaming of something else than what she has.

Recall the credit sequence in which Joan appears as a child anxious to become an adult, a child who soon learns to move 'straight on' and to manipulate people (especially men: the driver of the cart who gives her a ride home after school, the young man who takes her to dinner in the best hotel, rather than the movies). She is also a child, precociously able to articulate her desires, as in her childhood letter to Santa Claus that asks for a pair of silk stockings, *real* ones not artificial. Without indulging in complex psychology, and in spite of the light tone of this prologue, we sense that this is a young woman who, for some reason, was not allowed a childhood, and who compensates for this by both a precocious maturity and a canny suspicion of the adult world, which tends to offer inferior substitutes for real desires (we learn that she 'was twelve before she got her first pair of stockings – and they *were* artificial!'). When Joan models her wedding dress alone in her bedroom during her first night at Port Erraig, she resembles a child pretending to be an adult, as she did in the prologue writing her mercenary letter to Father Christmas. Our empathy with Joan comes from both the intensity of her desires and our realisation that she (touchingly and vulnerably) remains an unsatisfied child whose suspicion and calculation masks a childlike desire for the promises of adult life, a naïve attraction to all the substitutes consumer culture offers in order to fuel desire and acquisition. Michael Powell, describing Joan in his autobiography, says she considers money 'a good substitute', but cannily does not specify *what* it is a substitute for.[19]

On the train, the film segues into an extraordinary dream sequence, cued by the rhythmic sound and image montage, blending the headlong thrust of Joan's journey into a hypnotic power that flows into the realm of dreams. The soundtrack initially alternates between a masculine voice intoning the itinerary and a chorus of women's voices singing the film's theme song. Joan examines her itinerary and the map of her route, but repeatedly glances up from her reading with the faraway gaze of fantasy. The dream sequence proper begins with a camera movement from Joan asleep to her wedding dress, hanging sheathed in a shiny plastic container. As the camera tracks in on the transparent bag, swaying with the train's rhythm, the dress within suddenly vanishes.

Powell undoubtedly chose this plastic covering, (a rather recent technological novelty and presumably rare during this era of wartime rationing) as an emblem of the burgeoning world of consumer goods strongly anticipated in 1945, and only waiting for the end of the war to be offered to the public. Both Cook and Christie stress *IKWIG*'s critical relation to this looming consumer culture, already being announced to a public weary of wartime shortages.[20] This critique gains depth and avoids puritanical moralism partly by treating Joan sympathetically, but also by portraying how consumer culture acts parasitically on fundamental human desires, offering deceptive substitutes for the authentic hunger for adventure and love.

As the dress magically vanishes, leaving only this empty emblem of the shining world of visual attraction, the covering becomes a surface onto which desires are projected. A literal 'dream screen', this shiny surface remains superimposed over most of the images of the dream sequence. In place of the dress, Joan appears encased in the plastic, dressed in her wedding outfit for a satirical mock marriage to 'Consolidated Chemical Industries', performed by her father in sacerdotal robes. Behind him a series of large wheels, printed in negative, turn rhythmically. Interestingly, both Christie and Cook refer to these wheels as images of 'factories' or 'machines',[21] as indeed they first appeared to me. In fact, they are the balance wheels of large church bells, presumably wedding bells, printed not only in negative, but upside down in the frame. This confusion must have been intentional, revealing the mechanical nature of Joan's marriage to an industrial firm, as well as its inversion of her authentic desire. Likewise, the substitution of a steam whistle (which releases a spurt of vapor in close-up) for the 'I do' of CCI in this bizarre ceremony, followed by a shot of the locomotive charging towards the camera, plays with images associated with the mechanical, but also traditionally serving as substitutions (in cinema, from Von Stroheim to Hitchcock) for sexual power and desire.

Framed by the shiny plastic surface, Joan seems confined, a commodity herself, packaged for attractiveness – and for sale. In the shot following the locomotive, Joan becomes further transformed by a blonde wig, her face heavily made up and brightly lit, gleaming like the plastic cover we view her through. More than glamour, the image connotes a death-like stasis: she seems to be laid out in a coffin for viewing, as if she had suffocated in her plastic prison. I believe that Powell intends a direct fairy-tale reference here: Joan as Snow White in her glass casket, lost in a sleep that resembles death. The rhythmically spoken soundtrack invokes a flow of luxury consumer goods and money ('Charged to your account ... Five hundred guineas, five hundred guineas ... Lady Bellinger's car'). In the next dream shot, the bewigged Joan appears upright in the frame, but still catatonic, as a cascade of bills falls through the frame, visual images and sound reaching a climax of spending. This dream exemplifies Freud's claim that dreams present wish-fulfilments (remembering that the German *Wunsch* translates not only as 'wish', but as desire – although the fairy-tale aspect of wishing also belongs here). But, for Freud, wishes and desires are never straightforward; one wish hides behind another, and we see that behind Joan's wish to be Lady Bellinger, more subterranean desires stir, fused and confused on the surface.

The dream ends with the cartoon-like image of what Christie describes as 'tartan hills', a particularly witty dirty joke, as the toy train enters a tunnel just under the

What barrier has been crossed? Joan arrives at Erraig House on Mull on the way to her dream wedding in *I Know Where I'm Going!*.

mountain's kilt. Announcing the honeymoon spot of Gretna Green,[22] the male voiceover, oddly calm in contrast to the previous rhythms of acceleration, intones, 'You're over the border now'. What border has been crossed? The dream sequence, placed in the centre of Joan's determined journey and, in retrospect, supplying much of its urgency and motive force, hints at Joan's derailment long before the check she encounters at seaside from fog and storm. In her sleep – indeed, I think we have to say unconsciously – Joan has already crossed another border, one she does not yet recognise. This border crossing into unacknowledged desires prepares the way for the later physical crossing of thresholds, which, as Cook and Christie note,[23] visually punctuate Joan's stay on Mull.

From this point on, the film questions its own title: does Joan really know where she is going? The dream splits her in two: the artificial sleeping beauty who rushes towards her entombment in the bright and shiny but airless world of money, and, under this cover, a still young girl who knows only that she desires *something*, that she has not thus far been satisfied with all the substitutes life has offered her, although still drawn by the promise of their shiny surfaces. The drama that will take place on the island of Mull, where Kiloran looms on the horizon but cannot be reached, stages a struggle between these two Joans. The one, who dominates the opening sequences, has nearly lost herself in shiny substitutes. The other, who surfaces and ultimately triumphs as the film progresses (even as her journey stalls), possesses passions and desires that will come to the surface through her encounter – not only with a true love – but with the limits of experience.

Near the climax of the film, when Joan endangers her own life and the life of others by attempting to cross over to Kiloran during the gale, she tries to explain her action to Bridie (the young girl whose lover Kenny would pilot the boat) by saying, 'I'm on the brink of losing everything I ever wanted, ever since I could want anything.' Her impassioned statement anchors her wilful and reckless act (she does not know what she is doing) in an infantile wish and desire reaching back to an almost primal point, when she first wanted anything. The resonance of her self-defence, made to another young woman longing for marriage, comes partly from the ambivalence of the word 'want', so fundamental to the paradoxes of a love story. To 'want' means to 'desire', but also 'not to have', to be deprived, 'in want'. Again, speculation on Joan's childhood experiences of wanting are raised here, but not answered. Although I think they are worth speculating on, ultimately the issue exceeds personal biography. To love *is* to want, and love's great conundrum comes from the fact that it asserts both lack and the powerful desire born of that lack.[24] We do not need Lacan to tell us (since it is implied in every great love story, as well as every mass-market romance) that while needs can be fulfilled, desire never can, and thus it never ceases, until death. Here, we encounter again the resistance of love stories to closure, even though, classically, they would seem to provide the form of narrative fulfilment par excellence. Joan entices us into her drama, even when everything tells us she is marrying a rich and pompous ass, because we see her desire running beyond her needs, her bold devotion to what André Breton and the surrealists would valorise as *l'amour fou* – love beyond calculation of benefit or even self-preservation. Joan's foolish rush towards a man she does not really love paradoxically shows the sublime nature of her desire, her love of love itself.

MAGIC? WHO KNOWS?

If it were true – as conceited shrewdness, proud of not being deceived, thinks – that one should believe nothing which he cannot see by means of physical eyes, then first and foremost one ought to give up believing in love.

Søren Kierkegaard[25]

When the breeze snatches the itinerary from Joan's hand as she waits for the boat to take her to Kiloran, we know that the first leg of the journey and the first act of the film has come to an end. As Pam Cook puts it, 'There could hardly be a clearer sign that a frontier has been reached – one that will necessitate a change in direction and a major revision of goals.'[26] As I stated before, this is the moment when the headlong journey stalls and Joan lands in the space of transformation. Supported by the imagery that associates the island of Mull with the dark forests of fairy tales and romances, a different sort of narrative causality seems to take over, directly in opposition to Joan's straight-on trajectory (a product, we have learned, of both her deliberate planning and calculation, and of obscure desires). The wind that snatches this orderly plan from Joan announces a new force in the narrative that appears first as chance or contingency (accidents that waylay the best-made plans of mice and men), but increasingly seems to be not at all random, taking on the appearance of fate or destiny. Unseen and often non-human forces take on a dominant role, reducing – for the moment – characters' conscious decisions to a secondary role. As Christie puts it, 'what controls the working out of the narrative is almost entirely mythic'.[27]

This fashioning of a destiny out of pure chance makes up one of love's main forms of seduction. Lovers see a purpose behind the events that shape their falling in love – indeed, one could say falling in love consists of this growing sense of destiny embroidered over random happenings.[28] If autobiography is the story one tells oneself, love could be described as a story two people tell each other that allows them to see themselves as a couple. This sense of a fate willingly adopted – or constructed – by lovers gives the love story its narrative necessity, but their willing adoption of this fate (rather than a mere submission to it) must be a gradual process, overcoming resistances. This growing sense of destiny, of the power of love to shape one's life even without one fully knowing it, also carries a severe danger, that of losing oneself entirely through submission to dark forces, even death.

Here we encounter what Walter Benjamin, in his incandescent analysis of one of the world's greatest love tragedies, Goethe's *Elective Affinities*, calls the dark and fatal powers of the mythic.[29] Fatal love exists for Benjamin in a world bereft of freedom, ruled by a primal sense of guilt that demands the sacrifice of the innocent (in Goethe's novel, this sacrifice takes the form of drowning). Cinematic love melodramas (we might think of *Vertigo* as the most sublime example) unfold within this dark world of desire, retribution and sacrifice, rather than fulfilment. On the other hand, love stories that tend towards comedy, like *IKWIG*, flirt with this danger, indeed sometimes, as in *IKWIG*, confront it directly, veering into melodramatic mode – as in the climactic scene at Corryvreckan – but they ultimately escape from it. That is why events must oscillate between seeming to be simple accidents or revealing the hand of some other power. For this pattern to avoid becoming truly fatal, the recognition by lovers (and audiences) of another power shaping events must retain a playful aspect. In contrast to the doomed love of fateful lovers, in love comedies such as *IKWIG*, love appears as a necessity freely taken on, a destiny in which one discovers one's freedom – that is, one's true nature. Instead of pure submission to fate, love demands a moment of free decision. While the powers of the dark world force one (sometimes unknowingly) to the threshold of that decision by calling into doubt everything one previously took for granted, at the moment of decision a direct confrontation with those dark forces takes away their power – a moment of exorcism occurs. This acceptance and new understanding of the power of love (and the decision to embrace it), more than the satisfaction of desire, allows the closure of a love story, while hinting that this ending remains only a prologue to a long life that continues beyond the story's borders. We could say the final decision involves the alignment of one's wishes with one's most authentic desires, which is no easy thing to achieve, and needs both help – and opposition – from forces seemingly outside, or even opposed to, one's will.

If the simple breeze that blows her itinerary away provides our first visual emblem of unseen intervening forces, the weather more broadly embodies its power over the story as it halts Joan's trajectory and delays her marriage. Like the breeze, weather carries the connotation of divine intervention, a theme played with throughout Joan's stay on Mull. The segue between Joan's determined knowledge of where she is going and her encounter with other forces is carefully developed through her three prayers or wishes. The first occurs on her first night at Erraig house and is prompted by Torquil telling her an old Scottish superstition as they lean out of their respective bedroom windows: if she counts the beams on the bedroom ceiling before she falls asleep, her wish will come true. Joan's dual reaction to this superstition (flippant condescension to Torquil, then apparent credence when she sits in her bed alone) reveals how her childlike wishes persist beneath a veneer of sophistication. After shutting Torquil out by closing the window and lowering the blind, Joan obviously falls under the spell of her old-fashioned bedroom, lit only by an oil lamp. As we hear her counting, the camera tilts up to the central spot on the ceiling where the five beams converge on a grotesque face of a troll or monster. Joan expresses her 'wish' through a childlike prayer, as she intones, 'Please Lord, don't let the wind drop and let it blow the fog away'. Joan ends the prayer with a coquettish glance at the ceiling as if she were playing at praying. Her cocky glance is followed, however, by a close-up of the grotesque face, its long tongue sticking out from its mouth. It seems to ask, who is playing with whom?

This demonic face helps us define the nature of the force that seems to intervene in Joan's life and the film's narrative. It would be misleading to assume that Divine Providence operates here. The grotesque face that appears to receive Joan's prayer recalls demonic forces, rather than divine ones. Crossing the dark forest may ultimately lead the way to divine love, but initially the way is beset with monsters and demons – not Satan, the author of Evil, but 'little gods', whose actions resemble capricious pranks, forces that are cunning in their relations to mortals rather than succouring. As Christie points out in his commentary, the fulfilment of Joan's prayer plays with ambiguous meanings, as did traditional oracles. We dissolve from Joan's slumber to a montage of gale-force winds whipping tree branches and brush and driving surf against rocks. The wind indeed has not died down, it *has* blown away the fog, but in doing so, it calls up a gale that renders any voyage across the bay of Kiloran impossible. The answer to Joan's prayer exploits the ambiguity that has begun to sprout in her desire, sowing doubts not only about how to get to where she is going, but about what it is she really wants. Joan's voyage now becomes subject to devious guides that reflect both the intensity and the ambiguity of her desire. As Torquil tells her the next day, 'You wished too hard'.

Joan's second prayer occurs the next night after a day spent with Torquil exploring Mull. Joan has moved into the modern hotel in Tobermory. The sequence begins with Joan pausing in the middle of writing a letter to 'Daddy, my darling'. The fragment reads: 'You thought you had a grown-up daughter who knew her own mind and could manage without anybody's help. Oh, darling I wish … ' The object of her wish lingers, unspoken (or unwritten). Joan gets up and paces her room as the wind blows the curtains at her window and the rough sea beyond (a movie cliché of female sexual frustration). Clearly Joan no longer knows what she wishes. She lies upon her bed, brightly (if not particularly realistically) illuminated by a pair of electric lamps that contrast with the oil lamp in the earlier scene. With none of her previous playfulness, she begins a prayer, 'Please God … ', but pauses and looks up at the ceiling.

The camera tilts up, but no grimacing demon looks down on her, only two delicately scalloped florets of light, cast by the lamps. Joan looks down pensively and begins her prayer again: 'Please let the gale drop. I must get over to the island tomorrow. You know that I must.' The ending of the prayer sets a curious kink in the theme of knowing in this film. Joan's insistence that God knows where she must go reveals her growing doubt that she still possesses the knowledge she has counted on throughout her life. Indeed, from this point on, Joan tries to invest others with knowledge that would underwrite her actions, as when she tries to avoid dancing with Torquil at the ceilidh, telling the host, 'Kiloran knows I must get back'. But Torquil refuses to take on this responsibility, responding firmly, 'Kiloran knows nothing of the sort'. The film does not tell us what God knows. We do not know if, like Torquil, God refuses to shore up Joan's growing uncertainty, or even if he rules in this transitional space, which may be entirely under the sway of mischievous demons. In any case, Joan's second prayer remains unanswered, even deviously. A shot of her hand switching off the electric lamp dissolves into a shot of raging surf, unchanged from the day before.

Joan's third prayer may be the most ambiguous. It occurs during the film's climax, the attempt to cross Kiloran bay during the gale, a voyage that ends on the edge of the Corryvreckan whirlpool, threatening to destroy the passengers in the boat, Torquil, Kenny and Joan. I will discuss this sequence in more detail later, but the prayer marks its literal turning point. After the boat has survived wind and rain, its motor suddenly fails, and Torquil labours to repair it before the tide changes and sweeps them into the maelstrom. Before he tries to restart the motor, Torquil barks at Joan, 'Pray!'. The motor turns over, and he tells Joan, 'Your credit must be good in heaven'. Joan responds, 'They know a good prayer when they hear one'. At last, one of Joan's prayers seems to have a direct effect. But curiously, compared to the previous prayers, which we hear on the soundtrack and which are accompanied by strong visual images, this prayer remains unmarked. We do not hear it, nor does Joan give any outward sign of praying. It may be that she has abandoned prayer, or that her praying has taken on a form beyond any direct representation. In spite of Joan's apparent avowal, I tend to believe the first alternative, partly because of the bedroom scene that follows her safe, but weary, return to shore. As she extinguishes the oil lamp, Catriona repeats to Joan the folklore that if she counts the beams, her prayers will come true. But Joan responds this time, 'I am not praying tonight'. The camera does not tilt to the ceiling, but pans over to the wind-blown curtains at the window. Ironically, the dissolve that follows shows the curtain in daylight unstirred by wind; the gale has ended. Joan's non-prayer has been finally answered (or was fulfilment simply delayed?).

THE PERIL AND USES OF MYTH: IRONY, SACRIFICE AND THE BREAKING OF TABOOS

> On one of these occasions [boat trips to Corryvreckan] I said to Pamela [Brown]: 'Do you
> realize that we nearly got drowned just them?'
> 'Yes,' she said.
> 'Would you have minded?'
>
> Michael Powell, *A Life in Movies*[30]

Pam Cook and Ian Christie, and, I would wager, most viewers of *IKWIG*, spot a mythological dimension once Joan has arrived at the Port Erraig.[31] Both compare the first strikingly backlit, silhouetted shot of Catriona Potts (née MacLaine, played by the magnificent Pamela Brown),[32] returning from the hunt with her hounds on leash, to Diana, Goddess of the hunt. When Joan arrives at Port Erraig, strange archaic powers *do* seem to emerge to greet her, in a cluster of images that contrast sharply with the images of modernity in the film's opening journey – such as the clichéd Gothic imagery of the fog-shrouded ruined castle of Moy and its curse. Mythic animals also appear, not only Catriona's hounds, but Colonel Barnstaple's falcon (not to mention his missing eagle), the exotic oxen Bridie herds through the fog-enveloped streets of Port Erraig and the uncanny sound coming from the sea that the locals tell Joan is 'the seal's signal'.

But we must catch the complex nuance of these images and their role in marking the space – and process – of transformation. Like the appearance of the goatherd in the opening of *A Matter of Life and Death*, the 'timeless' aspect of these images has a deceptive and ironic aspect. Port Erraig never really becomes a realm of classical mythology, nor even of traditional folklore; rather, the film presents something of a parody of these realms, a carnivalesque mixture of high and low. Catriona's dramatic backlit 'Diana' must be balanced by her subsequent entrance into Erraig house – stunning, dramatic and filled with energy, but hardly a goddess, with her wet tousled hair, her kilt-like plaid skirt and the leather coat that she flings to the floor like an eight-year-old home from school. Barnstaple's sudden entry to welcome Joan, with his hunting garb and falcon on his wrist, while startling and at first unsettling, quickly settles down into a traditional comedy of manners, evoking eccentricity rather than ancient mystery. The space of transition remains a space of minor gods and demons, tricksters and shape-shifters, who oddly carry a numinous aura into domestic circumstance. With this mixture of the familiar and the unfamiliar, these figures embody Freud's concept of the 'uncanny', the *unheimlich*, rather than the more stable meanings of the sacred or of myth.

As the transformation space exists primarily to undermine previously established order, to reroute trajectories and metamorphose identities and desires, it draws near to, but cannot maintain, a revival of mythology, which would invite the regression that Ricoeur warns us movement back into primal space and time tends to risk[33] (interestingly, Cook also claims that *IKWIG*'s nostalgia for vanished ways of life 'lays the film open to accusations of regressive sentimentality'[34]). *IKWIG*'s attitude towards mythology avoids simple regression by maintaining a sense of humour and irony about vanished traditions. If the old gods haunt the dark forest, they do so as dethroned deities, distorted reflections of former glory, daemons and devils, recalling the grotesque face on Joan's ceiling. Aspects of *IKWIG* recall the satiric treatment of mythology in Jacques Offenbach's operettas[35] (Pressburger had scripted a film about Offenbach in Germany in 1935, Powell and Pressburger collaborated on a film of Offenbach's *The Tales of Hoffmann* in 1951, and curiously the Farcarolle from that operetta is briefly quoted by Allan Gray's score after the escape from the whirlpool), or in Reinhold Schünzel's 1935 comic German operetta film *Amphitryon* (Pressburger had scripted several of Schünzel's films in Germany in the early 1930s). Rather than a revival of mythology, the space of transition functions as an anarchic reversal of the ordinary world, with demonic overtones.

This less than pious attitude may have been hinted at already by the lyrics of the film's theme song. The first line, the film's title, asserts Joan's original independence, while the second, 'I know who's going with me', raises the aspect of the film that remains uncertain throughout her stay on Mull: who *will* accompany Joan, who seems thus far to have made her journey alone? The next line, therefore, also comes into question, 'I know who I love'. Does she, indeed? But the fourth line poses an enigma that threatens to become philological. The subtitles for the Criterion DVD transcribe it as 'But the day knows who I'll marry', clearly a mistake (like the later transcription of the Scottish song as 'Naught Brown Girl'!). The lyric is often given as 'But the dear knows who I'll marry' (as in Padraic Colum's 1922 *Anthology of Irish Verse*[36]), and Michael Powell cites this version in his autobiography,[37] which makes more sense, but not a lot more. Another transcription of the song, which I found by searching the web, gives this line as 'But the de'il knows who I'll marry', 'de'il' being a one-syllable contraction of 'devil'. In this version, the line contrasts with an alternate third line, 'The Lord knows who I love'. To my ear, admittedly often confused by British accents – let alone dialects -the line sung in the film sounds more like 'de'il' than 'dear'. As the film has already raised the question of what Joan knows, and of what God does, or does not, know, the possibility that the devil knows who Joan will marry becomes irresistible. We could wonder if the devil alone knows what is happening on Mull and perhaps even has a hand in it. (After all, in her penultimate line to Torquil, Joan speaks of 'all the hell I raised'.)

If the various invocations of myth clustered around Joan's arrival at Port Erraig have an ironic, or even comic, undertone, two ancient myths appear in the film not as fragmented, ambiguous images, but as complete narratives: 'The Legend of Corryvreckan' and 'The Curse of Catriona MacLaine'. Both are doubly inscribed in the film: recited on the soundtrack and visually presented through the engraving in the post office of the legend and the rock carving of the curse revealed in the film's final scene. Torquil recounts the legend to Joan as she waits for the radio connection with Sir Robert (although, significantly, his telling is interrupted by the radio communication, and Torquil only finishes the story on the boat during the gale), while we hear the voice of Torquil's old nurse recite the curse, and the story of violence that explains it, as he explores the forbidden castle of Moy at the film's end.

The playful fragments of mythology, the realm of folklore and Offenbach-like satire that throng about Port Erraig help distract Joan from her rationalistic, and ultimately selfish, calculation and one-way logic in order to open her up to her deeper desires (wants that cannot be fulfilled by shiny consumer goods). But these complete myths possess a greater and more dangerous power, the dark fatalism that Benjamin saw brooding over Goethe's *Elective Affinities*, demanding sacrifice not of objects but of innocent lives: the death-drive of Thanatos that threatens to overwhelm and defeat the powers of Eros, transforming it into a vengeful Eros Tyrannos by fusing these forces together.

Torquil and Joan's nearly fatal encounter with the whirlpool of Corryvreckan provides a complex climax for the film. As in Lillian Gish's extraordinary rescue from the ice floes at the climax of D. W. Griffith's *Way Down East* (or, as Cook insightfully points out, the storm on the lake in F. W. Murnau's *Sunrise*[38]), with this sequence, *IKWIG* crosses into the melodramatic mode of physical action and contest with natural forces (not, incidentally, represented in all three films by the changeable power of water). This melodramatic climax provides an emotional catharsis, as well as an objective correlative of the turmoil raging within the lovers. Initially, the action expresses the last gasp of Joan's apparently stubborn determination finally to complete her journey and reach her rich fiancé on Kiloran. This is how Torquil reads it: as a sign of her selfishness and arrogance, endangering the lives of others. However, Catriona, who has silently observed Joan throughout the film and especially as she makes this reckless decision, understands that Joan is no loner running towards something, but running away – away from her growing love of Torquil. As Joan confesses to Bridie, she is no longer 'safe' on Mull; she is becoming aware not only of her love for Torquil, but of the transformation of her self that it demands – and it terrifies her. But both of these motives provide too simple a motivation for Joan's desperate act, whether running toward the one she loves or away from him. The pull of the darkly mythic enters, challenging Joan to face it.

Joan has heard of the legend of Corryvreckan and knows that to withstand the deadly pull of the whirlpool constitutes a test of true love (as it was for the Norwegian prince in the legend who sought to win the hand of the daughter of the Lord of the Isles by anchoring his ship for three nights within the whirlpool, but failed when his magical rope snapped due to an unfaithful maiden). Although the confrontation of the whirlpool seems to be another accident (attributable to the confluence of Joan's foolhardy action, the gale and the failed boat engine), on the mythic level Joan must undergo this ordeal and test her love. The mythic forces demand a sacrifice, and Joan seems to offer a boatload.

Setting off from Mull into the realm of water, transformation space sheds its comic aspect and reveals its most sinister and serious energies. Everything is at stake now. Ricoeur quotes from the historian of religions Mircea Eliade to express this aspect of the quest romance through a discussion of Ulysses, 'the trapped voyager':

> His voyage was a voyage toward the center, toward Ithaca, which is to say, toward himself. He was a fine navigator, but destiny – spoken here in terms of trials of initiation which he had to overcome – forced him to postpone indefinitely his return to hearth and home. ... as in the Labyrinth, in every questionable turn, one risks 'losing oneself.' If one succeeds in getting out of the Labyrinth, in finding one's home again, then one becomes a new being.[39]

Rather than running away from Torquil, or towards Sir Robert, in rushing to the brink of the vortex, Joan runs both towards and away from herself, seeming to abandon herself to fatality rather than risk her 'safety' by staying with Torquil.

Ironically, Torquil has accompanied her on this attempt to escape him, boarding the boat to help both Kenny and Joan during the perilous crossing. Earlier, in a scene played with remarkably close physical intimacy between the two yet-to-be-acknowledged lovers, Joan had asked Torquil to ferry her across to Kiloran. Torquil indicated that he would only set out in this gale if 'people are in danger and need help'. Joan turns to him and, in her most confessional moment so far, tells him, 'I want help desperately'. This moment, as Joan and Torquil stand on the brink of true communication,

Powell was attracted to the legend of Corryvrecken by its resemblance to Poe's 'A Descent into the Maelstrom'.

Joan knows that to withstand the whirlpool is a test of true love. But who is she running towards or away from on the brink of the vortex?

is interrupted by the clanging of a gong as Colonel Barnstaple, ridiculously arrayed in turban and apron, rushes in with news of his eagle. The grotesque and comic mythic forces turn hostile for the moment, even as they appear at their most silly, blocking intimacy between the lovers. Torquil does not respond or understand Joan's plea for help, and it is only later, when Catriona explains it to him, that he realises his own role in Joan's apparently selfish decision and rushes out to join her in this final voyage.

At first, the voyage to Kiloran seems simple enough. Joan undergoes a Holly-wood-like 'comeuppance' of the sort dealt out to independent women in screwball comedies (another point where the film flirts with regressive resolutions – the independent woman disciplined – a resolution I think the film ultimately escapes, although it skirts it, like the deadly tides of Corryvreckan), receiving swells of water full in the face as she stands arrogantly in the boat prow. Torquil demonstrates his seamanship and stays on course until a storm blows up that strips Joan of the possessions she transported so comfortably in her train compartment – her suitcase and, most symbolically, her wedding dress. But what still could be a comic sequence transforms darkly, as the failure of the boat's engine provides the ultimate check in Joan's forward momentum, and the circular pull of Corryvreckan threatens to convert her linear sense of direction into a vortex that turns simply on itself and pulls one down into the realm of death.

Powell indicated that the legend of Corryvreckan attracted him because it recalled 'his favorite story in the world, almost', Poe's masterful 1841 tale 'A Descent into the Maelström'.[40] In this extraordinary fictional narrative of a Norwegian sailor sucked into a powerful whirlpool, Poe provides a vivid description of the Romantic Sublime and its temptation toward submission to the fatal attraction of being over-whelmed, even onto death. Swirled about, the sailor recalls: 'I began to reflect how magnificent a thing it was to die in such a manner, and how foolish it was in me to think of so paltry a consideration as my own individual life, in view of so wonderful a manifestation of God's power.'[41]

Such delight in the triumph of force over life exemplifies the fatal pull exerted by the dark forces of mythology, the temptation towards self-destruction inherent in romantic love. It is hardly accidental that the swirling vortex, representing loss of personal identity, stands as the central image of the greatest cinematic expression of overwhelming fatal desire, Hitchcock's *Vertigo*.[42] While surrendering to this destructive force would destroy Joan, sacrificing not only her illusions, but her self (and the lives of Kenny and Torquil as well), *confronting* the whirlpool, sailing to its brink and then turning away from it, may be the act necessary for Joan to become able, finally and truly, to turn about and redirect her energies and desires. She must 'risk losing her self' in order to emerge as 'a new being'. The combined efforts of Torquil, Kenny and Joan cause the boat to regain power and reverse direction, sailing home (if Port Erraig could be home for Joan —as it obviously is for Kenny, and perhaps Torquil), avoiding the grim fatality the myth of Corryvreckan demands.

Why has Joan escaped? We might recall the story of Isaac and Jacob and see the drowned wedding dress as a substitute sacrifice to mythic forces (when Joan later wonders what happened to her dress, Torquil speculates that 'A mermaid will marry in it'). But survival of the whirlpool's ordeal does not magically resolve Joan's dilemma. Mythic forces have been braved, but they must still be exorcised by a free decision. The next morning, after a night without prayers, the sea is tranquil and the boat sent by Sir Robert approaches, and Joan prepares to meet it. Torquil has resumed his Navy officer's uniform, rather than the kilt he has worn since the first morning in Port Erraig, the Laird of Kiloran again becoming an ordinary military officer. It might seem we have come full cycle. The space and time of transformation seems to have reached its end, like the gale that has blown itself out, but, apparently, nothing has changed. The confrontation with and escape from the vortex may have been cathartic, but its process of regeneration remains unfulfilled.

In fact, the process of transformation has not been completed, particularly on Torquil's part. He remains in thrall to mythic forces through his fear of the Curse of Catriona MacLaine. If the encounter with Corryvreckan constitutes the action-filled climax of the film, Torquil's penetration into the cursed castle of Moy moves us toward true transformation. Roger Livesey's wonderful performance imbues the role of Torquil with such humanity and personal magnetism that one almost forgets what a potentially static and even self-satisfied character he could appear to be (especially in contrast to Joan's dynamism and inner tension). Compared to Joan, what has he risked? Even his heroic action at the whirlpool seems entirely consistent, part of his identity as local boatman and naval officer.

Torquil's crossing the threshold of Moy Castle, after it seems Joan has finally departed for her wedding on Kiloran, carefully develops and resolves a number of themes, revealing new aspects of his character and allowing for a final transformation of both lovers. His previous refusal to cross the threshold occasioned his revelation to Joan of his status as the traditional Laird of Kiloran, shattering her fantasy of becoming the Lady of the Island through marriage to Sir Robert, who, Torquil firmly informs her, only rents the island. The shot of Torquil backlit and silhouetted at the castle threshold recalls not only the similarly composed shot when Joan stood there earlier and invited him to enter, but the shot of her arrival at Erraig House (a similarity both Christie and Cook have noted).[43] This similarity puts Torquil in Joan's place: instead of returning home to a place where everyone knows and recognises him, and where he is familiar with every detail of history and custom, he must now, like Joan, enter a place where he has never set foot, a place not only unfamiliar, but potentially threatening.

In contrast to the warm welcome Joan receives from the eccentrically mythologised characters she meets inside Erraig House, Torquil's own dark shadow looms before him, a literal projection of his fears. Later, Torquil will tell Joan he lied when he said he was afraid of the castle. His performance as he slowly enters and examines the interior of this Gothic ruin does not encourage us to believe this (although we easily believe that he is overcoming his fear, and that by the time he speaks to Joan he is no longer afraid). Even if he does not believe in the castle's supernatural threat, nonetheless he is breaking the tradition of his family, as he explained earlier to Joan, 'of my father, my grandfather, and his father'. At the very least, Torquil breaks a continuity of patriarchal tradition. Further, his entrance into this enclosed, womb-like space involves a strong element of regression, as the voice of his child-hood nanny appears on the soundtrack. As he defies the practice of MacNeil fathers for generations, Torquil becomes surrounded by female voices, not only his nanny, but the outraged and vengeful curse of Catriona, recited as the scene ends.

This sequence parallels and completes the scene at Corryvreckan, only now Torquil must experience the fear that he so firmly repressed through his expertise as he engineered the escape from the whirlpool. Water and drowning appear here as well, only as an image of past horrors, the murder of Catriona MacLaine and her lover by the Laird of Kiloran. In this past action of masculine violence against women, Torquil encounters the mythological guilt the curse embodies and whose burden he shares. In his commentary, Christie compares the ruin to a labyrinth, and the overhead shot looking down through the circular hole in the floor into the watery realm in which Catriona and her lover were drowned visually recalls the vortex imagery of the whirlpool, a compositional echo doubled by the shot of Torquil mounting a spiral stairway to read the curse that is etched in stone on the castle ramparts.

The final exorcism of dark mythic powers in the film comes not only through Torquil's courage in breaking with family tradition and defying the curse, but most elegantly and wittily, by redefining the curse itself (which has never before been specified, only referred to – repeatedly – as a 'terrible strong curse'). The curse laid on the Laird of Kiloran who dares to cross the threshold of Moy Castle poses another ambiguous oracle – not a contract legally designed to have a single unequiv-ocal meaning, but poetic words whose interpretation can, indeed *does*, transform its meaning from curse to blessing: 'He shall be chained to a woman till the end of his days and shall die in his chains'.

Finally, the mythic powers are dispelled by the characters' free decisions. The lag between Joan's drama at the whirlpool and her celebratory return, serenading Torquil with pipers hired by Sir Robert to play at their wedding, after seemingly parting from him forever, dramatically delays her decision to dump Sir Robert for Torquil, emphasising that it is her assertion of a newly won freedom, rather than simply a magical transformation. Torquil's crossing of the threshold likewise not only frees him from a family taboo, but is freely done. Torquil can gain the hand of Joan because, like her, he confronted the fatal sacrifice, but instead of losing his life, regains it, shedding his relation to what Christie calls 'the dead hand of tradition', paying for his forefather's guilt toward women by accepting a punishment that is, in fact, no punishment. Like Melville's Ishmael ('Who ain't a slave?') or even Milton's Samson Agonistes, Torquil accepts his chains, but finds them light. The film ends with the ambiguous curse recited by the nanny on the soundtrack, the shot of the stone inscription dissolving to an image of Joan and Torquil walking off into the dis-tance. The difference might not be great, but I find it significant that *IKWIG* avoids ending with a kiss (the lovers' first and only screen kiss comes at the moment of their apparent parting). As the lovers declare their love for each other by embracing within the cursed castle, they each confess previous lies: Joan acknowledging her love of a free life rather than the luxury she claimed to desire, and Torquil (as previously mentioned) declaring his lack of fear of Castle Moy. After each confession, the other one delightedly replies, 'I know'. They are now joined in a new sort of knowledge and together walk out of the film in the same direction. Do we know where they are going? They do.

NOTES

1. Dashiell Hammett, 'Tulip', in Lillian Hellman, ed., *The Big Knockover*, New York: Random House, 1966, p. 334.

2. Ian Christie, audio commentary, *I Know Where I'm Going!*, Criterion DVD (catalogue no. KN0030); Pam Cook, *I Know Where I'm Going!*, London: BFI, 2002, p. 8.

3. Possibly the most insightful criticism written about films centred on love has been written by Stanley Cavell. It is striking that he has written on both love comedies (in *Pursuits of Happiness: The Hollywood Comedy of Remarriage*, Cambridge, MA: Harvard University Press, 1981), and melodramas (*Contesting Tears: The Hollywood Melodrama of the Unknown Woman*, Chicago: University of Chicago Press, 1996). *IKWIG* clearly relates to Cavell's discussion of comedies of remarriage.

4. These issues are well developed in Virginia Wright Wexman, *Creating the Couple; Love, Marriage and Hollywood Performance*, Princeton, NJ: Princeton University Press, 1993; and David Bordwell, Kristen Thompson and Janet Staiger, *The Classical Hollywood Cinema*, New York: Columbia University Press, 1986.

5. William Blake, 'The Little Black Boy', in *Songs of Innocence and of Experience*, ed. Andrew Lincoln, Princeton, NJ: Princeton University Press, 1998, p. 41.

6. Bordwell *et al.*, *Classical Hollywood Cinema*, p. 16.

7. Roland Barthes, *S/Z*, trans. Richard Miller, New York: Hill and Wang, 1974; Victor Shklovsky, *Theory of Prose*, trans. Benjamin Sher, Elmwood Park: Dalkey Archive Press, 1990.

8. Ovid, *The Art of Love and Other Poems* trans. J. H. Mozley, Cambridge, MA: Harvard University Press, 1999, pp. 114–15.

9. Jorge Luis Borges, 'The Garden of Forking Paths', in *Labyrinths: Selected Stories and Other Writings*, trans. Donald A. Yates, New York: New Directions, 1964, pp. 19–29.

10 See, for instance, Tzvetan Todorov, 'The Grammar of Narrative', in *The Poetics of Prose*, Ithaca, NY: Cornell University Press, 1977, p. 111.

11 David Bordwell, *Narration in the Fiction Film*, Madison: University of Wisconsin Press, 1985, p. 35.

12. Paul Ricoeur, 'Narrative Time', in W. T. J. Mitchell, ed., *On Narrative*, Chicago: University of Chicago Press, 1981, p. 180.

13. For a brilliant structuralist analysis of the narrative system of a film, see Stephen Heath's discussion of Welles's *Touch of Evil*, 'Film and System: Terms of Analysis, Part One', *Screen*, vol. 16 no. 1, Spring 1975, pp. 7–77. The diagram on p. 71 shows the arc of narrative resolution.

14. Ricoeur, 'Narrative Time,' p. 180.

15. Ibid., p. 181.
16. Franz Kafka, 'A Little Fable', in *The Complete Stories*, ed. Nahum N. Glatzer, New York: Schocken Books, 1976, p. 445.
17. Cook, *I Know Where I'm Going!*, p. 27.
18. Christie, DVD commentary.
19. Michael Powell, *A Life in Movies: An Autobiography*, New York: Alfred A. Knopf, 1987, p. 469.
20. Christie, DVD commentary; Cook, *I Know Where I'm Going!*, pp. 57–64.
21. Christie, DVD commentary; Cook, *I Know Where I'm Going!*, p. 29.
22. Or so Ian Christie's DVD commentary informs me.
23. Cook, *I Know Where I'm Going!*, pp. 45–46; Christie DVD commentary.
24. See my essay, 'The Desire and Pursuit of the Hole', in *Erotikon*, Chicago: University of Chicago Press, 2004.
25. Søren Kierkegaard, *Works of Love*, New York; Harper and Row, 1964, p. 23.
26. Cook, *I Know Where I'm Going!*, p. 45.
27. Christie, DVD commentary.
28. Freud pointed out that both lovers and psychoanalysts believe in the significance of seemingly accidental acts. 'The Psychopathology of Everyday Life' in Sigmund Freud, *The Standard Edition of the Complete Psychological Works of Sigmund Freud*, vol. VI, London: The Hogarth Press and Institute of Psychoanalysis, 1953–74, p. 153.
29. Walter Benjamin, 'Goethe's *Elective Affinities*', trans. Stanley Corngold, in *Selected Writings*, vol. I, 1913–1926, Cambridge: Harvard University Press, 1999, ed. Marcus Bullock and Michael W. Jennings, pp. 297–360.
30. Powell, *A Life in Movies*, p. 480.
31. Cook, *I Know Where I'm Going!*, p. 38; Christie DVD commentary.
32. Having already exceeded my allotted length, I reluctantly forgo a discussion of Catriona (possibly the only woman who could divert me from my devotion to Joan, although somehow I do not think she would have me). The scene between her and Torquil in which their love for each other was explored was excised from the film and limits the possibility of a full development of her character and significance. But the coincidence of the fact that she has the same name as the author of the curse holds more significance than simple genealogy. In some ways she, more than any other single character, embodies the intervening narrative force that allows the couple's love to blossom (a role I also see ironically hinted at in Cheril – played so delightfully by the young Petula Clark – who reads fairy tales, asks Joan probing questions about her marriage to Sir Robert and who, we are told by her mother, 'knows everything').
33. Ricoeur, 'Narrative Time', p. 181.
34. Cook, *I Know Where I'm Going!*, p. 41.
35. For a discussion of Offenbach's satires on Olympus, see Siegfried Kracauer, *Jacques Offenbach and the Paris of His Time*, New York: Zone Books, 2002, especially, pp. 200–8.
36. Padraic Colum, *Anthology of Irish Verse*, New York: Boni and Liveright, 1922, p. 37.
37. Powell, *A Life in Movies*, p. 460.
38. Cook, *I Know Where I'm Going!*, p. 18.
39. Mircea Eliade, *L'Epreuve du labyrinthe*, Paris: Pierre Belfond, 1978, p. 109, quoted in Ricoeur, 'Narrative Time', pp. 181–2.

40. Powell, *A Life in Movies*, p. 465.

41. Edgar Allan Poe, 'A Descent into the Maelström', in *Poetry and Tales*, New York: Library of America, 1984, p. 443.

42. I discuss this figure in, 'The Desire and Pursuit of the Hole'. Cook also sees a reflection of the vortex in the image of the ceiling beams converging on the grotesque face. *I Know Where I'm Going!*, p. 55. It might be worth noting that Celtic interlocking spirals, whirling in and out of the centre, are often interpreted as symbols of death and rebirth.

43. Christie, DVD commentary; Cook, *I Know Where I'm Going!*, pp. 45–6.

7 Life and Death in *A Matter of Life and Death*

Philip Horne

> When you see millions of the mouthless dead
> Across your dreams in pale battalions go,
> Say not soft things as other men have said,
> That you'll remember. For you need not so.

Charles Hamilton Sorley,
'When You See Millions of the Mouthless Dead', 1915

> It's not a matter of life or death
> But what is, what is?
> It doesn't matter if I take another breath
> Who cares, who cares?

Elvis Costello, 'Hoover Factory'

We are told to be concerned with a matter of life and death', coming at the end of a world-historical event, an all-convulsing war in which millions have lost their lives. It is striking, then, that Powell and Pressburger's title refers 'only', as it were, to the outcome of a love affair – between an English pilot, Peter Carter (David Niven) and an American servicewoman named June (Kim Hunter). Bob Trubshaw (Carter's 'Sparks', played by Robert Coote) and Dr Frank Reeves (Roger Livesey) pass from the earth in the course of the action, but they are, of course, far from being the only ones: we see French and British and American airmen arriving in the heavenly training department in large numbers. So even if our individual hero manages to escape, the war that is about to end in Europe has taken an appalling toll of others. We are, in fact, offered in the trial scenes a sublime, poetic vision – the poet Peter Carter's vision – of the 'pale battalions', the hosts of the dead, those who have 'gone before'.[1] The film's combination of tones, of a light touch and a more serious register, which is perhaps particularly marked in the ability of Allan Gray's music to darken or lighten the mood in an instant, balances the embrace of life and the confronting of death.

It is a matter of life *and* death, because that is what the war has been a matter of, and because the film is concerned, in various ways, with the relations between the living and the dead. It is equally possible to say that the film erects its elaborate scaffolding of fantasy and romance as a pretext for making its points about Anglo-American post-war relations, as requested by Jack Beddington of the Ministry of Information's Films Division. There is undeniably a good deal of interest in the study of the political aspects of the project – its commissioning, its effect as an intervention in a particular situation, its propagandistic techniques, its political implications, its reception and so forth. But this chapter will take the propaganda commission more as a pretext for Powell and Pressburger, as artists, to construct an elaborate world of fantasy and romance, perhaps a model of the relations between the living and the dead 'in the mind of a young airman'.

A Matter of Life and Death (hereafter *AMOLAD*) can be read as an entry in a genre or a tradition of films concerned with the interplay between life and death. Certain kinds of narrative, with inventive plots, allow films to discuss seriously matters that cannot be known, only speculated about (particularly the afterlife). There is sometimes a profound rationale underlying films that would normally be categorised (and that used to be routinely dismissed) as fantasy. We can gain a good deal from establishing their grounding and their sense.

The inexplicability of Peter's survival in *A Matter of Life and Death* contributes to his despair about his otherworldly law case.

According to the *Oxford English Dictionary*, the word 'film' comes from the Old English 'filmen', meaning 'membrane, caul, prepuce'. One of its obsolete, pre-cinematic senses is 'membrane, animal or vegetable', including the skin of an egg. This is a palpable thing, albeit exceedingly thin; but in other senses, 'film' becomes less physically concrete. The *OED* also includes the following definition: 'Often applied to the emanations from the surfaces of bodies… which in the philosophy of Epicurus were supposed to be the objects of perception.' This seems to suggest that in normal vision we see not bodies but the 'films' that emanate from them. Another entry reads: 'slight veil or covering of haze, mist, or the like, *lit.* and *fig.*'. But the most appropriate definition for my purpose here is: 'A morbid growth upon the eye. Also said of the growing dimness in the eyes of a dying person; sometimes *film of death*.' The blurring that afflicts Peter Carter in his idyllic glade, which we share through a subjective view of a strangely obscured June, might represent this 'film of death' in *AMOLAD*. Against this I would want to set film's, that is cinema's, cultivation of the life and brightness of the eye, as in the words of the great cinematographer John Alton in his 1949 book *Painting with Light*, where the resistance of such dimness is an article of faith: 'There is always a hot spot, an illuminant which, when reflected in the mirrorlike, moist surface of the eyeball, gives it lustre, pep, life.'[2] The celluloid surface registers the reflection of such heat and light in the actor's eye, and in due course, the reviving light of the projector-bulb casts the image onto another reflective surface, the cinema screen, from which its eye-beams connect with the spectator's in a process that is a sacrifice as well as an apotheosis of the original actor (who, in a sense, is a raw material used up in the operation). Of course, this elegiac dimension of interpretation or feeling lies dormant in most films; only a few seem at all consciously to evoke it. *AMOLAD* is, I think, among them. The eyes of David Niven and Kim Hunter, and especially the tears of the latter, as lit by Jack Cardiff, carry the expressiveness of life. It is not as an American girl that Peter Carter first loves her: 'I love you, June. You're life, and I'm leaving you.'

AMOLAD is partly a comedy, and although the chief other work to which it alludes is English – *A Midsummer Night's Dream* – and is indeed in some ways a model, a stronger influence is exerted by what one might call the Hungarian connection.[3] In *A Life in Movies*, the first volume of his memoirs, Powell recalls the genesis of *AMOLAD* in Pressburger's characteristic imaginative reaction to the Ministry of Information's Anglo-American commission: 'For this a fantasy is best.' Powell calls such a response

> basic Hungarian dramatists' thinking. They like to treat serious themes lightly. They like to keep tragedy in reserve as the hidden weapon of comedy. They like to think that it is they who control the audience, not the actors. I thought of *Liliom* (a play), and of how beautifully life and death were blended in that love story.[4]

As a member of the Hungarian diaspora in England, which also included Alexander Korda, Arthur Koestler and George Mikes, and as an alumnus of UFA

(Universum Film Aktiengesellschaft) in Berlin, where Lubitsch, Murnau, Lang, Wilder, Siodmak and innumerable others had worked, Pressburger represented an urbane European tradition and sophistication that was comparatively alien to British film-making. Powell's reference to *Liliom* is to the 1909 play by the Hungarian Ferenc Molnár (1878–1952), which was first filmed in Hungary in 1919 by Michael Curtiz (it was reportedly never finished). There was an American version by Frank Borzage in 1930, as well as then one shot in French in 1933 by Fritz Lang when he was in Paris en route to Hollywood from Berlin. Rodgers and Hammerstein adapted it as *Carousel* in the 1940s, a musical that was rather stodgily filmed in 1956 by Henry King. Such a continuity of adaptation testifies to a rare capacity to catalyse and inspire, fertile ground for variations on its situations and invented universe, where the struggle between love and death is dramatised through a struggle of individuals against a celestial parody of earthly bureaucracy and authority.

Molnar's Liliom (seen, *left*, in a stage production) is a fairground barker who operates a carousel, a handsome ladies' man, brutal in manner but good-hearted. He falls in love with a servant girl, Julie, and sets up house with her. Without money, he cannot support her and their forthcoming baby; he becomes frustrated and strikes her; takes part in a futile robbery and gets caught; and stabs himself. Two men in black, the 'Heavenly Policemen', take him to 'the Beyond', to a heavenly police court, where he is case number 16,473. He is given a chance to repent and return once to earth to make amends, by doing a good deed that will determine his fate – but he defiantly refuses to admit that he is sorry. Nevertheless, after sixteen years in 'the crimson fire',[5] he comes back down to earth to see his daughter Louise, and gives her 'a glittering star from Heaven' wrapped in a handkerchief (VII, p. 134). She refuses it, and again frustrated, he hits her hand with a resounding slap; Julie, who has been sitting with her back to Liliom, comes over to see what has happened and Louise explains that something strange has occurred:

> Mother — the man — he hit me — on the hand — hard – I heard the sound of it – but it didn't hurt — mother — it didn't hurt — it was like a caress — as if he had just touched my hand tenderly. (p. 135)

Liliom is led away by the Heavenly Policemen, but the play ends with the awestruck Julie as she tells Louise that 'It *is* possible, dear – that someone may beat you and beat you and beat you – and not hurt you at all'.(VII, p. 137).[6] This representation of the relation between the dead and the living seems to me to have been extremely influential, both in its wryly knowing satire on earthly bureaucracies, and in its picture of how the dead only detach themselves gradually from their affections and preoccupations when alive. The 1933 Fritz Lang film starring Charles Boyer (difficult to see outside archives) is hard-edged, as one might expect from Lang, and sardonic, but also achingly tender.[7]

Perhaps the most poignant of what one might call, without prejudice, the *Liliom* derivatives is Thornton Wilder's 1938 play *Our Town*, with its heartbreaking evocation of the pain of ghostly revisitings to still-living loved ones. It was in one production of this play that Powell recalled spotting Sergeant John Sweet, who would star in *A Canterbury Tale*.[8] Powell remembered weeping uncontrollably at the end, and commented that 'It is a great play, almost foolproof to any cast, but made particularly moving on this occasion by the fact that all the parts were being played by young servicemen and – women, in the middle of a war from which many of them would never return.'[9] Its ending takes place in the small American town cemetery (the dead sit on chairs, which represent graves), where the just-dead Emily chooses to go back with her dead consciousness and relive her twelfth birthday amid her family, only to find the weight of hindsight, the pressure of unspoken love and pity, too much to bear, so that she breaks down: 'I can't. I can't go on. It goes so fast, we don't have time to look at one another.'[10] Her final recognition: 'Oh, earth, you're too wonderful for anybody to realize you …. Do any human beings ever realize life while they live it? – every, every minute?'[11]

Philip van Doren Stern recorded that he had the idea for his short story 'The Greatest Gift' (1943), the basis of Frank Capra's 1947 film *It's a Wonderful Life*, in February 1938, which, one can note, was eight days after the New York opening of *Our Town*. The notion of a man slowly realising the value of his own life only when granted a vision of his world from the perspective of lifelessness seems traceable both to *Our Town* and back to *Liliom*. There is no space here to do justice to Capra's wonderfully dark, subtle and overwhelming movie, which cannot have influenced *AMOLAD*, as it was shot between April and July 1946, five months after shooting on the British film had finished. Nonetheless, I will point out some parallels with Powell and Pressburger's masterpiece, as the comparison is suggestive. The opening shots of space are strikingly similar in both films. However, Capra's space is a whimsical realm, in which stars become angels and are given voices, whereas Powell and Pressburger's vision is scientifically up to date, with novas, globular clusters and so on. Both have sympathetic, doubtfully competent other-worldly messengers specifically sent to deal with the hero's case (though Clarence is dispatched to save George Bailey, whereas Conductor 71 is sent to convey Peter Carter to Death). Both make conspicuous, narratively daring use of freeze-frames. Both cast leading actors – James Stewart and David Niven – whose pre-war stardom had been seriously interrupted by military service, and whose return to acting thus both involved some anxiety and brought a new depth of experience. Both are located specifically at the very end of the war (in a sense, their common theme): *It's a Wonderful Life* reaches its climax on Christmas Eve 1945; *AMOLAD* seems to go from 2 May 1945 to (although it is not specified) VE Day, 8 May 1945 (hence at the end, 'We won' – 'I know, darling.') Both films, therefore, address the question of life after war. Doubtless, it elides many important differences

to say that both films are affirmations of a love of life (life evoked as long-lasting marriage) in the context of an intense evocation of possible death by a leap from a height
into dark water.

There are connections with several other 1940s films, analogues that may amount to
sources. *Heaven Can Wait* (1943), directed by Ernst Lubitsch, is a cynical-senti-

mental tour de force based on another Hungarian play, by Laszlo Bus-Feketé, whose
upper-class hero is a guilty lifelong philan-
derer (Don Ameche) who nonetheless never
ceases to love his wife. When he dies and
goes to Hell's reception-room, he humbly
tries to persuade the Devil that he should be
damned (the film is a series of flashbacks
from Hell as he recounts his escapades).
Finally judged to have no harm in him, he is put in the lift up to Heaven. His
despairing, cynical, self-condemning attitude recalls Liliom's, albeit in a different
social register (as perhaps does Peter Carter's own sense of doom).

Hungarians do not enjoy a monopoly in this preoccupation, as Ian Christie suggests in his BFI Classics book on *AMOLAD*. Another closely related film is Victor
Fleming's *A Guy Named Joe*, with Spencer Tracy (1943; remade by Spielberg as
Always in 1989). It contains a number of elements that recur in *AMOLAD*: British
fog; the notion that a flier's 'number is up', so that when he gets to the next world
'We've been expecting you here for some time'; an officer who heroically remains in
his burning plane after the crew have baled out; the idea (maybe *Liliom*-derived) of
a pilot rebelling against the administration of the afterlife (he is told, 'I don't think
you understand at all', but then – unlike Peter – realises his mission and learns his
lesson); and finally, the idea of sacrificial guardianship, the protection of the living
by the dead.

And then there is Alexander Hall's odd comedy *Here Comes Mr Jordan* (1941), a
whimsical fantasy of reincarnation, which takes death no more seriously than Noel
Coward's play *Blithe Spirit*, written in the same year. It does, however, hinge on the
incompetence of a heavenly messenger, played by the bumbling, officious Edward
Everett Horton (familiar from the Astaire–Rogers films), who recruits the hero to
the ranks of the dead before his due time: it turns out that 'There's no "Pendleton,
Joseph" listed.' Joe's body is unfortunately cremated while he is detained in a higher
place, and the rest of the film, which is pretty flimsy, concerns his dogged, matter-
of-fact attempts to get a suitable body so that he can become a boxing champion (he
had been a boxer poised for a big fight).

We could almost imagine that Peter Carter had seen *Here Comes Mr Jordan* between
bombing missions and seized on its portrayal of an incompetent heavenly emissary
as a saving precedent in the projection of his own imaginative resistance to death.

Also that, as a student of European history, he thinks of a French aristocrat from the days of the guillotine for Conductor 71 precisely because of the pun on the expression 'I lost my head', which becomes a joke in the fantasy.

Why do such suggestions make any sense? Because, I would suggest, much of the power of *AMOLAD* lies in the *precision* of its framing, the logical embedding of the fantasy.[12] With *It's a Wonderful Life*, one needs to mount a defensive argument, claiming that in Capra's masterpiece it is not important for the spectator to *believe in* what Pope, discussing the system of Rosicrucian sylphs in his poem *The Rape of the Lock*, calls the 'machinery': that is, in bumbling guardian angels like the charming Clarence.[13] It seems right to say that, as in Dickens's *A Christmas Carol*, from which it derives so much, the film's supernatural agency has a metaphorical significance, standing for some inner moral process of imaginative recognition. The somewhat offputting sentimental aspect of George Bailey's despair, then, should not distract us from the force of the film's grim but enlivening recognition of the unlived life and its dramatisation of George's recoil, temporary though it may be, from despair into a moment of full, joyful human experience. The bitterness in James Stewart's performance, the impunity of the film's villain Potter, the acknowledgment of the grind and disappointment of 'decent' small-town life – these establish a complex reality that is unmitigated by the angelship of Clarence, whose limited powers cannot give George the money he needs, but only grant the imaginative vision of the world he thinks he wishes for, the world in which he has not been born.

AMOLAD needs no such disclaimers. The film states its premise at the start in a title:

> THIS IS A STORY OF
> TWO WORLDS
> THE ONE WE KNOW
> AND ANOTHER
> WHICH EXISTS ONLY
> IN THE MIND

It may be the human mind in general, we start to think, or the mind of the film-makers; but then the title starts to roll upwards and we read on. It is not just 'THE MIND', but 'THE MIND ...'

> ... OF A YOUNG AIRMAN
> WHOSE LIFE AND IMAGINATION
> HAVE BEEN
> VIOLENTLY SHAPED BY WAR

The comedy in the film's depiction of the Other World is thus not at all necessarily a mark of whimsy on the part of the film-makers, but characterises the imagination of Peter Carter. As the screenplay says more exactly: 'The Other World is seen only through the imagination of our pilot, its limits are the limits of his imagination and

Dr Reeves' case notes on the
other world will stand him in
good stead when he becomes
Peter's counsel.

of his knowledge and of his sense of awe and his sense of humour.'[14] And the same
point is actually made within the film by a medical authority, Dr Frank Reeves, in a
conversation with the American surgeon:

> And he's had several talks with this heavenly messenger. Hallucinations, of course, but you never
> saw such an imagination. I've been taking tips on the other world – laws, system, architecture.
> Here's the interesting point – he never steps outside the limits of his own imagination … Nothing
> he invents is *entirely* fantastic. It's invention, but logical invention.

This talk of 'invention', however, does not mean that all aspects of the Other World
are entirely under Peter Carter's imaginative control: the scenes register the struggle
between life and death taking place in his brain-damaged condition. And in an
earlier scene, when Frank reveals his diagnosis to June he very suggestively describes
Peter in terms that would apply also to us as a film audience: 'He's having a series of
highly organised hallucinations comparable to an experience of actual life, a combination of vision, hearing and idea.' As film viewers, we are partial creators of what
we see, like Peter; but the film is also, crucially, external to us, and unrolls like a work
of fate.

  As one might expect, there seem to be some minor discrepancies in the Powell
and Pressburger accounts of the genesis of the idea (though they may not be incompatible). In his biography of his grandfather, Kevin Macdonald describes how

> The inspiration for Peter's medical condition came from the semi-autobiographical novel, *A
> Journey Round My Skull*, by the Hungarian novelist Frigyes Karinthy, in which the narrator wit-
> tily and ironically recounts the onset of hallucinations and the brain operation he had to get rid of
> them.[15]

Several elements in *AMOLAD* occur also in Karinthy: the precise sequence of the
attacks, with hallucinations (of train sounds, then fully visual also),[16] headaches,

fainting and pallor; the patient's hallucination during the operation of 'my mind seeming to move freely about the room'[17] (which is introduced thus: 'The following pages come before my eyes like a sequence from a film');[18] and the idea of a parallel between a medical and a judicial 'case':

> The medical examination and confinement in hospital of a patient before he is treated exactly correspond to the detention of an accused man before trial. The accused has only one idea in his head – namely, is he going to be declared guilty and, if so, what will his sentence be?[19]

Macdonald's 'wittily and ironically' is right; but for all its plucky air of writerly detachment, the book is also informed by an underlying fear, as Karinthy himself (wittily) commented: '[I] went from humorist to tumorist.'[20] People around Karinthy, as well as the author himself, keep up a brave, cheerful tone: 'Everything was going to turn out all right. And yet … if that were so … what was this strange anxiety coming over me?'[21] The hallucinations were the result of a brain tumour, which the operation in Stockholm did not cure: Karinthy, who has been credited with inventing the theory of the six degrees of separation (in his 1929 short story 'Chains'), died in 1938, a year later (and a year before the English translation was published). Although Karinthy seems to have written his book under the impression that the operation had saved him, it nonetheless closes with a sense of existential solitude: 'I wonder whether you will understand me when I say that, in the depths of my heart, I always felt that each one of us was alone and abandoned.'[22]

In interviews he gave much later, Michael Powell liked to emphasise *his* insistence on the grounding of the whole set-up in medical reality. In 1973, speaking to Kevin Gough-Yates, he claimed that

> Emeric wrote the first script of *A Matter of Life and Death* as a fantasy, just as fantastic as *Here Comes Mr Jordan* … I couldn't wear that, I said. First it was because it didn't fit into the war atmosphere and second, I didn't think it was very interesting.[23]

What makes aspects of the fantasy interesting, is their traceability to something real and serious. In 1970, Powell had told Gough-Yates, claiming less credit, how proud he was of the film. It remains a good account of the film's premises:

> It is the most fascinating to me because of all this fantasy miracle actually taking place in a medical case, inside somebody's damaged head, so there was a good sound medical reason for every fantasy image that appeared on the screen. This appeals to me for I like to have my fantasy based on something real because life is far more fantastic than fantasy and although most people won't understand it I just can't go with pure fantasy. Although I'm good at fantasy, at pure fantasy I would be no good at all. I'm too practical. Emeric had sequences in this which I puzzled over for a long while where people appeared and disappeared, where you saw shots where the window curtain was moving and he was gone. I simply said, 'I can't do it.' But I started reading medical textbooks. Out of those I got the facts that hallucinations take place not in time but in space.

That was a turning point because that meant I could stop time. And then there were all the other things like the pressure on the eyes and the smell of fried onions, which all came from textbooks. I rewrote the script entirely and everything came out of natural ideas.[24]

In other words, no suspension of disbelief in an Other World is necessary for the spectator: 'everything came out of natural ideas', there is nothing supernatural.[25] Powell told David Badder in 1979 that he reworked Pressburger's original draft of the script (on the boat going to America to cast June)

from a medical point of view; I had all my notes in a special file on medical cases which I'd been looking up through my brother-in-law, who is a great surgeon. I don't think I ever stated what was wrong with the young flier (David Niven) after he's crashed in the bomber. A previous injury had caused adhesions on the brain ...[26]

The fantasy, the highly organised series of hallucinations, seems to begin when Peter bales out of his plane without a parachute at the end of the extraordinary opening scene. Pausing only briefly for thought, he plunges into the fog, expecting to join his 'Sparks' Bob Trubshaw, whose dead, goggling eyes have just appeared gruesomely on screen. He is about to discover whether they will be wearing 'a prop or wings'. When the fog clears, we see Peter lying unconscious or dead in the sea, and hear a distorted voice: 'a prop, or wings'. The next scene of the rows of wings awaiting the dead affords our first glimpse of the Other World and is the first to be shot in monochrome. The transition fairly clearly indicates on one level that the Other World is a figment of Peter's imagination, directly embodying and dramatising his last conscious concerns: but on a less sceptical level, of course, it gives us an answer, revealing that indeed we do wear wings in the Beyond. Bob is waiting in for Peter; in other words, we can infer that Peter is expecting to die and join him. But the scene ends as the alarm bell on the Other-Worldly clock goes off, which appears to signal the fact that is revealed in the next scene, in colour, that Peter, deposited by the tide on the vast beach, is slowly coming back to consciousness and thus life, that he has not died after all.

It is the next scene that raises some particularly interesting questions.[27] Peter's eyes open and he stares up at the sky and clouds. Assuming he has died and gone to the Other Side, he slowly gets to his feet. He immediately feels his head, perhaps because of his headaches, perhaps because he is testing the conditions of sensation in the afterlife. He looks round and sees dunes in the distance, mostly obscured by mists – fairly convincing as an other-worldly landscape. Getting up, he says out loud (as he is alone, and earthly decorums no longer obtain, why wouldn't he?) 'I wonder where I report.' The discipline of years of war bureaucracy is contained in the question, as well as an ironic comment on it. He strolls away from the sea, meditatively discarding his wet things (presumably on the assumption that in the afterlife there will be no need for earthly clothes). He notices his shadow: his body, unlike that of a vampire, has retained another of its solid earthly properties, the capacity to cast a shadow – he shakes his leg experimentally to test it. Coming to the dunes, he discovers a 'Keep Out' sign, and, ruefully, not wanting to disobey instructions, he goes back another way. As he walks through the dunes, a dog barks, and he comes over and greets it, saying to himself, 'Oh, I always hoped there would be dogs'. Then he hears some distinctly other-worldly piping – which turns out to come from the dog's owner. Here is Powell's own description of the next episode:

> The script called for a boy with some animals … I made the boy a naked boy, playing on a reed pipe a little tune composed by Allan Gray, while his goats cropped the sparse marram grass on the sand dunes. It looked charming, like a scene from Theocritus. David kneels down and talks to the child, and gradually begins to realize that he is not dead, that he's alive.[28]

There are some surprising elements in this account. While the scene has a weird charm, it certainly seems to raise the question of incredibility: if this *is* the real world, England in 1945, what is this boy doing here, playing a pipe in classical mode and without a stitch of clothing? In particular, why does he make no attempt to cover himself up when a strange man approaches?[29] The mention of Theocritus perhaps offers a clue here: this seems like a poet's vision, and, of course, Peter Carter is an educated poet.[30] However, as at this moment we are not supposed to be registering what we see as being Peter's fantasy, but rather as living reality, the pastoral stylisation has a disturbing effect. I am not sure that the sense of unreality is dispelled by the dimness and banality of the boy's speech when Peter interrogates him. *Is* this the sort of event that would make one begin to realise one is not dead? And that flicker of doubt may remain with us throughout the film, a catalyst for our anxiety.

If we are with Peter in the business of reality-testing, we might well be disconcerted at the coincidences that follow: Peter has washed up, the boy tells him, at Lee Wood, near Lee Wood House where June told him on the radio she lived. A clue has been planted about this in the opening scene, where Peter asked her if it was an old house:

> JUNE: Very old.
> PETER: Good, I'll be a ghost, and come and see you. You're not frightened of ghosts, are you? Be awful if you were.
> JUNE: I'm not frightened.

When Peter sees a figure on a bicycle and runs across to it to find that it happens to be June, one might say that the sense of unbelievable miracle – coming on top of the mystery of surviving a fall without a parachute – has been stretched to maximum. The recognition – 'You're June' / 'You're Peter' – presents them to each other bodily, allowing them to realise the potential that on the radio seemed doomed never to have a chance ('I could love a man like you, Peter'). Their kiss at the end of this scene represents a union between a living person and one presumed certainly dead. One way of reading the scene, indeed, is as a dying man's fantasy of survival, framing the action – as in *Incident at Owl Creek* (1962), or David Thomson's ingenious readings of *Point Blank* (1967) and *Citizen Kane* (1941) – as an elaborate evasion of the inevitable, a flight into wish-fulfilment perhaps generated as Peter plummets from the flaming bomber.[31]

This is one of the puzzles that makes the film so involving, and just what Powell intended probably cannot be resolved, as he declaredly believed that 'life is far more fantastic than fantasy'. But I do have a suggestion to make about the *artistic* and psychological reasons – if not the 'good sound medical reasons' – for the piling-up of unbelievabilities in this mysterious scene. It is one of the necessary conditions of Peter's (medical) case that he should have no persuasive account to give of how he came to survive his baling-out, that he should find it in some sense unbelievable that he is still alive. This scene has that function: it stresses the inexplicability of Peter's

survival, which Dr Reeves, with medical authority, claims is one of the contributing causes to his despair about his other-worldly law case.

Finally, I want to suggest something about the fact that the film's action appears to end on VE Day, 8 May 1945. (Powell began shooting on VJ Day, 14 September 1945.) *AMOLAD* is among other things about sur-

vival and guilt, about the incredibility of having survived six years of war, of not yet having joined the hosts of the dead. This is a feeling many in the first audiences might have shared. Peter Carter has flown on sixty-seven operations; the appalling rates of casualties in the RAF during the war make this alone a cause for wonder. And we have seen from the start that he has made up his mind to die, as illustrated by his quotation of Sir Walter Ralegh's 'The passionate man's Pilgrimage/Supposed to be Written by One at the Point of Death'. When Dr Reeves asks him, 'What was the cause of your father's death?', he spookily replies, 'Same as mine.' 'Brain?' 'No, war.' He has to reconcile himself to not having died in war as expected; and the force that impels him is love of June, which is love of life.

The film evokes both the duty of continuing and, more vividly, the newly urgent desire to live on after the war, to turn from conflict to love, to rebuild, or build, the life so much had been sacrificed to defend. Underlying its cheerful humour is a sense of existential solitude and terror, crystallised in Allan Gray's chilling stairway theme, which may have come from Karinthy; the stoical English wit of denial, indeed, sim- ultaneously manifests courage and movingly allows Peter's fear to show. Powell and Pressburger startlingly dramatise, too, the sense in which every loving relationship is a product of a sequence of implausible coincidences against overwhelming odds – so that ordinary life, rendered in its precious fragility, appears with the rich, mirac- ulous glow of Technicolor.

NOTES

1. Most of those in the contemporary audience of AMOLAD would have known people who had died in the war: the audience at the trial scene in the film could be thought of as a representation of those lost ones, as, in fact, a kind of ghostly, familiar cinema audience on the Other Side. I owe my Sorley epigraph to a tip from Charles Barr; and here gratefully acknowledge help from several other people: Ian Christie (whose learned and helpful book on the film, *A Matter of Life and Death*, London: BFI, 2000, has been published since I wrote the first version of this chapter); Thelma Schoonmaker-Powell; Ian Smith; Peter Swaab; Valerie Wilson; and Henry Woudhuysen.

2. John Alton, *Painting with Light*, Berkeley, LA: University of California Press, 1995 (first published 1949), with an introduction by Todd McCarthy, p. 104.

3. It would be misleading to claim any exclusivity for Hungarians in dramatic and cinematic treatments of the afterlife, or indeed as direct inspirations for *AMOLAD*. German cinema had treated the subject with intense poetic seriousness. Fritz Lang's silent *Destiny* (*Der Müde Tod*, 1921), for example, another romantic fantasy in which sacrificial 'Love is as strong as Death', and which contains a visionary staircase scene where the upper steps are bathed in white light, is mentioned by Powell as among the films 'dazzling and bewitching me' that had been made by 'Fritz Lang, the German movie director who had been my idol ever since … about 1923 or 1924'. Michael Powell, *A Life in Movies: An Autobiography*, London: Heinemann, 1986, p. 516.

4. Powell, *A Life in Movies*, p. 458.

5. Ferenc Molnár, *Liliom: A Legend in Seven Scenes and a Prologue*, trans. Benjamin F. Glazer, New York and London: Samuel French, 1945, VI, p. 121.

6. When in the 1956 Henry King version the hero returns and strikes his daughter, Julie replies mysteriously that 'It is possible for someone to hit you, to hit you hard, and it not hurt at all.' The play's toughness is attenuated by this reduction of habitual wife-beating to a single blow, and, paradoxically, we cannot easily swallow this blander account of domestic violence. The twisted sacrificial truth of Molnar's text to something human is a chilling honesty that is lost in the rancid cheesiness of the 1956 movie's ending.

7. As Valerie Wilson notes, Lang, who elaborates the satire on heavenly bureaucracy and introduces a material set of scales of justice to register Liliom's spiritual progress, adds a scene that seems a direct source for Powell and Pressburger's use of June's tear as evidence to present before the celestial tribunal: 'Just as June's tear is the evidence that sways the court in *A Matter of Life and Death*, it is the tears of Liliom's long-suffering and selflessly loving wife that, literally, tip the scales in Liliom's favour.' Valerie Wilson, *The Representation of Reality and Fantasy in the Films of Powell and Pressburger: 1939–1946*, unpublished PhD thesis, University of London, 1999, p. 192.

8. However, according to Kevin Macdonald in *Emeric Pressburger: The Life and Death of a Screenwriter*, London: Faber and Faber, 1994, p. 238, 'they had seen [Sergeant John Sweet of the US Army] playing a small part in an amateur production of Maxwell Anderson's *The Eve of St Mark*'.

9. Powell, *A Life in Movies*, p. 442.

10. Thornton Wilder, *Our Town, The Skin of Our Teeth, The Matchmaker*, Harmondsworth: Penguin Books, 1964, p. 88.

11. Ibid., p. 89.

12. Even the speculation about the afterlife has a scientific basis of a serious sort. As Ian Christie points out, much of the phraseology about the afterlife in the film – e.g. 'the survival of human personality after death' – comes from the systematic work of William James's associate Frederic (F. M. W.) Myers of the Society for Psychical Research. Christie, *AMOLAD*, p. 26.

13. Alexander Pope, 'To Mrs Arabella Fermor', *The Rape of the Lock* (1714), ed. Geoffrey Tillotson, London: Methuen, 1971, p. 26. It is pleasing to note that the actor who plays Clarence, Henry Travers, was in the original Broadway production of *Liliom* by the Theatre Guild in 1921.

14. Foreword to '1945 Screenplay', quoted in Wilson, *Representation of Reality and Fantasy*, p. 198. I am grateful to Kevin Macdonald and Thelma Schoonmaker-Powell for permission to quote it here.

15. Kevin Macdonald, *Emeric Pressburger*, London: Faber, 1994, pp. 256–7.

16. Including one of a suave doctor (analogous to Conductor 71), who tries to lure the victim to submit to a diagnostic test that Karinthy later discovers would have proved fatal, and that some instinct (like Peter's on the heavenly escalator) prompts him to distrust (Frigyes Karinthy, *A Journey Round My Skull*, trans. Vernon Duckworth Barker, London: Faber and Faber, 1939, chapter 13, 'Death Tempts Me', pp. 144–8).

17. Karinthy, *Journey*, p. 241.

18. Karinthy, a former medical student, also describes early in the book watching a documentary film of brain surgery being performed ('one could see the grey matter of the brain trembling in its bony case'). Karinthy, *Journey*, p. 21.

19. Ibid., p. 85.

20. Quoted at www.Frankfurt.matav.hu/angol/irok/karinthy/public.htm (unsourced; consulted 11 November 2004).

21. Karinthy, *Journey*, p. 91.

22. Ibid., p. 286.

23. 'Michael Powell', article and interview by Kevin Gough-Yates. Published on the occasion of Europalia 73 Brussels: Filmmuseum/Palais des Beaux-Arts October 1973, pp. 12–21, p. 17.

24. 'Interview with Michael Powell', by Kevin Gough-Yates, 22 September 1970, in Gough-Yates, *Michael Powell: In collaboration with Emeric Pressburger*, London: BFI, 1971, unpaginated pages.

25. Diane Broadbent Friedman has established that Powell is likely to have derived much medical and surgical detail from his brother-in-law's associate, Hugh Cairns, Professor of Neurology at Oxford. She comments that 'this film depicts clinical details in such an accurate way that a clinician might diagnose the probable site of the lesion'. 'A Matter of Fried Onions', *Seizure* no. 1, 1992, pp. 307–10, p. 307.

26. David Badder, 'Powell and Pressburger: The War Years', *Sight and Sound* vol. 48 no. 1 Spring 1979, pp. 8–12, p. 12. This remark of Powell's draws our attention to an oddity in the plotting of Peter's condition that may not strike us at first. It is *not* in any way caused by the extraordinary events we see, but is pre-existent: it is revealed that the headaches started six months ago (from a concussion incurred two years earlier). It is odd to think that had Peter *not* fallen and been washed up at Lee Wood, he would doubtless not have met Dr Reeves, not

have been assigned the best surgeon available, and would very possibly have died of his 'chronic adhesive arachnoiditis'. Friedman's hypothetical diagnosis takes the common-sense line by attributing more significance to Peter's recent fall: 'Recent concussion resulting in increased intra cranial pressure and complex partial seizures due to an epidural haematoma or a subacute subdural haematoma.' Friedman, 'A Matter of Fried Onions', p. 307.

27. It is a scene that John Ellis mentions as bizarre, but in a different aspect, in his article 'Watching Death at Work: An Analysis of *A Matter of Life and Death*', in Ian Christie, ed., *Powell, Pressburger and Others*, London: BFI, 1978, pp. 79–104.

28. Powell, *A Life in Movies*, pp. 542–3.

29. Speaking to David Badder in 1979, Powell mentions the sequence with 'the little boy piping with the goats all around. It was all a spoof, of course …'. And shortly after this, he goes on, suggesting there is no simple key to the enigma: 'Fortunately, I hadn't any crass producer to say, "What does that mean?" because half the time I didn't know what it meant either. I just felt it was right.' Badder, 'Powell and Pressburger: The War Years', p. 12.

30. Ian Christie observes that by making Peter Carter a poet, the film picks up on the poet-airman connection established in *The Way to the Stars* (1945), the most popular British film of the war (*A Matter of Life and Death*, p. 10). This would not be mere opportunism, cashing in on the huge success of the other film, but a way – through Peter's necessarily exceptional imagination – of justifying the whole created other world. The move thus constitutes part of the solid grounding of the fantasy structure of the film.

31. According to Thomson, the Lee Marvin character's 'expressive somnambulism is not just a search for vengeance and satisfaction, but the signs of sleep and inertia in a man actually slipping away from the world, defeated by it but inventing a story in which he triumphs as he dies'. And 'every apparent point of view in the film is warmed by Kane's own memories, as if the entire film were his dream in the instant before death'. David Thomson, *The New Biographical Dictionary of Film*, London: Little, Brown, 2002, pp. 95, 925.

8 The Invisible and the 'Intruder Figure': Perfume in *Black Narcissus*

Jean-Louis Leutrat

… a primeval gulf; and drops it to the ground,
There where, like Lazarus rising, his grave-clothes half unwound,
And odorous, a cadaver from its sleep has stirred:
An old and rancid love, charming and long-interred.
Charles Baudelaire, *Flowers of Evil*[1]

The cinema recognises certain 'limit points', such as sounds in 'silent' cinema and colours in black and white.[2] These limit points are always interesting and somehow revelatory, because their impossibility obliges the film-maker to search for an equivalent or substitute. In the cinema, the mere fact of mentioning a colour (in a title, such as *Green for Danger*) lets us know that it exists and can even allow us to locate it. The same is true of perfumes. Some remain in our memory thanks to a flash of humour attaching to them: when Wyatt Earp leaves the barber's shop in *My Darling Clementine*, he exudes the scent of honeysuckle. Other perfumes signal a psychological trait or define a character by his or her main activity – *Scent of a Woman*, for example.[3]

In a sequence from Michael Powell and Emeric Pressburger's *Black Narcissus* (1947), the character of the young General, struggling with some typing, suddenly produces a dark-blue handkerchief from which emanates, as he unfolds it, a strong perfume. Two women are present: Kanchi, the young native girl, and Sister Ruth, one of the nuns who have come to Mopu to set up a hospital and school. Kanchi appears to be intoxicated by the scent and clearly drinks it in hungrily. The actress, Jean Simmons, mimes a voluptuous pleasure, with her eyes closed, to express its penetration. Sister Ruth, on the other hand, bridles at the smell, remarking curtly that she does not like perfume. These two symmetrical and opposite reactions indicate that something important is happening at this moment around this perfume, which the young General announces, is called Black Narcissus – the title of both the film and of Rumer Godden's novel from which it is taken.[4]

There are several ways of expressing perfume in a film. Usually it is sufficient for an actor to mime it, for the audience to understand that it is present, as in the scene described. Another approach is to use substitutes, in which case we have to talk about synaesthesia; for in the film the various qualities inherent in colours, jewellery, the sound of the wind and flowers all contribute to the evocation of perfume. The film mentions, or shows, many flowers, some in the form of pictures: in the gardening catalogue, where we pass from a page of vegetables to one of petunias, and in the alphabet book that Joseph Antony leafs through, where the letter I is illustrated by an iris. The list of flower names in this book, which is used to teach children, is, in order: forget-me-not, sweet pea, daffodil, Japanese peony, Chinese lily, tulip, honeysuckle, delphinium.[5] Narcissus does not figure in the list, though

the daffodil and Chinese lily are of the same family. On another occasion, the nuns' discussion of the Prince's jewels summons up a flashback of the emeralds that Clodagh's grandmother had promised her. Kanchi, whose luxuriant locks, black and fragrant, are adorned with a flower, and who is susceptible to jewellery, steals one necklace and is given another by the young General, just as Conrad gives Clodagh a brooch. *Black Narcissus* is a very colourful film. Green occupies an important place – it is the colour of emeralds, matching Clodagh's Irish origins. Red is no less important. In the novel, characters blush very easily. The book also features interiors in which blue dominates, a detail that is also adopted by the film. And finally, like the wind, perfume penetrates everywhere, and like the wind, it is perceptible by its effects. The film emphasises the presence of the wind and the fact that Mopu Palace is pervaded by draughts, which enable all the smells to penetrate from outside.[6] The bodies and minds of the nuns are, like the palace, spaces to be penetrated.

A range of themes traditionally associated with perfumes is deployed in the film, notably their sensuality, with scent functioning as a trigger for desire. This is probably the origin of the film's insistence on the themes of sickness and contagion. All the nuns, without exception, are affected by a rash of spots when they arrive at Mopu, and Sister Ruth is presented as sick even before she leaves home. She is consequently the most vulnerable. The all-powerful perfume spreads, like the genie released from an oil lamp. It insinuates itself into beings and changes their state of mind. The nuns run the risk of yielding to their senses, and Mr Dean is willingly enslaved to his. Abstinence, with the perfume's scent inciting the call of the flesh deep inside Sister Clodagh: this is exactly the subject of *Black Narcissus*.

Proceeding by suggestion, perfume belongs – along with music – in the world of what Baudelaire calls *mémoranda* ('things to be remembered'). The evocation of Black Narcissus and of the person who first mentions the name, the young General, brings with it by association the memory of the jewels he wears in abundance. Likewise by association, memories are reawakened in Sister Clodagh. The film then moves on to a series of flashbacks.[7] One of these concerns a fox-hunt and the elation of the gallop. A sort of vertigo of the senses is suggested by the series of tracking shots, interrupted only by a sudden fixed framing, shot from a distance. It is a quality of those perfumes characterised as 'heady' that they provoke this kind of vertigo. The image of the abyss, representing the interior hollow of the conscience, recurs each time the sisters ring their convent bell, which is sited, appropriately, at the edge of the precipice. Sister Clodagh is not the only one with memories. In the past, the palace had been the 'house of women', and the frescoes on the walls show lines of naked dancers wearing heavy necklaces. The name given the mountain facing them, 'the naked goddess', emphasises this aspect. A painting, which Sister Clodagh orders to be taken down, illustrates Mopu's voluptuous past.[8] It is this past that is hovering on the brink of rebirth and that the local spirit, Angu Ayah, who witnessed this period, would like to see return. When we first see the young General, he is asking the nuns for permission to study with them and explains his desired timetable, declaring that he wants to learn physics from 'the physical sister'. The expression is obviously a double entendre, formed by the misuse of the word 'physical'. In the next scene, Kanchi dances alone in a room, a reincarnation of the figures depicted on the wall.

This perfume has been given a flower's name, a colour and an origin. First, black: a blackness prolongs Clodagh's search for Conrad in the dark, while Sister Ruth's voice is heard saying 'It's called Black Narcissus and it comes from London'. Going into the blackness suggests simultaneously night-time, absence and perfume, the name designating a characteristic.[9] 'Black Narcissus' is a bold juxtaposition of words as well as an impossibility, for there are no black narcissi or daffodils. As a flower, a 'black narcissus' is an intruder in the species, a cuckoo in the nest. As an expression, 'Black Narcissus', then, is emblematic of the whole. The juxtaposition of opposites does in fact shape the film on several different levels. The perfume Black Narcissus comes from London, a metropolis usually associated with the idea of luxury.[10]. As well as the contrast between natural and artificial perfume (in the film we find only two other references to smells that are described as unpleasant: that of the human body, according to the young General, and that of the natives, according to Sister Ruth), an opposition is established between East and West. However, the film immediately offers a remarkable transformation of these two clichés, reversing the association with the perfume. The East is reputedly pervaded by intoxicating odours, yet the perfume comes from Europe, from The Army and Navy Stores. One could be forgiven for believing it to be cheap and nasty, but in fact *Narcisse noir* is the name of a Caron perfume of the 1930s.

The choice of flower is not inconsequential. The narcissus makes us think of mythology and a figure important to the Symbolists[11], and it is also poisonous. Narcissus is both a proper noun and a common noun. The name 'Black Narcissus' is very

appropriate to the person who wears the perfume, the young General, as Sister Ruth realises: 'That's what I'm going to call him. It's a beautiful name for him. He's so vain, like a peacock, a fine black peacock.'[12] The nun uses 'narcissistic' here in its common meaning of vain and self-satisfied, with the peacock's feathers at the same time resembling flowers (one can put them in vases). At the end of her dance, Kanchi greets the arrival of this messenger in her own way, standing in front of a mirror that is shaped like a peacock feather. The name 'Black Narcissus' also relates, possibly, to Joseph Conrad's 1897 novel, *The Nigger of the Narcissus*, a figure associated with the young General.[13] And then, by extension, to Mr Dean. As if to explain the title, the film is framed, so to speak, by Mr Dean, whose voice-over describes the palace at the beginning of the film and whose face in close-up appears almost at the very end.

But 'Black Narcissus' could also refer to Sister Ruth. In this case, 'Black Narcissus' could represent the dark side of the ego and Ruth the hidden face of Clodagh. We understand that 'the physical sister' is Sister Ruth, while Sister Clodagh is shown at the beginning of the film teaching mathematics. The list of classes that the young General wants to take starts with mathematics and ends with physics. They are mirror images, inverted images. The link between the two nuns is marked in the novel by the green colour of Ruth's eyes (Ireland again). In an important scene in the film, the two nuns confront each other across a table. Specular double symmetry comes into play here; that is, the symmetry relating to both the vertical plane of the mirror and to the sagittal plane (which is perpendicular to the plane of the mirror and passes through the median axis of the person looking into it). It is an imagined and an inverted symmetry. Sister Ruth and Sister Clodagh are each the other's dream (imagined symmetry). The novel tells it differently, and links them by the perfume:

> Sister Clodagh was very angry when she heard that Sister Ruth had nick-named the young General 'Black Narcissus'. She was angry and astonished at its neatness; what had made Sister Ruth echo her own dream with a name? In her dream, Dilip and Con had held mirrors in the palms of their hands, and she had tried to attract them but could only echo what they said. And now Sister Ruth had put her dream into words.[14]

Ruth abandons her vows and puts on a crimson dress (like the whore of Babylon).[15] She puts into action Clodagh's secret desire to go to the home of the man (Mr Dean). Ruth's death allows Clodagh to come to her senses and regain her equilibrium (that is, to stop being 'superior').

As they confront each other in *Black Narcissus*, Sister Ruth and Sister Clodagh enter each other's dream.

The juxtaposition of opposites contained in the words 'Black Narcissus' extends to the whole of the film. The perfume is associated with seduction, with desire, but also with puerile vanity. The young General is at times compared to a cuckoo, at times to a peacock. The colour red is associated with the blossoming of azaleas, with a triumphant sensuality, but at the same time with the failure of that sensuality. Sister Ruth's faint when rejected by Mr Dean is represented by a punctuation steeped in this colour. The environment of Mopu is supposed to be desolate and arid, yet the palace has enjoyed a luxurious and sensual past that is now slumbering. The 'house of ill repute' has become a cloister. Mr Dean is like an angel of annunciation, but he is a coarse man, not to be praised to the heavens, as Sister Clodagh warns Sister Ruth. A significant pairing of opposites in both film and novel is 'servant, superior'. The formula 'The Superior of all is the servant of all', sets up this oxymoron in the very first scene.[16] The shot in which Sister Clodagh and Mr Dean watch the holy man, for example, combines high and low, spiritual and physical in the form of Mr Dean and the holy man, who stands on the top of a hill dominating the valley below, in a shot that juxtaposes opposites.

We can recognise in the film a set of themes common to the literature and painting of the second half of the 19th century: strong perfumes, clashing colours, strange flowers, the figure of Narcissus, peacocks, the colour black.[17] We can also discover in it Pre-Raphaelite sensibilities, and not only in the colours. In a painting by Charles Allston Collins entitled *Convent Thoughts* (1850–51, Ashmolean Museum, Oxford), a nun, surrounded by flowers (lilies, forget-me-nots, water lilies, etc.), stands dream-ily before a stretch of water at her feet. In one hand she holds a passion flower, in the other a prayer book. This same mixture of nervous sensuality and profane spirituality is present in *Black Narcissus*, the precisely rendered studio sets exuding something of the cold and meticulous technique of artists such as Collins. Before taking the veil, Sister Clodagh's red hair had resembled that of Dante Gabriel Rossetti's *The Beloved*, and other details relating to this character also seem to have been taken from paint-ings. For example, the open prayer book in her hand, as in *Convent Thoughts*,[18] while on another occasion she is seen embroidering, like Mary in Rossetti's *Girlhood of Mary Virgin* (1848–9, Tate Gallery, London). The same attention shown to the very con-spicuous flora in the film is also present in the Pre-Raphaelite paintings. A close inspection of Millais' *Ophelia* (1851–2, Tate Gallery, London) will reveal pansies, pop-pies, daisies, forget-me-nots, bluebells, etc. However, the Pre-Raphaelites' preferred flower is the white lily (the words 'sicut lilium' appear at the top of *Convent Thoughts*, and a painting by Mary Stillman is entitled *Cloister Lilies*, Ashmolean Museum, Oxford), while the film embraces the black narcissus. If the film deals with 'convent thoughts', they are very different from those suggested by Charles Allston Collins.

The Pre-Raphaelites treated the theme of the Annunciation in several different ways. Millais painted an unusual version in *Mariana* (1851, private collection), of which Ruskin wrote that it depicted 'no Annunciate Maria bowing herself, but only a Newless Mariana stretching herself'.[19] Burne-Jones's *King Cophetua and the Beggar Maid* (1884, Tate Gallery, London) is another variation on the Annunciation.

According to Mr Dean, Kanchi is familiar with the story of the Prince and the Beggar Maid,[20] while in France, there is the story of the Prince and the Shepherdess.[21] In fact, behind the Prince and the Beggar Maid lies the King (Cophetua) and the Beggar Maid, an allusion from Shake-speare.[22] Tennyson wrote a poem based on the tale (1833), which was followed by Burne-Jones's painting on the same theme.[23] The Beggar Maid is Kanchi – but also Ruth (who will go begging to Mr Dean); and even Mr Dean himself, when confronted by Sister Ruth: the superior woman and the base man. Through an enforced reversal, the King is at the Beggar Maid's feet. In one scene featuring the young General and Kanchi,

Cloister Lilies by Marie Stillman.

the latter rushes to pick his scarf up off the ground and looks up to find the young man staring down at her. Later on, he is standing while a crouching Kanchi raises her eyes towards him.[24] This time it is the male protagonist who is troubled. The film breaks down the scenario of the King and the Beggar Maid into two parts. Inserted between these two scenes (which are very close to one another) is the episode in which the young General disperses the fragrance from his handkerchief. It is the perfume that brings about the exchange between the two characters.

The first shot after the opening titles shows the Sister Superior as if in a Vermeer painting, with the window and light on the left. The reference is surprising, especially when we think of the Pre-Raphaelite elements in the film (though the relationship to the latter is thematic rather than figurative). However, a woman, alone and immobile in a room, wearing a cornet-shaped headdress, will almost inevitably call to mind the figures of the Dutch painter. Gilles Aillaud emphasises how Vermeer paints time – not Proustian time, 'but time that is in the act of passing, the infinitesimal moment in which a thing exists, static and monumental, as a presence'.[25] It is a time to which perhaps only the very old nun and the holy man can gain access, the one being the incarnation of wisdom and the other embodying a life of contemplation, both brought to the point of perfection. The fact that the nuns' order is an active one is just one more paradoxical juxtaposition. Vermeer's subjects, too, are often caught in the midst of activity (the milkmaid, the lace-maker, etc.), but as if detached from the time frame of the everyday.

It has been noted that Vermeer's work does not usually include an 'intruder figure', as represented by a male character, no erotic resonance associated with an allusion to venal love. One can imagine the angel of the Annunciation as such a figure, and almost all the characters in the film are in their own ways intruder figures, except Angu Ayah. Daniel Arasse notes that Vermeer instigated 'the articulation of interior space that was his own. He sets aside an interior within the interior, an inner interior; he shows the privacy of the private ...'[26] It is this very protected space that the perfume invades. It is the perfume itself that is unbidden, that is 'the uninvited', or rather the representative of the 'intruder figure'. In other words, the representative of the invisible, the invisible squared, so to speak.

Thus, *Black Narcissus* develops a literary and iconographic theme that intersects with the tradition of fairy tales and embroiders a New Testament story. The film suggests, among other contradictory associations, a mix of genres that are *a priori* different because this is both a colonial story (India) and a religious film (taking place in a convent). Its subject is the awakening of a buried sensuality[27] and its title almost recalls films noir such as *The Blue Dahlia* (1946) or *The Blue Gardenia* (1953).[28] And, finally, it takes up a whole set of 'Gothic' themes. The film begins with a scene where a character is given a mission to travel to a distant place with which she is unfamiliar, as in Jacques Tourneur's *I Walked with a Zombie* (1943) or Jack Clayton's *The Innocents* (1964). Exerting a pernicious influence on the character, this place has its own ghosts, to which will be added those of the heroine's past, as in *The Amityville Horror* (1979). The theme of the doppelgänger emerges here, as does a rhetoric appropriate to the horror genre: namely, the unmistakable point of view of an invisible observer, as in the final scene in the chapel, which is punctuated by two shots of Sister Ruth appearing furtively. Sister Ruth's grave is another 'Gothic' image of the abyss that haunts the nuns.[29] And perfume is the horror film subject par excellence. Indeed, perfume, substituting for a person, is in fact the ideal messenger. Through it, 'this presence is understood as an absence. Perfume is the touch of another being.'[30] This is why it can play such a fitting part

Black Narcissus offers a mix of genres – colonial story, religious film and *noir* thriller – as well as recapitulating a whole series of Gothic themes.

in ghost stories, as in *The Uninvited* (1943), where the ghost is revealed by the scent of mimosa. The invisible becomes palpable via a fragrance that, of course, the audience cannot experience. *The Uninvited*, and the title of its French version, *La Falaise mystérieuse* (The Mysterious Cliff), accords well with *Black Narcissus*, for is the cliff not symbolic of the temptation aroused by this surprise guest? These two novels by Dorothy Macardle and Rumer Godden share a number of themes – as do, of course, the films based on them.[31]

Yet the relationship to the cinema (and literature) of the supernatural is not the most important. It does no more than signal the magic that is the basic mechanism of the cinema. The perfume here is like the tear absorbed by the blotting paper in Jack Clayton's *The Innocents*, the ephemeral or intangible proof that testifies to the powers of that other kind of visibility that lies at the heart of cinema. 'Black Narcissus' also brings to the fore the power of the words that shape the film between images and sounds, invisible as perfume.

Translated from French by Clare Kitson

NOTES

1. Charles Baudelaire, *Flowers of Evil*, trans. Edna St Vincent Millay, New York: Harper and Brothers, 1936.

2. See Suzanne Liandrat-Guigues's text 'Les Couleurs du noir-et-blanc', in *La Couleur en cinéma*, Milan: Mazzotta, 1995, pp. 53–62.

3. If cinema, enclosed in the logic of a 'realistic rendering', cannot allow us to 'smell', any more than it can afford us a taste (cf. *The Taste of Cherry*, not to mention *The Taste of Saury Fish*, which is the Japanese title of Ozu's *Autumn Afternoon*), the novel can describe the nature and effect of the perfume. Its capacity to suggest via words is a clear advantage in this area.

4. If we compare these works, we are, of course, struck by several details, all differences, such as the absence in the film of certain characters from the novel, or the importance given at the beginning of the film to Mr Dean's letter, which serves to introduce the Mopu landscape and is not present in the novel. The action takes place in a relatively precise geographical region, which is the same in both works (in other transpositions, it can happen that a spatial or temporal displacement is effected). The film was shot in London and proudly proclaims the artificiality of its sets and special effects. So while the action is indeed supposed to take place in the same location as that of the novel, at the same time, the set designs tell us something different. The director had the choice of shooting in real locations (which, of course, could or could not be those in which the action takes place – a further choice) or in studio sets. The solution chosen necessarily entails certain consequences.

    Smells and perfumes pervade the whole book. The following two examples are separated by a single page: 'the wood was stacked in the passage and the house smelled of it'; and 'at the smell of the belladonna she almost vomited'. Rumer Godden, Black Narcissus, New York: The Modern Library, 1947, pp. 114–15.

5. All of these flowers, as well as some others, appear in the novel – notably pp. 155–6 and 203. Sister Philippa talks of foxgloves in the film, a flower that cannot be found in Godden, and is

probably suggested by the fox-hunt, a scene that, of course, prefigures another Michael Powell film, *Gone to Earth* (1950).

6. 'At Mopu Palace you lived with the sound of the wind and a coldness always about your ears and ankles. … In summer the wind smelled of roses and the languorous orange flowers from the groves far below in the foot-hills above the valley' (Godden, *Black Narcissus* p. 25). 'The flimsy walls did not shut out the world but made a sounding box for it; through every crack the smell of the world crept in, the smell of rain and sun and earth and the deodar trees and a wind strangely scented with tea' (p. 73).

7. Forgetting and remembering are intertwined in the film: the forgetting and recollection of the past, the forgetting inherent in being a nun, the forgetting of God… right up to the name of the forget-me-not.

8. The frescoes and painting do not appear in the book.

9. In France, an advertisement promoting the aroma of a coffee proclaims: 'Carte Noire – a coffee named desire'. The colour black, the desire, the aroma and the way it insinuates itself come together as in *Black Narcissus*. It is striking that the scent of Roland Barthes's Bayonne childhood is associated with black, with darkness (see *Roland Barthes par Roland Barthes*, *oeuvres completes*, vol. III, Paris: Éditions du Seuil, 1995, pp. 198–9). And we should not forget Gaston Leroux's *The Perfume of the Lady in Black*, both the novel and the film.

10. Thus the perfume comes from the place whence Western values are exported to India. The year of the film (1947) is not inconsequential in the history of India. The situation regarding the British Empire had been different when Rumer Godden's novel was published in 1939.

11. André Gide's *Traité de Narcisse* appeared in 1891 and Gustave Moreau painted his *Narcisse* in 1895. The first draft of Paul Valéry's poem 'Narcisse parle' dates from 1891: 'O frères! tristes lys …' ('O brothers! sad lilies …'). The notion of narcissism first appeared in Freud's writings in 1910.

12. Godden, *Black Narcissus* p. 161.

13. Another flower is associated with one of the film's characters, but in a more immediate way. When Joseph, reading out the list of flowers, says the word 'honeysuckle', Sister Honey, who is nearby, raises her head and smiles.

14. Godden, *Black Narcissus* p. 164.

15. Red is the distinguishing colour of this character: the blood that has splashed on to her, the crimson dress she has ordered in Calcutta, the lipstick she puts on in the presence of Sister Clodagh – prefiguring one of the final shots of Jean-Luc Godard's *Je vous salue Marie* (*Hail Mary*). The red lips of the children of Ireland recur as a leitmotiv in the novel.

16. Godden, *Black Narcissus* p. 11. The young General is surprised by the expression designating the nuns as the servants of Mary. He asks whether the Superior's name is Mary. The first title after the opening credits emphasises the word: 'The Convent of the Servants of Mary. Calcutta'.

17. Like Huysmans's hero Des Esseintes in *A rebours* (*Against Nature*, 1884), Dorian Gray is also initiated into the science of perfumes and dedicates himself to the study of gemstones. His creator, Oscar Wilde, was known to like lilies and blue porcelain.

18. Sister Clodagh's fall in the film, because she has dozed off, could have been suggested by the character in this painting, lost in thought.

19. In his 1878 lecture entitled 'The Three Colours of Pre-Raphaelitism'.

20. The second mention of this story (which, unlike the first, is not in the book) occurs at the moment of the final departure. The young General reports that Mr Dean has advised him, when telling the story of his adventure with Kanchi, to talk about the Prince and the Beggar Maid.

21. Other titles come to mind: *The Prince and the Pauper* (Mark Twain, 1882), *The Young King* (Wilde, 1888), *The Happy Prince* (Wilde, 1885).

22. In several plays, including *Romeo and Juliet*.

23. The Pre-Raphaelite painters were greatly influenced by Tennyson. Burne-Jones' picture inspired Julien Gracq's story *Le Roi Cophetua*, in which he develops the 'serving girl-mistress' theme.

24. He stands up to conjugate the verb 'to sit'. In the Burne-Jones picture, both of the main characters are seated.

25. Gilles Aillaud, Albert Blankert, John Michael Montias, *Vermeer*, trans. Jane Brenton, New York: Rizzoli, 1988, p. 11.

26. Daniel Arasse, *Vermeer: Faith in Painting*, trans. Terry Grabar, Princeton, NJ: Princeton University Press, 1994, p. 67.

27. It is similar in this respect to *Senso* and *La Chienne*, two otherwise very different films.

28. As Ian Christie has suggested to me, Powell and Pressburger are probably also remembering *Casablanca* (1943) here.

29. Seen at the end of the film, the grave echoes the empty chair at the beginning, marking Sister Ruth's place. The character is seen from the very beginning as absent. Sister Clodagh entrusts with Mr Dean the mission of maintaining Ruth's grave (which means, one imagines, keeping it supplied with flowers).

30. Jean-Pierre Richard, *Poésie et profondeur*, Paris: Éditions du Seuil, 1955, p. 107.

31. We even find in *The Uninvited* (the novel) a reference to Ireland and a Pre-Raphaelite atmosphere attaching to the character of Stella: pale-blue painted walls, marguerite-patterned curtains, Florentine madonnas, a white rose in a glass vase. Dorothy Macardle, *The Uninvited*, London: Corgi Books, 1966, p. 191.

9 The Light that Fails: A Commentary on *Peeping Tom*

Laura Mulvey

PRE-CREDIT SEQUENCE

The eye opens onto a street at night. A man approaches a prostitute, whistling faintly. A 16mm camera, hidden under his duffle coat, carries his movement forward. The film's camera is forced out of focus and subordinated to this voyeuristic camera eye – as is the audience. We see the space between the one who is watched and the one who is surreptitiously watching. But there is no voyeuristic thrill in this male–female sexual encounter. The spectator's gaze is not erotically involved or glamorised, but insistently absorbed into the camera as it tracks its prey.

For a moment, the camera's aggressive look is halted by a cut, then continues inexorably on its way. When the spectator's look is aligned for so long with the camera's look, both become self-conscious: the conventional association between the camera's look and the male gaze becomes uncomfortable as it becomes visible. The gas fire, the nylon stockings, the poor bedsit room – briefly, the film's social observation and realism overwhelm voyeurism. But as Dora starts to undress, almost imperceptibly voyeurism shifts into its close associate, sadism. The camera's active look bears down on its passive object, the music begins, and the space created by looking is closed by fear. Dora sees something and her eyes freeze with terror.

THE CREDIT SEQUENCE

The camera records a scene, one specific moment in time, which is then fossilised, 'mummified', as André Bazin memorably put it. Once projected, that moment can be replayed and repeated: the camera's look at the scene becomes the spectator's look at the screen. Here, as Mark projects his film, the different times of spectatorship are doubled again. The screen changes size, becoming a screen within a screen, as it shifts between the time of the story when Mark Lewis watches his film and the time when any audience watches *Peeping Tom* in the cinema. While the credits roll, these layers of time that are usually invisible become uneasily visible for the audience of this film. The story is showing us an extreme, a perversion of the cinematic look, but it also reflects outwards, onto the cinema's intrinsic fascination with looking, and the ease with which it can make peeping toms of us all. The credits also show that the makers of *Peeping Tom* acknowledge their complicity: the cinematographer Otto Heller's name appears at the climax of the scene, and Michael Powell's is superimposed on the projector.

DAY 1

The scene shifts to the next morning, but the shot through Mark's camera recalls the night before. Although the secret nocturnal crime has become public spectacle in the light of day, the same camera eye is there, observing. Now the *film's* camera has to assert its control over the telling of the story, by reversing the field of vision. The audience is curious to see *who* is behind these images, though at first Mark is shielded by his camera, until a bossy bystander's inquisitive gaze moves him into the eye of the film camera. A wry joke – that he works for the *Observer*, Britain's oldest, most prestigious Sunday newspaper – acknowledges the complexity of the vision plot.

The scene of the murder is Newman Passage, described by Powell as 'a narrow arched passageway that gives you goose pimples just to look at it. They say it was associated with Jack the Ripper.'[1] Whatever the truth of this rumour, the curious crowds and newspapermen gathered around the body of a murdered prostitute place the scene in a long tradition of English subculture, dating back to the 19th century. Sex murders have long fed a public appetite for shocks – the shock of violence and of scandal – from lurid Victorian papers to tabloid newspaper reporting and the horror genre itself. David Pirie places *Peeping Tom* within the horror genre that flourished in Britain in the 1950s, and further locates that genre within the English tradition of the Gothic, with its taste for excess, dualism, deformity and cruelty – and its obsession with vision.[2]

Newman Passage leads into Rathbone Place, where a newsagent's shop already existed when Powell shot exteriors for his first film in 1931 and still does in 2005, although its pin-ups are now in magazines on open display. This is the northern edge of Soho, London's red-light district in the 1950s, and the scene in the newsagent's establishes first the confidential space of pornography, through Mark's secret glance and the customer's furtive whisper, then rapidly transforms into the public space of respectability by a little girl's entrance, which both normalises and abnormalises the scene. Here, *Peeping Tom* not only captures the repressed atmosphere of London in the 1950s, but more specifically the nuances of the English class system. Powell said of the actors Bartlett Mullins and Miles Malleson, the proprietor and customer respectively, that together they amounted to a complete vaudeville act, playing out the unbridgeable gulf between the lower and upper middle class.

We move from the scene of consumption to the scene of production, in the studio above the newsagent's where Mark takes the pornographic pictures that Mr

Peters sells. The opening of *Peeping Tom* is constructed as a series of fragmented scenes focusing on different facets of voyeurism, explicitly addressing the sexual pleasure of looking and its place in our culture, in subcultures and in the cinema. But the layering of looks and the audience's enforced complicity also distance the spectator. In the studio scenes with the models Millie and Lorraine, the film reflects ironically the way that the pleasure of looking is built around an image of women displayed as a spectacle, moulded and fashioned for the male gaze. Millie's pose under a street lamp in a cardboard set evokes Dora, the murdered prostitute. When Mark sees Lorraine's deformed face and pulls out his own camera to film her, the film associates male voyeurism with sadism – not necessarily as systematic cruelty, but as an instinct to dominate and subordinate by means of a controlling gaze.

For Freud, the sexual instincts and their inversion into opposites would be present in any individual psyche, male or female, but in culture they tend to be personified according to gender, masculinity as active and femininity as passive.

What distinguishes *Peeping Tom* from most films about psychoanalysis is its use of puns and double meanings, creating puzzles that hide their meaning and, like the language of the unconscious, need to be decoded. The writer of *Peeping Tom*, Leo Marks, had worked as a code-breaker during the war, and his original project with Powell had been to make a film about Freud, until news of John Huston's *Freud the Secret Passion* forced them to change direction. Leo Marks suggested a story about 'a young man with a camera who kills the women he photographs'.[3] So Mark is an obsessive cameraman, acting out the implications of the voyeuristic and sadistic gaze that, Marks and Powell imply, is inevitably present in the cinema. But their use of verbal and visual codes suggests that psychoanalysis can interpret these perversions and bring them to the surface. In the photographic studio scene, Mark asks the model to 'look at the sea', which we can translate into a coded reference to seeing. And when the film cuts from this modernised Gothic scene to a middle-class birthday party in the house where Mark lives (and also owns), the cut from pouring a cup of tea to a glass of whiskey is a visual pun that turns social convention upside down, while linking Mark's two worlds. In spite of the run-down respectability of his lodgers, Helen's mother Mrs Stephens, blind and alcoholic, retains a suggestion of the Gothic. And the cut to Mark, peering in at the window, enacting the title of the film, recalls the classic monsters of the horror genre: sad and isolated, yet mysteriously threatening.

From the moment when Mark invites Helen into his flat, the scene begins to take on a distinct symmetrical pattern. The opening and closing shots are wide, allowing the whole room to be seen, with a gas cooker giving a touch of pathos to its former grandeur. Thereafter, the organisation of shots follows Helen's penetration into Mark's space. When she looks towards the mysterious room at the back, the camera stays 'with its back to it', refusing any reverse shots in that direction. Anna Massey's large eyes draw attention to Helen's look and the curiosity she represents. When she starts interrogating Mark, as though to change the subject from the back room, the camera moves into a series of shot-reverse-shot close-ups that mark the middle of the sequence as a whole. Mark puzzles Helen, as he had puzzled Millie earlier in the day. But now his answers relate to his father and the house, which was his father's.[4] The audience knows Mark's secret, but Helen's questions reflect their curiosity about how this shy, sensitive young man has come to acquire his double, his other self. As the scene pivots on the close-ups, Mark finally invites Helen completely into the room, opening up its space again. Her interrogation moves on to a new and more dangerous stage, emphasising the split between what she knows and what we know about Mark. Her questions are drawn, as though by a second sense, to his films and the back room, although for a moment the sounds of the party below seep back into the scene, as though to tempt Helen with a rival object of desire.

As Helen follows Mark through the heavy curtains, we are treated to one of the most beautiful scenes in the whole film. The red darkroom light fuses with her red hair and red dress, and the scene is shot with a crane so that the camera can follow Helen fluidly, without the distraction of cuts: now nothing can distract her in this strange new world that she finds so exciting. Here, the whole of film-making technology is collected in a single room: the cameras, lab, projector and screen. And when Mark projects his father's home movie for her, she will find the outward traces that the father left on his son's interior world, his memories and his tortured psyche.

Professor Lewis (played by Michael Powell) was a scientist working with behaviourist psychology, which has nothing to do with Freudian psychoanalysis. He studied outward reactions, with no regard for the unconscious mind, and in the film of Mark as a child (played by Powell's own son, Columba), we see the sexual curiosity of the young voyeur as he climbs a wall to watch a couple courting in the adjacent park. There are three looks here: the adult child Mark's, Professor Lewis's as he films the scene, and the film's spectator's superimposed on and distanced by the black-and-white film. Freud associated children's voyeurism with sexual curiosity: here, the framing and shape of the projector emphasise Mark's eyes as he watches himself being watched. Once again, as Mark turns the spotlight onto Helen, we see the probing light, familiar from Dora's murder when it first alerted her to the fact that something was wrong, similar to the flashlight his father used to wake the young Mark from his sleep. Now the music and editing combine to transform the home movies into a horror movie. Close-ups magnify a small lizard that is dropped onto the young Mark into a monster.

Given that both screenwriter and director were interested in Freud, these scenes of childhood trauma fill the screen like small fragments of Freudian scenarios: the Oedipal drama and a cruel enactment of the castration complex forced by the father himself. Helen demands an explanation of the riddle; her driving desire to see has been overwhelmed by the desire to understand, to decipher the images she is watching. Her look is still foregrounded, but it is now directed beyond the surface of the screen to the enigma that lies behind it.

Another aspect of the Oedipal drama is acted out as the child is seen mourning his dead mother, his original love object that the father denies him, now literally –

and in keeping with the conventions of the horror genre – through death. The father has replaced his son's dead mother with his own object of desire. Critics have frequently pointed out her similarity to the blonde eroticised women who have become the objects of Mark's aggression. The woman, of course, is unable to dominate the mechanics of the look – as she appears out of focus, Dr Lewis/Michael Powell appears to reassert control. He would later say in an interview: 'I understood the story well enough to know that I couldn't ask an actor to play the part of the father with his son'.[5] The Oedipal scenario is consummated with a gift, a gift that fills the previous scenes of loss and trauma. The unwelcome castrating 'gift' of the lizard and the lost mother are displaced onto this final gift: the phallic gift of a camera. The father's legacy is the film camera as fetish object and instrument of voyeurism. The horror of the home movies affects Helen and, as he feels her emotion, he is compelled to film her. But – and this is a turning point in the story – she refuses to become the object of the camera's look. The act of looking, its sadistic aggression, cancels out the process of understanding that Helen represents. As she rebels against his look, she switches off the projector herself.

The film's camera sweeps her out of Mark's haunted room, reversing the drive that had taken her in originally. But back in the light, she is undaunted: she questions the morality of a scientist's investigation into his child's fear. Here, the object of spectacle earlier associated with women (with Dora, Millie and Lorraine) is shifted onto Mark's childhood experience as spectacle for his father's experiments. In his interview with *Midi-Minuit Fantastique*, Powell spoke of the camera as 'something very frightening … I don't think there is anything more frightening than a camera that is running, watching you'.[6] As Mark leans back against his father's collected works, Helen's eyes watch him and challenge his father's hold. Living in his father's study, Mark is caught in the past and in the legacy of his father's gift. As a powerless child, he was subordinated to his father's camera, which he now turns on women. But Helen has introduced another aspect of femininity into the film, in contrast to subordination that goes with the exhibitionism of the pin-up and the prostitute, that of curiosity.

DAY 2

The scene shifts to the film studio where Marks works as a camera assistant. Powell treats the business of film-making satirically, with a number of in-jokes and coded references. 'Don Jarvis', the head of the studio, is clearly John Davis, J. Arthur Rank's successor as head of the Rank Organisation, with whom Powell had a stormy relationship as he presided over the collapse of serious British production. Shirley Anne Field, who plays the star of the film being made, had previously starred in *Horrors of the Black Museum*, where, in David Pirie's words, 'she was hopelessly unable to register emotion in front of the camera' – precisely the problem she has in the fictional production 'The Walls Are Closing In'. The film's director, 'Arthur Baden', is played by Esmond Knight, who had been partially blinded during the war, and who thus literally cannot see what he is doing, quite apart from the associations of his name.[7] And Moira Shearer plays the star's stand-in, bringing an internationally known name to a minor part, as well as the associations from her previous roles with Powell and Pressburger. In the film that launched her screen career, *The Red Shoes* (1948), she played the young dancer Vicky who is driven to suicide by the impossibility of mediating the demands of her mentor Lermontov and her husband Julian. In *The Tales of Hoffmann* (1951) one of the roles she played was the mechanical doll Olympia, and here her dance for Mark also has something mechanical, robotic about it.

Shearer's 'Viv' takes the story, for the first time, away from Mark's point of view. We see her in her dressing room, making up in preparation for her 'screen test'. The colour tones of the room and of Viv's costume are beige and brown. But the colour of her make-up case, a pale yet saturated blue, is so prominent that this insignificant object inevitably catches the spectator's eye. Knowing what we do, we watch her walk into a trap from which there is no escape as she prepares to dance for Mark. Blinded by the studio lights, her look is blocked and she is subjected to a caricature of the father's power. Mark's project is to film the moment when his victim sees her own death, the moment of terror that transfixes her on the exact threshold between life and death. This fleeting second can only be captured by the camera, which is also, with its dagger tripod, the murder machine. When he tells Viv that he is 'searching for perfection', Mark is like a Romantic artist reaching out to the sublime. His emotional investment is not in the murder, which is a necessary step in the process of achieving the image. Mark will have to wait for the moment of projection when, realising his failure, he exclaims 'the light failed'.

But Mark's perverted search for the sublime is inevitably charged by the psychotic residues left by his father's experiments, and psychoanalytic theory weaves a chain of links between the themes that have been surfacing across the film. The simple opposition between masculine voyeurism directed at feminine 'to-be-looked-at-ness', tinged as it is with sadism and aggression, may also be a form of masculine defence – a defence against the woman's body as wounded and concealing an inner void or emptiness. As she looks through the camera, Viv brings back memories of Mark's stepmother behind his father's camera and the moment, recorded on film, of the camera gift – a fetish object offered in cynical recompense to a traumatised child by a castrating father. Critics have often commented on the phallic nature of Mark's tripod, his instrument of death with its fold-out dagger blade. Now, in the deserted studio, with the props left from the day's shooting, a blue trunk begins to play a part in Viv's dance of death, its colour and the symbolism of the box both prefigured by Viv's make-up case. The empty void of the box stands in a symmetrical relation to the phallic symbolism of Mark's tripod. In myths and legends, and in the movies, the woman's body over and over again suffers under the fantasies projected onto her. The castration anxiety aroused by the father's aggression is displaced onto the woman's body, in a gesture of displacement and appeasement. The camera follows Mark as he closes in on Viv with a slow tracking movement, only broken by a sharp, disturbing cutaway to the empty box. Mark's scenario of death recalls the Medusa,

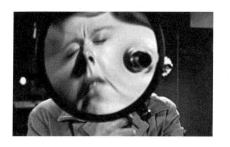 

the image of castration itself, according to Freud. Mark literally creates the wound as he kills; and he kills with the gaze. During the last moments of Viv's dance, the film reiterates the aggressive phallic advance of the camera and the vulnerability of its subject by cutting between them; and Viv's surface, the masquerade of femininity, begins to disintegrate into terror.

The film returns abruptly to a medium close-up of Mrs Stephens. There is a structured opposition between Helen's blind mother and Mark's all-seeing father. The film displays its pattern of meaning as a series of clues, but deciphering these involves an effort of the mind that is partly intuitive and partly intellectual. It involves seeing beyond the surface of a sign and displacing dependence on sight as a source of truth. A film that is overtly about voyeurism and the fetishisation of sight – a film that draws its cinema audience's attention to the voyeuristic nature of the cinema – demands to be viewed with 'second sight' – the second sight of the blind, who figure out the meaning of things without being blinded by the obviousness of vision.

Helen's second visit to Mark's room shows him trying to escape the world of his father's legacy and live more fully in the world of the present, which is coming alive for him through his relationship with Helen. He offers her a birthday present, which is more 'normal' than his previous present of the childhood movies; but the brooch he gives her is in the form of a dragonfly, which is reminiscent of the lizard in the home movies. The atmosphere of Mark's room changes with Helen's presence and as she tells him about the children's book she is writing, loses its claustrophobic quality. In the tradition of Grimm, Hans Christian Andersen and Lewis Carroll, Helen's book about a magic camera offers Mark the chance to turn his fantasies, locked in his childhood, into a fantasy for children. Not a fantasy he has to live out, compulsively, but one that lies within the cultural tradition to which his character belongs – essentially stories of the double by Edgar Allan Poe and Robert Louis Stevenson, which depict the split between the unconscious and everyday normality.[8] However, the developer timer rings in the darkroom calling Mark back from his exchange of looks with Helen to the footage of Viv's death and the underworld of perverse filming that still claims him.

DAY 3

Back at the film studio, the director and crew are blocking out a scene, unaware that opening the trunk that contains Viv's body will make their black comedy real, and unaware that they are also enacting a scene for Mark's 'documentary'. As he prepares to film the discovery of the body, music starts on the soundtrack, ironising the realism of documentary. *Peeping Tom* turns the conventions of the thriller genre upside down. As Hitchcock pointed out, thrillers depend on a mixture of mystery, suspense and surprise. As the audience has always known that Mark is the murderer, an important element of narrative mystery has been eliminated from the first moments of the film. Helen's questioning has revealed the origins of Mark's psychosis. But as the police arrive to investigate the body found in the trunk, an element of suspense is introduced that makes an ironic comment on the audience's process of identification. Although we know that Mark is a psychotic murderer, once the police begin to close in, he too becomes a victim. The police are, of course, excited to be working in a film studio, blinded by its glamour from seeing what is really happening. Their conventional attitude to cinema is contrasted with Mark's fellow technician, a middle-class reader of *Sight and Sound* who goes to see films at the Everyman in Hampstead. Mark says he is making a documentary, which would normally place him in the realist, anti-glamour tradition, represented in the late 1950s by the Free Cinema movement. But Mark's inability to distinguish between life and art, which leads to death, places him on the side of Romanticism,

The police do not notice Mark's symptoms, but the film's camera allows the audience to see his reaction when the inspector takes his 16mm camera away from him. This camera adjusts its angle to foreground Mark's 16mm camera, placed tantalisingly out of his reach. Separation from his camera makes him profoundly uneasy, and his hands reach for it involuntarily as the film-struck policeman plays with it. As Helen will observe later, the camera has started to grow into an extra limb. But after he escapes detection at the studio, despite dropping his pens from the roof in a celebrated slow-motion shot, he returns to the house in Melbury Road and the more searching interrogation of Mrs Stephens's sightless eyes. As he and Helen go out for dinner, Helen also succeeds in separating him from his fetish camera, acting with quiet, almost maternal authority. In Freudian theory, a fetish object acts as a disavowal of the mother's castration; and as Mark overcomes his resistance and surrenders the camera to Helen's safe keeping, he takes a further step into a present tense, into the lived reality of the relationship she offers, and hence a way forward out of fantasy and psychosis. They leave the house on their date almost like children discovering the world of grown-ups.

The magic camera that is the subject of Helen's book finalises the series of exchanges between Helen and Mark. It takes voyeurism back into a world of childish curiosity, out of the world of sexual domination and anguish. Here, the film suggests that, as in fairy stories, the monster Mark might be saved by Helen's love. But, of course, it is too late; and the timer ticking in the darkroom is a reminder that time is running out. As Elliott Stein said of the film, 'there is no more moving, doomed love affair'.[9]

Mrs Stephens's uncanny appearance in Mark's room sets up another layer of symmetry in the film's structure. This scene balances with their first meeting earlier in the evening, when she had seemed to see into his mind as she held his hand between hers. But that unspoken exchange now erupts in full-scale conflict, like a battle scene in which both sides are struggling from weakness rather than strength. Mark hides behind the spotlights, but he is trapped in his other, nether world – a world that Mrs Stephens knows to be the site of his psychotic unconscious, without knowing precisely the full horror of its content. She lives under his room, exercising her own form of surveillance – 'the blind always live in the rooms above them'. Mrs Stephens's pointed stick caricatures Mark's bayonet and drives him back to the projector and the footage of Viv's death. The camera angles are awkward and disturbing. While the scene is a grotesque re-enactment of Helen's visit to Mark's 'cinema', the blind mother is unable to see the full horror of the father's legacy. As Mark's latest experiment in 'perfection' plays out on the screen, the dead woman's face is superimposed on his crucified body in one of the most extraordinary images of the film. Like the artist in Kipling's novel, *The Light that Failed*, who is searching for the perfect melancholia, Mark is in the grip of a mad drive for perfection that will always elude him. The excess of this scene reinforces *Peeping Tom*'s place in the subculture of the English Gothic, here amplified by a fleeting allusion to Hoffmann's tale of Dr Dapertutto, who steals reflections, and appeared in Powell and Pressburger's earlier *Tales of Hoffmann*.

Mark cannot, in his despair, turn to Mrs Stephens to realise his project of photographing fear, as she can not see his bayonet or her own image. Mark collapses at the mother's feet, clutching his fetish object, in the exact place where fetishistic disavowal is born. And as he gives her back her stick, he enacts the fantasy of the phallic mother. Mrs Stephens is able to reassert her control over him, as they both know that she has found him out. It was the blind seer Tireseis who told Oedipus the truth that his unconscious resisted. The camera slowly tracks her movement back to the front room, pushing Mark forward. Once again, the invisible, instinct, is contrasted with the visible as a source of knowledge. She knows that Mark will never be cured if he cannot tell his own story, which is the opportunity that Helen has offered him. But it is too late – he is searching for the ultimate image on film, the fetishistic obsession that fuses madness and art. As they part in the hall, the camera reproduces the framing and placing of Mark and Helen's goodnight. Mrs Stephens dissolves the distance of vision, the father position of cold observation, into the intimacy of touch, the mother's touch and concern. This is the only moment in the film that is allowed an erotic edge.

DAY 4

When Mark decides to talk to a psychologist (who is advising on the murders for the police) about his father and voyeurism, he takes them up in a studio elevator – not so much for privacy, we infer, but to reach the controlling position he associates with both of these subjects. This was the position from which he watched Viv enter the studio, from which he invisibly controlled the lights that blinded her. The film uses the searchlight motif to condense the scientist's (father's) observation of his material with the voyeur's (Mark's); and the lights in the film studio elide the two into one. Voyeurism, or 'scoptophilia', as Dr Rosen calls it, belongs to both the visible and invisible worlds. The sexual perversion invests its erotic drive in the visible, the surface appearance of its object; and voyeurism may combine with fetishism to produce an anxiety about what a surface may conceal. But these are also symptoms of the unconscious, belonging to a nether world with its own perverse and symptomatic subculture, the world of *Peeping Tom* itself. The police also belong to two worlds, the world of clues and deciphering and the world of surveillance. Helen, however, represents imagination and the curiosity that is attributed to women and children.

When Mark returns to the newsagent's studio, the film's narrative starts to retrace its steps, returning to its opening scenes and creating a symmetrical pattern that will rhyme the end with the beginning. The atmosphere of the upstairs room has changed. The lighting is very different from the first scene with the models: the windows now open up the space to daylight, unlike the shadows and rich colours of the earlier *mise en scène*. Mark had filmed the police, discreetly, after the discovery of both Dora's and Viv's bodies; now he films them from the upstairs window while under their surveillance. The music, the artificial wall that serves as a set and, finally, Mark's shadow falling across Millie – like the shadow of the child murderer played by Peter Lorre in Fritz Lang's *M* – all introduce the last murder. Powell's attitude to storytelling is also reminiscent of Hitchcock's, and *Psycho* would be released shortly after the critical and financial demise of *Peeping Tom*, a film with a very similar theme, yet a different destiny. However, *Peeping Tom* is in many ways closer to Hitchcock's 1925 film *The Lodger*, subtitled 'A Tale of the London Fog'. In both films, the main character lives above the girl he falls in love with and the suspicious mother listens to his footsteps overhead. Both films can be seen as influenced by German Expressionism: *The Lodger* more directly, having been made in the midst of that movement's international popularity and after Hitchcock had worked in Germany; while Powell's filmography before *Peeping Tom* had included many collaborations with Germans and Hungarians, and this film was shot by the Czech-born cinematographer Otto Heller, whose prolific career had included shooting Max Ophuls's *De Mayerling a Sarajevo*, Thorold Dickinson's *The Queen of Spades* and Alexander Mackendrick's *The Ladykillers*.

In 1964, Powell made a neo-expressionist film of Béla Bartók's opera *Bluebeard's Castle*, and certain themes in *Peeping Tom* are reminiscent of the Bluebeard story. Mark's inner room, where he keeps on film the 'bodies' of the women he kills, is similar to the mysterious locked room where Duke Bluebeard keeps the bodies of his former wives. Mrs Stephens says, 'This is the one room I expected to find locked', but Mark was never allowed to lock his room by his father. Helen's curiosity has drawn her further and further in, until she is forced to realise, like Bluebeard's latest wife, that she has fallen in love with a psychotic and sadistic murderer. But Helen's desire to know is greater than fear: she needs to see in order to understand something that can not ultimately be seen.

In Mark's story, he is shown to be trapped in a look that takes the woman as object and compulsively records his victims with phallic cruelty. As a child, the reverse was the case. He was subordinated, feminised, by his father's filming. His split character exists on both sides of the look. His position is reversible, from one of power to its opposite. The moment he is striving for is not present in the act of murder. As he explains to Viv, it is not enough to kill you; his project is to capture the rigid look of terror, and the process of filming is secondary to that of projection – 'look at the sea/see and 'see the look'.

Mark unveils the final mystery to Helen. At last the audience sees the ultimate horror of his murder weapon: a mirror forces the victim to see her face, distorted with terror in a distorting mirror, as though enacting the moment when the Medusa's castrating look was turned towards her, reflected in Perseus's shield. Helen's gaze does not flinch, saving her from death, but pushing Mark into the final phase of his tragedy. Mark's suicide is also a murder. The sadist is released into masochism. The victim's gaze will turn on the male voyeur and finally succeed in turning the all-seeing father into its object. Mark will then be able to 'kill the father' by killing himself: his project was designed to culminate with his own suicide.

We see Mark's suicide figured doubly as a death drive: a drive to *his* end and to the end of the story. The spectacle of his death balances and retrospectively transforms the opening spectacle of Dora's murder. The 16mm camera dominated the film's look in the first sequence. In the final sequence, cinema has been replaced by a series of still cameras, wired to go off in sequence when activated by Mark's movement past them to impale himself on his own apparatus. This reproduces one of the key experiments that prefigured the invention of cinema: Eadweard Muybridge's analysis of movement by means of stills taken in sequence is here reversed into a movement towards stillness. The film creates a metaphoric image of its own end: the stillness that is the end of every story, once its protagonist has carried his narrative mission through to its conclusion.

Powell's own voice is heard on the soundtrack and the legacy of Mark's father's experiments comes to an end. Helen has lost her struggle to change the course of the story determined, years earlier, by Professor Lewis. The moving image returns to a still photograph as the projector runs down. Then the empty screen within the film fills the cinema screen, just as the opening eye had opened the movie.

NOTES

1. Michael Powell, *A Life in Movies: An Autobiography*, London: Faber & Faber, 2000, p. 217. This essay is based on a commentary originally written to accompany the Criterion Laserdisc release of *Peeping Tom*.
2. David Pirie, *A Heritage of Horror*, London: Gordon Fraser, 1973.
3. Michael Powell, *Million Dollar Movie*, London: Heinemann, 1992, p. 393.
4. The film is set in 7 Melbury Road, north of Kensington High Street and south of Holland Park. Michael Powell lived across the road at number 8, and both houses were designed by the architect Norman Shaw. Powell said: 'The house, with its finials, pinnacles and chimneys and windows had created a perfect setting for me. There is something looney about its absorption in ornament and detail, as there is in me.' (*Million Dollar Movie*, p. 395.)
5. Interview with Powell by Bertrand Tavernier and Jacques Prayer, *Midi-Minuit Fantastique* 20, 1968, p. 4.
6. Ibid.
7. Baden-Powell was the founder of the Scout movement for boys. Or was the name 'Baden' arrived at through association with 'Powell', as another instance of self-inscription?
8. Poe's 'William Wilson' and Stevenson's *Dr Jekyll and Mr Hyde*.
9. Elliott Stein, 'A Very Tender Film, A Very Nice One: Michael Powell's *Peeping Tom*', *Film Comment*, September 1979.

10 *They're a Weird Mob*: Powell in the Antipodes[1]

Graeme Harper

'ANTIPODEAN' PROPOSITIONS

The opening sequences of Michael Powell and Emeric Pressburger's 1966 film *They're a Weird Mob* make two significant propositions with regard to European cinema.[2] First, they propose, through cinematic form, a clash between a European and a non-European ideal of space and place. Second, they propose grounds for a much wider, and much more detailed, examination of European-ness in film, film-making and film criticism. The significance of the proposals made in *They're a Weird Mob* might well require us to revisit critically much of the work by twentieth century film scholars offering socio-historical or socio-economic readings of world cinema.

While these proposals should not be seen as criticisms of European-ness they do invite us to consider whether full attention has yet been given to the filmic manifestations of a European worldview: that is, of an outlook endowed with ideas we might with confidence label as distinctively 'European', an outlook that supports these ideas both within and beyond the geographic region known as 'Europe'.

The first of Powell and Pressburger's sequences is a spoof 'informational' pointer to the nature of Australia: children stand in front of a world globe, their backs to the camera; the globe spins and reveals Australia, the voiceover describing Australians as living 'down under' and suggesting that this is like being 'flies on a ceiling'. The shot flips, and we are presented with an upside-down series of frames: the fly-on-the-ceiling viewpoint. The frames then return to European 'normality' and we cover what are described as some key cultural pointers: Australians as a nation of sportsmen, definitions of 'doing ya block', 'a schooner', 'sheilas or beaut sorts' and, ultimately, examples of the English language Australian-style.

The second sequence is more obviously a romanticised travelogue, but not a real one. It is spoof travel sequence. A vista opens up: an extreme high shot of a stark white cruise ship entering the sunny expanse of Sydney Harbour is accompanied by a musical number, whose chorus begins as follows: 'It's a big big country …'. This ends at the words 'a life you'll understand', pausing the music to insert the exclamation, 'And you're so bloody wrong!'

From there on, the title sequence overtakes the images, but the backdrop is the first part of the central character's arrival-from-Italy emigration narrative, and the musical number at this point contains such lines as 'a man's got to prove he's a man', 'an Antipodean man must be …' and 'it's a man's country, sweetheart'. This, of course, is all tongue-in-cheek – at least on the surface of the film's discourse.

They're a Weird Mob is a film adaptation of the 1957 book of the same title by Nino Culotta, the Italian pseudonym of Australian writer John O'Grady. O'Grady's book is a comic consideration of the nature of European emigration, and an equally comic investigation of European expatriate society – with an emphasis on the misunderstandings generated in translating meaning from one European language to another, made more difficult by a colonial transference to non-European space and place.

And yet, to treat Powell's film as a straightforward adaptation of O'Grady's book would be to miss a number of key points. The film varies the thrust of the book and actively highlights similarities between resident Europeans and their Antipodean cousins; not least, those similarities engendered in a shared socio-economic and pol-

'Go South young European!' Nino Culotta (Walter Chiari) finds himself lost in Antipodean space in Powell and Pressburger's *They're a Weird Mob*.

itical worldview connected to identifiable European ideals about the character and role of work, social status and cultural integrity. In effect, *They're a Weird Mob* calls into play the technologies and aesthetics of film in order to assert a distinctive European politics of space and place that are merely presented on the surface of the discourse of O'Grady's book.

There can be little doubt that this degree of oppositional substrata in the film was unplanned; rather, that it came about naturally through Powell's own Britishness, connected explicitly with the background of his collaborator, the Hungarian-born screenwriter Emeric Pressburger, in this case writing under one of his pseudonyms, Richard Imrie. While the book was a bestseller in its home Australian market, it was virtually unknown elsewhere at that time, and had no cultural currency beyond that narrow and, indeed, minor English-language film market. It was, in that sense, a 'clean' property and its option was acquired largely because the 'option-taker', the American film actor Gregory Peck, had a passing connection with what might be broadly called 'Antipodean adventure films'.

Peck had previously starred in the 1959 adaptation of Nevil Shute's novel *On the Beach*, in which nuclear war wipes out humanity in the northern hemisphere, and an American submarine finds safety in Australia, only to come face to face with a growing post-war angst. And yet, despite Peck's enthusiasm for *They're a Weird Mob*, the property was passed from its original backers to Powell when the American interests baulked at the idea of making what Peck thought could well end up as very fine 'Ealing comedy' – a comment that is less unifying than it seems, given that Ealing comedies were not entirely generic, but reflecting on the fact that what Peck was considering was, to his mind, identifiably a British film. As James Howard points out in his book on Powell, Peck had hoped that such a comedy would be capable of 'winning a medal at the Cannes Film Festival'.[3]

Whether the failure of Peck and his American associates to pursue the option related to the backers' dislike of Ealing's comedies, or whether it was because the material in O'Grady's book offered very little scope for a 'world market' film, is difficult to tell. But certainly, *They're a Weird Mob* remains even today one of the least likely prospects for a blockbuster film in either the American or the European markets.

The film's subsequent lack of international success did not prevent Powell maintaining his interest in 'European' Australia. He went on to work there with another international leading man of not dissimilar stature to Peck, the British actor James Mason, who both starred in and co-produced Powell's *Age of Consent* (1969). In that film, adapted from a book by Norman Lindsay, an Australian artist with a reputation for flamboyantly erotic subject matter, Mason plays an ageing, disgruntled painter who moves to an island to try and recapture his artistic vigour, and does so with the assistance of a young girl – a scenario that picks up neatly on Mason's role as Humbert Humbert in Stanley Kubrick's earlier adaptation of Vladimir Nabokov's *Lolita* (1962).

The striking thematic similarity between *Age of Consent* and *They're a Weird Mob*

– something akin to the theme of 'a second coming-of-age in uncharted colonial territory' or 'Go South, Young European!' – suggests this thematic interest might well have been Powell's, which sits neatly alongside the biographical fact that his elder son was at the time considering a move to Australia to work in that country's infant media industry. The Australian media industry in the mid-1960s was little more than an offshoot of its British counterpart. As Bill Rout has pointed out:

> From 1946 to 1969 an average of just over two films a year were made in Australia – and none at all in 1948 and 1963–4. More than a third of these were 'foreign' productions. Increasingly, 'Australian films' came to mean films made in Australia – by Britain (Rank and Korda, among others), by Hollywood (including *On the Beach* and *The Sundowners*), by France, and even, briefly, by Japan.[4]

Thus, the making of *They're a Weird Mob* afforded a personal Antipodean opportunity for Powell and a link to Pressburger's own immigration story, while, simultaneously, maintaining a well-established tradition of European production in the southern hemisphere. Herein lies a dilemma in the interpretation of the film.

Culotta's book is a comic investigation of a colonial society populated largely by those of European descent – those of Anglo-British background being the largest group. It is not an argument with, or for, the nineteenth-century concept of European nation state, nor is it a particularly concerted vehicle for the aesthetic foundations of a European worldview: that is, of an outlook in which European ideals of beauty and taste are strongly promoted. And yet, Powell and Pressburger's treatment alters the book's themes to favour exactly such a nation-state premise and to promote more strongly a European aesthetic – if not a 'pan-European' one, then certainly cross-continental in the meeting of Hungarian screenwriter and British director. From its outset in its spoof travelogue and glossy high shot, the film echoes Ananda Mitra's point, made in relation to the Western lens and Indian cinema, that the 'image attempts to produce a geographical space that is simultaneously splendid in appearance and hostile in nature'.[5] For example, while the film makes some specific references to the Pacific climate of Australia, and to the environment's brown, gold and red colourings, it does so negatively, placing these either as difficulties to be overcome or as part of a contrast with 'civilised' European life. Likewise, while the film is based on a comic clash between Anglo-Australians and 'New Australians' – that is, between Britons and recently emigrated Mediterranean Europeans, represented by Nino Culotta – it shows this confrontation to be much less significant than the impact of the Pacific's 'alien' geography.

They're a Weird Mob focuses on the economic impératives of Nino Culotta, presenting not only a certain style of mercantilist mentality, which might identifiably be labelled 'European', but also a vision in which work is both fine filmic spectacle and a moral imperative. In this way, Powell and Pressburger's film shifts monologic European economic orthodoxies to the forefront, sidelining the original text's focus on the dialogic – not only in the Bakhtinian sense, in which the original text involves the clash and formation of new languages, but also in that the book is heavily conversation-based, while the film is more evenly balanced between visual set pieces and its lively immigrant-meets-local dialogue.

The 'weird mob', in that way, becomes not Europeans transported to non-European environments – as is the case in O'Grady's book – but non-European space and place itself, a far more pathetic fallacy than O'Grady himself ever intended, and a much more revealing premise than the book presents. In *They're a Weird Mob*, the Asia-Pacific region is in effect portrayed not as another, non-European, region, but as the Europe made disconcertingly weird. While the clash between the emigrant Italian and the settler Briton certainly remains, such comical clashes are presented as evidence of a bond of European-ness, suggesting that such a notion of a 'pan-European' association, far from being a tool for denying the national identity of individual European nation states – in this case, Italy and Great Britain – is actually a deeply felt and enduring association.[6]

WEIRD OR NOT? POWELL'S TYPOLOGY

Australia, of course, represents just one example of a predominantly European population emigrated, or transported, to a non-European space and place, largely under the auspices of colonialism. Suffice it to say, such widely read post-colonialist theorists as Bill Ashcroft, Gareth Griffiths and Helen Tiffin consider the USA a colonial society now in a latter stage of 'post-colonialism'. As the films and film-making of Europe are frequently discussed in relation to the impact of US film and film-making on Europe – specifically Hollywood's impact – it is imperative that a new view of European-ness in film considers whether Hollywood and European films are, in fact, ever properly placed in direct opposition. We might, perhaps, rightly begin to question Jean-Luc Godard's comment that 'If World War I enabled American cinema to ruin French cinema, World War II, together with the advent of television, enabled it to finance, that is to say ruin, all the cinemas of Europe.'[7]

However, the fact may be that American cinema, far from ruining the cinemas of Europe, represents an extension of European-ness into the geography of the New World, a mechanical reinvention of non-European space, and the most forceful example of the reinterpretation of space and place undertaken in the 20th century. It is important to note that such an argument does not represent a Europeanising of Hollywood cinema; rather, it simply gives due recognition to the enduring cultural heritage of the vast majority of the American population and suggests that such a heritage identifiably carries with it aesthetic, ideological and economic history that cannot be ignored, and should not be denied.

Powell and Pressburger's *They're a Weird Mob* and Powell's *Age of Consent* might well stand as exemplars of this particular movement and, if so, be key texts in an understanding of the European origins not only of much Australian cinema, but of much Hollywood cinema as well. To use a descriptive metaphor, what Powell and Pressburger's Antipodean films prove is that, in this very important sense, the

Hollywood camera lens is not a pair of eyes – a common critical description – rather the external portal of a refractive mirror. As Europeans, like Powell and Pressburger, we see what we mechanically reproduce in our own image. Such a suggestion goes to the very heart of theories of both European and Hollywood cinema.

There is not room here to separate the aesthetics of literature from that of film, suffice to say that the USA was more capable of rapidly developing an indigenous European literature to replace the imported European literature of its past than were countries such as Canada, New Zealand and Australia. Continued economic, social and political dependency, a lack of a key point of revolutionary zeal and a fundamental problem of space and place – that is, distance and/or geographic size – meant that for many years these countries remained net importers of European cultural artifacts rather than as successful settler-creators. In many ways, they remain exactly that today.

In film terms, the USA matched its own interest in technological, economic and indeed artistic independence from Europe with an ability to draw on its largely European heritage, and a willingness both to adopt and adapt European models. It is absolutely no coincidence that many of Hollywood's earliest and most successful directors and producers were recently transplanted Europeans, fuelling a Hollywood film culture that gave no room for an alternative Amerindian eco-political agenda or, indeed, a transported African aesthetic – to name just two possible alternative histories of cinematic dominance in the USA.

It is worth recalling that, however obvious it might be, as an art form film came into being at the time of the modern European age of imperialism, which stretched roughly from the early 1890s to the period of severe world financial crises in the late 1920s. In fact, film developed through one of the key periods of imperialist activity by European and European-fuelled societies. If the USA today continues to reflect largely a European 'New World', its population still mostly descendent from Europeans, then, to an even greater extent, the artistic, political and cultural framework in which film has operated has been decidedly about maintaining its Euro-origins. Godard's disgust at the influence of a neo-imperialist Hollywood becomes, in effect, little more than a parent's frustration with the independence of its child.

Of course, to broaden out the argument from Powell and Pressburger's example, exchanges between Western film-makers and non-Western film-makers have not always operated in one direction. To take a well-known case: Japanese director Akiro Kurosawa's work has been identified as influencing Western form as much as being influenced by it. Kurosawa himself protested any notion that he had been Westernised, declaring 'I don't think I'm Western at all. … I feel among Japanese directors today I must be the most Japanese.'[8] Kurosawa's own influence on American and European directors such as Sam Peckinpah and Sergio Leone is well documented, and his homage to Sergei Eisenstein in *The Hidden Fortress* (1958) is equally undeniable. Contestation between Kurosawa and his Japanese contemporaries – directors such as Nagisa Oshima – further complicates the discussion. The question of who is more Westernised, Oshima or Kurosawa, revolves largely around whether Oshima independently adopted a European political use of film, adding to this a general artistic interest in Brechtian distancing devices, or whether Kurosawa's interest in a Western film aesthetic constitutes an abrogation of an indigenous Japanese temperament. One or other of these directors is taken to be a net receiver of European influence. This argument is largely rhetorical, and a Western construct.

The question raised by Powell and Pressburger's *They're a Weird Mob*, and to a lesser extent by Powell's *Age of Consent*, remains: in what sense have the origins of film, and of filmic culture and filmic discourse, been driven by European ideals and objectives – of which space and place are primary tools, as well as important goals? This is not to accuse Europeans such as Powell and Pressburger of unprecedented and unyielding imperialism. To use historiography in that way – to slice off periods of history and make them definitional – falsifies the fluidity of time; or, as Henri Bergson might have said it, calls into relief the true nature of matter. Certainly, the term 'Euro-centrism' seems to offer little if any assistance in locating the aesthetic motivations behind film's success, the socio-cultural or economic imperatives that have developed around it or the possible challenges that arise to it. But, equally, there are gaps in the critical record of film that reveal evidence of a link between cinema's historical 'roll out' worldwide and the history and influence of Europe and Europeans. An examination of both *Age of Consent* and *They're a Weird Mob* adds further weight to this discussion.

THE REFRACTIVE MIRROR

Classical colonialist theory, particularly in relation to literature, tells us that 'One of the main features of imperial oppression is control over language'.[9] If anything, a film like *Age of Consent* shows evidence of a control over *visual* language. Here, scenery of Australia's Great Barrier Reef is presented as if in a travelogue: attractive, unusual - indeed exotic - and available. Characters, drawing from the exoticism of Norman Lindsay's original novel, are themselves visual feasts as much as psychological studies; the film's underwater scenes are particularly spectacular; while the film's editing favours visual impact rather than narrative drive. The list continues, and the overall effect is to highlight the refractive nature of the European eye when placed in a non-European environment. In other words, what Powell interprets from Lindsay's novel, and therefore films, is not necessarily what is seen in actuality by the indigenous population.

Although the question of whether cinema is *purely* a language remains vexed, there is enough evidence in a film such as *Age of Consent* to suggest that a visual version of this linguistic metaphor works, and that treating film as a language, however discursive, multi-dimensional and multi-faceted, is a useful way of coming to understand it. Imbued as it is with such artistic generativity, film offers its consumers a particularly strong aesthetic experience, utilising and appealing to the physiology of the eye and ear, to the processing capacities of the right hemisphere of the brain, and to the fluid, non-linear activities of the left hemisphere, memory and the imagination. Powell's European refraction in *Age of Consent* is in keeping with the highly generative nature of film art.

Age of Consent highlights the 'refractive nature of the European eye' in its portrayal of Australian landscape as seen by a returning native.

To offer a suggestion for a new, future study, stimulated by thinking on the visual nature of *Age of Consent* and its colonialist links to another Powell and Pressburger film, *Black Narcissus* (1947): what is now the world's largest film-producing nation, India, might well stand as a primary subject for a consideration of just how far a colonial situation operated in the cinema, even prior to any 'neo-colonialism' inherent in the more general economic hegemony of the USA. This would be a 'new' study, in that not enough has yet been done to determine the role of indigenous aesthetics and local arts in appropriating film form for the maintenance of non-European ideals. Such a study should not be based solely on either cultural comparisons or semiological or aesthetic analysis, but would need to embrace the same multi-dimensional approach that film itself adopts. To use Anthony Gidden's term, it would need to be 'structurationist' in approach[10], include aspects of the economic and social structures inherent in film and filmmaking, relate the role of institutions and societal and individual human agency to the product itself, and give such an analysis historical and comparative spatial scope. Few film scholars would currently be capable, or indeed interested, in undertaking such an important but surely massive study. Without such a reassessment, film criticism today remains an essentially European activity, re-confirming its own value judgments, and given over to assessments of genre, form and response that unfortunately pay very little attention to the notion of an alternative worldview.

LIVING WEIRD

They're a Weird Mob was released in 1966, having been partly funded by Australian sources and partly by the National Film Finance Corporation, London, and the Rank Organisation, who would be the film's British distributors. In Europe, the film was greeted with what can only be described as lack of interest. British critics, according to Powell, received 'the film in dead silence'.[11]

Ian Christie has suggested that the film contains an 'affectionate mockery of Australian customs and the poignancy of the migrant's experience'.[12] This is true, at least on the surface of the filmic discourse. But satire, like metaphor, often under-plays any complexity in the substrata of its meaning in order to allow the viewer or reader to follow more readily its primary shift in plane of reference. That is, like metaphor, it both recreates and reinforces meaning. The 'joke' contained in satire depends on this, and Powell's film manages this shift much less broadly than O'Grady's book. Powell and Pressburger concentrate on the visual clash of Culotta and his environment, using the verbal clashes between the central character's Italian and the other characters' English to provide points of simple slapstick, and even reduces one moment, in which the heat of the Antipodean environment turns Culotta's camera-eye viewpoint to a whirling, blurred shot of cement in a cement-mixer, to an expressionist transition. Interestingly, the transition works structurally but fails to work on the level of visual coherence. It appears crudely televisual and roughly cut, and the viewer is left wondering if the joke is not just a little on the film-makers themselves, in that the comedy of the moment is lost in the fore-grounding of such technical difficulties.

Logistically, in adapting O'Grady's book, the script ignores the first seven pages and picks up on small paragraph on page 14 describing Culotta's ship entering Sydney Harbour. Yet, in the missing seven pages, the references are explicit and hardly superfluous to the book's meaning. In relation to the 'author's' wife: 'she's a nice wife. She's an Australian. Not a black one. The ordinary kind, with one Irish ancestor and one French ancestor and some other kinds further back.'[13] In describing the 'author's' European background:

> Many foreigners came to Milano, and I couldn't find out much about them, because I couldn't understand them. So I studied languages very diligently … I also got a job with a big publishing house, interviewing foreigners and writing stories about them in the magazines. The French people were troublesome because they said so much in answer to a question that much had to be left out of the articles; and the English people were troublesome because they said so little that I had to fill up from my imagination. What I imagined was not always true, and some of the English people could read Italian, and my troubles were plentiful.[14]

And he has this to say in relation to translation:

Suppose you were writing about one of your friends, and what you wrote had to be translated into a foreign language, you could describe his physical peculiarities, his dress, where he lived, where he worked, what he ate. But unless he spoke correct grammatical English, you could not translate what he said. Some colloquialisms you could manage, but in general, the conversations people have with each other cannot be produced in another language.[15]

Adaptations, of course, are filled with questions related to textual fidelity and, at the level of the narrative, questions can rightly be raised about why the script changed the story structure of the original work. The answer seems plain: that Pressburger (if this was his decision) chose what would suit his primary British market, an adaptation that strikingly ignores the possibility of a more European-versus-European themed film in favour of creating a scenario focused on the clash of Europeans with a non-European environment. Interestingly, Pressburger did not start on the project as screenwriter, but was brought in after Powell and O'Grady had tried and, in Powell's view, failed to produce a satisfactory script.

Of course, film relies not only on narrative but also on mechanical duplications of reality, figurative and non-figurative images, music and sounds, the attendant aspects of movement, colour and shape. The opening sequences of Powell and Pressburger's *They're a Weird Mob* further exploit these to set up a text that diligently reiterates the claim that 'the pioneers of cinema as we know it ... were Europeans'.[16] From the outset, the European viewer enters a weird and yet familiar world. People – no 'black ones', to use O'Grady's tongue-in-cheek phrase – battle unfamiliar heat, difficult soil, strange insects, a warm but wild ocean and a light that blinds as much as it reveals. Established European media genres are referenced: media forms and functions that made up none of the basis of O'Grady's original text. These can be broadly described as: the neatly sequenced informational slot; the glossy travelogue; the finely honed character acting; the continuity style; the camera positions and the movements untouched by non-European narrative shapes, storytelling styles or, indeed, versions of non-European notions of beauty. Even the indigenous characters in Powell and Pressburger's film are European pioneers; whereas, in O'Grady's book, they are settler-creators, willing to adopt Nino Culotta, but contemptuous, as is Culotta, of

those who 'are still mentally living in their homelands, who mix with people of their own nationality, and try to retain their own language and customs'.[17] The language and customs *They're a Weird Mob* are indeed pan-European, oppositional and intentional. What use the film makes of the indigenous resources of the southern hemisphere is merely to reinforce the refractive image the filmmakers bring to the set.

The close artistic proximity of *They're a Weird Mob* to the British-ness of Powell and Pressburger's other films is plain. But so is the similarity to the less revolutionary European films of the same period, and the place of British film culture comparative to that of continental European cinema. While the film is not imbued with any strong sense of artistic experiment or intention, there is at least some minor connection with the French New Wave and British 'kitchen sink' films of the period in the obvious determination to place the central character in the heart of a European metropolitan experience – however displaced, spatially unfamiliar and experientially alarming that European metropolis might be. Equally, it displays something of the exuberance of the British pop group films of the period such as *A Hard Day's Night* (1965), *Help!* (1965) or John Boorman's debut, *Catch Us if You Can* (1965). And, perhaps alarmingly some might say, it is not so far removed from the slapstick of Gerald Thomas's *Carry On* films. In fact, 1966 was the year following the release of *Carry on Cowboy*, another film that took British comedy out of Britain, in that case to the American West.

The connection between the two films is not as tenuous at it at first seems, though it is indeed largely based on the physical comedy brought about by a European clash with 'alien' environments. Joel S. Kahn's observation that travellers in the service of Empire often viewed themselves as time travellers has relevance here, in that both films present places seemingly in earlier, less-developed stages of their socio-cultural histories.[18] In *Carry on Cowboy*, Stodge City, in the grip of the Rumpo Kid, and poorly protected by Marshal P. Knutt, is only one small step removed from the rambunctious imperial Sydney of *They're a Weird Mob*, though *Carry on Cowboy* is much closer to a music-hall farce and never approaches the penetration of satire. In both films, the settings and circumstances appear to be 'out of time and place', steps backward to a less 'civilised' and less sophisticated world. In *They're a Weird Mob* the message is more powerful and complex, and its satirical turn even employs the tenets of melodrama, for example in the love story of Nino Culotta and Kay, as well as the stock characterisations of moral deficiency: Tony Bonner as an irate lifeguard, not so much saving Nino from drowning as sinking him with browbeating; Keith Petersen as a drunken jingoist holing up 'foreigners' on a ferry;

Jack Allen as a fat man in a bar insisting Nino match him drink for drink. Whereas O'Grady's book ends with a call to 'learn the language' of the European Antipodes and to 'thank God for letting us be here',[19] Powell and Pressburger's film returns the audience to the rollicking choruses and comedic challenges of its opening sequence, leaving the viewer with the suggestion that this European trip to the southern hemisphere has been little more than a break in time and place, its European aesthetic, politics and socio-economic relations unchanged. Ironically, it would appear to be Powell and Pressburger who are 'still mentally living in their homelands…(retaining) their own language and customs'.[20]

And thus the challenge for the future. The problem of grounding Powell's *They're a Weird Mob* and, to a lesser extent *Age of Consent*, is more complex than it at first seems. Grounding it at all depends on matching a textual and cultural analysis, which initially is revealing in part, with an analysis of the institutionalised relations, social practices and human agency that also produced and received it. The film's undeclared ironic twist that it is the 'weirdness' of contemporary European-ness when shifted to the Pacific, and thus displaced from contemporary Europe, is well matched by its poor reception in Britain. Equally, this must be tempered by the observation that the poor reaction to the film might well be specifically related to its subject matter, and that this does not negate the idea that it may be the familiarity of contemporary Hollywood that draws European audiences to it. In other words: Powell and Pressburger's Europe shifted westward – not necessarily in economic relations or, indeed, methods of producing of film, but certainly in the way in which these films carry forward a European view of beauty, an aesthetic sense, and how this has fed figurative and non-figurative images, dialogue, music and sounds, and all films' attendant aspects of movement, colour and shape. In this way, it carries along with it at least some, if not a great many, elements of story, theme and subject, stories and themes, as it turns out, that owe their origins to Australian authors John O'Grady and Norman Lindsay, but their eventual appearance on screen very much to the European sensibilities of Powell and Pressburger.

NOTES

1. A different version of this chapter appeared in the 'Quo Vadis European Cinema?' issue of the journal *Spectator*, vol. 23 no. 2, Fall 2003, published by the University of Southern California and edited by Luisa Rivi.

2. The script of *They're a Weird Mob* is attributed to 'Richard Imrie', a pseudonym for Pressburger (often addressed as 'Imrie' by Powell). According to Powell, Pressburger rewrote a script already drafted by himself and John O'Grady (Powell, *Million Dollar Movie*, London: Heinemann, 1992, p. 453), so the degree of Pressburger's collaborative involvement should not be overestimated.

3. James Howard, *Michael Powell*, London: Batsford, 1996, p. 88.

4. Bill Rout, 'The Emergence of Australian Cinema', in G. Nowell-Smith (ed.), *The Oxford History of World Cinema*, Oxford: Oxford University Press, 1996, p. 426.

5. Ananda Mitra, *Through the Western Lens: Creating National Images in Film*, London: Sage, 1999, p. 177.

6. The word 'Eurocentric' seems to offer no significant advantage here, so I have avoided it.
    Some European languages scholars have been critical of the term (see Wendy Everett, ed.,
    European Identity in Cinema, Bristol: Intellect, 1996, p. 5) and, although not necessarily
    agreeing with them, it seems true to say that the term has lost its critical strength. 'European-
    ness' seems a less reactionary term, and one that allows the discussion to focus on
    manifestations of socio-economic, cultural and aesthetic type, rather than historical reversal of
    the kind that sees culture as 'singular' or 'pure'.

7. Ginette Vincendeau, *Cassell/BFI Encyclopaedia of European Cinema*, London: Continuum,
    1995, p. xiii.

8. Steven Prince, *The Warrior's Camera: The Cinema of Akiro Kurosawa*, Princeton: Princeton
    University Press, 1991, p. 18.

9. Bill Ashcroft *et al.*, *The Empire Writes Back: Theory and Practice in Colonial Literatures*, London:
    Routledge, 1989, p. 7.

10. Anthony Giddens, *The Constitution of Society: Outline of the Theory of Structuration*, London:
    Polity Press, 1984. See also Christopher Lloyd, *Explanation in Social History*, Oxford:
    Blackwell, 1986, in which Lloyd notes: 'The fundamental claim of structurationism is to be a
    framework for linking action, consciousness, and structure, to study how intentional and
    unintentional action structures the world and how social structures enable and disable action
    and consciousness' (p. 308).

11. Howard, *Michael Powell*, p. 89.

12. Ian Christie, *Arrows of Desire: The Films of Michael Powell and Emeric Pressburger*, London:
    Waterstone, 1985, p. 89.

13. Nino Culotta (aka John O'Grady), *They're a Weird Mob*, Sydney: Ure Smith, 1957, p. 8.

14. Ibid., p. 9.

15. Ibid.,. p. 12.

16. Vincendeau, *Encyclopedia of European Cinema*, p. xiii.

17. Culotta, *They're a Weird Mob*, p. 204.

18. Joel S. Kahn, *Culture, Multiculture, Postculture*, London: Sage, 1995, p. 76.

19. Culotta, *They're a Weird Mob*, p. 205.

20. Ibid., p. 204.

Collaborators

11 Another Life in Movies: Pressburger and Powell

Ian Christie

Emeric Pressburger's unique relationship with Michael Powell has made distinguishing the contribution of each to their joint work extraordinarily difficult – which is almost certainly how they would both have wished it. As late as 1977, they collaborated closely on a novelised version of *The Red Shoes*, which offers considerable insight into the sources and setting of the film;[1] and the recently published transcript of their last joint public appearance, in 1985, shows a close intuitive partnership still at work, in the wake of the successful restoration of *The Life and Death of Colonel Blimp*.[2] The second volume of Powell's memoirs ends with an imagined visit to Pressburger at his cottage in Suffolk, during the course of which Powell has him say:

> You know all those writers on film… are always trying to explain: 'Written, Produced and Directed by Michael Powell and Emeric Pressburger'? You and I know what it means, but they don't. They think there is some secret about it. I'll tell you what it is, Michael. The only secret about it is that we are amateurs. … Telling a story Michael is not a business. It is an art, and we are different from other artists, because we were left alone by Arthur Rank for ten years to go our own sweet way thinking we were professionals.[3]

The day of the imagined visit is that of Pressburger's death, in February 1988, and the fact that Powell's memoir was itself published posthumously five years later gives this account added poignancy as a final 'joint' account of their partnership. But is its invocation of artists as amateurs also subtly misleading? Neither Powell nor Pressburger enjoyed talking about the mechanics of their work, believing this should speak for itself, or remain a tantalising mystery. (Pressburger spoke of 'trapping magic' through the structure of a screenplay; Powell would quote Kipling's 'all art is one', and invoke the great tradition of cinema's craftsmen as his peers). In this, they were no different from most film-makers of their generation, many of whom found the enquiries and speculations of film scholars baffling, if not impertinent. We

cannot now press the film-makers for their explanations, but we can try to understand, as critics and historians, the process that produced, at their best, such miraculously fused works.[4]

   We might start by going back to near the beginning of that period when Pressburger and Powell were 'left alone' by Rank, which was of course a more anxious
time than it later seemed after all that happened subsequently. Among the limited
number of Pressburger's papers that have been preserved, we can find a rare conjunction: a diary entry for the day on which the first clear account of the structure of
Blimp was written down. Pressburger's intermittently kept wartime diary, as Kevin
Macdonald has noted, offers a mixture of personal and professional information, as
well as a commentary on the progress of the war. On 10 February, it records: 'I was
writing in the morning without much success. Blimp is a tough nut to crack …'.[5]
Blimp may have been tough, but a handwritten draft also dated 10 February is
headed 'II After research' and provides the following outline:

> I want to tell this story in three parts.
> The times of each of these are:
>
> I   1902   During the Boer War
> II   1918   During the last few months of the war
> III 1942   ~~An ambulance driver~~ He comes home to join up from Vancouver (or Victoria)
>
> There are 3 girls in the story: a governess
>   a girl from a very good family
>   an ambulance driver
>
> Blimp meets the first girl   in Berlin. He marries somebody else.
> the second   at Victoria Station. She dies in influenza.
> the third   (?)
>
> I want to tell the story from the girl's point of view. She is expressing the author's views.
> Blimp must be looked on from the bird's view.
>
> She sees Blimp   1) as a fool who wants her to hunt, to ride and has little idea
>   about life.
>   2) On the same level, seeing Bl's qualities at war, but also his
>   terrible setbacks about a sporting war, about civilians etc. She
>   would change him. She dies in influenza.
>   3) The third girl sees him a pathetic [?]. He thought she would
>   marry him but she hadn't thought of that.

The significance of this outline lies not so much in what led to its modification, as
in the analytical clarity of the scheme. Three periods; three girls; three points of view
– 'all expressing the author's views'. We know from other surviving papers that Pressburger had already carried out extensive research on all three periods: about the position of governesses, on the changing role of women and on German customs, which

led to him finding the duelling manual that would decisively shape the Berlin episode. We also know that he had already planned the prologue, 'war starts at midnight', very much as it exists in the finished film, up to Blimp's confrontation with the young soldier of today, followed by the shift back to 1902. But what matters here is the schematic underpinning: a plan to look at Blimp externally, 'from the bird's view', and so span forty years of British history.

There is no way of knowing if the scale and structure of *Blimp* was influenced by the example of *Citizen Kane*, which had reached Britain within the previous four months. More immediately, we can guess that the role of the contemporary girl was influenced by Emeric's attraction to the glamorous ex-model Wendy Green, whom he would marry in 1946, and who was then working as an ambulance driver.[6] In any event, the original structure was changed. *Blimp* became in many ways a film about love, and particularly about male inhibition. Instead of three women seeing Blimp critically, the point of view was reversed to become *his* idealised view of womanhood, seen in three phases. The central emotional relationship of the film becomes that between Clive Candy and Theo Kretschmar-Schuldorff, his former rival in honour and love, which may well reflect the close bond now formed between Pressburger and Powell (as Macdonald suggests), but also represents an allegorical relationship between England and Germany that is asserted in the face of the Nazi aberration.[7]

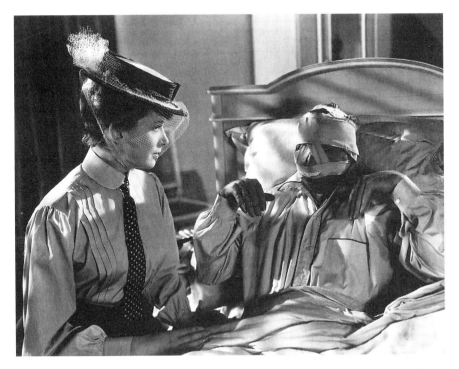

Clive's bandages as he recovers from his duelling wounds in *The Life and Death of Colonel Blimp* make him a kind of invisible man, for us as well as for Edith.

In spite of this displacement, which we may assume was motivated by a combination of propaganda and personal considerations, there remain crucial traces of the original women's point of view in the finished film. After the Berlin duel that leaves both Clive and Theo recuperating in a nursing home, the governess, Edith Hunter (the first girl), visits Clive on orders from the British Embassy and finds his head swathed in bandages.[8] Their meeting becomes comic as he nods helplessly in answer to her questions, but also pathetic, as it reveals the emptiness of his personal life, consisting only of his London club, his Aunt Margaret and game hunting. After the 'Khaki episodes' of the Great War, when Clive takes steps to find the nurse he has seen fleetingly who recalls Edith, their few scenes together precisely stress Candy's limitations (the original 'setbacks'), culminating in a fireside scene where 'Barbara' tenderly asks him not to hum, to which he replies, 'What'll I do if I don't hum?'. We learn from Powell that he found this scene, as written, 'a little short, and besides I wanted something more intimate for the last glimpse of Clive Candy's beloved wife'.[9] So he improvised 'a bit of business which scandalised Emeric – the anti-feminist'.[10]

The effect of this 'business' is not only to create believable intimacy between Clive and Barbara (Powell proudly recalled William Wyler watching him shoot the scene and giving a thumbs-up sign.)[11] It also conveys exactly and concisely Pressburger's original idea that 'she would change him', and contributes to the

Powell improvised some business for Pressburger's original scene between Clive and Barbara in *Blimp* to provide 'something more intimate'.

sense of Clive's essential naivety or emptiness. Here, and when the third girl, Angela, now an ATS driver, discusses him with Theo in 1940, we again see him as if from the outside in a more subtle articulation of dramatic point of view. Elsewhere in the film, Clive's 'emptiness' is displaced onto such elaborate figures as the performance of *Ulysses* he attends with the 'wrong' girl, a latter-day warrior returned to an uncertain reception, and the procession of hunting trophies that chronicle his lonely years of imperial service before the Great War. In each of these instances, where Powell the director elaborated something already in Pressburger's script, or added some improvisation, the effect is invariably to realise the underlying intentions; but also, in a sense, to take co-ownership of the intentions and nuance them. We know from his memoir that Powell was at this time powerfully attracted to the actress Deborah Kerr, who might otherwise have seemed too young and inexperienced for this triple role – as the women in Clive's life had become, after the change in perspective.[12]

Pressburger's original fireside scene stopped with Barbara's submissive response to Clive's recollection of his evening with Theo, having assured him that 'Germany would soon be on its feet again'. Simply: 'She bends down and kisses him.' Instead, in the film as shot, her mention of his 'little habit' speaks volumes about their relationship and makes the impending oblique announcement of her death, from a newspaper notice insert, all the more poignant. Now we know what Clive lost – and also, in microcosm, how the Powell–Pressburger partnership worked.

We learn from the diaries how critical and self-critical Pressburger could be. Kevin Macdonald writes of his concern that *One of Our Aircraft Is Missing* had structural weaknesses; and the already quoted entry of 10 February 1942 records a trip to the cinema to see the production of his story 'Victorious Defeat' as *Breach of Promise*, directed by Roland Pertwee and Harold Huth, which he found 'unbelievably bad'. After the generally appreciative reception of *Blimp* – apart from its much-publicised political difficulties with Churchill and the War Office – the following three Archers' productions would represent the climax of Pressburger and Powell's ambition to make films that satisfied their own creative ambitions as well as meeting the ideological demands of the time.

In terms of their conception, *A Canterbury Tale* and *I Know Where I'm Going!* (henceforth *IKWIG*) can be seen as occupying two poles of Pressburger's narrative imagination, and producing correspondingly different responses from Powell. The former is 'schematic', working through a pattern in order to reveal a paradoxical truth, while the latter is more linear: a form of quest, or 'adventurous expedition', which also reaches a paradoxical conclusion.[13] Interestingly, in view of Powell's characterisation of Pressburger as 'anti-feminist', both have female protagonists; although in *A Canterbury Tale*, this role is split between three characters: the land girl Alison, an American soldier on leave and a British soldier preparing for the D-Day landings.

A Canterbury Tale proposes an 'estrangement' of the familiar, to invoke the Russian theorist (and screenwriter) Viktor Shklovsky's concept.[14] Around the central theme of an American discovering the 'real England' is woven an attempt to explain the country to the city, and the past to the present.[15] A synopsis of the proposed production, dated 22 April 1943, makes clear this strategy. First, the link between the familiar title and this 'new tale' is established:

> Everyone has read or heard of Chaucer's 'Canterbury Tales', tales told by pilgrims of the 14th century about the England they saw around them as they rode, leisurely, upon their pilgrimage to the shrine of St Thomas a Becket in Canterbury Cathedral.
>
> Our Canterbury Tale is a new tale, about the England of 1943, a tale of three pilgrims and of a village on the old Pilgrim's Road.

Then the local magistrate who has 'some very strong views about the English countryside' is introduced, as well as the mystery of the repeated 'slashing' of girls' dresses when they go out with soldiers stationed near the village. The synopsis ends by reflecting on the 'shape' of the story:

> This is an upside-down crime story. Three people (the Girl, the American soldier and the British soldier) set out to find the criminal. All three are successful. But the longer they search for evidence against the offender the less they are interested in his punishment. And when the day comes that he can be handed over to the police there is nobody to hand him over.
>
> As we said at the beginning: our Canterbury Tale is a new tale about the old road and the old town, about a man of Kent who loved the English countryside and about the three pilgrims to Canterbury: one who came seven thousand miles, one who came three hundred, and one, the furthest of all, who came from the great city of London, fifty miles away.

A crime that evaporates – and the shortest distance that turns out to be the greatest. These must inevitably recall the master of paradox, G. K. Chesterton, whom we

know was highly regarded by both Powell and Pressburger, with Powell underlining the fact that he was 'revered' in Pressburger's native Hungary. Chesterton's most enduring creation, Father Brown, is a priest who acts as a detective by means diametrically opposite to those of Sherlock Holmes. Whereas Holmes is an expert in many things, Brown has no expertise except in 'the human heart ... and is only capable of detecting murder mysteries because he is the murderer himself – only, as it were, *in petto*'.[16] What appears initially fantastic in the crimes solved by Brown is revealed to be mundane. Similarly, Chesterton's celebrated use of paradox – 'the rich are the scum of the earth', 'thieves respect property', etc. – is, as Marshall McLuhan observed, greatly indebted to Oscar Wilde's earlier deployment of 'rhetorical paradox and epigram', to challenge conventional thinking, as enshrined in familiar phrases, by reversing these.[17] Chesterton in fact proposed the idea of turning the Prologue and framework of *The Canterbury Tales* into a modern novel, to show what would and would not work in modern terms, and also to underline the novelistic dimension of Chaucer.[18] And *A Canterbury Tale* is probably the most Chestertonian of all the Powell–Pressburger films. I have written elsewhere about the influence Chesterton had on Pressburger, and quoted Jorge Luis Borges on the Father Brown stories as aimed at dispelling a magical view of the world.[19] But the movement of *A Canterbury Tale* is only superficially to demystify the nocturnal assailant and his well-signposted identity. Thereafter, a series of filmic strategies are used to mystify, or perhaps mythologise, Colpeper, so that by the time the characters reach Canterbury, he will not only be able to confer a halo on Peter, but will appear and disappear throughout the town like a sprite or magician.

Borges also speculates of Chesterton that 'something in the make-up of his personality leaned toward the nightmarish', counteracting the dominant British view that his eternal optimism limited his profundity.[20] The effect of Pressburger's imagining of deepest Kent recalls Chesterton's account of his own 'vague and visionary revolt against the prosaic flatness of a nineteenth-century city and civilisation', which would lead to the nightmare climaxes of *The Napoleon of Notting Hill* and *The Man Who Was Thursday*.[21] In Pressburger's version of 'our village', lying 'just a few miles south of Canterbury', 'something shocking' has been happening, night after night. An unknown assailant has been 'slashing' girls' dresses, until 'no girl dares to go out with a soldier; there is a sudden run on the camp library and a remarkable attendance at lectures and discussions'. Powell records how Roger Livesey turned down the role, finding it 'distasteful' because 'he didn't understand the part', which led to Eric Portman – 'who did understand it' – accepting the part, and thus giving Colpeper 'the face of a medieval ascetic'.[22]

For contemporary viewers, Portman's face would also have been familiar as that of the Nazi diehard, Lieutenant Hirth, from *49th Parallel*. But even apart from such associations and Portman's steely confidence, we may wonder why The Archers did not anticipate that slashing women's clothes or pouring glue on their hair – if anything could be more sexually suggestive – would be unacceptable to British critical opinion. Of course, in Shklovskian, and apparently Pressburgerian, terms it is merely a 'device', an excuse to motivate the plot (Alison becomes a victim, so has a motive to discover the perpetrator). However, it is a device that symbolises the violence of Colpeper's beliefs, and one that goes too far – leading to revulsion by the critics, and to Powell's later self-reproaching for not having communicated his doubts to his partner.[23] Where might the ill-advised slasher/glue man have come from? The most obvious source of such motifs was German Weimar cinema, which had already portrayed the most notorious of 'slashers', Jack the Ripper, in two films: Paul Leni's *Waxworks* (*Das Wachsfigurenkabinett*, 1924) and Georg Pabst's *Pandora's Box* (*Die*

The most Chestertonian of the Powell–Pressburger films? Eric Portman well understood the part he was offered in *A Canterbury Tale* as Colpeper, giving him 'the face of a medieval ascetic'.

Conrad Veidt kept in a coffin by his master in *The Cabinet of Dr Caligari*.

Büchse der Pandora, 1929). The progenitor of this genre, *The Cabinet of Dr Caligari* (*Das Kabinett des Dr Caligari*, 1920), had launched Conrad Veidt as Cesare, Caligari's zombie predator; and the main author of *Caligari*, Carl Mayer, lived in London for a decade, and was well known to Pressburger.[24] And apart from the nocturnal attack, there is a distinctly Expressionist quality about such aspects of *A Canterbury Tale* as the interrogation of the village idiot and the magistrate/glue man's hypnotic lecture about the tangibility of the past. Nothing may have been further from Pressburger's or Powell's intentions than to evoke real violence or sexual menace, but the charge of unpleasantness or presenting 'something for the psychologists' would stick, later to be repeated in relation to *The Red Shoes* ('spoiling a fairy tale') and *The Tales of Hoffmann*, and of course revived for Powell's *Peeping Tom*.[25]

The slasher and his replacement the glue man, if they can be attributed firmly to Pressburger, point up what is in fact a general feature of his work as a scriptwriter.[26] For this is one example of a 'literalism' that draws unwanted attention to itself, out of the many that perform their narrative function more inconspicuously or appropriately. The term 'literalism' was introduced into film theory by Paul Willemen in the context of a discussion of verbal language and visual imagery, to avoid presumptions about metaphor, and one of the examples he gives is from a film by Ernst

Famous monsters come to life in Paul Leni's *Waxworks*, including Jack the Ripper.

Lubitsch, *The Mountain Cat* (1921). In this, the hero 'declares his love for Grishka by taking a cardboard heart from under his coat and offering it to her'. She accepts it and demonstrates her 'consuming passion' by eating the heart.[27] However closely wedded to silent-era dramaturgy this may seem – think of Chaplin's many such literalisms – it is Willemen's and my contention that vestiges of such verbal-visual exchange remain present and active in cinema. In the case of *A Canterbury Tale*, it seems likely that, whatever reasons of taste or expediency may have governed the shift from 'slasher' to 'glue man', the latter literalises the idea of 'pouring knowledge'. Certainly, such artistic choices cannot be reduced to single determinations, and this might also be a distant allusion to the 'Sand Man' in E. T. A. Hoffmann's story of the same name, said to throw sand in the eyes of naughty children as a means of scaring them to stay in bed.[28] However, there is enough evidence from across Pressburger's career to suggest that realising literalism played an important part in his creative method: from Clive Candy in *Blimp* 'caught with his trousers down' in a Turkish bath, and the convergence of Peter Carter's medical and legal 'cases' in *A Matter of Life and Death*, to Sammy Rice's nightmare 'fight with the bottle' in *The Small Back Room*.[29]

When The Archers were unable to pursue *A Canterbury Tale*'s theme of Anglo-American relations in *A Matter of Life and Death*, due to a shortage of Technicolor equipment, Pressburger produced a new script at high speed to meet their production commitments. We know that *IKWIG* had a spontaneous and exhilarating origin: 'it just burst out, you couldn't hold it back'; and this has been linked, not implausibly, with the recent birth of his daughter Angela, making it a kind of Yeatsian 'film for my daughter'. Pressburger's initial idea has been reported as 'a film about a girl who wants to get to an island', but is prevented by a storm, and when it becomes possible she no longer wants to go. Again, we are fortunate to have his first notes:

> 1. One foggy night a man and a girl meet in the only hotel of a small port. He is a naval commander, she a young architect. He has come to spend a week's leave on his island. She has come to marry a famous architect who rents the island for the duration.
>
> Somebody has lost his way in the fog and is calling for help. That is how the other two meet. The lost man is the best man.

It is easy to imagine Pressburger's delight in the wordplay of lost man/best man, and indeed to deduce that such play may have contributed to the idea of a best man becoming the cause of 'losing' the marriage. During the remainder of this first sketch, the best man plays a kind of chaperone/marriage-broker role, taking the girl to a house that he designed for some rich people, while a variety of devices are used to throw the girl and the naval officer together and also keep them apart, as the romance grows between them. Without venturing further into the elaboration of *IKWIG*, let us focus on the opening idea or image: 'one foggy night a man and a girl meet … in a small port' (the film's working title was 'The Misty Island'). In many ways, this harks back to the lyrical simplification attempted in such late silent-era films as Germaine Dulac's *L'Invitation au voyage* (1927) or, in the same year, Friedrich Murnau's *Sunrise*. The former took its inspiration from Baudelaire's poem of the same title and portrays a married woman's brief promise and fantasy of escape from a loveless marriage in the company of a sailor. *Sunrise*, written by Pressburger's friend Carl Mayer, is subtitled 'a song of two humans', and its story remains boldly elemental: a Woman of the City bewitches The Man, a young married farmer, tempting him to kill his wife to follow her to the city.

Pam Cook has already suggested a comparison between *Sunrise* and *IKWIG* in terms of an 'unconscious relationship' and a shared 'dream-like quality'.[30] However, my concern is with this as an example of how a film-maker who is not working in an avowedly experimental mode can preserve the integrity or simplicity of the orig-inating image, while developing an acceptable narrative. Another of Shklovsky's con-cepts is relevant here: that of 'retardation', or holding back the too-rapid unfolding of plot. There is a well-documented tradition of poets trying to preserve the spon-taneity of their *données*. Coleridge claimed to have dreamed 'Kubla Kahn' while in an opium-induced sleep and merely transcribed it, until he was interrupted; and, in terms that foreshadow Pressburger, Robert Browning said of his 'Childe Roland to the Dark Tower Came':

Powell's deep love of Scotland and delight in shooting on Mull for *I Know Where I'm Going!* made him contemptuous of documentaries that just showed 'a lot of waves and pretty pictures'.

> Childe Roland came upon me as a kind of dream. I had to write it, then and there, and I finished it the same day, I believe. But it was simply that I had to do it. I did not know then what I meant beyond that, and I'm sure I don't know now.

Recently, the German film-maker Tom Tykwer identified this dilemma in explaining the unusual form of his *Run, Lola, Run* (*Lola rennt*, 1998), and the psychoanalyst Annegret Mahler-Bungers has commented on his discussion by making a comparison between Freud's 'dream work' and 'film work', in which unconscious thoughts are translated into visual images by means of such procedures as displacement, condensation and the like.[31]

In *IKWIG*, the original idea was considerably elaborated, giving Joan a childhood and extensive detail for her journey to Mull, before she does eventually appear – in one of the film's most memorable images – as 'a girl on a foggy night' in a small port. Before reaching this threshold moment, one of the film's elaborations is in fact a dream sequence. As Joan travels north on the sleeper, her marriage is fantasised as a business arrangement (she is literally marrying her husband's company, symbolised by its imposing buildings), while her journey to Scotland translates into a model landscape draped in tartan and a toy train. The primary – perhaps we could say, following Freud, 'manifest' – function of the dream within the film is clear: it conveys Joan's inner doubts, in spite of her outer confidence about knowing 'where she's going'. In this respect, it belongs to a notable trend in both British and American cinema of the 1940s, involving 'symptomatic' dreams. It also marks the beginning of Powell and Pressburger's use of dreams and hallucinations in almost all of their subsequent films, from *A Matter of Life and Death* to *The Tales of Hoffmann*, reflecting a growing preoccupation with divided protagonists.

We cannot know for certain which of the partners originated the dream sequence, but there are grounds for thinking it may have been Powell, responding to the intentions of Pressburger's developing script and also adding his own interpretation.[32] In his first film with a Scottish island setting, *The Edge of the World* (1937), Powell had already used extended superimposition to create a memory or 'vision' effect, apparently influenced by his essentially romantic view of Scotland. But although this attitude is still apparent in *IKWIG*, notably in the scenes around Erraig House and the castle of Moy, the film's protagonist at least starts out as a brisk, unsentimental Englishwoman. We might therefore assume that the tartan-clad hills of her dream imply an Englishwoman's tourist view of Scotland; while we might also note that the motif of the heroine's fantasy/desire in Dulac's *L'Invitation au voyage* was a model ship. However, there is a further possible implication. In his memoirs, Powell expresses particular disdain for documentary, dismissing Flaherty's *Man of Aran* as 'just a lot of waves and seaweed and pretty pictures', and citing the GPO's *Night Mail* as evidence that 'documentaries are for disappointed feature film-makers and out-of-work poets'.[33] Harry Watt's widely admired film shows the mail train racing northwards, rhythmically accompanied by Auden's verse and Britten's music. Might not the toy train of *IKWIG*, accompanied by Allan Gray's rapidly modulating variations on the eponymous folk tune and the solemn station announcements, be a typically Powellian jibe at this most famous of 1930s documentaries – an ironic *clou* deftly punctuating Pressburger's narrative?

Yet from what information there is about the production of *IKWIG*, it soon becomes clear how Powell's romantic infatuation with the Scottish coastal landscape – and with the figure of Catriona as played by Pamela Brown, who takes Joan in while she is stranded by the weather – closely served Pressburger's original vision. Without Powell's determination to convey 'the fabled Hebrides' in cinematic terms,[34] we would not have Joan stepping precariously into the world she does not yet know is her destiny; and without the equally striking silhouette image of Catriona hunting (like 'a modern Diana', as Cook aptly describes her) – apparently all that Pressburger would allow of what Powell shot on location with Brown – we would not have the evocative prefiguring of a life that potentially awaits her.[35]

Although Powell and Pressburger stopped working together regularly in the mid-1950s and formally dissolved their partnership, they continued to co-operate on a variety of projects, some of which remained unsuspected due to the use of pseudonyms, and others because the films were never made. Unrealised projects, however, can be highly revealing about their respective attitudes towards the con-

Pressburger on set with Anton Walbrook during the shooting of one of The Archers' last films, *Oh Rosalinda!!*

struction of a film. And all the more so when they were living far apart and obliged to communicate by letter. One such project of the late 1960s was *Night on a Bald Mountain*, a Cold War spy story, no doubt considered promising due to the success of the Bond films and of recent John Le Carré and Len Deighton adaptations. Several letters survive from Pressburger, then living in Austria, to Powell, commenting on the evolution of the script as it travelled between them. One of these is worth quoting at length for the insight it gives into Pressburger's subtle approach to motivation and structure:

> I'm sorry to admit, but I can't think of a better ending for Kalesch [a Czech or Slovak collabo-
> rator with the Russians]. (I don't say there isn't a better ending, I just can't think of one.) What
> would a basically simple minded fellow in Kalesch's predicament do when he realises he has been
> cheated into refraining to use his weapon which gave him such confidence all through the night?
> Would he shoot himself? Would he just say something profound? Would he, in blind rage, just
> fire his gun after them, watched by Kanek who could remark (with understatement and sympa-
> thy) 'They're out of range comrade'. They *are* out of range, of course. So far out of range, in fact,
> that they wouldn't even hear the shots. The last statement is not merely the author's way to round
> up his story with a literary phrase, but with the hope that a way may be found to convey it to the
> viewer, thus blowing up Kalesch's tragedy out of all proportion.[36]

Earlier letters on the project had dealt in minute detail with considerations of naming the characters and dialogue, but in this extract we can hear both Pressburger's scrupulous weighing of the implications of different endings, and his appeal to his old partner to 'convey to the viewer' what can only be a literary phrase on paper. This is more than merely a division of labour between Pressburger the writer and Powell the practical film director. It goes to the heart of why the two had joined forces nearly thirty years earlier, when they realised that through intimate co-oper-ation they could achieve much more than by working separately.[37]

NOTES

1. Michael Powell and Emeric Pressburger, *The Red Shoes*, London: Avon Books, 1978 (written in 1977).
2. David Lazar, ed., *Michael Powell Interviews*, Jackson: University of Mississippi Press, 2003.
3. Michael Powell, *Million Dollar Movie*, London: Heinemann, 1992, p. 579.
4. I have already investigated the sources of *The Life and Death of Colonel Blimp* in an edition of the screenplay published in 1994 (London: Faber & Faber), and those of *A Matter of Life and Death* in a monograph of the same title (London: BFI, 2000).
5. Quotations from this and other unpublished papers by Emeric Pressburger appear by courtesy of the Pressburger estate.
6. On Pressburger's relationship with 'Wendy', see Kevin Macdonald, *Emeric Pressburger: The Life and Death of a Screenwriter*, London: Faber & Faber, 1994, pp. 210ff.
7. On the production history and interpretation of the film, see my introduction to the screenplay.

8. Sequence 41, Christie, ed., *The Life and Death of Colonel Blimp*, pp. 151–5.

9. Michael Powell, *A Life in Movies*, London: Faber & Faber, 2000 [paperback edition, revised], p. 411.

10. Powell's account is confirmed by the fact that this exchange does not appear in the original typescript: see Christie, ed., *The Life and Death of Colonel Blimp*, p. 243–4.

11. Powell, *A Life in Movies*, p. 411.

12. Ibid.

13. To use category 9. D (1) from Georges Polti, *The Thirty-Six Dramatic Situations*, trans. Lucille Ray, Boston: The Writer, Inc., 1977, p. 36. (This is translated from Polti's *Les Trente-six situations dramatiques*, Paris: Mercure de France, 1912, which is in turn based on Carlo Gozzi's analysis of the 18th century, discussed by Schiller and Goethe. Polti has since enjoyed a new lease of life within the teaching screenplay-writing community.)

14. Also referred to as 'defamiliarisation' in Russian Formalist theory. For an account of 'estrangement' based on examples from Tolstoy, see Viktor Shklovsky, *Theory of Prose* (1929), trans. Benjamin Sher, Illinois: Dalkey Archive Press, 1991, pp. 6–9. Shklovsky worked as a screenwriter and script doctor in Soviet cinema from the mid-1920s to the 60s.

15. See my other essay in this volume, 'History Is Now and England'.

16. Ronald Knox, paraphrasing Chesterton's *The Secret of Flambeau*, in 'Chesterton's Father Brown', in Denis J. Conlon, ed., *G. K. Chesterton: A Half-Century of Views*, Oxford: Oxford University Press, 1987, p. 135.

17. H. Marshall McLuhan, 'Where Chesterton Comes in', in Conlon, ed., *G. K. Chesterton*, pp. 76–7.

18. G. K. Chesterton, *Chaucer*, London: Faber & Faber, 1932, p. 163.

19. Ian Christie, *Arrows of Desire: The Films of Michael Powell and Emeric Pressburger*, London: Faber & Faber, 1994 (2nd edn), p. 7. See also: Ian Christie, 'Alienation Effects: Emeric Pressburger and British Cinema', *Monthly Film Bulletin* vol. 51 no. 609, October 1984, p. 318.

20. Jorge Luis Borges, 'On Chesterton', in *Other Inquisitions 1937–1952*, New York: Washington Square Press, 1966, p. 87.

21. G. K. Chesterton, *Autobiography* (1936), London: Arrow Books, 1959, p. 126.

22. Powell, *A Life in Movies*, p. 441.

23. Ibid.

24. Pressburger's diary records giving the impoverished Mayer money in 1941: 'he is so nice and so helpless'. Macdonald, *Emeric Pressburger*, p. 186. In a later interview, at the time of *Peeping Tom*, Powell appeared to confirm the Weimar origins of Colpeper's violence, describing it as 'a Continental idea that did not fit into an English film'. 'Mr Powell on Making Horror Films', in Lazar, ed., *Michael Powell Interviews*, p. 23.

25. The two female reviewers of *A Canterbury Tale*, C. A. Lejeune in the *Observer* and Dilys Powell in *The Sunday Times*, both referred to the glue-man motif as inviting psychiatric or psychological diagnosis (both 15 April 1944). Two reviewers of Powell's *Peeping Tom* in 1960 returned to the theme: William Whitebait – '*A Canterbury Tale* and *A Matter of Life and Death* more than hinted at morbidity (*New Statesman*); Derek Hill – 'the more bizarre tendencies of [Powell's] mind in *A Canterbury Tale*' (*Tribune*). See Ian Christie, 'The Scandal of *Peeping Tom*', in Christie, ed., *Powell, Pressburger and Others*, London: BFI, 1978, pp. 54–5.

26. Pressburger accepted full responsibility for the glue man in a joint interview conducted by the author with Powell and Pressburger at the National Film Theatre in 1985, transcribed in Lazar, *Michael Powell Interviews*, pp. 127–8.

27. Paul Willemen, 'Reflections on Eikhenbaum's Concept of Internal Speech in the Cinema', *Screen* vol. 15 no. 4, Winter 1974–5, p. 64.

28. Hoffmann's story is one of the main texts discussed by Freud in 'The Uncanny' (1919), in Albert Dickson, ed., *Art and Literature*, Penguin Freud Library, vol. 14, London: Penguin Books, 1985. It would also have been familiar to Pressburger, who had lived in Germany for a decade.

29. In my earlier essay, I suggested that Pressburger's use of literalism might have been reinforced by the experience of changing language, as he did three times. Arthur Koestler, a fellow Hungarian refugee, wrote of the 'rediscovery of the cliché' as a trap awaiting writers who learn a new language, without knowing its baggage. However, what might disable a writer of books could also profit a screenwriter.

30. Pam Cook, *I Know Where I'm Going!* London: BFI Film Classics, 2002, pp. 16–17.

31. Annegret Mahler-Bungers, 'A Post-Modern Valkyrie: Psychoanalytic Considerations on Tom Tykwer's *Run, Lola, Run* (1998)', in Andrea Sabbadini, ed., *The Couch and the Silver Screen*, London: Brunner-Routledge, 2003, p. 83.

32. A reason for attributing the dream to Pressburger might be his early collaboration with Erich Kästner and Max Ophuls on *Dann schon lieber Lebertran* (*I'd Rather Have Cod-liver Oil*, 1930), which involves a children's fantasy about heaven. But surrealistic and expressionistic dreams had been a familiar feature of the 1920s European cinema that shaped both Powell and Pressburger.

33. Powell, *A Life in Movies*, p. 241.

34. Ibid., p. 464.

35. On Pressburger having 'ruthlessly excised' most of Powell's location exteriors, see Macdonald, *Emeric Pressburger*, p. 246. Cook sees Catriona and Joan as 'reverse images' of one other, sharing 'an androgynous quality, a fighting spirit and an arrogance'. Cook, *I Know Where I'm Going!*, p. 39.

36. Letter from EP to MP, 13 April 1969, from Thiersee, Austria. The last part of this letter, dealing with Pressburger's novel in progress, is quoted in Macdonald, *Emeric Pressburger*, pp. 389–90.

37. Andrew Moor has taken a welcome step towards analysing the unmade projects with his account of the proposed Richard Strauss biography, *The Golden Years*, Screen 46:1, Spring 2005.

12 Hein Heckroth and The Archers

Nanette Aldred [1]

Our business was not realism but surrealism. We were storytellers, fantasists ... We storytellers started with naturalism and finished with fantasy. [2]

In his autobiography, *A Life in Movies*, Michael Powell stated this film-making aim and it was, I shall argue, largely through their collaboration with the painter, Hein Heckroth, that Powell and his partner Emeric Pressburger, most fully achieved their fantastic storytelling. How this collaboration was achieved has to be seen as an alchemical reaction of various elements, including Heckroth's aesthetics, his work as a fine artist and stage designer, and Powell's and Pressburger's film-making practice in relation to contemporary British film.

In Britain, Heckroth is known primarily for his designs for *The Red Shoes* (1948). However, it was not as a film designer that he first came to the attention of the modern English art world. In May 1943, he held his first London exhibition (which consisted of his Surrealist paintings) at the Modern Art Gallery in Charles Street, off the Haymarket. The highly regarded, influential critic and current champion for the Surrealist movement, Herbert Read wrote a foreword to the catalogue. [3] Complementing his work as a cultural commentator, Read was supporting political refugee artists in a number of ways: he had found positions for some artists and designers in London and was one of the supporters of the call to allow Heckroth to return from Australia where he had been interned as an 'enemy alien' since the beginning of the war. [4] The campaign succeeded, and Heckroth came back to England, where his wife Ada had remained with their daughter Nandi; Ada was working as a fashion-plate painter for *Vogue* and costume designer on a number of films, including Humphrey Jennings's *The True Story of Lili Marlene* (1944). In 1934, Heckroth had left Germany, where he was working as theatre designer with the Ballet Jooss, travelling to Paris to join Ada and Nandi, who had been living there since 1933 (as distant members of the Rothschild family, they had left the country

Hein Heckroth had already worked as a theatre and ballet designer before he entered cinema and took full responsibility for production design on *The Red Shoes*.

as soon as Hitler became Chancellor). Heckroth had worked on theatre design in Essen, where he taught at the Folkwangschule, and had already achieved recognition for his earlier Ballet Jooss designs, specifically for *The Green Table*. Known as a part of the Neue Sachlichkeit group of painters, he was a friend of Oskar Schlemmer (also associated with that group) during the 1920s when Schlemmer was working on innovative theatre and ballet designs.[5] Their engagement with 'new objectivity' or 'magic realism' led to a metaphysical notion of the resonance of the 'thing-in-itself' to carry meaning. This element would take on a quality of uncanniness in Heckroth's later work on films like *The Tales of Hoffmann* (1951) which exhibited an expressionist painting style. Heckroth was also associated with the Mutter Ey Gallery, as were Otto Dix and Max Ernst, the former associated with Neue Sach-lichkeit, the latter with poetic Surrealism.[6]

Heckroth had been introduced to Read by Roland Penrose and his wife Lee Miller (who knew him from Paris) shortly before Heckroth started teaching art at Dartington School near Totnes in Devon in 1935. Dartington Hall had been bought by Leonard and Dorothy Elmhirst in 1925 in order that they might establish an independent school based on their belief in the importance of the arts in education. By the mid-1930s, Dartington had become renowned as a centre for the arts and was regarded as a radical educational experiment in London cultural circles. Heckroth had been given responsibility for the school of fine art, and while he was teaching there, Penrose lent his collection of modern art to the department.[7] Heckroth's knowledge of and reputation in theatre design was an added attraction for the Elmhirsts, who would later invite the Jooss Ballet to make Dartington their base.[8] Walter Gropius, a refugee from the Bauhaus, was involved in rebuilding the large barn as a theatre; the American artist Mark Tobey was already at Dartington; and, in 1938, Cecil Collins, who had shown in the 1936 International Surrealist Exhibition, joined them. David Mellor has argued that the dominant notion of the artist in the late 1930s at Dartington was of a special being who could stand for the 'other' of the war and its concurrent rational and industrial society. This was a theme that The Archers would explore later in their films designed by Heckroth. Mellor goes on to argue that 'probably the main intellectual current at Dartington Hall at the end of the 1930s … was the Apocalyptic, Expressionist ballet-drama. There it was performed by the Ballet Jooss and [designed by] the painter Hein Heckroth.'[9]

That the theatre designs were instrumental in giving Heckroth the visibility and support he needed as an artist was emphasised in Read's introduction to the wartime exhibition in London. Read argued that an important relationship existed between Heckroth the stage designer and Heckroth the painter, and stressed how the activities enhanced each other rather than the one being merely a necessity or even a prostitution of his art. Read emphasised that Heckroth's earlier interest in Cubism had given him an understanding of what the Cubist idiom offered for three-dimensional design; when Heckroth later explored a Surrealist mode, Read considered it as a continuation of this exploration of formal and stylistic innovation rather than a plundering of available registers: 'each canvas', he thought, 'is a miniature theatre in which a surreal drama is enacted, and in which, incidentally, the artist displays his considerable gifts for decorative colour and composition'.[10] While Read noted that this was Heckroth's first painting exhibition in Britain, the tone of the piece suggests that its audience would be familiar with his ballet designs, some of which had been seen in The Dance Exhibition at the Leicester Gallery in 1938. A larger audience would have known of his designs for *The Green Table* (which had won the first prize in the prestigious Les Archives Internationales de la Danse in 1932 in Paris) and for *Pandora*, which had been exhibited around Britain in national and municipal galleries under the auspices of the wartime Council for the Encouragement of Music and Art (CEMA). Read was pleased that the Modern Art Gallery exhibition was bringing 'somewhat belatedly to our attention an artist who, already famous in his own country, has been expelled by political events [and for whom it would be necessary] to rebuild his reputation in a land of exile.'[11] Read also mentioned that Heckroth had designed the Arts Theatre Club production of *War and Peace* that same year (1943). In fact, Heckroth had come to England to design *A Kingdom for a Cow* by Brecht and Weil for a production financed by Edward James, and it was after seeing this earlier production that the Elmhirsts invited him to Dartington.[12] It was also after seeing *War and Peace* that Vincent Korda[13] (art director and brother

Powell (centre) with Jack Cardiff (l) and production designer Alfred Junge (far r.) on location for *A Matter of Life and Death*.

of the influential film producer Alexander Korda) introduced Heckroth to Tom White, the production manager of the Denham Studios, which meeting led to Heckroth's involvement in films.[14] His first designs were for the soldiers' costumes in Gabriel Pascal's film of G. B. Shaw's *Caesar and Cleopatra* (1944). Heckroth established a reputation for historically and culturally specific designs on this production, and as a result was taken up by another significant European designer, Alfred Junge, who had already worked on a number of Powell and Pressburger productions and was preparing his designs for *A Matter of Life and Death* for The Archers.[15]

Powell was looking for someone who could help him realise his ambition for visual narrative: to explore the possibilities of using imagery to tell the story. He was interested in filming ballet, especially in what film could offer ballet as an art form and what ballet could offer film as a total experience, and, as we have seen, Heckroth had already worked at the centre of modern ballet. This quest came at a crucial intersection in the recent history of British visual culture. Since the late 1930s, Britain had been developing its own native ballet tradition and, with its increased exposure through CEMA support for touring companies, dance had achieved a good critical reception. Ever since Diaghilev (some say the model for Lermontov in *The Red Shoes*) had established a precedent for using the best among contemporary easel painters for his ballets earlier in the century, the new ballet companies had used prominent contemporary artists like Graham Sutherland (whom Heckroth would get to know in 1951), John Piper, Edward Burra, Leslie Hurry and John Armstrong for new productions at London's Sadler's Wells theatre. A similar development had

taken place in relation to British films; the prominence they had achieved occasioned
by the relative wartime isolation had excited film-makers and critical commentators
with the possibility of a thriving British film industry in the future.

> Hein Heckroth was my contact with European art, when England, my England, threatened to
> smother me, or starve me out.[16]

In order to understand the significance of the introduction of Heckroth to The
Archers production company, it is necessary to consider the dominant style and
theory of British film at that time. Its critical reception largely depended on the
theoretical accounts published by film-makers associated with the documentary
movement. If Britain claimed a native film aesthetic, it was that promoted by the
influential London Film Society and those commentators associated with the documentary movement in the 1930s whose theories and practice gave film-making a
serious social and political role. In its 'creative treatment of actuality', documentary
aimed to show 'real' people in 'real' environments, and would come into its own as a
style in many British wartime films and the post-war productions from the Ealing
Studios, eventually feeding into the British 'kitchen sink', new wave films. Documentary realism in films was coded though framing and lighting, emotional

Powell had met many artists while working in Nice for Rex Ingram, seen here (r) with the
dancer Hubert Stowitts, a former protegé of Pavlova, who appeared in *The Magician*.

responses evinced by a serious musical or literary soundtrack that often used contemporary composers like Benjamin Britten, writers such as E. M. Forster and
Laurie Lee and painters like William Coldstream and the polymath Humphrey Jennings. These 'high' art elements of the documentary movement were reworked in
The Archers' opera and ballet films. Powell came from outside the British tradition,
having originally worked in silent films in France with the Americans Rex Ingram
and Harry Lachmann, who emphasised spectacle in their films and made the visual
composition carry the narrative. Although by the time that Powell began working in
film, such cinema of spectacle was largely mistrusted, he aimed to revive the tradition, and The Archers' narratives worked increasingly in a nonverbal understanding of the images themselves (although Pressburger, unsurprisingly, always believed
in the importance of dialogue.) Powell called *The Red Shoes* a 'Freudian ballet',
believing that images could directly address the subconscious in a way that verbal
narrative might not. [17] He aimed to transform, not to record, reality, and with Heckroth as production designer, it seemed a target that The Archers could achieve.

As we have seen, British film criticism had not developed a way of successfully
engaging with cinema's own aesthetic – with the visual – and its critical language was
often unable to articulate the concerns of The Archers' films. Indeed, The Archers
drew attention to cinema language often by breaking its conventions: in the direct
address to camera, the arrested movement with a continued soundtrack and the jokes
about 'Technicolor' earth – all of which appear in *A Matter of Life and Death*, for
instance. Powell's first personal film, *The Edge of the World* (1937), worked within the
documentary aesthetic. Like other figures in the poetic documentary films, the characters became mythical British folk in their elemental struggle within a mystical
British landscape, a theme that he developed to greater dramatic effect with The
Archers in such films as *A Canterbury Tale* (1944) and *I Know Where I'm Going!* in
the following year. Their final landscape film was in a totally different register. *Gone
to Earth* (1950) was in colour and designed by Heckroth, who used both colour and
images of the landscape symbolically and emotively. The pivotal love scene at the
centre of the story between Hazel Woodus and Squire Reddin is rendered as a silent
film episode, the whole weight of the momentous scene carried by the visuals and
the soundtrack. There is no dialogue.

The Red Shoes, in its early sequences, does gesture towards a documentary approach
in its study of Covent Garden market and the world of the ballet also associated with
that part of working London. But, like *The Tales of Hoffman*, it does something else
too: it attempts consciously to make film into a significant art form; in fact, the ultimate art form, as a form of Wagnerian synaesthesia, the ideal medium for bringing all
the arts together in a spectacle that included word and image, music and movement.
In seeing commercial mainstream film as a vehicle for serious art, The Archers dif-
fered from the contemporary film aesthetic and aspiration.[18] The most apparent manifestation of this serious engagement with art was in the designs and paintings that
Heckroth produced as integral to the films. His paintings did not merely provide a
model for the film set; they often actually were the place where the events took place.

A gesture towards documentary? The Royal Opera House interior reconstructed at Pinewood for early sequences of *The Red Shoes*.

The importance of Heckroth to this radical process was that he was first a painter rather than a film designer, and thus used film to create images as he would on the two-dimensional canvas, rather than the architectonic illusionism of the stage.

> I have a poetic approach…I have to find a theme or something that appeals to my imagination and work it out from there. [19]

Heckroth worked on all The Archers' films between 1946 and 1956, during which time the group created some of the most memorable screen images in Britain. An important aspect of working with The Archers was the encouragement they offered to individuals to explore the formal and technical possibilities of film, combined with the discipline of working collaboratively. Heckroth started as a costume designer on The Archers' production of *A Matter of Life and Death* (1946) and *Black Narcissus* of 1947 before becoming production designer on subsequent films like *The Red Shoes*, *The Small Back Room* (1949), *Gone to Earth*, *The Elusive Pimpernel* (1950), *The Tales of Hoffmann* and *Oh … Rosalinda!!* (1955). He was artistic adviser for *The Battle of the River Plate* (1956), and he invited Powell to work with him on the independent production of *The Sorcerer's Apprentice* (1956) and *Bluebeard's Castle* (1964). He won an Oscar for his designs for *The Red Shoes* and a special prize at Cannes for *The Tales of Hoffmann.* There were other abortive joint projects, of which *The Tempest* would have been the most interesting and probably would have shown the Powell–Heckroth collaboration at its finest.[20] In this chapter, I want to concentrate on *The Red Shoes* and *The Tales of Hoffmann.*

The production designer of the earlier films was Alfred Junge, and it is important to note why he was not included in The Archers' films after 1946. After all, it was Junge who had given some of the earlier films their distinctive style. In Powell's words:

> It was a case of realism versus fantasy. Alfred was the realist. It might be assumed that the man who designed *A Matter of Life and Death* would be the right man to design an original Freudian film-ballet, but it was not so. Everything in Alfred's Other World had been strictly literal and logical ... when I told him that once the curtain had gone up for the performance [of 'The Red Shoes'], we would no longer be in a theatre but inside the heads of two young people who were falling in love, what would he say then? ... He said what I feared he would say: 'Micky, you want to go too far.' ... And when one of my collaborators tells me that I want to go too far, that's the end of the collaboration.[21]

Powell considered that magic and special effects should be the job of the art department, rather than technicians, and took on 'a staff of real painters in charge of costume, décor and make-up'.[22] It is also possible, however, that Junge was replaced because he was too overbearing and intransigent, less willing to compromise or collaborate.[23] As they discussed the project, it was clear that Heckroth understood what Powell had wanted and was capable of taking it further as a performance than even Powell originally imagined.

BEYOND THE LIMITS OF NATURALISM: *THE RED SHOES*

Heckroth had not had overall responsibility as production designer on a film before this, but, as we have seen, he had worked extensively in the theatre. The challenge of *The Red Shoes*, for him, was in creating the designs for a staged ballet that would metamorphose into a filmic ballet able to transcend time and space. During the following year, he produced 130 oil paintings as well as numerous colour sketches, a prodigious output at any reckoning. The next radical move was the decision to choreograph the ballet around the designs and, to this end, Heckroth's paintings and sketches were put together to animate a 17-minute film sequence where he worked with the composer Brian Easdale to construct the ballet of 'The Red Shoes'. In the ballet scene in the film, Powell probably came as close as he would ever come to realising his ambition of making a 'total' film, whereby the elements were synthesised from the basic ingredients of sound and image adding the movements and gestures of the dancers, the light and shade provided by the lighting technicians, the expressionist colour of the paintings, the colour and form of the costumes and the camera shots and rhythm of the editing and music. In the Romantic-Symbolist tradition that Powell espoused, he wanted films to attain to the condition of music, and this he was able to achieve through

An impossible region of surreal landscape: the *Red Shoes* ballet was first painted by Heckroth, then realised in the studio and lab using mainly matte techniques, so that there was 'seventeen minutes of painting'.

his editor Reginald Mills. Mills (like Pressburger) loved opera and was able to edit the film by following the score. He and Heckroth, the painter who had extensive experience in theatre and opera design and a real love of ballet, were crucial to The Archers here.

Pressburger's original story concerned a young dancer who declares she is prepared to live only for her art. A ballet based on Hans Christian Andersen's fairy tale is written especially for her, but subsequently her 'real' life begins to echo the fate of the fairy tale character. The power of Heckroth's original paintings determines the reading of the film in its final form. The tone of the ballet scene is constructed through his haunting image of the over-towering church and the townscape, whose buildings are elongated for emotional resonance over the small figure of the wearer of the fatal red shoes. The ballet starts within a conventional stage setting but, as it develops, opens into an impossible region of a surreal landscape. The significance of Heckroth's contribution lay in his ability to move the action between the stage and his painted visualisation. His earlier paintings within the surrealist idiom played a significant part in this imaging, enabling him to free the *mise en scène* representing the ballerina's fantasy world through painting. In this way, The Archers' film goes beyond cinema's usual reliance upon the very notion of the 'real' to re-present the world as constructed reality: as a fantasy. The film-makers Buñuel and Dali created their version of Surrealist film by the bizarre juxtaposition of real objects – burning trees, giraffes, etc. – in an unlikely sequence (following the poet Lautréamont's influential assertion that Surrealist beauty was like 'the chance meeting on a dissecting table of an umbrella and a sewing machine'). With Hein Heckroth, The Archers reworked another definition of Surrealism, with its painterly (rather than literary) emphasis on the personal symbolic marks of the unconscious – an automatist all-over use of the space of visual representation.

A number of Heckroth's images and concerns in the films had been apparent in his Surrealist paintings since 1937. Versions of the demons that appear to Vicky from her subconscious had populated Heckroth's paintings from *Vogelmenschen* in 1943, but were reworked in the film within the expressionist coding of the mask. This painting also recalls the final scene of 'The Red Shoes' ballet where Vicky dances to the sea and sees the figure of Lermontov, the impresario, as an oceanic god transmogrified from the shoreline rocks. *Free Love* and *Nina* of 1939 contain references to textures like the cellophane and gauze that Heckroth employed (more successfully) in his film work. *Free Love* uncannily prefigures the fragmentation of Olympia's body in *The Tales of Hoffmann*, while the red boots in the painting seemed to be symbolically empty, waiting to be filled like the red ballet shoes in the film.[24] The deep, recessive space between the two walls that lead Vicky into her subconscious is a key scene in Heckroth's work and one that indicates a mental journey into one's past. In his late German television film, *The Wall* (1969), he would use the same motif to explore his own inner world. That construction of space had been coded for anxiety in Giorgio de Chirico's *The Mystery and Melancholy of a Street* (1914) and reappears in Max Ernst's painting *Two Children*

A pre-war painting by Heckroth prefigured the fragmentation of the doll Olympia (Moira Shearer) in the first act of *The Tales of Hoffmann*.

Threatened by a Nightingale of 1924. De Chirico's paintings also use shadows as suggestively and threateningly as Heckroth employs the shadow of the shoemaker in the ballet to indicate his presence in distorted and monochrome expressionist terms[25] – terms of which Powell was fully aware from his love of silent film, and Pressburger knew from his work in the German film studios.

METAMORPHOSIS AND *TROMPE L'OEIL: THE TALES OF HOFFMANN*

The French composer Jacques Offenbach based *The Tales of Hoffmann* on a selection of tales by the German Romantic writer E. T. A. Hoffmann, with a prologue and epilogue derived from a pseudo-biographical account of the conditions of their telling. The tales are macabre fantasies of love and danger with a chorus of doppelgängers, soul-stealers, automata, mysterious scientists and figures of death. They blur the distinction between dreaming and waking and explore the psychology of perception. The main characters of the opera are Hoffmann and his two doubles – one evil and one good (played in the film by Robert Helpmann and Pamela Brown) – who have accompanied him in his romantic quest for love. The complex circular narrative concerns Hoffmann and Stella, the dancer with whom he is in love. She seems perfect, not least because she combines the qualities of his previous three loves. These relationships have been with a doll, a courtesan and an artist; each of whose stories is played out in turn. Each episode of *The Tales* is recounted between the first and last acts of Stella's ballet performance, and each of the tales prefigures the end of their relationship.[26]

From the beginning, the emphasis is on the visual and, as such, the direction follows the convention of silent film, with its abrupt close-ups, mask-like make-up, dramatic camera angles and visual clues, while during the length of the overture the only verbal signifiers are handwritten ones. A long-held shot emphasises Lindorf's (Helpmann's) tail – his long cloak. Lindorf's 'tail' is always present in Hoffmann's 'tale'. In the first two tail/tales, the pun is obvious. In the third, the Lindorf character (now disguised as Dr Dapertutto) merely wears a very long cloak to suggest a tail. In the final sequence, as Dr Miracle, he wears only a short coat, but the tail is depicted in the scorpion brooch pinned to his cravet, a metaphor that suggests these tales will contain a sting in the end. This visual pun clarifies the narrative and informs the spectator that each of the sinister characters is, in fact, the same harmful doppelgänger of Hoffmann's split psyche.

A similar use of a visual pun emerges in another dominant motif. At first, the gilt flower-headed cherubim of Olympia's story seem to be purely decorative, but the meaning is more complex. In the second episode, the cherubim have metamorphosed into a single gilt Medusa's head that occupies a central position in Guilietta's room. Heckroth continues the Medusa theme throughout the scene by making it unclear whether certain figures are human or sculptural. In the third episode, the gilt motif refers to the musical instruments of Antonia's art, and the metaphor extends beyond this, in that Antonia (the artist) is herself gilded, adorned by the brilliant golden light coming from her dead mother (a statue that comes to life in a reversal of the previous scene). In the final scene, it is Hoffmann's constant companion (played by Pamela Brown in drag) who is gilded to metamorphose into his faithful muse.

It is through recurring motifs and visual continuity that the narrative moves forward, and it is through visual discontinuity of colour and style that each separate episode is constructed. Heckroth uses colour symbolically to indicate the different episodes, a practice he described in a 1950 article written with Powell, 'Making Colour Talk'.[27] He used yellow to connote frivolity, and in the first tale (Olympia the clockwork doll), he achieved a luminous transparency by creating space from floating gauze dyed to an intense yellow that could be opened up, tied into extravagant swags and lit from behind to give a sense of great depth and lightness. The colour moves into a more threatening register in the Venetian scene, where purple and black, the colours of death and passion, prevail. In the final scene, the dominant ethereal blue and white suggest purity, the Madonna and the sea, all of which are appropriate to the tale. The technical delight in colour resurfaces with the use of red in *Oh ... Rosalinda!!* Here, the interiors of the hotel cupboard occasion an opportunity for the purely stylistic use of saturated colour. Heckroth used colour more symbolically (and disturbingly) by making each room in his *Bluebeard's Castle* a different colour for expressive and dramatic ends.

Heckroth's Venice in *The Tales of Hoffmann* is that of the Northern Romantic imagination: a city where passion is closely associated with danger and death.

As with colour, style is used to give each tale its own distinguishing features. However, style is used so deliberately as to suggest the impossibility of representation without recourse to it: to demonstrate the coding of representation, each episode of *The Tales* is articulated in its own stylistic mode, each of which is taken from a Romantic archetype. Heckroth's Venice is the Venice of the northern Romantic imagination, a city where passion is closely associated with danger and death; his story of Antonia is transported from the Munich of Hoffmann's original story to the *Island of the Dead* in Arnold Böcklin's 1880 painting in a classical setting. It also refers to de Chirico's designs for Diaghilev's production of *Le Bal* (1929).

In *The Red Shoes*, art and imagination transformed the world; in *The Tales of Hoffmann*, they construct it. With the symbolic use of the spectacles in the first of Hoffmann's tales, Heckroth/Powell pursue a fascination with the transforming powers of the imagination and, at the same time, an interest in the technical means of achieving this: an interest that remains in Heckroth's work through to the last paintings like *Undine, Kuhleborns Reich* (1966). Coppelius's magic glasses transform the world, just as cinema does. Heckroth explored the possibilities offered by this metaphor by literally filming through glass panels. He had developed the matte shot with Technicolor during the filming of *The Red Shoes*.[28] Using this method, it was possible to film through painted glass to create the surreal world around already filmed images of the dancers.[29] Heckroth made *The Tales of Hoffmann* depict the different kinds of reality that exist behind surface appearances. For instance, through the magic glasses, painted abstractions become figures, and marionettes appear to be real dancers. Towards the end of the film, each of the women Hoffmann has loved is seen with a figure who, peeling off the masks of his separate identities, reveals himself on each occasion to be Helpmann, Hoffmann's sinister opponent. The opening of the second scene in Venice is immediately unsettled as the rippling reveals it to be a reflection in the water, again emphasising the deceptiveness of appearances. Using a similar device in *The Red Shoes*, Heckroth presents the dancer's perception of the funfair on painted cellophane, which, as it crumples and falls to the earth, reveals it to be an illusion.

In many ways, the fantastic *Tales of Hoffmann* had everything to make a perfect Archers collaboration (although it was actually Sir Thomas Beecham's idea to film it). Holding, as it does, such significance for the Romantic (and Freudian) imagination, the opera was eminently suited to follow *The Red Shoes*.[30] Heckroth designed a number of versions of it both before and after 1951. But, however much he employed Romanticism in its various forms in the film, as a painter, Heckroth was also interested in the modernist emphasis on surface. Each of these opera/ballet films transforms natural space into something further and vaster. An extended space is possible in this artificial construction of the world of colour, light and different surface textures. But Heckroth also does something very different in *The Tales*. Rather than expanding space, as he had in *The Red Shoes*, the images often delight in a modernist two-dimensionality. The overture starts boldly with flat images of the cut-out silhouettes that connote a fantasy 'Germania' in Heckroth's schema, then suddenly one of the flat images abruptly swirls into the third dimension. (The cock on the weathervane turns round in the wind disarming our understanding of the image.) This is significant, as Heckroth plays with perspective, filmic codes and the *trompe l'oeil* of creating three dimensions on a flat cinema screen. As Herbert Read had pointed out in 1943, Heckroth had explored Cubism for its formal and spatial possibilities in his theatre designs and paintings. The two paintings entitled *Stilleben* (Still Life) of 1939 show its influence. In the construction/confusion of the glass panels in the tale of Olympia, Heckroth uses flat planes to articulate a Cubist construction of space, which thereby emphasises the flatness of the image; but by constructing the planes from painted glass panels, he was able to explore flatness and allow Hoffmann to figure in actual space. The panels also allowed him to fill the screen with an all-over decorative richness in a modernist emphasis of the surface, as he had in paintings like *Schlafende* (Sleeping) in 1937. Like Matisse, he used line to define objects in a monochromatic space: Olympia's bedroom consists of a swinging bed, the colour yellow and a series of gilded cherubim emphasising the flatness of the image. This play between flatness and depth becomes pure pantomime when Frederick Ashton, as the puppet master, unrolls a vast staircase on the floor of the ballroom, then by altering the camera angle to a crane shot, Olympia appears to dance *down* it, as if it were three-dimensional. Flat and rounded staircases appear in a number of *The Tales* and function like Miro's use of the ladder as an image that plays with perspective on a flat, painted surface: is the ladder flat or in perspective? Heckroth inserts a ladder motif among calligraphic marks, segmented circles and line figures on his painted glass screens. The line figures had appeared in his paintings and collages like *Gestalt mit Schatten* and *Zwei Figuren* of 1935. The mobility of the camera to frame the shots allows Heckroth to take this spatial ambiguity further than he could in painting, and the ability of film editing to disorientate the spatial continuity is engaged in the third story. As Antonia tries to escape the evil Dr Miracle, she runs out of one room only to discover that she has re-entered it as in a nightmare. In this spatial wonderland, she finally runs from the front of the constructed space, only to throw herself into the distance and off the island itself. This signals the move beyond the space of the stage set through a landscape to re-emerge from the auditorium of a painted theatre.

One of the most fascinating images in the first tale is the scene in the bank. Helpmann moves through naturalistic space to present his cheque. Then the shot changes to the flattened silhouette of the bank clerk in an abstract expressionist all-over image. Interestingly, this scene is drained of colour, so that it resembles the black and white of Picasso's bullfight drawings of 1948, which seem to be a model here (just as the reference to *Le Jour* in the duet in 'The Red Shoes' ballet had referred to Picasso's use of collage). They also anticipate the black and white drawings of Jackson Pollock (as filmed by Hans Namuth), but rather than an appropriation of a new way of describing space, they are an exploration of the technical means by which this could be achieved cinematographically. To create this effect, Heckroth had the scene filmed through the ink-spattered glass pane of the bank so that the ink spots changed scale to encompass the figure.

Coppelius presenting his cheque in the 'Tale of Olympia' is stylised by Heckroth with echoes of Picasso and Jackson Pollock.

Heckroth wanted to remain part of The Archers after the mid-1950s, but the company itself was coming apart and their popularity waning, as they struggled with the conditions of production in the post-war British film industry. They were still regarded by 'the men upstairs' as too visual to be trusted, and their films were considered the work of visionary aesthetes or perverted stylists with nothing to say. Heckroth decided to take a post in Frankfurt when it was offered and returned to Germany in 1954 (though he was credited as artistic adviser on *The Battle of the River Plate*). He did work on two more films with Michael Powell, *The Sorcerer's Apprentice* and *Bluebeard's Castle*, and a number of other proposed schemes would have enabled them to collaborate once more, but they would never again find the necessary financial backing. The reputation The Archers gained through their emphasis on painterly values encouraged Powell to consider the possibility of working with other artists like John Piper, Graham Sutherland and even Picasso, though these plans were never realised. Heckroth's work had been recognised in Britain, where he was invited to submit ideas for the 1951 Festival of Britain funfair in Battersea Pleasure Gardens. While the proposal came to nothing (the commission went to Roland Emmett, who had designed films like the *Titfield Thunderbolt* for Ealing) it would have given him the opportunity to design for the real world something of what he had created on screen and that had become part of the British filmic con-

Heckroth had already taken a theatre post in Frankfurt before he served as artistic advisor on
The Archers' *Battle of the River Plate*.

sciousness. As a painter, Heckroth had spanned the modernist modes of Romanticism, Expressionism and Surrealism and had absorbed the formal lessons of Cubism
and Constructivism. Powell and Pressburger were film-makers in whose Romantic
sensibility the subjective dominated over the discursive and mimetic forms of realist
art. The Archers repudiated established cinema codes and radically exploited cinematic resources. As such, their films rupture dominant conventions through a kalei-
doscope of Gothic horror, fantasy, grotesquerie, puppet and marionette Grand
Guignol traditions, the use of visual leitmotif's and an almost post-modernist collage of styles to create another form of cinema. Contemporary reviewers found the
films visually fascinating but often too close to the macabre; but their value was to
reassert the freedom of the imagination and the possibilities of art within a popular
mode – an achievement that would have been impossible without Hein Heckroth.

NOTES

1. This essay was first published by the Deutsches Filmmuseum in 1991 as part of its
   retrospective exhibition of the work of Hein Heckroth.
2. Michael Powell, *A Life in Movies: An Autobiography*, London: Heinemann, 1986, p. 523.
3. Read, with Humphrey Jennings and Roland Penrose, had been responsible for the popular and
   successful 1936 International Surrealist Exhibition at the Burlington Galleries in London.

4. Other supporters included Kenneth Clarke, director of the National Gallery and Keeper of the King's Pictures, and Roland Penrose, painter, collector of Picasso and of many Surrealist painters.

5. Ada Heckroth, interviewed by the author in Lewes, Sussex, on two occasions in 1990 and at her home in Frankfurt later that same year.

6. Heckroth and Ernst were in Paris together. There they met Jankel Adler (who would also be based in Britain later), Man Ray and other members of the Surrealist group. Heckroth also became friendly with Georges Braque through the art historian Carl Einstein, with whose family Ada and Nandi had been living.

7. Much of his collection would later go to the Tate Gallery in London.

8. The Kurt Jooss ballet were in the USA when war was declared; they made Dartington their base when they came to Britain in 1942, the same year that they were funded by CEMA (Council for the Encouragement of Music and the Arts) to tour Britain, thereby figuring in the development of an audience for ballet in Britain that would help to make *The Red Shoes* a success.

9. David Mellor, *A Paradise Lost: The Neo-Romantic Imagination in Britain 1935–55*, London: Lund Humphries/Barbican Art Gallery, 1987, p. 20.

10. Herbert Read, *Hein Heckroth: The Surrealist Paintings*, London: Modern Art Gallery, 1943, unpaginated.

11. Ibid.

12. Edward James was a wealthy English patron and collector of works by the French Neo-Romantic and the Surrealist painters (especially Salvador Dali, to whom he had paid a regular income during 1936–7, and Rene Magritte). James was also involved with supporting ballet and was for some time married to the British dancer Tilly Losch.

13. Vincent Korda had also trained as a painter and had a successful career in Paris before his brother asked him to act as designer for London Films. His appointment marked a change in attitude to film design. Korda looked for suitable easel painters rather than the usual interior designers. Hitchcock would famously take this approach to extremes in his use of Dali's designs.

14. Heckroth already knew the painter, photographer, writer and film-maker Humphrey Jennings, as well as the famous documentary film-maker Robert Flaherty, who had already suggested he try to work in cinema, convinced that his paintings would work on film. It is interesting that Heckroth's first contacts in film were with the Documentary movement, a very different proposition from the fantasy films that ensured his name in film history – although for all of these film-makers the image was of great significance.

15. Formed in 1943, The Archers included a regular team of technicians like Chris Challis and Jack Cardiff, who had trained at Technicolor and understood more than most contemporary cameramen about how colour film worked. At the opening of an exhibition of Heckroth's work at the German Film Museum in 1991, Cardiff generously acknowledged Heckroth's role in The Archers.

16. Powell, *A Life in Movies*, p. 149.

17. Ibid., p. 629.

18. Although the idea of presenting 'high' art through a popular medium could be seen as part of the then current attempt to democratise culture as CEMA metamorphosed into the Arts Council of Great Britain.

19. Quoted from Kevin Gough-Yates's pioneering interview, *Michael Powell in Collaboration with Emeric Pressburger*, London: National Film Theatre, 1971.

20. When Powell's career in films was cut short after *Peeping Tom*, according to Ada Heckroth, it was her husband, back in Germany since 1954, who remained faithful to their vision of filming and supported him at his lowest financial and personal point (from conversations between the author and Ada Heckroth in Frankfurt and Lewes, 1990). *The Sorcerer's Apprentice* was made in Hamburg in 1954.

21. Powell, *A Life in Movies*, p. 629.

22. Ibid., p. 635.

23. Jack Cardiff, for example, has hinted at this. See J. Cardiff, 'Technicolor Tyke', *Sight and Sound* vol. 2 no. 7, July 2001, p. 66.

24. To suggest a definite connection, it is worth noting that the boots in the painting are in the fourth position of classical ballet.

25. There are many connections to be explored between de Chirico's ballet and theatre designs and the work of Heckroth. De Chirico's ideas about the psychology of space were largely informed by the German theatre theory that he had encountered in Munich in the early 20th century. He was particularly interested in the theories of George Fuchs, as well as Adolphe Appia and Edward Gordon Craig, both of whom were influences on Heckroth.

26. It is interesting to compare the narrative structure with that of *The Life and Death of Colonel Blimp* (1943), in which Pressburger uses three episodes to recount Blimp's three (fetishistic) loves, all played by Deborah Kerr. Similarly, he starts his story just before the end in chronological terms, returning to the past loves as episodes within the overall narrative movement. It could also be compared with the spatial construction of Heckroth's narrative painting *Erinnerung an Oberhessen* (1939), in which a series of past episodes in Heckroth's life form a circle above his home (*heimlich*) landscape.

27. Michael Powell and Hein Heckroth 'Making Colour Talk', *The British Studio Supplement of the Kinemagraph Weekly*, 9 November 1950, and reprinted in Gough-Yates, *Michael Powell in Collaboration with Emeric Pressburger*.

28. See Powell, *A Life in Movies*, pp. 667–8: 'I used to go with Hein to the workshop assigned to us behind the Technicolor Laboratories at Heathrow … it was there that our matte painters were working on the most spectacular shots of the ballet. There were several hundred set-ups in the "The ballet of the Red Shoes" and each one had been sketched out by Hein and then carefully drawn by draughtsmen so that we could shoot the live action in the studio first … the matte painters were working on the "dead areas". Small projectors, at the speed of one turn, one picture, were projecting the scene with the live actor onto glass. Then, working from Hein's original sketches, they painted, on a separate piece of glass, the permanent décor which was not going to change during this sequence of dancing … there was no setting or props … but only seventeen minutes of painting.'

29. Heckroth would have seen the composite shots that enabled the Himalayas to be reconstructed in the Pinewood Studio when he was designing the costumes for *Black Narcissus*. In that film, the sense of vast space was created, in part, by filming a landscape painted onto glass next to the action in the 'women's house'.

30. The first tale, 'The Tale of Olympia', had been used by Freud to illustrate his theory on 'The Uncanny' (1919), which is interesting, in that Powell had called *The Red Shoes* a 'Freudian' ballet. Red shoes are, of course, a potent Freudian image, and Powell's 1960 film *Peeping Tom* was based on Freudian notions of voyeurism. All of these themes would anticipate much of contemporary film theory, though the Surrealists had already discovered them.

Gender Matters

13 Bending the Arrow: The Queer Appeal of The Archers

Andrew Moor

EPISODE ONE

Scene One. Location: a quiet beach. A good-looking young Englishman walks from the shore. He is upper middle class, classically educated, poetically minded, devoted to his mother and sisters. He comes upon a boy, a goatherd, playing pipes. The boy is completely naked. Is the boy real, or is he the Englishman's fantasy? In the late 19th century, Baron Wilhelm von Gloedon photographed similar 'classical' images of naked Sicilian adolescents, with an 'artistic' alibi.

Scene Two. Location: some woods. A strange young man – aristocratic, and French – emerges magically from the bushes and tries to tempt the young Englishman away from his new girlfriend. The stranger is effeminate, impertinent, lusciously dressed, and although he is charming, the Englishman resists.

EPISODE TWO

Location: Mopu, India. A preening, narcissistic young Indian, bedecked in a coat of white ermine and feathers, gazes adoringly as a drunken Englishman, a jungle roué, sings in a hearty baritone about being 'too fond of pleasure'. 'I love his voice', the Indian beams, unselfconsciously. 'So strong – and masculine!'

EPISODE THREE

Location: a village square. A boy and girl – they are lovers – encounter a queer cobbler, who tempts the girl with a pair of luscious red shoes. Once he intervenes in their romance, the fairy-tale course of their love is doomed.

EPISODE FOUR

Location: a magic world of chiffons, gauzes and colourful drapes, endlessly shifting. Masks are worn; masks are removed, to reveal yet more masks. Roles are performed, and identities are labile. Everything is balletic. Hoffmann, a romantic, whose companion Nicklaus is played by a woman, is bemused by this chimerical world, and defeated in his pursuit of the women in his life.

It may be perverse to run these episodes together, and irresponsible to claim that they constitute evidence of a secret narrative of consistent queerness in Powell and Pressburger's work, but impishness is one of the weapons queer readers have recourse to. Queer arrows, fired at mainstream culture, have circuitous trajectories and tend to hit their target from an oblique angle. This can produce readings that are ironic, negotiated, resistant or, where political radicalism is the impetus, downright terroristic. Queer readings worm their way seditiously into the 'innocent' discourse of the culture to subvert its heterosexual assumptions from within.

This chapter offers queer readings of Powell and Pressburger's films, and as the term 'queer' is notoriously slippery, some guiding premises are best laid down first. In a sense, I want to have it both ways, suggesting that queerness is a matter of reception, but *also* that it can lurk in the texts themselves. When I argue that 'queer' is in the eye of the beholder, I want to insist that the concept says more about viewing strategies than it does about texts. This is not to invoke the sense of ideal or abstract spectatorship suggested by some branches of (Althusserian–Lacanian) film theory. Rather, I

The Tales of Hoffmann: a magic shifting world where masks are worn, roles performed and identities remain labile.

want to suggest that those who are subculturally positioned, and who occupy what Alan Sinfield calls 'partly ... alternative subject positions',[1] are likely to participate in the culture in ways that are informed by their own race, ethnicity, gender, class and sexuality. As Brett Farmer's consummate account of gay spectatorship points out, the very concept is grounded in the notion that forms of gay activity that exist '"outside the theater" affect and help structure spectatorial relations "inside the theater"'[2]. This is not to assume that all gay spectators will find the same path to and from their text, or that they will be equally good at it, but I want to hold on to the idea that queer readings expose the often tortuous, sometimes playful, but always complex ways in which dispersed or marginal groups engage with the culture. They can therefore offer important evidence of subcultural work in action.

It is difficult to think about 'queerness' without using established labels of sexual identity ('gay', 'bisexual', 'straight'), as Alexander Doty has noted.[3] Hence, my previous paragraph slips between the terms 'gay' and 'queer', although the latter term, with its anti-essentialist impulses, refutes the stable notion of the former – or of any similarly fixed identity position, for that matter. Queerness is a broader and more flexible concept, containing a range of non-straight, 'perverse' positions and activities, yet undeniably it is informed by the histories of gay, lesbian and bisexual people. Queerness is necessarily open to straight critics too, where they scrutinise heterocentrism, where they critique homophobia or where they comment on other forms of prohibited or 'deviant' sex. However, when queerness is defined broadly as a 'thorough resistance to the regimes of the normal',[4] it can lose some of its radical edge and its sexual specificity. This is why Judith Butler stresses that 'queer' is a 'site of collective contestation' that must interact with other languages of power – racism and misogyny – to maintain its political impetus.[5]

What, then, can a political reading 'do'? This essay follows Butler to suggest that '"queering" might signal an enquiry into (a) the *formation* of homosexualities (a historical inquiry which cannot take the stability of the term for granted ...) and (b) the *deformative* and *missappropriative* power that the term currently enjoys.'[6] The task is not simply to ascribe (homo)sexuality to a text, if such a thing were possible, because texts have many meanings, and the notion of a fixed sexual identity is anathema to 'queer studies' anyway. The goal of a queer reading may be to assert tenancy or ownership of a cultural artefact or practice where the labour of gay men and women in its production has historically been erased: a flag-planting act of reclamation. Or it may be a ruder intrusion, claiming squatters' rights; or it might be just to stake a foothold in a text by demonstrating how and what it signifies to a queer constituency. Either way, territorial issues are at stake, yet not all texts get queered. Although they are probably all susceptible, some are luckier than others. Whether or not I approach the films of Powell and Pressburger purposefully and jauntily sporting my queer hat, it seems to me that they offer up peculiar stories, oddly told tales, disruptive outbursts of sensual excess, camp performances and curious closures that have a particular resonance to gay spectators and make them ripe for requisition. What interests me is why my queerness feels more or less 'at home' in many of

The Archers' films. What do I identify with, and how far is it my queerness that does the identifying?

It is not as if gay or bisexual men and women prevailed in the production process. Neither Powell nor Pressburger were gay – although there is certainly scope to talk queerly about their close collaboration. As Alexander Doty has noted, the notes and letters in their archives, with Michael's affectionate pet names for Emeric, are ripely interesting here, but what they show is male-to-male friendship, expressed through the commonplace, playful language of an old boy from an English, single-sex public school.[7] This established homosocial discourse evades censure by taking tactical flight into an ironic register when it needs to neuter any implications of over-familiarity, marking the culture's anxiety about men talking to men. True, Powell sometimes pushed this further than most – he notably referred to his working part-nership as a marriage – but when it comes to praising their own sex, gay men do not have a monopoly on terms of endearment. Some of the other members of The Archers' team – Eric Portman, Anton Walbrook, Leonide Massine, Robert Help-mann and Judith Furse (hardly a front-line player) – may well have been gay or bisexual, but the 'outing' game does not necessarily reveal very much. We should not undervalue the crucial importance of acknowledging and celebrating gay achieve-ment – it is still too often occluded – but it can be more interesting to focus on the intersections of actors, star personae and roles, and the apparently queer kudos of Conrad Veidt, Walbrook and Helpmann does seem to inform some of the parts they play: spies or tricksters with hidden intentions; gods or monsters with outsiders' per-spectives and hypnotic powers. For Harold Beaver, despite (or because of) the range of vicious stereotypes of homosexuality in our culture, the homosexual is covert, 'a double-dealer, moving incognito ... – a marauding alien, an unscrupulous bogeyman plotting devious sexual revenge, a masked avenger, ... a secret agent crossing the shadow line of dreams'.[8] Powell and Pressburger's films often employ striking instances of characters like this. By imagining homosexuals as exiles penetrating the secure borders of heterosexual society and roaming invisibly within it, Beaver uses a language of geographical displacement all too familiar to Pressburger, for more lit-eral reasons. Where the exilic experience informs Pressburger's screenplays, his stories strike a chord with aspects of gay life, because of the metaphors of displace-ment that have figured in the development of Western homosexual culture. Exiled and gay people have strategies of camouflage, and as Hamid Naficy – a writer whose primary focus is exilic cinema – points out, both groups also have a habit of drama-tising their existence in a heightened way, of 'turning naturalized reality into reality-effect and normative identity into identity-effect'.[9] I want to argue, then, that the sharply 'camp' identities, split personalities and masquerades, and the dynamics of assimilation, exclusion and visibility at work in Powell and Pressburger's films – strange accents that can be attributed in part to Pressburger's experience of exile – are particularly meaningful to gay/queer reception.

Unsurprisingly, there are no signs of manifest same-sex desire in the films, let alone gay activity. It would take a remarkably acute symptomatic reading to find

Paradise interrupted in *49th Parallel*: Leslie Howard's wilderness idyll is rudely interrupted by Nazis on the run, who are openly contemptuous of his aestheticism.

that. There are homosocial groups in *49th Parallel, One of Our Aircraft Is Missing, The Battle of the River Plate, Ill Met by Moonlight, The Life and Death of Colonel Blimp* and *Black Narcissus*, and the same sex dynamics within them could be coaxed out. Genre explains the gender bias in most of these films, but the last two instances have dramatic same-sex pairings that are worth flirting with: Clive and Theo; Clodagh and Ruth. There are moments where the grammar of classical editing splices these characters together in ways that open up the possibility of erotic desire, however much the films disavow it. Shot-reverse-shot close-ups, when Clive first meets Theo for the duel in *Blimp*, intend to record the men carefully inspecting their opponent's mettle, and they certainly register mutual recognition and respect. Could this admiration of martial skill, military rank and athletic physique spill over into something more erotic though? The camera cranes away to the heavens almost before this thought can register. The answer, it seems, is a decisive 'no', but the question still hovers. There is a headier erotic charge to the face-off between Ruth and Clodagh towards the end of *Black Narcissus*. Ruth has always been a bit of a 'problem'. By the time of her key confrontation with Clodagh, she sits in her red dress applying lipstick; Clodagh, who has fled to the Order to escape the vicissitudes of heterosexual love, clutches her Bible defensively. Beads of sweat tremble on Ruth's forehead, and Clodagh's frigidity quivers. The moment is charged with possibility, but it culminates in Ruth's sudden dash to Mr Dean. By placing Dean between the women as

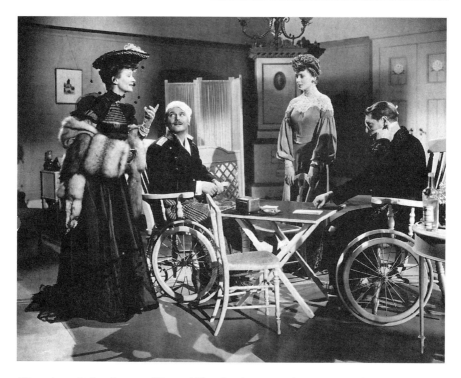

Blimp places the love between Clive and Theo in a heterosexual romance storyline, with parallel narratives for the two men, rather than the triangular one it really is.

the object of erotic attraction, insinuated lesbianism is displaced into a traditional, straight love triangle. *Blimp* similarly places the love between Clive and Theo into a heterosexual romance storyline, although it actually supplies two romances and two women, Edith and Barbara, creating parallel narratives for the two men rather than a triangulated one. But of course it *is* a triangle, because both women are Deborah Kerr: Clive and Theo have one each. The dominant reading of this is that the multiple casting reveals Clive's morbid, repetitious pursuit of an ideal woman, or his inability to differentiate between real ones. Circumvent that reading, and the marriages, which are there to close off the possibility of same-sex desire between the men, actually perpetuate an intimacy that has been established early on. When the three characters first celebrate Theo and Edith's engagement in Berlin, the two men jokingly wear Edith's hats. Clive's subsequent pursuit of Barbara may well bring him psychologically closer to Theo's wife, his 'original ideal', but this inevitably brings him close to the man as well. Exactly how far does Clive identify with Theo? Where are the boundaries drawn? Toasting the engagement, Clive drops defensively into 'military-speak', but does this moment of token cross-dressing clue us into the way the masculinity of these traditional military men is queered through matrimony? Certainly, it worries the image of military manhood (and at one level of significance, marriage will effeminise Clive, for after his wedding he incorporates Barbara's family

After Clive's and Theo's early closeness in Berlin, the defeat of Germany in the First World War casts a temporary shadow over their relationship.

name – Wynne – into his own). The intimacy between Clive and Theo is vital of course: the film's purpose is to elide the geographical border separating the Englishman and the German, to propagate the image of the 'good' German, to wrench Nazism from its ideological foundations in the German land and to leave it as a rootless anomaly. Yet when it queries the national boundary, it also blurs the socio-sexual one.

Without resorting to simplistic biographical projection, elements of Michael Powell's 'creative subjectivity' – the culture he developed in and which he expressed – find their way into his films and are amenable to queer reception. Queer readings are often 'against the grain', exposing silenced or covert codes of non- or anti-normative desire, but it is possible for the contours of putatively mainstream texts to *coincide* with some of the underlying structures that have informed gay or queer experience, and for readers who are positioned in those subcultures to align themselves more comfortably with them. Some of Powell and Pressburger's work shows a resistance to bourgeois culture. This is not in itself surprising: 'straight culture' is quite capable of resisting hegemonic values, just as gay subcultures can be remarkably reactionary on matters such as race, class or gender. In the dialogue between the mainstream and the marginal, the counter-Establishment elements in Powell and Pressburger's films mirror the formation of modern gay history.

Look at *A Canterbury Tale*. It endorses a pre-capitalist, rustic ethos in the manner of the Arts and Crafts movement, with its medievalism and its reaction against metropolitan commerce. Powell's memoirs touch on this discourse – it is there in the ruralism of the early childhood sections, in his resistance to big business, and it is one of the central 'messages' in both *A Canterbury Tale* and *I Know Where I'm Going!*. His qualified anti-bourgeois stance perpetuates a tradition of nineteenth-century 'middle-class dissent'. His public-school education and class position suggest it, his aesthetics champion it and his films express it repeatedly. In the history of emergent nineteenth-century British gay culture, the oppositional current that *A Canterbury Tale* invokes is typified by Edward Carpenter, the influential author of *The Intermediate Sex* (1908). He extolled Whitmanesque, manly comradeship and rural craftsmanship, finding a queer, anti-metropolitan home in the greenwood. I do not say that the character of Colpeper is a direct descendant of Carpenter – Colpeper is too fastidious, too solitary and too closeted for that – but I do think that the counter-hegemonic impulses that he represents, and the anti-materialist tradition he articulates, approximate to some of the experience of gay history by opposing the rush of mainstream culture. There is a resemblance between their respective experiences of the margins.

Eric Portman's Colpeper incarnates an anti-materialist and anti-metropolitan tradition of dissent that owes something to Edward Carpenter's queer example.

This may, though, be just be a way of saying that the anti-materialism in the film is de facto an oppositional stance that queer readings can fall in line with, and its weakness is that it fails to focus on sexual desire, to the degree that *any* unorthodox or non-mainstream reception might experience the same frisson of recognition. But the film puts queerer elements in motion. Colpeper's aversion to the village girls' flings with local soldiers is puritanical, and one of the purposes of his 'glue-man' campaign is to instil a social order that will help maintain established, stable heterosexual relationships through the difficulties of wartime separation. Clearly, though, his methods are too perverse to be merely moralistic. By disrupting so vehemently these pastoral and therefore 'natural' couplings, Colpeper starts to accrue queerer credentials. He is also unmarried and lives with his mother. He organises 'men-only' events at the Colpeper Institute. The plot barely raises the possibility of romance between him and Alison (Sheila Sim). More pressingly, his nocturnal alter-ego is a secret, and his glue-man disguise is hidden in a closet in the corner of his court house. The vicious misogyny of his attacks is excessive: it is too morbid a reaction against sex. Early drafts of the screenplay show Pressburger's intention to have Colpeper slash the girls' skirts with a knife, but this violent quasi-rape was shifted into the habit of pouring glue into their hair. Either way, the attacks imply perversity, a failure to function along customary heterosexual lines, and queerness has always been ready to accommodate perversities.

It is not only Colpeper who trades in duplicitous appearances. Reflexively, the film suggests that its own representation of English village life is worth scrutinising too. The highly artificial 'village idiot' sequence is clearly shot on a studio set, with a self-conscious cuckoo-call on the soundtrack mocking its use of a clichéd country stereotype. The scene makes the natural unnatural, queerly punctuating the film's classical illusionism and forcing us to reassess its reliance on less obviously mediated location footage. Eventually, its oddly inflected patriotism resolves itself into a more conservative image of the British nation uniting. *A Canterbury Tale* is ultimately governed by the ideology of wartime, and this propagandising mission finds the urban/rural cleavage in society distressing. Hence, the film teaches us, as Colpeper learns, that the perplexed nation should come together, that differences of gender, region and habitat should be effaced. We see this dynamic in action in the closing image of the cathedral congregation, after which people of *both* genders are seen heading to the Colpeper Institute as the credits begin to roll. These are images of incorporation, characteristic of the 'People's War', and while they may well strike a subliminal chord with the wing of non-queer gay activism that preaches assimilation, the radical anti-Establishment ethic of queerness makes a virtue out of the marginalised, dispersed position of gay men and women, refusing incorporation and pinning its radical reputation on its refusal of bourgeois norms. Ultimately, *A Canterbury Tale* is conformist, with a holistic view of society, but its utopian closure only just succeeds in containing its strangeness.

Like *A Canterbury Tale*, *The Red Shoes* draws from a well of nineteenth-century dissenting culture and flows in the slipstream of Romanticism, although in other respects, its emphasis is very different from the earlier film's, with its faith that 'Art' can escape the rigours of the material base, and that it offers a space for creative, individual expression. Again, it is the sort of language Powell and his readers are familiar with. Ultimately, *The Red Shoes* is a film about oppositionality, and Boris Lermontov's ballet company is a site of radical resistance. Walbrook's performance as Lermontov, with its charming dismissiveness, anal precision, masked feelings, aesthetic acuteness and distanced contempt for the bourgeoisie, owes something to the image of the aristo-dandy, and of course it was in the dandified persona of Oscar Wilde that artistry, leisure and refinement coalesced iconically with effeminate homosexuality. Wilde's vivid, flamboyant stance was a square-faced opposition to British imperial masculinity, a great refusal. *The Red Shoes* figures things differently: Lermontov is not particularly effeminate, nor is he 'leisured', and Sergei Diaghilev is the obvious model rather than Wilde, but a clear queer code is still in play. The film centres on the theatre – *the* gay creative industry par excellence, a stronghold for gay men and women that is often constructed as a distinctively gay space. The specific subculture of the Ballet Lermontov is 'passed off' as a centre of artistic distinction speaking to all, and the queer productivity in the film is masked by its assertion that 'Art' is universal. The specifically gay labour that produced 'The Red Shoes' ballet is thus overlooked,

In the spotlight: Massine (l) had danced for Diaghilev, who was clearly the model for Lermontov and the 'queer code' that governs his company in *The Red Shoes*.

just as – beyond the film – the homosexual following Diaghilev's sensuous ballets excited gets little critical attention.[10]

The film's blatantly homosexual origins lie in the true story of Diaghilev's relationship with his chief male star, Vaslav Nijinsky, who then left the Ballets Russes company to marry Romola de Pulsky. The film tries to straighten this history by means of gender realignment, but the reversals just underscore its queerness. The dancer who now catches the impresario's eye is a woman, Victoria Page (Moira Shearer), and the partner she abandons him for is now male, Julian Craster (Marius Goring). Alexander Doty judges the general tendency to see the film simply as a heterosexual reworking of the Diaghilev story to be heterocentrism in action, and this seems valid, although Pressburger's original 1930s screenplay had actually charted a traditional love triangle between Lermontov, Vicky and Julian, and the skeleton of this structure just about survives in the rewritten final script.[11] In the finished film, the signs of romance between Lermontov and Vicky are vestigial, and it is difficult to see how Lermontov could any longer be assigned heterosexual status, because by the time the script had been reworked, he no longer has any clearly expressed sexuality at all. He admits to loving Vicky, but 'not in any way' that [Julian] would understand' – an elusive comment pointing to the codified nature of the film's realigned queer romance. His reaction against marriage is extreme, and so is his conviction that dance is incompatible with it. Importantly, then, the artistic excellence Lermontov embodies is located beyond the structures of married life and the family. The film's conflation of Art with Religion invites us to take Lermontov's anti-marriage stance as an endorsement of celibacy (echoing Colpeper's anti-sex campaign), but the implication is that, like the Church, the Ballet Lermontov is a marginal, homosexual space. Partly through the charming, magnetic pull of Walbrook's performance, *The Red Shoes* asks us to see his world as more vital than the dull-looking married life Vicky opts for with Julian. When Vicky dances 'The Red Shoes' ballet, her repressed desires and fears are expressed. These fantasies mark the limits of her upper-class British upbringing: prostitutes and primitive-looking natives are summoned up by her as she dances to the jazz-like score. There is danger here, as Vicky explores an arena beyond her bourgeois experience, but there is also sensuality, and Hein Heckroth's colourful, fluid designs capture both. It feels dangerously yet vibrantly illicit.

Even while the film straightens and then desexualises its love triangle, the queerness at its core fizzes to the surface emerging in the camp, excessive performance of Léonide Massine, who plays Grischa Ljubov. Massine had replaced Nijinksy as Diaghilev's principal male dancer and, for a while, as his lover, so his presence in the film advertises what the narrative has censored. In the ballet of 'The Red Shoes', he dances the central role of the Shoemaker, the diabolical character who intervenes in the romance plot between the Girl (Vicky/Shearer) and the Boy (Boleslawsky/Helpmann), tempting her into the red shoes and away from any mythologically heterosexual happy ending. Massine's dancing stands out: it is angry, angular, athletic and confrontational, often facing the camera like a defiant anti-hero, and in the film's pattern of contained tales and surrogate role-playing, the Shoemaker contains a gallery of queer characters: Ljubov, Massine, Lermontov (Vicky's tempter) and Walbrook, with the spirit of Hans Anderson, the homosexual writer of the ballet's source tale, ghosting through as well. Or, rather, the Shoemaker fails to 'contain' them, because Massine's performance is so remarkably excessive. Even outside 'The Red Shoes' ballet, he is flamboyant, grinding and contorting his words through a heavily broken accent, twisting his body unnaturally, squealing hysterically when he cannot find the red shoes before curtain up, and queen-like, he always craves the centre-stage, petulantly rebuking a slack technician for failing to keep up with his moves during a private rehearsal: 'Spotlight sur moi!. Toujours sur moi!' Pure camp like this clearly adds to the film's queer currency.

Campness of this sort does not make the film frivolous: that would be to misread the seriousness of camp, but it would also to be to overlook the film's graver aspect. Because Lermontov is placed outside social norms, extracted from the narrative of heterosexual romance, he is said by those around him to have 'no heart' and to be 'a monster'. He wears shades to protect him from the sun, and at times he lurks alone in darkness, vampiric, deathly and unnatural. The demonisation at work here counters his established association with (artistic) vitality. This can be partly explained by noting how the impresario himself is not a 'creative' person (unless we grant creativity to entrepreneurship and solid accounting). Instead, he relies on the artistry of his team, and so could be seen to be parasitic. I think more is at stake, though. Powell and Pressburger clearly take a Romantic view about the primacy of Art, and the ballet world is constructed as superior, but they counter their own positive enthusiasm by allowing Lermontov's critics to damn him for his inhumanity. The film refuses to settle this ambiguity. The Ballet Lermontov is both vital and fatal – an impossible combination that undoes the binary opposition between Life and Death. What is more, the insistence on Lermontov's monstrosity echoes a magisterially heterosexist line of reasoning that sees matrimonial heterosexuality as uniquely procreative, and which consequently views homosexuality to be sterile. Queer artistic creativity is thus interpreted as a displacement of procreation, and Art is constructed as a site of non-familial activity: decadent, and to the heterocentre, fundamentally unnecessary.[12]

Lermontov personifies this anti-domestic trend, but he is just one of a line of supreme, aristocratic authoritarians in Powell's films: troubling isolated men ranging from Conrad Veidt's characters in *The Spy in Black*, *Contraband* and *Thief of Bagdad*, through those played by Eric Portman in *49th Parallel* and *A Canterbury Tale*, by Roger Livesey in *A Matter of Life and Death* and by James Mason in the late work, *Age of Consent*. These are not surrogate father-figures. They remain unincorporated into family structures and lack the sense of heterosexual mastery that fatherhood confers. Indeed, they can be seen to accrue their terrific power precisely because they are not brought within the taming family institution. Conversely, though, and mediated through remarkable layers of self-reflexivity, Powell's own cameo appearance as his fictional protagonist's 'real' father in *Peeping Tom's* home-movie footage is an extreme, and self-mocking, instance of the type, a man whose

The Red Shoes invites us to see Lermontov's religion of art and celibacy as more vital than married life with Julian.

abuse of power is more worrying because the young 'victim' is played by Powell's real son, so that the abuse can be read as intra-familial while it stays in line with the film's consistently ironic play on the 'real'. These men are fascinating, phallic visionaries, and they disturb us because they are powerful yet attractive, because they exist outside the disciplinary regime of the commonplace (or above it) – and queer culture is quick to claim them because of their deviance.

   Lermontov, the transcendent power overseeing his company's ballets, is an arbiter of taste, one of those artistic homosexuals who are, in Harold Beaver's words, 'producers of signs, … so-called deviants [who] above all are the agents of culture'. As he sees it,

> [t]hough relegated to the borderlands and sick ghettos of bourgeois culture (with other scape-goats and victims) the homosexual's role, far from parasitic, is central: as an index of cultural complexity and self-awareness (in all symbolic activities, including language) that floods traditional discourse with irrational needs and desires.[13]

This mapping of the homosexual artist's position captures well the tension in Powell and Pressburger between centrality and marginality, but they are so fascinated by the magus role that they raise it to an aristocratic plane, valiantly – and Romantically – shedding it of victimhood. This can be seen most emphatically in the ending of *The*

Red Shoes, where the last shot of Massine holding the red shoes to the camera entices the film's bourgeois audience to sample Lermontov's outcast brilliance, despite Vicky's tragic death (or because of it: queer culture adores its iconic female martyrs). Note the contrast here with *A Canterbury Tale*, which ends with images of social cohesion. Without the centralising social impetus of wartime propaganda, *The Red Shoes* keeps its separatist edge. Tellingly, Lermontov is last seen alone in the shadows of his theatre box, unlike his predecessor Colpeper, who joins the mixed congregation filing into Canterbury Cathedral.

Massine holding Vicky's shoes directly to the camera; Massine's excessive performance; the shift between Heckroth's surreal designs for 'The Red Shoes' ballet and the more realist frame narrative; the invitation to the dance directly mimed to the cinema audience: all this illustrates the anti-classicism of Powell and Pressburger's films. Models of 'classical narrative cinema' emphasise its efficient storytelling and the way it subordinates all other elements of film language to the narrative imperative. They also stress its need for rounded closure, with no loose ends. Paradigmatically, classical narratives are advanced through the actions of a (typically) male protagonist, towards an Oedipal resolution and heterosexual union. Aided by patriarchal heterosexual dynamics that structure ways of viewing to the advantage of male (straight) viewers, it can be seen why cinema should so often have been regarded as a powerful apparatus hooking viewers into its operations by offering visual pleasure and narrative resolution, but then channelling these viewers along its heterocentric, masculinist grid. The task of feminist (and queer) critics has been to throw a spanner into the works, pointing out the fracture-points in the system, or showing how viewers might resist it. Just as feminist film theories have suggested ways in which female audiences negotiate films with problematic endings, blinkering themselves from misogyny in order to reap pleasure from disruptive moments of pleasurable excess, so too can gay viewers disregard the formal dynamics of classical narrative to revel in their own imaginative responses to texts. Powell and Pressburger give us licence to do so.

Formally, their narratives are often figured around arrested rather than continuous developments: journeys are halted and left uncompleted while goals are renegotiated. Contained tales such as *Tales of Hoffmann* highlight the storytelling process, as do episodic narratives such as *49th Parallel*. Many of the films do without heterosexual closure, although those starring David Niven do resolve themselves this way. The films are often fragmented stylistically, shifting to and from colour in *AMOLAD* or to and from surrealism in *The Red Shoes*. Changes like these, along with other motifs that foreground the voyeuristic nature of the cinema experience, point to the way the films are systems of representation, violating the supposed 'invisibility' of classical cinema. In some of the post-war 'art' films, there is an interest in the aesthetics of formal design, and a concomitant detachment from contemporary concerns (detachment like this has often been seen as a defining characteristic of the camp, dandified homosexual, persisting into the perceived hedonism of contemporary gay club culture). Under Hein Heckroth's art direction, we are given sensuous surfaces, textures and colours that are fascinating in themselves. Marius Goring's French aristocrat, Sabu's Indian General,

Walbrook's mannered impresario and Helpmann's various roles in *Hoffmann* draw attention to themselves and point up the coded performativity of the actors' work. There is, then, a strong case to be made for Powell and Pressburger's anti-classicism and for locating the source of it in a diverse range of factors – from their transnational experience and international aesthetic to their interest in formal experimentation (visually, and narratively). With this claim comes the proposition that the audiences they invite are required actively to participate in constructing the film's meaning. Powell certainly hoped to attract audiences like this, and such tactical engagement is grist to the queer mill, for gay men and women have long been adept at negotiating their way round cultural artefacts. Because neither Powell and Pressburger's films nor many gay people dovetail neatly into any one dominant cultural space, and because both have a particular interest in forces of inclusion and exclusion, there is a charged sympathy between the two.

NOTES

1. Alan Sinfield, *The Wilde Century*, London: Cassell, 1994, p. 184.

2. Brett Farmer, *Spectacular Passions: Cinema, Fantasy, Gay Male Spectatorship*, London: Duke University Press, 2000, p. 32.

3. Alexander Doty, *Making Things Perfectly Clear: Interpreting Mass Culture*, London: University of Minnesota Press, 1993, p. xvi.

4. Michael Warner, *Fear of a Queer Planet: Politics and Social Theory*, London: University of Minnesota Press, 1993, p. xxvi.

5. Judith Butler, *Bodies that Matter: On the Discursive Limits of Sex*, London: Routledge, 1993, pp. 228–9.

6. Ibid.,

7. See Alexander Doty, 'The Queer Aesthete, the Diva and *The Red Shoes*', in Ellis Hanson, ed., *Out Takes: Essays on Queer Theory and Film*, Durham and London: Duke University Press, 1999, pp. 46–71.

8. Harold Beaver, 'Homosexual Signs (In Memory of Roland Barthes)', in Fabio Cleto, ed., *Camp: Queer Aesthetics and the Performing Subject: A Reader*, Edinburgh: Edinburgh University Press, 1999, p. 162.

9. Hamid Naficy, *An Accented Cinema: Exilic and Diasporic Filmmaking*, Oxford: Princeton University Press, 2001, p. 274.

10. Emmanuel Cooper confirms the view that the work of Diaghilev gave a huge boost to the search by homosexuals for an art around which their sexual identity could be centred. See E. Cooper, *The Sexual Perspective: Homosexuality and Art in the Last 100 Years in the West*, London: Routledge & Kegan Paul, 1986, p. 135.

11. Doty, 'The Queer Aesthete', p. 57.

12. Sue Ellen Case explores this denigration of homosexuality on the grounds of its perceived sterility. See S. E. Case, 'Tracking the Vampire', *Differences: A Journal of Feminist Cultural Studies* vol. 3 no. 2, 1991, pp. 3–4.

13. Beaver, 'Homosexual Signs', p. 168.

14 That Obscure Subject of Desire: Powell's Women, 1945–50

Natacha Thiéry

Michael Powell's filmography testifies to the importance he accorded his female characters, from the 'quota quickies' (such as *The Love Test*, 1934) right up to *Age of Consent* (1969), and including *Contraband* (1940), *A Canterbury Tale* (1944) and *Luna de miel* (1959). But this phenomenon is especially noticeable in the six films that he made in collaboration with Emeric Pressburger between 1945 and 1950. Neither icon nor foil for her masculine counterpart, neither femme fatale nor self-effacing companion, the Powell woman is either a partner in the full sense of the word (*A Matter of Life and Death*, 1946; *The Small Back Room*, 1949) or else the main character (*I Know Where I'm Going!*, 1945; *Black Narcissus*, 1947; *The Red Shoes*, 1948; *Gone to Earth*, 1950). Furthermore, the narrative often presents the woman's point of view and attracts audience identification. This trait, characteristic of The Archers' films, is unusual in the cinema and should be emphasised. It is in sharp contrast to most classic Hollywood fare and also that of post-war Britain.[1] In this exploration, which is by no means exhaustive, I look at the narrative and aesthetic treatment that defines the female characters at the heart of these films as (suffering) subjects of desire. From *I Know Where I'm Going!* (hereafter *IKWIG*) to *Gone to Earth*, the woman – whether wild child or urbanite, nun or dancer – is subjected to ordeals, each of which relates to her position, not only vis-à-vis the man but also relative to the society with which she comes into conflict, not being fully integrated into it. We are struck by the fact that the female character cannot be considered independently of the question of desire – both the desire she inspires and also, more unusually, the desire she herself experiences. Whether she accepts or rejects it, desire, always associated with danger, is the source of conflict within the character and thus within the fiction itself.

Although the woman is central to The Archers' films, although she is the object of sympathy as well as curiosity, and is even the one who attracts audience identification, yet she is not the subject of a feminist view of the relationship between the sexes. Rather, the films reveal the difficulty experienced by female characters in finding their place and escaping the alienation produced by a society fearful of an independent woman (independent, that is, in her desire). Neither is the malaise provoked by the woman the result of rejection – for we shall see that death is never a punishment – but of a realisation of failure, stated bluntly and quite magnificently. Seen as a stumbling block, the woman's place – uncertain, fragile, subject to chance – is the mainspring of the fiction and the *mise en scène*.

FEMALE STATES: THE TABOO OF DESIRE

Despite their diversity, the six films of the period from 1945 to 1950 all portray women who are, despite their obvious charms, less objects than subjects of desire. The films are the dramatisation of this distinctive trait. One tries to resist it by deploying an energy proportionate to the strength of the attraction she feels (Joan in *IKWIG*); another braves death in order to prolong the state of being in love (June in *A Matter of Life and Death*); a nun renounces her vocation to become a woman at last, while a poor Indian teenager dreams of a prince (Ruth and Kanchi in *Black Narcissus*); a dancer gives up her art to follow and marry a composer who has fallen from favour (Vicky in *The Red Shoes*); a woman being courted chooses instead her impotent colleague (Susan in *The Small Back Room*); and a naïve young girl projects

Female desire finds its fullest realisation in *Black Narcissus*, where everything suggests sensuality, from the palace's décor to the wind and vertiginous drops that surround it.

into nature the signs she is hoping for in response to her lovesick yearnings (Hazel in *Gone to Earth*). The male characters reciprocate with a longing to be chosen, to become the target of this desire.

Black Narcissus is probably the film in which female desire finds its fullest realisation. In contrast to the nuns' position and the demands of convent life, everything in the film suggests sensuality, from the palace environs – profuse and brightly coloured vegetation and vertiginous drops – to the wind that penetrates the building, via the frescoes of half-naked courtesans in lascivious poses. What is remarkable about this film is that the male is eroticised here, in the persons of two masculine characters, Dilip (Sabu) and Dean (David Farrar). The young Indian General is characterised by attributes that the nuns had to give up when they abandoned their femininity. He wears coloured outfits cut from costly fabrics, jewellery and a perfume, Black Narcissus, a scent that makes Ruth feel ill but delights Kanchi, who strains, eyes closed, to capture this invisible fragrance. As for Dean, his physical appearance demonstrates Powell's intention to eroticise him – with humour and in visible stages. As the film progresses, the shots of Dean gradually close in on his body to frame his virile torso and face. His shirts become more and more unbuttoned as the narrative unfolds, until his naked torso is finally revealed. When the nuns summon him urgently, following the death of a small baby and the natives, departure from Mopu, Dean bursts into the room where they are gathered, dressed only in his hat, shorts and sandals. A low-angle medium shot emphasises his imposing virility. This unusual scene shows this tanned, near-naked man in the midst of nuns who are covered from head to toe in their uniform white habits, one of whom, sister Ruth, both anxious and fascinated, approaches for a closer look, as if to touch him, to breathe him in.

Yet the exercise of desire, inasmuch as it leads the female character to change her situation, is a source of conflict, if not an actual taboo. Nathalie Heinich's book *États de femme. L'identité féminine dans la fiction occidentale* (States of Women: Feminine Identity in Western Fiction) offers some understanding of this paradox.[2] Although the author deals mainly with nineteenth-century novels (in the West), with some other examples taken from theatre and cinema, her approach is actually pertinent to an analysis of the Powell and Pressburger films, for in these, as in the works discussed by Heinich, 'the basis of the plot is a change in the state of the heroine or a female protagonist or, at the very least, an ordeal that is related to her state'.[3] The definitions of the various female conditions relate, for the author, to their relationship with sexuality, whether legitimate or not. Thus she suggests, for example, a distinction between the girl 'to be taken', still a virgin, and the woman, who has entered a masculine, sexual world to which she has agreed to sacrifice her girlhood and, thus, her virginity. And this is the point: whether a virgin, a woman despite herself or even a nun, the heroine resists the dead end of which conjugality is the symbol.[4] In *Gone to Earth*, for example, the sensuality of the main character sets up from the very beginning an ambiguity in identifying the heroine as girl or woman. Still a girl, and with an innocence that is emphasised by her closeness to nature, Hazel actually presents a disjunction, with sensuality as the misleading indicator. Although this quality incites men to look at her as

Hazel's chaste marriage to the pastor in *Gone to Earth* is a trap: proclaimed but not consummated, it leaves her sexuality unresolved.

a woman (such as Reddin, played by Farrar again, whose omnipresent and voyeuristic gaze prefigures the sexual act, or her cousin Albert), she is still in an undefined space, where she floats between two distinct and irreconcilable states at the beginning of her suffering – and of the narrative. The difficulty experienced by the female character played by Jennifer Jones in passing from the state of girlhood to womanhood finds its most striking expression in the question of marriage. The girl 'to be taken' is taken, but badly, for physical love remains dissociated from conjugal love. Hazel's difficulty in escaping the grimness of the community and its religion, as well as the alienation brought about by relationships with the opposite sex, is acute.[5] Hazel lives in a world where, as Heinich writes:

> marriage is, typically, the moment when it happens, the shift from virgin to wife-and-mother, from girl to woman; the moment of passing from the world not inhabited by man … to the world inhabited by men, the world shaped by the difference between the sexes and haunted by sexuality.[6]

Hazel undergoes this shift, but it manifests itself in an unexpected way. Her experience throws into relief the fundamental paradox of the question of union – which suggests, by its semantic ambivalence, both marriage and sexuality. The entry into the sexual world here crystallises the failure of the character, preparing the way for her death at the end of the film.

First, Hazel's marriage is the result of a strange vow made before her father Abel. As a vow, it is thus a trap that Hazel has set herself, for in one of the following

scenes, she admits to the pastor that she has no wish to marry. Second, the marriage
is realised in two contradictory ways. When Hazel marries Edward Marston, the
pastor, she spends the wedding night alone. Later, she goes to Jack Reddin and is
taken, physically, by him, thus becoming an adulteress in the eyes of the community.
So the marriage is first proclaimed but not consummated, and then it is consummated but not proclaimed. This chiastic construction is hinted at by an elliptical *mise
en scène* that is strewn with clues. On the night of their marriage, Edward kisses
Hazel at the door of her bedroom and then goes off to his own. The wedding night
has been validated by nothing more than a chaste kiss. Thus, Hazel does not experience the sacrifice (of her girlhood) that marriage implies. More precisely, she is not
incited to this sacrifice by her husband, who is too respectful of her feelings. In
acting this way, Edward is above all keeping his promise to God, given on the night
of his proposal to Hazel: 'I promise that I shall ask nothing of her, nothing until she
wants to be a wife to me'. Although their mutual commitment has been blessed in
church, Hazel is not really Edward's wife. In short, the characters' commitment is in
both cases expressed by a performative utterance, both spoken formula and act,
which causes them to give up their liberty. Later, another sequence functions as a
subtle counterpoint to Hazel and Edward's official wedding. Hazel, having believed
(or wanted to believe) she could read signs of encouragement in the nature around
her, goes to the assignation arranged by Reddin. One important detail attracts our
attention: the white dress Hazel is wearing is the same one she wore for her wedding to Edward.[7] So Hazel is in her wedding dress, clutching in her hand a bouquet

When Hazel is taken by the
squire, Reddin, in *Gone to Earth*,
physical love is fatally dissociated
from conjugal love.

of red meadow flowers. Thus, the *mise en scène* suggests that she is marrying for the second time, but without the blessing of a priest. The act, which cannot be redone without first having been undone, is thus almost immediately replicated. As the man approaches, at first out of shot, his shadow precedes him and progressively covers Hazel's body from the feet upwards. The virginal dress is inexorably obscured. Then the embrace is signified indirectly, via close-ups of the characters' feet, Hazel's bare and Reddin's booted. The former stands on tiptoe and drops her bouquet, while Reddin picks her up and crushes the flowers. A dissolve then marks an ellipsis: married to Edward, Hazel has now experienced her wedding night – her deflowering – with Reddin. The *mise en scène* has signified very literally the double meaning of the verb 'deflower' (both to take away someone's flowers and to take someone's virginity). The paradox of the duality of the marriage in *Gone to Earth*, which invalidates it in both cases, shows clearly how impossible it is for Hazel to pass from one female state to another. After her union with Reddin, she is certainly no longer a girl, but if she is a woman, it is an adulterous woman.

Elsewhere, the condition of the female characters is again problematic. As they have dedicated their existence to religion, the female protagonists of *Black Narcissus* have a very specific status. More precisely, their status as nuns has obliged them to renounce their basic femininity. As a nun, one is no longer a woman. The film depicts the suffering that is born of this rending of their identity. Though in different circumstances, Vicky in *The Red Shoes* is confronted by the same interdict – indeed Lermontov has actually defined dance as 'a religion'. Although some commentaries on *Black Narcissus* have seen in the film a confrontation between two conflicting religions, I, on the contrary, see in the characters' status no more than the pretext for a radical experiencing of desire. It is because it is taboo that the desire they are vainly trying to resist constitutes such an ordeal for the nuns. Faith is not the subject of the film, and is only ultimately significant inasmuch as it presupposes, and demands, consent to a refusal of femininity. What interests The Archers about the figure of the nun is the woman in her who resists, the body that revolts.[8] Through the double portrait of Clodagh and Ruth, *Black Narcissus* exposes the cruelty of the nun's position, in which she finds herself in an environment that never ceases to remind her that she is – or was – a woman, while being obliged constantly to renew her forgetting of that fact.

The confrontation between Clodagh and Ruth and their positions facing each other during the night scene in which the latter, under the fascinated eye of the former, puts on lipstick, suggests an inverse symmetry between the two characters. Ruth expresses what Clodagh represses, namely the assumption of her femininity and her desire. She is the one who releases a turmoil of the senses and dissidence around the community. Furthermore, if the growing violence of the character is so frightening to the other nuns and most of all Clodagh, the Sister Superior, it is because it is proportionate to the violence of her desire. The two merge. Though she is still a nun, Ruth already behaves like a woman, when those two states are mutually exclusive. Her insistent watching of Dean, seeking his company and continually checking his comings and goings at Mopu, provokes a malaise resulting from a strange and disturbing disjunction, namely that Ruth's behaviour belies her habit: the woman is hiding behind the deceptive appearance of the nun. As for the symptoms she suffers, from insomnia to her rivalry with Clodagh, though these are continually perceived as indications of a physical problem and mental disturbance stemming from a questionable faith, they actually evoke rather more strongly her amorous obsession. In this respect, one scene in particular represents brutally the paradoxical conversion of Ruth into a woman, long before she discards her nun's uniform. When Dean is in Clodagh's office, she bursts in without warning and in a state of extreme excitement, recounting the scene she has just witnessed and participated in. She has seen a native bleeding profusely and has managed rapidly to staunch the flow. But this stemming of spilled blood has signified at the same time the liberation of her own emotions. Under the effect of a fascinating, terrifying and yet intoxicating danger – the blood – her resistance gives every appearance of having collapsed for good. And Ruth's expression does indeed radiate a wild elation. From then on, she is more woman than nun. Her white habit, splashed with blood, indicates the sexing of the character. In the same image, menstrual blood and the symbolical loss of virginity are displayed, as they will be again later in the red dress that will replace the uniform and advertise her difference from the rest. The visual shock expressed in Clodagh's face – a superb superimposed image emphasises her stupefaction – is proportionate to the transgression that it announces in this literal manner. And the sternness of the Mother Superior's reaction conveys a twin reproof: not so much disapproval of the initiative taken by Ruth as of the sudden exposure in broad daylight of this sacrilegious femininity. The nun's body is indeed the privileged locus of a violent struggle between girl and woman. Desire, when taboo, throws the spirit into turmoil but is made flesh in physical symptoms, stigmata or fever.[9]

DESIRE AND DANGER, SOMATIC PERTURBATION AND PSYCHIC PROJECTION

In its feminine form, desire in *Gone to Earth*, *Black Narcissus*, *IKWIG* and, to a lesser extent, *The Red Shoes*, becomes taboo. But the assumption of desire lifts the taboo, thus exposing those affected to annihilation and death. Furthermore, desire is signalled by the sense of danger that it provokes. If the affable Torquil in *IKWIG* represents a threat to Joan that she is constantly trying to avoid, it is because she is promised to another and the attraction she feels to him risks destroying her commitment. But her flight ends in the paradox of a sea crossing, during which the danger this time becomes all too real and brings the protagonists face to face with death. The episode of the raging whirlpool at Corryvreckan expresses perfectly the equivalence of power between the ocean chasm and the young woman's feelings. In *Black Narcissus*, too, the man, by his presence alone, threatens the integrity of the religious order based on the nuns' 'forgetting' their original femininity. Thus, Clodagh tries to remove Dean from Mopu, while the integration of Dilip, the young Indian General, demonstrates the futility of this. But it is in *Gone to Earth* that the close relationship between desire and danger takes its most systematic form. Just as the film illustrates very literally Hazel's identification with her fox (Foxy), Reddin incarnates the 'black hunter', the terror of whom is fed by the book of spells and charms the young woman has inherited from her mother. In fact, the film is like a hunt, with Hazel as the prey. The development of the narrative, and certain sequences in particular, establishes a latent correspondence with Sandro Botticelli's polyptych entitled *The Story of Nastagio degli Onesti* (1483), which is inspired by an episode from Boccaccio's *Decameron* (1350). Both text and painting recount the violent story of a knight of Ravenna whose betrothed, having refused to marry him, eventually agrees once she has seen another woman condemned to be killed by her rejected lover, thrown to his dogs and eviscerated.[10] *Gone to Earth* maintains a silent dialogue with these works. Several shots echo the composition of the painting and concentrate Hazel's harassment by Reddin into a prismatic image: the tapestry in the bedroom at Undern shows hunting dogs, heads stretched up towards a deer, whose head projects from a thicket of green foliage. In the film's final sequence, an alternating montage between hunters on horseback with their hounds and Hazel, vulnerable, holding Foxy in her arms, suggests an unequal struggle and increases the sense of urgency of her flight. This headlong flight recalls the Botticelli painting. In the same shot, the spectacle of the lone woman and her multiple assailants, replicated over and over (hunting dogs and men, including her lover, on horses), is a stunning image. But the killing of the woman in the painting is not only used as a metaphor in the film. Hazel, in falling down the mine shaft, deprives her pursuers of a killing. For she literally disappears from sight. Only the sound of pebbles falling after her and the tearful cry of the pastor mark her fall, as well as low-angle shots of the dogs, their febrile excitement at the edge of the abyss now pointless.

Other shared themes between these works include marriage and the problems a female protagonist encounters in reconciling herself to it; the violence of a hunt in which the woman, replacing the animal, has become the prey; and lastly death itself. In Boccaccio, this is a punishment associated with damnation, but in the film it represents something quite different: a confirmation of the impossibility of the female character ever finding her place once she has fallen from her original state (nature), been absorbed into a repressive religious community (marriage) and violated by an illegitimate sexuality (adultery). In *Gone to Earth*, death appears at the end as a tragic way out. In these works (literary, pictorial, cinematic), male desire is realised in the form of a terrifying hunt, evoking the figure of Pan, and death intervenes as the only possible response to the woman's refusal of an unwanted assault: desire is thus by its nature 'panic'.[11] But it is also a response to the subjective projection of female desire: Hazel's (pantheistic) invocation of nature indicates her delusion that hearing supernatural 'fairy music' will lead to her joining Reddin, when it is in fact her own father, Abel, playing his harp on the other side of the hill. In these examples, it is obvious that the feeling of desire, whether repressed or accepted, does violence to the female body. The image, without revealing the secret of an always invisible inner disturbance, speaks of the suffering of the body in this state of emotional perturbation.

The body of the female in Powell's films is rarely her own, but is forced to flee – like Hazel running to her death in *Gone to Earth*.

Female desire in Powell's films reveals itself in recalcitrant images – a memory believed lost, imaginary creatures – or in physical symptoms, the harbingers of disorder. Coming from inside, it is revealed externally for all to see.

The body is only very rarely an erotic object in its own right. Rather, the Powellian image represents the body shot through by erotic emotion and more broadly by desire. The films thus reveal a problematic relationship with the female body. The object of domination (*The Red Shoes*), of concupiscence (*Gone to Earth*), either prevented from doing what it wants (*Black Narcissus*) or forced to do what it does not (*Gone to Earth*), the body of the Powell woman is not her own and she has no right to her own desire, which is necessarily illegitimate. In the clutches of desire, the body is in constant movement, crossing space, crossing the film frame, and never remaining still. But the movement of the body, in the context of a desire repressed either by the outside world or by the subject herself, is not aiming towards the object of that desire. On the contrary, it is inciting the body to deviate from its course, to flee. Hence Joan's equivocations and evasions (*IKWIG*) and Hazel's flight (*Gone to Earth*). Only Ruth moves with the single, monomaniacal aim of joining the object of her desire in an illusory union (*Black Narcissus*). But instead of union, she experiences dissolution as she faints out of shot and the image suddenly disappears, fading to red.[12]

Ruth has broken the tacit pact that bound her to the community and required from her that she remain 'bodyless'. This film depicts the return of the body in a (religious) context that had excluded it and a milieu (Mopu) that brings it back to life. Moreover, in *Black Narcissus*, desire manifests itself as an eruption: a dermatological eruption that affects each nun, one after the other; an outburst of tears in the case of Sister Philippa, bowled over by the beauty and sheer expanse of the landscape, and of Clodagh when, at the end of her tether, she tells Dean her story; an outburst of cries and lamentations from Sister Honey, when she sees a native baby quietly fade away; and finally an eruption of violence from Sister Ruth. In all cases the collision between desire and the interdict placed on it causes a boiling over, a spurting out, an excess, which sweeps away the reserve necessary for peaceful convent life. This collision is the mainspring of the fiction itself. It is initiated and nourished by the nuns' state of crisis. Although concealed beneath her habit, the body surges forth. Desire is signalled by the spilling of bodily fluids: tears, and the blood that splashes Ruth's garment. Hidden, the body kicks out beneath the habit until its sudden exposure: Ruth's red dress, her legs luminous in the dark, her hair loose, lips coloured the shade of blood, begging in vain before stealing a kiss on the hand of the man who is deaf to her desire.

In short, the body of the Powell woman, because invaded by an impossible desire, suffers the torment of uselessness or, if it chooses to rebel, of illegitimacy. Whether the heroine is treated compassionately or sadistically (or indeed both at the same time), it is the strangeness of the woman – and of this, her own desire, to which she has no right – that is in play and at the heart of these films. Powell and Pressburger integrate the mystery of female desire into their *mise en scène*. This dimension is contained within the sense of the fantastic that imbues *Gone to Earth*, *Black Narcissus* and even *IKWIG* and *The Red Shoes*. The fantasy quality of the Powell and Pressburger image suggests something of the same mystery that Jacques Tourneur explored in, for example, *Cat People* (1942) and *I Walked with a Zombie* (1943). Martin Scorsese's comment on Tourneur's work also sheds light on The Archers' films:

> [His films] undermined a key principle of classical fiction, the notion that people are in control of themselves. Tourneur's characters were moved by forces they didn't even understand. Their curse was not fate in the Greek sense: it was not an external force; it dwelled within their own psyche.[13]

Powell and Pressburger interrogate female desire and almost systematically establish its failure; a failure to which death adds a heart-rending fermata.

'AT THE END, SHE DIES …': THE VIOLENCE OF AN UNTHINKABLE POSSIBILITY

The films Powell and Pressburger made between 1945 and 1950 are marked by death. In three of them, it is a threat only eluded at the last minute: *IKWIG* (Joan and Torquil), *A Matter of Life and Death* (Peter), *The Small Back Room* (Sammy). More noteworthy in this respect are the three other films that end with the death of the main female character: *Black Narcissus* (Ruth), *The Red Shoes* (Vicky) and *Gone to Earth* (Hazel). In these three works, death has been anticipated or even announced at the beginning of the film and then confirmed by a network of converging clues. But here is a paradox: while the death is foreseen, that is to say articulated as a possibility, for the spectator it nevertheless remains unthinkable. As a result, its arrival at the end of the film produces a brutal, shocking effect. Although the viewer has been alerted at the beginning, he nevertheless hides from himself what he *already* knows about the character's death. He 'forgets' what had been predicted. Thus death, the outcome of the diegesis, operates by means of disappearance, of an eclipse.

The ways in which the death of the female character is announced in *Black Narcissus*, *The Red Shoes* and *Gone to Earth* are somewhat cunning, being at the same time both explicit and veiled. The films are sprinkled with advance indications that the viewer, however, persists in not identifying as such. First, in all three cases, the character knows the place of her death, as she has been there before. Thus, we have Vicky conversing with Julian at the edge of the balcony as a train passes beneath (*The Red Shoes*); Ruth, when we see her for the first time, elated, ringing the bell in front of a dizzyingly steep landscape (*Black Narcissus*); and Hazel almost falling into the depths of a mine shaft when travelling with her father to the pastor's fête (*Gone to Earth*).[14] Thus, Powell's *mise en scène* is based on anticipation fulfilled in two time frames: though the location of the future death is revealed, when comes it is none the less brutal in its unexpectedness. Indeed, the anticipation is only appreciated *a posteriori*, establishing a paradoxical 'retroactive foretelling'. Second, the three films are studded with multiple clues heralding the death. A detail of the image, a gesture or a word becomes an augury of disaster. Remember that Lermontov, when recounting Andersen's tale 'The Red Shoes', had used this strange phrase, 'time passes by, love passes by, *life passes by*', and had replied to Julian's question with this detached conclusion: 'At the end, she dies …'. The tale whose character dies at the end overflows the context of the stage and spills into the unfolding of the diegesis, the life of Victoria Page, who dances this role in the ballet. In *Black Narcissus*, death is somehow incarnate in the very character it will strike at the end, Sister Ruth. The nun, characterised above as the dissident element of the community, is – thanks to her extreme amorous rivalry and her compulsions now exposed to the light of day – the bringer of death. She heralds disorder, a surging violence and the bubbling over of a destructive element within the heart of the Order. Her death at the end not only tragically underlines the failure of the nuns in Mopu but is also the factor necessary for a return to order. But *Gone to Earth* (even the title can be construed as a return to the earth whence we came) is, of the three films, the one in which the suspension and, so to speak, permeation of death into the character's environment are the most systematic. The recurrence of the grave motif, and the profession of Hazel's father – he is a harpist and beekeeper but also makes coffins and wreaths – again signals the proximity of death.[15] Furthermore, the twilight effects, red and orange skies streaked with clouds, dark and twisted tree trunks and the wind that sculpts terrifying shapes in mineral outcrops form a Romantic landscape whose magnificence is proportionate to the catastrophe lurking beneath the surface. Death thus shapes these three films. It is a vaguely felt presentiment, but remains hidden in the images. It is a promise suspended (but never absent) and long deferred.

In the mind of the viewer, death is latently present in the films through a net-work of hints that are visible but at the same time hidden; whether it actually occurs or is finally avoided, it certainly belongs in the realm of the possible. But even so, it does not become necessary. It remains one possibility among others. Powell's cinema installs the possible but disappoints the viewer's expectation. Death is never where you expect it. Thus it is unthinkable and unthought. Cinema's mimetic illusion comes up against an impossible thought: though death is inexorable, waiting at the end of existence, viewers constantly forget about it, and even more so when watch-ing a film. The character on whose presence the story is based, and in whom they invest their emotions, cannot die. Death is not part of the possible. Furthermore, to the extent that death – when it concerns the main character of the film – presup-poses a cessation of the images, or at least an acceptance that the images, if they con-tinue to flow, will from now on be orphans, the audience, in their desire for the film, deny death and resist this prediction. Their 'blindness' is the twin of that other symptom, their amnesia where death is concerned.

In terms of the *mise en scène*, death always means a falling out of the field of vision, a disappearance, a sudden absence from the frame. A character, usually the one who was the main object of our attention, disappears suddenly. Powell illustrates death not only by ellipsis but also by an eclipse of the body. Vicky leaps from the parapet under a moving train (*The Red Shoes*); while trying to push Clodagh over the precipice, Ruth loses her balance and falls into the void at the foot of Mopu (*Black Narcissus*); and Hazel, cradling her fox, disappears into the bottomless pit of a mine shaft (*Gone to Earth*). They have all come up against an impossibility, that of finding a place to exist. In this respect, Ruth's faint when rejected by Dean is seen as the only possible response to the character's impasse. It is, as Nathalie Heinich puts it, the 'only way to demon-strate that she no longer has her place, that there is no longer a place where she can exist'.[16] But in *Black Narcissus*, this fading away is treated literally: the character fades from the image and under the effect of her anger, the shot, which has become subjec-tive and monochrome, now dissolves totally. It is on Dean's face and through the soundtrack that we can read that Ruth has lost consciousness. She occupies the scene by default, in an out-of-shot area that affects the visible field of action and alters it until it is totally absorbed into redness. The fainting, an ephemeral disappearance, nevertheless produces a shift and prefigures her definitive disappearance.

Likewise, in *The Red Shoes*, Vicky arrives at the balcony and, at the moment of her leap, we see Julian in a reverse shot reaching towards her with a cry. In a low-angle shot, the young woman's chest, head thrown back, sweeps down towards the camera. For a fraction of a second, her body in free fall, her flesh and the tulle of her dress cross the frame, merging together, out of focus and disordered. A strange suspension gives the illusion of weightlessness. This fixed framing is followed by another, identical to it, but the body has now silently removed itself. The eclipse of the body marks the death of the dancer. On the stage, the circle of light that had previously bathed the dancer now illumines an empty space. The sequence alternates shots of the stage with exterior shots of a bloodied body lying on the rails. *The Red Shoes* is the only film in which

Powell chooses to show the body of the dying protagonist. This does not, however, mark a break with his preferred device, that of disappearance. On the contrary, the immobile body, a counterpoint to what is unfolding without it on the stage of the theatre, accentuates the feeling of an intolerable absence. The violence done to our eye is not that of the blood but rather that of a confrontation between the presence of the body and its absence in the place it should occupy.

In *Gone to Earth*, Powell offers a visual translation of Hazel's death, through a sudden effacing, a final, syncopated appearance. It also functions as an ethics of absence. Hazel is somehow sucked into the abyss. Her fall leaves the viewer aghast.

The death of the female character, the obscure subject of desire, coincides with the audience being deprived of the principal object of their gaze. They are left with contradictory emotions. The subject of a paradoxical identification with the female character on whom they have concentrated their voyeuristic gaze, while also suffering along with her, they feel this final death – though announced in advance – as a harrowing event. This brutal, irrevocable disappearance from the screen imposes an absence that is unexpected and rendered all the more cruel by the presence of the character in every previous scene. It establishes the impossibility of the image and it interrupts the story. The scopic impulse is deprived of its object, and it is when the desire to see is at its highest point that it experiences its most violent frustration.[17] This double definition of desire, indissoluble from the notion of absence, and thus of a lack, has been taken up by psychoanalysis, in the writings of Freud and above all of Lacan. It describes very precisely desire as it relates to the cinema, which is based on the illusion of presence

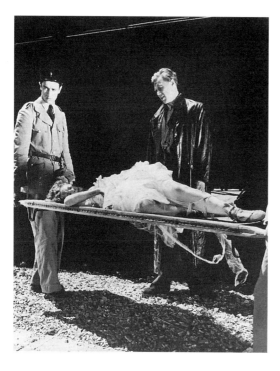

The Red Shoes is the only film in which Powell shows the dying protagonist, poignantly contrasted with her absence from the place she should occupy on stage.

and the reality of absence. This paradox, specific to cinema, is central to the thinking of Jean Louis Schefer, notably in *L'Homme ordinaire du cinéma*, in which the author recreates (from the audience's point of view) a relationship with the cinema that makes it an always paradoxical experience. This process, by which the viewer knows he is outside the film and yet merges into it, defines the particular experience that is induced by Powell's cinema. Furthermore, the film-maker shows, or rather requires of the viewer, the experience of privation, of ontological absence in the cinema image. A constituent of cinema fiction, which only functions through the tacit agreement whereby the viewer pretends to forget for a moment the perceptual illusion on which it is founded, absence is reiterated *in the image* – in the killing of the character, that is to say in her exclusion from the picture area, in the movement by which she crosses the frame to be exiled from it for ever.

An analysis of *The Red Shoes* and *Gone to Earth*, from the point of view of death, and more precisely the eviction of the object of desire, or the harrowing experience of its absence in the frame, leads to a reflection on the broader nature of Powell's cinema. The film-maker emphasises cinematic absence. It is, in fact, signified in two areas. According to Louis Marin:

> Representation is generally accompanied by the conviction that the represented object is absent but not lacking. Representation targets and brings to mind what is not there, but this object was once there and can be rediscovered. An object is absent if it cannot be directly perceived yet is present in representation.[18]

Here, the absence is double, functioning both in perception and in representation.

Being deprived of the object of desire – an object that is itself problematic, for it is an illusion and the reflection of an absence – is all the more cruel for that. In short, desire in Powell's films is always perilous, for it contains a threat of the revelation of absence and the absorption of the viewer's gaze.

In the films of 1945–50, the eminently problematic femininity of the characters crystallises into the difficulty of changing from one state to another, which, radicalised as far as death in three of the films, gives Powellian melodrama its specificity: a substitution for 'fate' of the projection of a suffering psyche, in which desire is synonymous with danger. Yet the woman, the desiring subject, struggles in vain to exercise an impossible desire, the mainspring of a narrative in which death alone, which is also a cessation of the images, resolves the impasse. Without a place where she can exist, the woman disappears with the final frames of the film.

NOTES

1. It was fundamental to the Gainsborough films: costume dramas that were certainly popular, but enjoyed a lesser legitimacy in terms of their critical reception.
2. Nathalie Heinich, *États de femme. L'identité féminine dans la fiction occidentale*, Paris: Gallimard, 1996, in the series *Essais*. The author brings together anthropology, psychoanalysis and the sociology of literature.

3. Ibid., p. 17.

4. Powell's oeuvre rarely associates marriage with happiness. Conjugality is problematic and marriage fails to crown a loving relationship.

5. Remember that the action of this film starts in 1897.

6. Heinich, *États de femme*, p. 24.

7. This essential detail, absent from the novel, was Powell and Pressburger's idea.

8. We can cite two other films featuring nuns, both based on the same historical material, where desire expresses itself through the metaphor of diabolic possession: *Mother Joan of the Angels* (1961) by the Polish film-maker Jerzy Kawalerowicz and *The Devils* (1971) by Ken Russell.

9. The ordeal of desire for the nun – seen in the character of Ruth, who is said, after her flight from Mopu, to have 'gone mad' – here takes the form of a hysterical delirium. (While the term 'hysteria' does not appear in the film, it is, however, used in Rumer Godden's novel.) It evokes what Gladys Swain, in *Dialogue avec l'insensé*, Paris: Gallimard, 1994, has identified as the historically durable assimilation of hysteria into the ecstasy of love.

10. The picture representing the story of Nastagio adorned a wedding chamber, thus offering a strange counterpoint to the celebration of a marriage. The denouement of the Boccaccio story appears to be an injunction to women to submit to 'men's desire' and, by extension, an exhortation to conjugality.

11. The etymology of 'panic' stems from the mythic reaction to the sudden appearance of the god Pan.

12. The body of Kanchi, by contrast, as an incarnation of the palace's frescoes, palpitates as they do and thus reconciles body with flesh.

13. Martin Scorsese and Michael Henry Wilson, *A Personal Journey with Martin Scorsese through American Movies*, London: Faber & Faber, 1997, p. 100.

14. This scene does not appear in Mary Webb's novel and is thus the result of a positive decision on the part of Powell and Pressburger.

15. When, at the beginning, Hazel takes refuge in her father's cottage, the camera marks the young woman with the seal of death. She appears in the centre, coming from the back of the shot. In the doorway, Abel has just assembled the sides of a coffin and is examining his work. When Hazel opens the door, her silhouette appears in a double frame formed by the door and by the outline of the coffin.

16. Heinich, *États de femme*, p. 98.

17. Later, the *mise en scène* of *Peeping Tom* (1960) will become the paradigm for this device.

18. Louis Marin, *To Destroy Painting*, trans. Mette Hjort, Chicago: University of Chicago Press, 1995, p. 147.

15 Officers and Gentlemen: Masculinity in Powell and Pressburger's War Films

Robert Shail

Richard Dyer's work on film stardom has provided a touchstone for those wanting to examine the representational aspects of film stars. At the centre of his influential *Stars* is the notion of star types, which he adapts from the earlier work of O. E. Klapp.[1] Dyer divides stars into distinct categories ranging from 'The Good Joe' to 'The Rebel', and defines them in relation to Western society's dominant value systems. He sees the majority of stars as acting to uphold and reinforce those values, while the rest fall into the category of 'alternative or subversive types' whose function is to provide a safety valve for societal anxieties or dislocations while containing them. One of the principal risks of his approach, which has been identified by subsequent film theorists, is a tendency to be too broad in these definitions (Dyer only provides five star types in total). In his collection of essays on British stars, Bruce Babington argues that whatever stars mean in the wider cinema 'they signify more complexly in relation to their original environment'.[2] The essays that Babington assembles covering the range of British stardom from the silent period to the present day amply support his position. By refining Dyer's approach, these essays indicate the specificity of stardom within a particular British context.

This approach has been most comprehensively applied to British cinema's male stars by Andrew Spicer in his study *Typical Men*.[3] Spicer extends Dyer's original list of five main types and arrives at a more complex and extensive list that reflects the distinctive nature of British male stardom. These range from the 'English Gentleman', the 'Civilian Professional' and the 'Action Adventurer' of the immediate post-war era through to more contemporary types such as the 'Lovable New Man' or the 'Damaged Man'. The development of these individual types is explicitly linked to changes in the wider British society and in the historically placed discourses of masculinity that they reflect. Here, I adapt this approach again to apply it to the very particular field of Michael Powell and Emeric Pressburger's war films. In doing so, I am defining 'war film' fairly broadly as referring to films that touch upon the effects of war. In the case of Powell and Pressburger, this can vary from the explicit propaganda of *One of Our Aircraft Is Missing* (1942) to the more oblique references of *A Canterbury Tale* (1944). I have focused on their mainstream projects, omitting the short propaganda pieces *An Airman's Letter to His Mother* (1941) and *The Volunteer* (1943), as well as the features *The Lion Has Wings* (1939) and *The Queen's Guards* (1961), which did not involve the contribution of Emeric Pressburger. Having outlined the broad attributes of five key types, I will proceed to examine their appearances in ten films that were made over a period of eighteen years. By working through the films chronologically, I aim both to indicate the recurrence of these figures and the ways in which they develop. The defining features of each type are by no means exclusive to one individual character in each film, as there are occasional combinations that blur the boundaries in a manner quite characteristic of Powell and Pressburger's work. In adopting this, admittedly slightly mechanical, approach, my intention was to look more closely at how these masculine types reflect both on Powell and Pressburger's depiction of war itself and on their response to notions of British, or more particularly, English national identity.

The most immediately striking and familiar of Powell and Pressburger's male types is one that I shall call The Sympathetic Foreigner. Ian Christie has shown, in his examination of the attempted government suppression of *The Life and Death of Colonel Blimp* (1943), how this aspect of Powell and Pressburger's work led them into conflict with the wartime British authorities (this figure recurs repeatedly in their films).[4] It is worth breaking down the two central elements that characterise this type. First, obviously enough, they are 'foreign', which in Powell and Pressburger's hands has a double-edged impact: while these characters are self-evidently different from 'us' in such basic features as their accents and clothing, they are also conversely just like us, in that beneath these surface appearances their basic humanity, as well as their cultural traditions, indicate their intrinsic familiarity. Second, they are 'sympathetic' in the sense that we are invited to engage emotionally with them, a fact that, as Christie shows, was more than enough to enrage the wartime censors when the characters concerned are frequently German. It is easy enough to trace the appearance of this character type to Pressburger's own experiences as a Hungarian expatriate in Britain, and it is confirmed by their willingness to employ non-British collaborators and technicians, starting with the designer Alfred Junge and cinematographer Georges Perinal.

The second distinctive type I have called The Father Figure or, if we were being less respectful, The Old Buffer. This figure is often reviled by younger characters and is sometimes treated with a degree of affectionate mockery by Powell and Pressburger themselves, but he is also a wise man, equipped with a lifetime's knowledge and experience; his value to the community, although easily overlooked, is almost inestimable. In times of crisis he is the man whom others turn to for advice. In addition, he is also frequently the embodiment of threatened values, the living indicator of what is being defended in wartime. A third type might suffice as the nearest Powell and Pressburger get to a villain, although even this figure is depicted with a good deal of sympathy. The False Prophet is a harbinger of new values in a changing world, but these are values that threaten to undermine those that are already long established. He is frequently strident and shrill, but above all else he is so convinced of the rightness of his own views that he fails to see the shared values that link all of the other types together.

The final two types are closely linked. The Romantic Gentleman is often Powell and Pressburger's hero. An embodiment of chivalrous virtues, he is brave, noble and kindly. He often has a liking for literature, particularly poetry, as well as an appreciation of philosophy and history. He relishes food, drink and entertainments of all varieties, but his attitude towards women is romantic to the point of sentimentality. Here, the tradition of courtly love is invoked, in that the longing for the loved one is almost as powerful as actually having her. This figure is also distinguished by the fact that he may be damaged, physically or psychologically, and by his gentleness, qualities all the more striking in the context of films dealing with wartime heroics. The final type shares many of these characteristics, but The Visionary is driven by a more singular, perhaps even mystical, notion of truth and honour. This leads to the kind of behaviour that The Romantic Gentleman would never contemplate, as The Visionary is willing to take drastic action to protect the things he values. This figure actually reaches its zenith outside of the war films in the character of Lermontov (Anton Walbrook) in *The Red Shoes* (1948), whose obsessive, semi-religious pursuit of his ideals succeeds in placing art above life itself.

Powell and Pressburger's first two war films offer us variations on the first of my types, The Sympathetic Foreigner. As Roy Armes suggests, both *The Spy in Black* (1939) and *Contraband* (1940) have their roots in the conventions of the 1930s spy thriller (as well as Hitchcock's films of the period). Despite the First World War setting of *The Spy in Black*, both films give expression to fears of impending invasion or subversion from within.[5] What remains striking in both is the degree to which these anxieties are countered by the appearance of one of their most sympathetic of foreigners in the form of Conrad Veidt. Veidt's characteristics remain fairly constant across both films. His dynamism is indicated by his bravery in taking on a suicidal mission in the first film and by his willingness to set off alone across blacked-out London to find the missing Valerie Hobson in *Contraband*. Germanic stereotypes are invoked by his severe facial expressions, the expressionistic lighting of his outline and the stern efficiency with which he sets out to complete his mission in both films. However, this is frequently undercut by currents of humour that humanise the stereotype. In *Contraband*, this is most evident in the way that he handles Valerie Hobson when she refuses to wear a life jacket while on board his ship. His attempts to discipline this 'difficult' woman openly invite a sexual reading, something confirmed by the flirtatious sparring of their dialogue and in the sequence in which they are tied up together. He is further softened by his obvious delight in eating and drinking. His joy at finding real butter after leaving the privations of his submarine in *The Spy in Black* and the extended sequence at the Danish restaurant in *Contraband* are evidence of this.

Expressionistic lighting for Conrad Veidt as the gallant Danish captain and quintessential
Sympathetic Foreigner in *Contraband*.

Even the 'otherness' of his accent becomes a source of amusement as Valerie
Hobson corrects his pronunciation of butter.

Above all, Veidt's characters are men of principle. His U-boat captain in *The Spy
in Black* would rather go down with his ship than be captured. His attempt to outrun
a British destroyer in *Contraband* wins him the respect of her captain. In *Contraband*,
this sense of purpose is contrasted fairly obviously with the deviousness of the chief
German spy, but more surprisingly in *The Spy in Black*, it is contrasted favourably
with the behaviour of the film's erstwhile hero (Sebastian Shaw), who is an apparent drunk and, strictly speaking, an imposter. Shaw's Lieutenant Ashington effectively becomes the film's False Prophet, apparently representing the forces of moral
order and the British national interest, but at best being little more than a shallow,
self-righteous spy. The rather disconcerting fact that the film invites the audience to
side with a German U-boat captain over a British agent was to become a characteristic Powell and Pressburger touch. Any confusion in the propaganda message is
avoided in the second film by having Veidt cast as a Danish sailor who finds himself
caught up in wartime intrigues and ends up helping the Allies combat a nest of
German spies. Similar contradictions occur again in *49th Parallel* (1941) in its story
of a German U-Boat crews attempt to evade capture as they flee across Canada. We
are certainly made to understand the evil character of Nazi Germany in the form of
Eric Portman's ruthless officer. His manic devotion to Hitler and his willingness to

murder innocent bystanders are contrasted with the humanity of the various Canadian characters he encounters. Even the members of his own crew are much more sympathetically drawn. However, the extraordinary single-mindedness with which Lieutenant Hirth leads his men back and forth across the Canadian landscape begins to take on surprisingly heroic proportions. In some respects, Portman's performance takes on elements of The Visionary and prefigures his own later role in *A Canterbury Tale*, as well as Anton Walbrook's appearance in *The Red Shoes*. His coldness makes him the film's villain, but the strength of his conviction almost makes him attractive.

Lined up against him are a number of variations on The Romantic Gentleman, from Anton Walbrook as the gentle, idealistic leader of a Hutterite community, through Laurence Olivier's dashing, courageous French patriot, to Leslie Howard as the embodiment of Western civilisation, whom Hirth accuses of being 'soft and decadent'. We discover him living in the mountains, where he carries out his studies of the Native Indians and protects his Matisse and his Picasso, along with the novels by Thomas Mann and Hemingway that he owns. The philistine Nazis trample on these symbols of enlightened achievement, but Howard is strong as well as sensitive and has his revenge on behalf of culture. Even Hirth's second-in-command, Vogel (Niall MacGinnis), provides a further interpretation of the role, in that this unwilling Nazi finds a home among the Hutterites, where he can again take on the job of

The Canadians encountered by the U-boat in *49th Parallel* represent a range of Romantic Gentlemen, including Laurence Olivier's dashing French patriot.

community baker as he had done in Germany before the war. These figures provide various shadings to the function of The Romantic Gentleman, whether it lies in gentleness, bravado or high-minded intellectualism. What links them is their willingness to uphold a set of values that are seen to be under threat. These values are contained in public symbols such as works of art, but also in an ethic of community and tradition that they all share despite their apparent differences.

The dynamics of a male group again form the centre of the narrative in *One of Our Aircraft Is Missing*, a more straightforward and less compromised exercise in war propaganda than *49th Parallel*. The film has obvious affinities with other war films of the period such as *In Which We Serve* (1942) and *The Way Ahead* (1944), where a small, disparate group of characteristic British males are thrown together by the circumstances of war and then bond together into an effective fighting force despite their individual differences. Here, that bond is almost taken for granted and the differences in background between the men are sketched in economically: one is northern, another from the West Country, the third is an ex-actor and their leader is a former diplomat. The group as a whole share many of the characteristics of Powell and Pressburger's Romantic Gentlemen (they take considerable pleasure in food and drink, they are respectful towards the women they encounter, they are surprisingly gentle for trained combatants), but their individuality is frequently submerged by the

The dynamics of a male group thrown together by war: members of the crew of 'B for Bertie' in *One of our Aircraft is Missing*.

need for them to operate as a team. There are two exceptions to this: Hugh Williams as Frank Shelley, the ex-actor, who although occasionally the butt of some of the other airmen's joke, exhibits more overtly aspects of The Romantic Gentleman, as is particularly revealed when he greets Googie Withers's resistance fighter by kissing her hand; the second, and much more significant here, is The Father Figure as played by Godfrey Tearle. George is clearly older than the other men, but he is the one they turn to once they are stranded in the Netherlands. He is also the embodiment of the values they are fighting for. He is given the honour of making the speech of thanks to the Dutch resistance, which he does with considerable feeling. His importance to the rest of the team is indicated when he is wounded during their escape and has to be cared for and protected by the others. At the end of the film, they refuse to leave him in order to make their own escape. The film's final statement of its patriotic intentions is indicated in the scenes that show the various members of the crew preparing to go out on another flight, including George.

The role of Godfrey Tearle, and in particular one deleted sequence in which he explains to the young Hugh Burden that despite their surface differences they are in fact very alike, provided the initial prototype for what is, perhaps, Powell and Pressburger's most complex male character, Clive Wynne Candy (Roger Livesey), in *The Life and Death of Colonel Blimp*.[6] The complexity of this character is confirmed by the fact that he defies simple allocation to one of the types I have devised; in fact, he bridges two of them. The older Clive is obviously enough our Father Figure and is clearly viewed this way by his young driver 'Johnny', played by Deborah Kerr. He is the embodiment of the virtues of old England, indicated by his obvious love of the traditions of the officer class (gentlemen's clubs, dressing for dinner, hunting and shooting) and by his unimpeachable sense of honour and duty. The instinctively conservative, and even reactionary, aspects of this 'Blimpish' persona are, however, revealed to be only part of the picture. This is most movingly conveyed in his relationship with the German officer Theo Kretschmar-Schuldorff (Anton Walbrook) and in his speech to the young officer (James McKechnie) who mocks him for his large stomach and moustaches. It is precisely this point, that appearances are untrustworthy, that lies at the heart of this speech and that is revealed in the extended flashback at the centre of the film's narrative. It is here that we witness the tenderness and loyalty of his relationship with Theo, which, as Christie puts it, provides an 'evocative vision of friendship that transcends nationality'.[7] This is starkly contrasted with the tone and manner of the young sergeant, effectively the film's False Prophet, who is strident, arrogant and offhand in his relationship with his fiancé and, at least for the moment, oblivious to the truth worth of Wynne Candy.

The young Clive Candy is every inch The Romantic Gentleman and finds his mirror image in Theo. Candy is literary (at least to the extent of reading *The Strand* and knowing Conan Doyle), is inevitably fond of dining and is romantic and flirtatious with women. His bravery, as evidenced by his Victoria Cross, is balanced with his regard for the enemy and his sense of honour in battle; he argues that Britain can still win with 'clean soldiering'. His romanticism initially takes the form of a courtly

The young Clive Wynne Candy (Roger Livesey) finds his mirror image as Romantic Gentleman in Theo Kretchmar-Schuldorff (Anton Walbrook).

The older Clive has become a Father Figure in *The Life and Death of Colonel Blimp*, but Theo retains his 'continental charm'.

longing of Edith, the woman who prefers his friend Theo, and is reaffirmed by his lifelong pattern of seeking out women who remind him of her. Even his big-game hunting is excused as a reaction to his personal losses, firstly of Edith to Theo and then at the death of his wife. Anton Walbrook's Theo is almost a pared-down version of the youthful Candy, whose romanticism is tempered by a thread of harsher common sense. Nonetheless, even here, as Andrew Moor puts it, his 'foreignness is the occasion for romance, and the continental charm of the star is celebrated'.[8] Powell and Pressburger's identification with these two characters is clearly strong and almost seems to provide a mirror of their own friendship. Theo's powerful speech describing the feelings of the refugee coming to Britain is a heartfelt echo of Pressburger's own circumstances, and Powell's intense Englishness is caught in the film's final scene as Wynne Candy defiantly reaffirms the fact that he, and his values, are still with us.

The growing complexity of Powell and Pressburger's male characters is confirmed by all three of the main figures who appear in *A Canterbury Tale*, but especially in the form of Eric Portman's Thomas Colpeper. Colpeper is probably the first real appearance of The Visionary and here is explicitly linked to what Raymond Durgnat called the 'hard-edged soft-centred mysticism' of Powell and Pressburger's work.[9] In some senses, Colpeper is another Father Figure, believing that he knows what is best for the young soldiers whose minds must be kept on the job in hand, which he tries to achieve by preventing them from coming into contact with the distractions of the opposite sex (even if this means sneaking about at night pouring glue into the hair of the unfortunate women concerned). Like Clive Candy, he is associated with traditional images of Englishness, particularly through the Kent countryside and his love of history. His office is a shrine to oak beams and suits of armour. Like so many Powell and Pressburger heroes, he is given opportunities to make speeches that outline his values, here in the form of the slide show he presents for the young soldiers. However, it is also here that he slips over into the more messianic role of The Visionary. Silhouetted against the light of the lantern, he is an almost sinister figure, a kind of shaman or magician who conjures up the past for his acolytes. His zeal pushes him past the easygoing self-belief of a Clive Candy into something harder and darker. Andrew Spicer points to the disturbing aspects of Portman's screen persona, placing him in his category of 'Post-war Psychotics'.[10] Colpeper is complemented by the two other male characters in the film. John Sweet's American sergeant, Bob Johnson, is an unashamed romantic who longs chastely for his absent lover and whose feeling for wood gives him an immediate connection to the village carpenter, which belies any differences in nationality. When he finally encounters Canterbury Cathedral, he decides that it is essentially the same as the wooden church built by his father back home in America. Peter Gibbs, played by Dennis Price, is initially the film's False Prophet. He is a cold cynic who refuses to exhibit belief in anything beyond his own self-interest. However, even he comes under the apparent spell of Colpeper, and arriving in Canterbury is given the chance to play the cathedral's organ, thereby achieving a kind of epiphany or redemption.

Such religious descriptions seem appropriate in a film where the visible manifestations of Englishness take on such a mystical quality and where they are upheld by
Eric Portman's almost divine Colpeper.

A summation of these masculine types, and the values they represent, is provided by *A Matter of Life and Death* (1946). David Niven's Captain Peter D. Carter
is the perfect encapsulation of Powell and Pressburger's Romantic Gentleman. His
opening speech (Powell and Pressburger's male heroes are prone to express their
deepest feelings in slightly theatrical speeches) encapsulates his philosophy of life,
as he longs for a world run according to the teachings of Plato and Jesus, admits
he would rather have been a poet like Raleigh or Marvell than had to fight against
Hitler and, at the point of death, is able to confess his true feelings of affection for
his mother. Here is the characteristic love of high art, veneration for tradition and
sense of chivalric longing that so often typify all of Powell and Pressburger's types
(with the exception of The False Prophet). His politics follow a similar train of
thought as he declares himself 'Conservative by instinct, Labour by experience'. As
Christie suggests, particularly in relation to *I Know Where I'm Going!* (1945), the
politics of Powell and Pressburger's films at the end of the war reflect, at the very
least, an ambivalence towards the election of a new Labour government. They do
this by rejecting socialist utopianism in favour of individualism (here represented
by Peter Carter's desire to escape the sterility of heaven and remain on earth, and
in Technicolor).[11] They certainly celebrate traditional values, but there is also a
strong sense of a new beginning or at least, a reaffirming of old values in a new
age, so that while Peter Carter may be a one-nation Tory at heart, he recognises
that these values might actually find their expression in the reality of a radical
post-war Labour government.

Peter Carter is also injured, anticipating David Farrar's physically and psychologically damaged scientist in *The Small Back Room* (1949). He is trapped within a
subjective world where the nature of his experiences cannot be easily defined, floating freely between physical existence and some spiritual dimension beyond surface
appearances (linking him back to the mysticism of Colpeper in *A Canterbury Tale*).

Abraham Farlan (Raymond
Massey) as False Prophet in the
heavenly trial of *A Matter of Life
and Death*.

In understanding the importance of this other level of knowledge, he is aided by a second advocate for romanticism in the form of Marius Goring's celestial messenger (and French aristocrat), who has no difficulty in identifying with Carter's forlorn love affair. Additional aid comes from Roger Livesey's Father Figure, who provides the necessary guidance to help him find his way back to earth. It is Livesey's Dr Reeves who pleads for Carter's life in the heavenly court against the film's version of the False Prophet, the American patriot Abraham Farlan (Raymond Massey). Reeves's humanity, optimism and warmth are again contrasted with the strident Puritanism of Farlan, whose self-righteousness is a cover for the personal nature of his resentment towards the British (having been killed by one in the American Revolution). He is in that long line of priggish zealots that stretches back to *The Spy in Black*. However, Reeves is a more complex character who also embodies elements of The Visionary. This is particularly apparent in the sequence where we find him in his camera obscura surveying the surrounding village. He adopts the same protective tone as Colpeper as he looks down on the people he loves. His ability magically to conjure their images from the ether mirrors the slide show of *A Canterbury Tale*, and both characters take on the appearance of magicians.

The remainder of Powell and Pressburger's war films play a series of relatively limited variations on these types. The most interesting is, perhaps, David Farrar's role as Sammy Rice, the crippled, alcoholic munitions expert in *The Small Back Room*, who achieves a kind of salvation by taking the place of his dead colleague and dismantling a German booby trap. Sammy might have been another of Powell and Pressburger's Romantic Gentlemen, the last of a dying breed of intellectuals who use their gifts to defend their country, but the characterisation here is pushed much further. Sammy is a deeply troubled man. His confusion and unhappiness are not only manifest in his drinking and occasional violence, but also in the *mise en scène* and cinematography of the film. As so often with Powell and Pressburger, the visual style expresses the subjective world of the central character. This is most obvious in the delirious dream sequence as Sammy tries to resist the lure of a giant bottle of whisky that follows him around his room, but also in the stifling interiors and oppressive darkness that seem to fill the film. There are enough False Prophets for Sammy to fight against in this materialistic post-war Britain, from ignorant government ministers (Robert Morley), to cynical, Machiavellian civil servants (Jack Hawkins). Sammy's more traditional values are contrasted with the shabby expediency of this world. Such interesting complexities are largely missing from the rather routine heroics of *The Battle of the River Plate* (1956), although again it is The Sympathetic Foreigner who steals the show. The victorious British naval officers, led by Anthony Quayle and John Gregson, are unremarkable, two-dimensional figures, whereas Peter Finch as Captain Langsdorff is every bit The Romantic Gentleman, dashing and skilful as a naval commander and thoroughly decent and honourable as a human being (as evidenced by his merciful treatment of his British captives and his willingness to scupper the *Graf Spee* in order to save lives). The film is at pains to show the regard in which he is held by the British

The Sympathetic Foreigner, in the shape of Peter Finch's German battleship commander, steals the show in *The Battle of the River Plate*.

officers, and Finch's charismatic performance, with his flamboyant cigar smoking, contrasts markedly with the blandness of his British counterparts. *Ill Met by Moonlight* (1957) is another story of bravery in foreign lands, as Dirk Bogarde leads an assorted group of British soldiers and Greek partisans in the daring kidnapping of a senior German officer. Bogarde is yet another Romantic Gentleman, with a dash of something more dangerous and free-spirited. He dresses in local Greek costume and describes himself as 'a latter-day Lord Byron'. If the film fails to generate much dynamism around this figure, it may be, as Powell himself suggested, due to the failure of Bogarde to engage fully with the role.[12]

Applying this form of typology to the films inevitably leads to some simplifications and omissions. However, consistent patterns in the depiction of masculinity do emerge when the films are considered in this way. Taking into account the fact that these films are linked by their concern with war, it remains remarkable that warfare itself is such a distant and abstracted element in most of them. It is almost a shock when Clive Candy actually finds himself on a First World War battlefield although even here we do not see any actual fighting. With the exception of *The Battle of the River Plate*, there is barely a scene of bloodshed, violent conflict or direct suffering in these ten films. Instead, Powell and Pressburger deal with war less as a tangible event than as a conflict of ideals. These films are less about the process of war than they are about what is being fought for and defended. Here, three of my character types are linked: whether it is the paternal Father Figure, the dashing Romantic Gentleman or the obsessive Visionary, these types are joined by their defence of a set of shared ideals. In addition, the function of The Sympathetic Foreigner is often to confirm that this set of ideals, although seen as characteristically English, is not necessarily nationally specific, but can be shared even by your enemy. Even the False Prophet, who sometimes acts to counter these ideals, often ends by recanting and grudgingly agreeing to support them as well.

Attempting to define these values is less easy. At their heart is a seemingly contradictory combination of the reactionary and radical. Christie examines the nature of this vision through reference to the influence on Powell and Pressburger of Kipling (as does Raymond Durgnat) and of G. K. Chesterton.[13] I would suggest a further point of reference in the essays of George Orwell.[14] This may not seem the most obvious comparison, considering Orwell's openly socialist viewpoint, as expressed in the essay 'Why I Write', particularly when Powell and Pressburger are commonly seen as intrinsically conservative in their values. However, Orwell's essays combine his radical belief in a world governed by principles of equality and fairness with a love of British traditions. This can be seen in such essays as 'In Defence of P. G. Wodehouse', 'The Art of Donald McGill' and, inevitably, 'Kipling' (which defends Kipling against charges of imperialism by arguing for the complexity of his account of Britishness). Orwell's essays combine the sentiments (even sentimentality) of a little Englander with the radicalism of a political Puritan. It is easy enough to trace this tradition in left-wing thinking right through to a more contemporary figure such as Tony Benn, whose socialist beliefs are combined with a love for the traditions of parliament and the joys of tea drinking. It is this odd conflation of seemingly disparate political leanings that characterise the ideals that Powell and Pressburger's masculine types defend in time of war. The other feature that distinguishes these men, and which is similarly contradictory (and typical of Powell and Pressburger), is that for all that they are officers involved in the violence and horror of warfare, they remain essentially gentle men.

NOTES

1. R. Dyer, *Stars*, London: BFI, 1998, pp. 47–59.

2. Bruce Babington, ed., *British Stars and Stardom*, Manchester and New York: Manchester University Press, 2001, p. 22.

3. Andrew Spicer, *Typical Men: The Representation of Masculinity in Popular British Cinema*, London: I. B. Tauris, 2001.

4. Ian Christie, 'Blimp, Churchill and the State', in Christie, ed., *Powell, Pressburger and Others*, London: BFI, 1978.

5. Roy Armes, *A Critical History of British Cinema*, London: Secker and Warburg, 1978, p. 218.

6. James Howard, *Michael Powell*, London: B. T. Batsford, 1996, pp. 42–3.

7. Ian Christie, *Arrows of Desire: The Films of Michael Powell and Emeric Pressburger*, London: Faber & Faber, 1985, p. 3.

8. Andrew Moor, 'Dangerous Limelight: Anton Walbrook and the Seduction of the English', in Babington, ed., *British Stars and Stardom*, p. 82.

9. Raymond Durgnat, 'Michael Powell', in Christie, ed., *Powell, Pressburger and Others*, p. 66.

10. Spicer, *Typical Men*, pp. 176–7.

11. Christie, *Arrows of Desire*, pp. 52–8.

12. Michael Powell, *Million Dollar Movie*, London: Mandarin, 1993, p. 363.

13. Christie, *Arrows of Desire*, pp. 6–8.

14. See George Orwell, *Collected Essays*, London: Secker and Warburg, 1961.

Filmography

Much of the fundamental work on developing this filmography from its origins in my *Powell, Pressburger and Others* was done by Markku Salmi, with additional information and corrections from many sources, including David Meeker and Steve Crook. Credits for films in which Powell was not extensively involved have been abbreviated. Otherwise all credits are as complete as possible. Wherever possible names are given in the order and style that they appear on the credits, or in contemporary promotional literature. Additional credits information appears in square brackets. All films were produced in Great Britain unless otherwise stated. No print is known to exist of titles marked *. *Ian Christie*

Mare Nostrum (USA)   1926

d – Rex Ingram. *p. c* – MGM. *p* – Rex Ingram, Harry Lachman, George Noffka.
p. manager – Harry Lachman. *sc* – Willis Goldbeck, based on the novel by Vicente Blasco Ibáñez.
ph – John F. Seitz. *ed* – Grant Whytock. [*art d* – Ben Carré]

main cast – Alice Terry (*Freya Talberg*), Antonio Moreno (*Ulysses Feragut*).

102 mins. US release – 15 February.

Rex Ingram had made his name in Hollywood with an adaptation of Ibáñez's earlier Great War novel, The Four Horsemen of the Apocalypse, in 1921. Now based in Nice, after falling out with Louis Mayer, he turned to Ibáñez's tale of a Spanish sea captain who is tricked into helping the German navy by a seductive spy. Ingram's wife, Alice Terry, played the spy who goes proudly to her death, and Moreno plays the upright captain. Powell got his first experience of production as a general assistant on the film at the Victorine Studios, eventually writing some of the intertitles.

The Magician (USA)   1926

d/p/sc – Rex Ingram, based on a novel by Somerset Maugham. *p. c* – Metro-Goldwyn-Mayer. *p. manager* – Harry Lachman [*prod. asst* – Michael Powell]. *ph* – John F. Seitz.
ed – Grant Whytock. *art d* – Henri Ménessier.

Alice Terry (*Margaret Dauncey*), Paul Wegener (*Oliver Haddo, the magician*), Ivan Petrovich (*Dr Arthur Burdon*), Firmin Grémier (*Dr Porhoet*), Gladys Hamer (*Susie Boud*),
Hubert Stowitts (*Dancing Faun*), Henry Wilson (*Haddo's servant*) [Claude and Gerald Fielding (*Fauns*), Michael Powell (*Man with balloon at snake charming*)].

83 mins. *US rel* – 24 October.

Maugham's 1907 novel drew on the notoriety of Aleister Crowley, self-styled 'Great Beast' and magician, whom he had known in Paris at the beginning of the century. For the Crowley figure of 'Haddo', Ingram secured the German actor Paul Wegener, famous for portraying the Golem, who needs the blood of a virgin to pursue his dream of creating life. Alice Terry plays a sculptress who falls in love with her doctor, but comes under the influence of Haddo and is taken to his castle, where she witnesses a fantastic witches' Sabbath. Powell, who had been a general assistant with the unit, made his 'debut as one of Rex's clowns' in a fairground scene. He described Ingram's comic sense as 'rudimentary'.

The Garden of Allah (USA)   1927

d/p – Rex Ingram. *p. c* – Metro-Goldwyn-Mayer. *p. manager* – Harry Lachman. [*asst d* – Michael Powell]. *sc* – Robert Hitchins (from his own novel), Willis Goldbeck, Martin Brown (titles). *ph* – Lee Garmes, Monroe Bennett, Marcel Lucien. *ed* – Arthur Ellis. *set dec* – Henri Ménessier. *m* – William Axt, Edward Bowes, David Mendoza.

Alice Terry (*Domini Enfilden*), Ivan Petrovich (*Father Adrien/Boris Androvsky*), Marcel Vibert (*Count Anteoni*), H. H. Wright (*Lord Rens*), Pâquerette (*Suzanne*), Gerald Fielding (*Batouch*), Armand Dutertre (*Priest of Beni-Mora*), Ben Sadour (*the sand diviner*), Claude Fielding (*Hadj*), Rehba Bent Salah (*Ayesha*), Michael Powell (*a tourist*).

96 mins. *US rel* – 2 September.

Robert Hitchins's romantic potboiler had already been filmed in 1916 and would be filmed again as a talkie in 1936. Powell suggests that Ingram accepted MGM's proposal because he was becoming interested in Islamic culture, and this film would require location shooting in North Africa. As well as assisting Lachman with the production, Powell received his first screen credit as a quintessential English tourist.

Riviera Revels (GB/France)   1927–8

d/p/sc – Harry Lachman [Michael Powell]. *ph* – G. Ventimiglia and Marcel Lucien.

Michael Powell (*Cicero Baedeker Symp*), Madeleine Guitry (*Mme Sidonie Papillon*), John Tudor (*Sheik Abdrool Krimp*), Georges Terof (*Rev. Blackton Beetle*), Henriette Terof (*Mrs Blackton Beetle*), Marie Anie (*Mlle Ophelie Beetle*), Gerald Fielding (*Apollo Naris*), Francis Mylio (*the guide*).

12 'one-reel *Travelaughs*', *c.* 10 mins each. *dist* – Wardour.

A series of knockabout silent comedies, filmed in picturesque locations around the Riviera, after the disbandment of Rex Ingram's company in Nice left Lachman and Powell unemployed. Powell played an eccentric English tourist, performing his own stunts and doing some direction. (Several episodes are preserved in the National Film and Television Archive.)

Blackmail   1929

d – Alfred Hitchcock. *p. c* – British International Pictures. [*p* – John Maxwell]. *sc* – Charles Bennett (from his own play), Alfred Hitchcock, Benn W. Levy [Michael Powell]. *ph* – Jack Cox (*cam. asst* – Michael Powell, Ronald Neame]. *ed* – Emile de Ruelle. *art d* – C. Wilfred Arnold. *m* – Lew Henderson, Buddy G. DeSylva, Herbert Bath. [*sd* – Dallas Bower].

Anny Ondra (*Alice White*), Sara Allgood (*Mrs White*), Charles Paton (*Mr White*), John Longden (*Det. Frank Webber*), Donald Calthrop (*Tracy*), Cyril Ritchard (*Mr Crewe, the artist*), Hannah Jones (*Landlady*), Harvey Braban (*Inspector*).

96 mins. *UK rel* – 30 June. *UK dist* – Wardour.

Powell revealed in his memoirs that he had helped Hitchcock with the adaptation of Bennett's original for what would become Britain's first talkie, improving the third act and apparently suggesting the British Museum as the scene of the final chase after the blackmailer Tracy. Powell also shot publicity stills of the Czech actress Anny Ondra, whose voice was dubbed by Joan Barry, and served as camera assistant.

*Caste   1930
d – Campbell Gullan [Michael Powell]. *p. c* – Harry Rowson (Ideal). *p* – Jerome Jackson. *sc* – Michael Powell, from a play by T. W. Robertson. *ph* – Geoffrey Faithful. *e* *d* – John Seabourne.

Hermione Baddeley (*Polly Eccles*), Nora Swinburne (*Esther Eccles*), Alan Napier (*Capt. Hawtree*), Sebastian Shaw (*Hon. George d'Alroy*), Ben Field (*Albert Eccles*), Edward Chapman (*Ben Gerridge*), Mabel Terry-Lewis (*Marquise*).

70 mins. *UK dist* – United Artists.

Already twice filmed in the teens, this story of a cockney girl who marries a young aristocrat, then comes to live with his family when he is reported killed in action, was updated from the Boer War to the Great War. 'A story about class', as Powell summarised it, gave him his first experience of directing a sound film during Gullan's frequent absences.

*77 Park Lane   1931
d – Albert de Courville. *p. c* – Players' Guild. *p* – William Hutter. *p. supervisor* – John Harding. *sc* – Michael Powell, with dialogue by Reginald Berkeley, from a play by Walter C. Hackett. *ph* – Geoffrey Faithfull, Mutz Greenbaum. *ed* – Arthur Seabourne. *art d* – Lawrence Irving. *sd* – Rex Haworth.

Dennis Neilson-Terry (*Lord Brent*), Betty Stockfield (*Mary Connor*), Malcolm Keen (*Sherringham*), Ben Walden (*Sinclair*), Cecil Humphreys (*Paul*), Esmond Knight (*Philip Connor*), Molly Johnson (*Eve Grayson*), Roland Culver (*Sir Richard Carrington*).

82 mins. *UK dist* – United Artists.

'A rich and debonair young man returns from abroad with a friend, goes to his town house and finds that, in his absence, a bunch of crooks have rented it and are running a gambling club there. All the action took place in the house [and] the situation gave scope for misunderstandings, comedy, thrills, fights, glamour, lovely clothes, stolen jewels and suspense' (Powell). Shot with three casts of principals – British, French and Spanish – as a 'multinational', a shortlived experiment of the early sound period.

*Two Crowded Hours   1931
d – Michael Powell. *p. c* – Film Engineering. *p* – Jerome Jackson, Henry Cohen. *sc* – J. Jefferson Farjeon. *ph* – Geoffrey Faithfull. *ed* – A. Seabourne. *art d* – C. Saunders.

John Longden (*Harry Fielding*), Jane Walsh (*Joyce Danton*), Jerry Verno (*Jim*), Michael Hogan (*Scammell*), Edward Barber (*Tom Murray*).

43 mins. *t. s* – 8 July. *UK rel* – 28 December. *UK dist* – Fox.

A murderer escapes from prison and tries to kill everyone who might give evidence against him, pursued by a detective who is helped by a taxi driver (Verno). Powell's first film as a solo director.

*My Friend the King   1931

d – Michael Powell. *p. c* – Film Engineering. *p* – Jerome Jackson. *sc* – J. Jefferson Farjeon, from
his own story. *ph* – Geoffrey Faithfull. *ed* – Arthur Seabourne.
art d – Charles Saunders.

Jerry Verno (*Jim*), Robert Holmes (*Captain Felz*), Tracy Holmes (*Count Huelin*), Eric Pavitt
(*King Ludwig*), Phyllis Loring (*Princess Helma*), Luli Hohenberg (*Countess Zena*), H Saxon Snell
(*Karl*), Victor Fairley (*Josef*).

47 mins. *t. s* – 23 September. *rel* – 4 April 1932. *UK dist* – Paramount.

Verno repeats his role in *Two Crowded Hours* as a comic taxi driver, this time caught up in a plot
to kidnap a young foreign king staying in London.

Rynox   1931

d – Michael Powell. *p. c* – Film Engineering. *p* – Jerome Jackson. [*sc* – Jerome Jackson, Michael
Powell, J. Jefferson Farjeon, Philip MacDonald]. From the novel by Philip MacDonald. *ph* –
Geoffrey Faithfull, Arthur Grant. *ed* – Arthur Seabourne.
art d – G. C. Waygrove. *construction* – W. Saunders. *sd* – Rex Howarth.

Stewart Rome (*F. X. Benedik*), John Longden (*Anthony X. 'Tony' Benedik*), Dorothy Boyd (*Peter*),
Charles Paton (*Samuel Richforth*), Leslie Mitchell (*Woolrich*), Sybil Grove (*secretary*), Cecil
Clayton, Fletcher Lightfoot (*Prout*), Edmud Willard (*Captain James*).

47 mins. *t. s* – November. *rel* – 7 May 1932. *UK dist* – Ideal.

A businessman is threatened by a mystery stranger and later found dead, but the insurance
inquiry reveals that he had invented his assailant.

*The Rasp   1931

d – Michael Powell. *p. c* – Film Engineering. *p* – Jerome Jackson. *sc* – Philip MacDonald, from
his own story. *ph* – Geoffrey Faithfull. *art d* – Frank Wells.

Claude Horton (*Anthony Gethryn*), Phyllis Loring (*Lucia Masterson*), C. M. Hallard
(*Sir Arthur Coates*), James Raglan (*Alan Deacon*), Thomas Weguelin (*Inspector Boyd*),
Carol Coombe (*Dora Masterson*), Leonard Brett (*Jimmy Masterson*).

44 mins. *t. s* – 3 December. *rel* – 11 April 1932. *UK dist* – Fox.

A young newspaper man finds a cabinet minister murdered with a rasp and makes his own
inquiries, calling into question the police's suspicion of the minister's secretary.

*The Star Reporter   1931

d – Michael Powell. *p. c* – Film Engineering. *p* – Jerome Jackson. *sc* – Ralph Smart, Philip
MacDonald. Based on a story by MacDonald. *ph* – Geoffrey Faithfull. [*add. ph* – Michael
Powell] *art d* – Frank Wells.

Harold French (*Major Starr*), Isla Bevan (*Lady Susan Loman*), Garry Marsh (*Mandel*), Spencer
Trevor (*Lord Longbourne*), Anthony Holles (*Bonzo*), Noel Dainton (*Colonel*),
Elsa Graves (*Oliver*), Philip Morant (*Jeff*).

44 mins. *t. s* – 10 December. *rel* – 9 May 1932. *UK dist* – Fox.

Described by *Picturegoer* as 'an unpretentious and fantastic story of a smash-and-grab raid, with a
newspaper reporter – in the American tradition – bringing the crooks to justice'.

Hotel Splendide 1932

d – Michael Powell. *p. c* – Film Engineering. A Gaumont-British Picture Corporation Ltd Presentation. *p* – Jerome Jackson. *story* – Philip MacDonald, Ralph Smart. [sc – Ralph Smart, from a story by Philip MacDonald]. *ph* – Geoffrey Faithfull, Arthur Grant. *ed* – Arthur Seabourne. *art d* – Charles Saunders. *m/sd* – Michael Rose.

Jerry Verno (*Jerry Mason*), Anthony Holles ('*Mrs LeGrange*'), Edgar Norfolk ('*Gentleman Charlie*'), Philip Morant (*Mr Meek*), Sybil Grove (*Mrs Harkness*), Vera Sherborne (*Joyce Dacre*), Paddy Browne (*Miss Meek*). [Michael Powell (*eavesdropping device operator*)].

53 mins. *t. s* – 23 March. *rel* – 18 July. *UK dist* – Ideal.

The innocent inheritor of a seaside hotel discovers that few of his guests are what they seem to be, and that the loot from a famous robbery was buried beneath where the hotel now stands. Long believed lost, *Hotel Splendide* was discovered in the late 1990s and first shown in 2000.

*C. O. D. 1932

d – Michael Powell. *p. c* – Westminster Films. *p* – Jerome Jackson. *sc* – Ralph Smart, from a story by Philip MacDonald. *ph* – Geoffrey Faithfull. *art d* – Frank Wells.

Garry Marsh (*Peter Craven*), Hope Davey (*Frances*), Arthur Stratton (*Briggs*), Sybil Grove (*Mrs Briggs*), Roland Culver (*Edward*), Peter Gawthorne (*detective*), Cecil Ramage (*Vyner*), Bruce Belfrage (*Philip*).

66 mins. *t. s* – 17 March. *rel* – 22 August. *UK dist* – United Artists.

Peter Craven becomes involved in elaborate efforts to dispose of a body he finds while trying to burgle a West End flat, encouraged by the girl most likely to be accused of her stepfather's murder, to whom he eventually proposes.

His Lordship 1932

d – Michael Powell. *p. c* – Westminster Films. *p* – Jerome Jackson. [*p. manager* – Walter Tennyson]. *sc* – Ralph Smart. Based on the novel *The Right Honorable* by Oliver Madox Heuffer. *ph* – Geoffrey Faithfull. *art d* – Frank Wells. *m/lyrics* – V. C. Clinton-Baddeley, Eric Maschwitz. [*m. director* – Maurice Winnick].

Jerry Verno (*Bert Gibbs*), Janet McGrew (*Ilya Myona*), Ben Welden (*Washington Lincoln*), Polly Ward (*Leninia*), Peter Gawthorne (*Ferguson*), Muriel George (*Mrs Gibbs*), Michael Hogan (*Comrade Curzon*), V. C. Clinton-Baddeley (*Comrade Howard*), Patrick Ludlow (*Hon. Grimsthwaite*).

77 mins. *t. s* – 2 June. *rel* – 5 December. *UK dist* – United Artists.

Rediscovered in the 1990s, this odd mixture of musical comedy and political satire – Jerry Verno's cheerful Cockney finds himself an unexpected peer and courts a Russian film star to please his revolutionary mother – shows off Powell's eccentric humour and willingness to mix genres.

*Born Lucky 1932

d – Michael Powell. *p. c* – Westminster Films. *p* – Jerome Jackson. *s c* – Ralph Smart. Based on the novel *Mops* by Oliver Sandys. *ph* – Geoffrey Faithfull. *art d* – Alan Campbell-Gray.

Talbot O'Farrell (*Turnips*), Renee Ray (*Mops*), John Longden (*Frank Dale*), Ben Welden (*Harriman*), Helen Ferrers (*Lady Chard*), Barbara Gott (*cook*), Paddy Browne (*Patty*), Roland Gillett (*John Chard*).

78 mins. *t. s* – 5 December. *rel* – 6 April 1933. *UK dist* – MGM.

Another low-budget musical, the 'simple story of a humble girl's rise to stage fame' (*Picturegoer*).

Perfect Understanding   1933
d – Cyril Gardner. *p. c* – Gloria Swanson Productions Ltd. A United Artists Picture.
p. manager – Sergei Nolbandov. *asst. d* – Thorold Dickinson. *sc* – Miles Malleson,
Michael Powell. Based on a story by Powell. *ph* – Curt Courant. *art d* – Edward Carrick.
m – Henry Sullivan.

Gloria Swanson (*Judy*), Laurence Olivier (*Nicholas*), John Halliday (*Ronnson*),
Sir Nigel Playfair (*Lord Portleigh*), Michael Farmer (*George*), Genevieve Tobin (*Kitty*),
Nora Swinburne (*Stephanie*), Charles Cullum (*Sir John*), Peter Cawthorne (*butler*), Rosalinde
Fuller (*cook*), Evelyn Bostock (*maid*), O. B. Clarence (*Dr Graham*), Mary Jerrold (*Mrs Graham*).

87 mins. *rel* – January. *dist* – United Artists.

Powell contributed the story and co-scripted what was generally considered an unsuccessful
attempt to make a Hollywood-style marriage comedy in Britain, teaming Swanson with the
rising young Olivier. Judy and Nicholas have an understanding that they will never disagree –
until Nicholas is attracted to another.

The Fire Raisers   1933
d – Michael Powell. *p. c* – Gaumont-British. *p* – Jerome Jackson. *sc* – Michael Powell, Jerome
Jackson [from an original story]. *ph* – Leslie Rowson. *ed* – Derek Twist.
art d – Alfred Junge. *costumeume* – Gordon Conway. *sd* – A. F. Birch.

Leslie Banks (*Jim Bronson*), Anne Grey (*Arden Brent*), Carol Goodner (*Helen Vaughan*), Frank
Cellier (*Brent*), Francis L. Sullivan (*Stedding*), Laurence Anderson (*Twist*),
Harry Caine (*Bates*), Joyce Kirby (*Polly*), George Merritt (*Sonners*).

77 mins. *t. s* – 18 September. *rel* – 22 January 1934. *UK dist* – Woolf & Freedman.

'A sort of Warner Brothers newspaper headline story' (Powell). A fire investigator builds up a
large business and maries the daughter of a Lloyd's underwriter. He also runs up large betting
debts and goes into partnership with an arsonist in an attempt to pay these off. When he is
unmasked, he goes to his own death, after rescuing another investigator.

The Night of the Party   1934
d – Michael Powell. *p. c* – Gaumont-British Picture Corporation. [*p* – Jerome Jackson].
asst. d – Bryan Wallace. *sc* – Ralph Smart. From the play by Roland Pertwee and
John Hastings Turner. *dial* – Roland Pertwee, John Hastings Turner. *ph* – Glen MacWilliams. *art
d* – Alfred Junge. *costumeume* – Gordon Conway. *sd rec* – S. Jolly.

Malcolm Keen (*Lord Studholme*), Jane Baxter (*Peggy Studholme*), Ian Hunter (*Guy Kennington*),
Leslie Banks (*Sir John Holland*), Viola Keats (*Joan Holland*), Ernest Thesiger (*Adrian Chiddiatt*),
Jane Millican (*Anne Chiddiatt*), W. Graham Browne (*General Piddington*), Muriel Aked (*Princess
Amelia of Corsova*), Gerald Barry, Cecil Ramage (*Howard*), John Turnbull (*Ramage*), Laurence
Anderson (*defence counsel*), Louis Goodrich, Roebuck. [Gordon Begg (*Miles*)].

61 mins. *t. s* – Feb. *UK rel* – 16 July. *UK dist* – Gaumont-British. *US rel* – 1935. *US title* – *The
Murder Party*.

A newspaper magnate gives a lavish party in honour of a visiting princess, and the guests are invited to play 'Murder'. When the lights are turned on again, the magnate is dead and almost everyone present is a suspect. Although his secretary Guy is charged, during the trial Chiddiatt, a foppish 'modern' novelist played in high-camp style by Ernest Thesiger – about to be seen in Whale's *Bride of Frankenstein* – becomes deranged and confesses, before killing himself.

Red Ensign   1934

d – Michael Powell. *p. c* – Gaumont-British. *exec. p* – Michael Balcon. *p* – Jerome Jackson. *dial* – L. du Garde Peach. Adapted from a story by Michael Powell, Jerome Jackson.
ph – Leslie Rowson. *ed* – Geoffrey Barkas. *art d* – Alfred Junge. *costume* – Gordon Conway. *sd rec* – G. Birch.

Leslie Banks (*David Barr*), Carol Goodner (*June MacKinnon*), Frank Vosper (*Lord Dean*), Alfred Drayton (*Manning*), Campbell Gullan (*Hannay*), Percy Parsons (*Arthur Casey*), Fewlass Llewellyn (*Sir Gregory*), Henry Oscar (*Raglan*), Allan Jeayes (*Emerson,* aka *Grierson*), Donald Calthrop (*MacLeod*), Henry Caine (*Bassett*). [John Laurie (*wages accountant*), Frederick Piper (*bowler-hatted man in bar*)].

69 mins. *t. s* – 2 February. *UK rel* – 4 June. *UK dist* – Gaumont-British. *US rel* – 1935/6. *US title* – *Strike!*

A Clydeside shipbuilder risks his business to develop a new design, but his board will not back him. Rather than risk defeat, he forges a signature to gain extra finance and is arrested, but the new ship is a success. With some location shooting in Glasgow, and a dynamic performance by Banks, the film struck an unusual note of topicality in British film-making after the Depression.

Something Always Happens   1934

d – Michael Powell. *p. c* – Warner Brothers. First National Productions Ltd, Teddington Studios. *exec. p* – Irving Asher. *sc* – Brock Williams. *ph* – Basil Emmott. *ed* – Ralph Dawson. *art d* – Peter Proud. *costume* – Louis Brooks. *sd* – Leslie Murray, H. C. Pearson.

Ian Hunter (*Peter Middleton*), Nancy O'Neil (*Cynthia Hatch*), Peter Gawthorne (*Benjamin Hatch*), John Singer (*Billy*), Muriel George (*Mrs Badger, the landlady*), Barry Livesey (*George Hamlin*). [Millicent Wolf (*Glenda*), Louie Emery (*Mrs Tremlett*), Reg Marcus ('*Coster*'), George Zucco (*proprietor of the Café de Paris*)].

69 mins. *t. s* – 21 June. *rel* – 10 December. *UK dist* – Warner Brothers-First National.

A carefree young motor salesman falls in love with a business tycoon's daughter, who introduces him to her father without revealing who she is. But the tycoon is not impressed by Peter's plan for a new chain of petrol stations, so he sells the idea to a rival concern.

*The Girl in the Crowd   1934

d – Michael Powell. *p. c* – First National. *exec. p* – Irving Asher. *sc* – Brock Williams. *ph* – Basil Emmott. *ed* – Bert Bates.

Barry Clifton (*David Gordon*), Patricia Hilliard (*Marian*), Googie Withers (*Sally*), Harold French (*Bob*), Clarence Blakiston (*Mr Peabody*), Margaret Gunn (*Joyce*), Richard Littledale (*Bill Manners*), Phyllis Morris (*Mrs Lewis*), Patric Knowles (*Tom Burrows*), Marjorie Corbett (*secretary*), Brenda Lawless (*policewoman*), Barbara Waring (*mannequin*), Eve Lister (*Ruby*), Betty Lyne (*Phyllis*), Melita Bell (*assistant manageress*), John Wood (*Harry*).

52 mins. *t. s* – 4 December. *rel* – 20 May 1935. *UK dist* – First National.

A bookseller marries one of the students who comes into his shop. She advises one of her friends, Bob, by phone on how to find a girl – and his choice turns out to be her. The friend ends up in court, accused of insulting behaviour, but all is sorted out by two 'new style' policemen who had been schoolmates of Bob's. 'A complete failure', according to Powell.

The Love Test   1934

d – Michael Powell. *p. c* – Fox British. *unit p* – Leslie L. Landau. *sc* – Selwyn Jepson, from a story by Jack Celestin. *dial* – Selwyn Jepson. *ph* – Arthur Crabtree.

Judy Gunn (*Mary*), Louis Hayward (*John*), Dave Hutcheson (*Thompson*), Googie Withers (*Minnie*), Morris Harvey (*company president*), Aubrey Dexter (*company vice-president*), Jack Knight (*managing director*), Gilbert Davis (*chief chemist*), Eve Turner (*Kathleen*), Bernard Miles (*Allan*), Shayle Gardner (*nightwatchman*), James Craig (*boiler man*). [Thorley Walters, Ian Wilson (*chemists*)].

63 mins. *t. s* – 2 December. *rel* – 1 July 1935. *UK dist* – Fox British.

The directors of a plastics company announce a competition to develop a new fireproof material, in order to decide who will become chief chemist, and Thompson is afraid of being beaten by Mary, the only female chemist in the lab. He therefore persuades John to distract Mary by pretending to fall in love with her, but the pretence turns real. Thompson tries to frustrate the romance, and claim John's discovery as his own, but is found out. An exceptionally stylish production with high-key lighting and elaborate camera movement in the lab scenes.

Lazybones   1935

d – Michael Powell. *p. c* – A Real Art Production. A Julius Hagen Presentation. *asst. d* – Fred V. Merrick. *adaptation* – Gerald Fairlie, from a play by Ernest Denny. *ph* – Ernest Palmer [and Arthur Crabtree]. *ed* – Ralph Kemplen. *art d* – James A. Carter. *m. d* – W. L. Trytel. *sd rec* – Leo Wilkins. *hair* – Charles.

Ian Hunter (*Sir Reginald Ford*), Claire Luce (*Kitty McCarthy*), Bernard Nedell (*Michael McCarthy*), Denys Blakelock (*Hugh Ford*), Mary Gaskell (*Marjory Ford*), Michael Shepley (*Hildebrand Pope*), Pamela Carne (*Lottie Pope*), Bobbie Comber (*Kemp*), Fred Withers (*Richards*), Sara Allgood (*Bridget*), Frank Morgan (*Tom*), Fewlass Llewellyn (*Lord Brockley*), Harold Warrender (*Lord Melton*), Paul Blake (*Viscount Woodland*), Miles Malleson (*the pessimist*).

65 mins. *t. s* – 17 January. *rel* – 24 June. *UK dist* – RKO.

'A comedy of impoverished aristocracy endeavouring to retrieve the family fortune by marrying the lazy elder son to an American heiress' (*Monthly Film Bulletin*, 1935). Sir Reginald thinks he has solved his problem by marrying Kitty McCarthy, until he discovers that she has also been disinherited. Building on the laid-back charm Ian Hunter had already displayed in *Something Always Happens*, Powell described *Lazybones* as 'about a man who couldn't get up in the world'.

The Phantom Light   1935

d – Michael Powell. *p. c* – A Gainsborough Picture. A Gaumont-British Picture Corporation Ltd Presentation. *assoc. p* – Jerome Jackson. *sc* – Ralph Smart. Based on the play *The Haunted Light* by Evadne Price and Joan Roy Byford. *dial* – J. Jefferson Farjeon, Austin Melford. *ph* – Roy Kellino. *ed* – Derek Twist. *art d* – Alex Vetchinsky. [*m* – Louis Levy]. *sd rec* – A. Birch.

Binnie Hale (*Alice Bright*), Gordon Harker (*Sam Higgins*), Donald Calthrop (*David Owen*), Milton Rosmer (*Dr Carey*), Ian Hunter (*Jim Pierce*), Herbert Lomas (*Claff Owen*), Reginald Tate (*Tom Evans*), Barry O'Neill (*Captain Pearce*), Mickey Brantford (*Bob Peters*), Alice O'Day (*Mrs

Owen), Fewlass Llewellyn (*Griffith Owen*), Edgar K. Bruce (*Sgt. Owen*), Louie Emery (*station mistress*).

75 mins. *t. s* – 9 January. *rel* – 5 August. *UK dist* – Gaumont-British. [Reissued 1950.]

After the death of his predecessor, a new keeper arrives at a lighthouse near where some mysterious sightings have also been reported. An undercover naval officer and a female detective appear on the scene, and discover a wreckers' plot to black out the lighthouse and lure ships ashore to be plundered, but their plan is thwarted in an exciting climax.

*The Price of a Song   1935

d/p – Michael Powell. *p. c* – Fox British. *sc* – Michael Barringer, Anthony Gittens. *ph* – Jimmy Wilson.

Campbell Gullan (*Arnold Grierson*), Marjorie Corbett (*Margaret Nevern*), Gerald Fielding (*Michael Hardwicke*), Dora Barton (*Letty Grierson*), Charles Mortimer (*Oliver Broom*), Oriel Ross (*Elsie*), Henry Caine (*Stringer*), Sybil Grove (*Mrs Bancroft*), Eric Maturin (*Nevern*), Felix Aylmer (*Graham*), Cynthia Stock (*Mrs Bush*), Mavis Clair (*Maudie Bancroft*).

67 mins. *t. s* – 24 May. *rel* – 7 October. *UK dist* – Fox British.

Grierson, a bookmaker's clerk, is short of money and forces his daughter to marry an unpleasant, but successful, song-writer for his fortune. When she leaves the song-writer after falling in love with a newspaper reporter, Grierson plots the perfect murder, in the hope that she will inherit the song-writer's money. But he makes a fatal mistake.

*Someday   1935

d – Michael Powell. *p. c* – Warner British. *p* – Irving Asher. *sc* – Brock Williams, based on the novel *Young Nowheres* by I. A. R. Wylie. *ph* – Basil Emmott, Monty Berman. *ed* – Bert Bates. *art d* – Ian Campbell-Gray.

Esmond Knight (*Curley Blake*), Margaret Lockwood (*Emily*), Henry Mollison (*Canley*), Sunday Wilshin (*Betty*), Raymond Lovell (*Carr*), Ivor Bernard (*Hope*), George Pughe (*milkman*), Jane Cornell (*nurse*).

68 mins. *t. s* – 17 July. *rel* – 18 November. *UK dist* – Warner Brothers-First National.

Curley is a lift-boy in a block of flats who falls in love with Emily, a maid, although they do not have enough money to marry. After she has been in hospital, Curley plans a surprise supper for her in a 'borrowed' flat, but the tenant returns unexpectedly and a fight ensues, before all ends happily.

Her Last Affaire   1935

d – Michael Powell. *p. c* – New Ideal Productions Ltd. *p* – Simon Rowson, Geoffrey Rowson. *asst. d* – Sidney Stone. *sc* – Ian Dalrymple, based on the play *S. O. S.* by Walter Ellis. *p* – Leslie Rowson. *cam. op* – Harry Gillam. *ed* – Ian Dalrymple. *art d* – J. Elder Wills. *sd rec* – George E. Burgess.

Hugh Williams (*Alan Heriot*), Francis L. Sullivan (*Sir Julian Weyre*), Viola Keats (*Lady Avril Weyre*), Sophie Stewart (*Jody Weyre*), John Laurie (*Robb*), Googie Withers (*Effie*), Felix Aylmer (*Lord Carnforth*), Cecil Parker (*Sir Arthur Harding*), Henry Caine (*Inspector Marsh*), Eliot Makeham (*Dr Rudd*), Shayle Gardner (*Boxall*), Gerrard Tyrell (*Martin Smith*).

78 mins. *t. s* – 21 October. *rel* – 25 May. *UK dist* – Producers Distributing Corporation.

The secretary to a leading politician wants to marry the politician's daughter, Judy, but first has to clear his name, as his father died with a tarnished reputation. He devises an elaborate plan to persuade the politician's wife to provide evidence of his father's good name, but she dies unexpectedly, due to a mistake in dispensing her medicine, and the secretary falls under suspicion. In the end, her confession clearing his father is discovered and he is free to marry Judy.

*The Brown Wallet   1936

d – Michael Powell. *p. c* – Warner Brothers-First National. *exec. p* – Irving Asher. *sc* – Ian Dalrymple, from a story by Stacy Aumonier. *ph* – Basil Emmott.

Patric Knowles (*John Gillespie*), Nancy O'Neill (*Eleanor*), Henry Caine (*Simmonds*), Henrietta Watson (*Aunt Mary*), Charlotte Leigh (*Miss Barton*), Shayle Gardner (*Wotherspoone*), Edward Dalby (*Minting*), Eliot Makeham (*Hobday*), Bruce Winston (*Julian Thorpe*), Jane Millicam (*Miss Bloxham*), Louis Goodrich (*coroner*), Dick Francis, George Mills (*detectives*).

68 mins. *t. s* – 25 February. *rel* – 20 July. *UK dist* – Warner Brothers-First National.

An impoverished publisher who has asked a wealthy aunt for help finds a wallet full of money in a taxi, but then learns that his aunt has been poisoned and her safe robbed. He is accused of murder, but saved by the real murderer's confession.

Crown v. Stevens   1936

d – Michael Powell. *p. c* – Warner Brothers. First National Productions Ltd, Teddington Studios. *exec. p* – Irving Asher. *sc* – Brock Williams. Based on the novel *Third Time Unlucky* by Laurence Meynell. *ph* – Basil Emmott. *art d* – Peter Proud. *ed* – Bert Bates. *sd rec* – Leslie Murray, H. C. Pearson.

Beatrix Thomson (*Doris Stevens*), Patric Knowles (*Chris Jansen*), Glennis Lorimer (*Molly Hobbs*), Reginald Purdell (*Alf*), Allan Jeayes (*Inspector Carter*), Frederick Piper (*Arthur Stevens*), Googie Withers (*Ella Levine*), Mabel Poulton (*Mamie*). [Morris Harvey (*Julius Bayleck*), Billy Watts (*Joe Andrews*), Davina Craig (*Maggie the maid*), Bernard Miles (*detective*)].

66 mins. *t. s* – 26 March. *rel* – 3 August. *UK dist* – Warner Brothers-First National.

Chris goes to visit a pawnbroker, only to find him dead, and sees his own employer's wife Doris, a former dancer, leaving the premises. She asks him to say nothing, but he goes to her house and discovers his employer dead in the garage. When he confronts her, Doris breaks down, explaining how she hoped to collect her husband's insurance, and gives herself up to the police.

*The Man Behind the Mask   1936

d – Michael Powell. *p. c* – Joe Rock Studios. *p* – Joe Rock. *p. manager* – Stanley Haynes. *sc* – Ian Hay, Sidney Courtenay. Adapted by Jack Byrd from the novel *The Chase of the Golden Plate* by Jacques Futrelle. *ph* – Ernest Palmer. *cam. op* – Erwin Hillier. *ed* – Sam Simmonds. *art d* – George Provis. *sd* – William H. O. Sweeny. *m. d* – Cyril Ray.

Hugh Williams (*Nick Barclay*), Jane Baxter (*June Slade*), Maurice Schwartz (*The Master*), Donald Calthrop (*Dr Walpole*), Henry Oscar (*officer*), Peter Gawthorne (*Lord Slade*), Kitty Kelly (*Miss Weeks*), Ronald Ward (*Jimmy Slade*), George Merritt (*Mallory*), Reginald Tate (*Hayden*), Ivor Bernard (*Hewitt*), Hal Gordon (*sergeant*), Gerald Fielding (*Harrah*), Barbara Everest (*Lady Slade*), Wilf Caithness (*butler*), Moyra Fagan (*Nora*), Sid Crossley (*postman*).

79 mins. *t. s* – 24 March. *rel* – 24 August. *UK dist* – MGM.

On the night he plans to elope with June, Nick is attacked at a masked ball and his assailant takes both June and a valuable heirloom that her father had acquired for his collection. Nick eventually traces the kidnapper and the shield, but falls into the clutches of the international criminal who had masterminded the plot, before being rescued at the last moment. Making what Powell described as this 'horrifically bad thriller', led to its American producer Joe Rock agreeing to back Powell's long-cherished Hebridean story *The Edge of the World*.

The Edge of the World 1937

d/sc – Michael Powell. *p. c* – A Joe Rock Production. [*p* – Joe Rock]. *p. staff* – Gerard Blattner, Arthur Seabourne, Vernon C. Sewell, W. H. Farr, George Black [and Sydney S. S. Streeter]. *ph* – Ernest Palmer, Skeets Kelly, Monty Berman. *ed* – Derek Twist. *asst. ed* – Bob Walters. *props* – W. Osborne. *m. d* – Cyril Ray. *choral effects* – women of the Glasgow Orpheus Choir, *conducted by* Sir Hugh Robertson. *orchestrations* – W. L. Williamson.
sd – L. K. Tregellas. *sd rec* – W. H. O. Sweeny.

The Manson family: John Laurie (*Peter*), Belle Chrystall (*Ruth, his daughter*), Eric Berry (*Robbie, her brother*), Kitty Kirwan (*Jean, their grandmother*). *The Gray family*: Finlay Currie (*James Gray*), Niall MacGinnis (*Andrew Gray*). *And* Grant Sutherland (*John, the Catechist*), Campbell Robson (*Dunbar, the Laird*), George Summers (*trawler skipper*) 'and all the people of the lonely island of Foula where this story was made'. [Margaret Grieg (*baby*), Michael Powell (*Mr Graham, the yachtsman*), Frankie Reidy (*Mrs Graham*), Sydney Streeter (*man at dance*)].

81 mins. *t. s* – 6 July. *rel* – 10 January 1938 [pre-release in London: September 1937). *UK dist* – British Independent Exhibitors (Distribution). *US rel* – 9 September 1938 [74 mins]. *US dist* – Pax Films. *UK reissue* – December 1940 [62 mins]. *NFTVA restoration* – 1990 [74 mins].

Inspired by the evacuation of St Kilda in 1930, Powell created two families who stand for the two factions within the dying island community of 'Hirta'. The Mansons want to stay and eke out a living in the traditional ways, while the Grays conclude the time has come to seek a better life on the mainland. This conflict threatens the love between Andrew and Ruth; and Ruth's brother Robbie dies in a cliff race with Andrew, undertaken to decide the island's future. Later, during the evacuation, Ruth's father Peter also dies, but her baby that has been born during Andrew's absence is saved from death by emergency medical treatment. Powell's first truly personal project was shot entirely on location on the remote island of Foula and in Lerwick. Despite modest commercial success, it attracted critical praise on both sides of the Atlantic and led to a contract with Korda. Powell published an account of the film's making: *200,000 Feet on Foula* (London: Faber & Faber, 1938).

The Spy in Black 1939

d – Michael Powell. [*p. c* – Harefield]. *presented by* – Alexander Korda. *p* – Irving Asher. [*asst. d* – Patrick Jenkins]. *sc* – Emeric Pressburger, from Roland Pertwee's adaptation of a novel by J. Storer Clouston. *ph* – Bernard Browne. *sup. ed* – William Hornbeck. *ed* – Hugh Stewart. *asst. ed* – John Guthrie. *p. designer* – Vincent Korda. *art d* – Frederick Pusey. *m* – Miklos Rozsa. *m. d* – Muir Mathieson. *sd* – A. W. Watkins.

Conrad Veidt (*Captain Ernst Hardt*), Sebastian Shaw (*Cdr. Davis Blacklock*), Valerie Hobson (*Joan, the schoolmistress*), Marius Goring (*Lt Schuster*), June Duprez (*Anne Burnett*), Athole Stewart (*Rev. Hector Matthews*), Agnes Lauchlan (*Mrs Matthews*), Helen Haye (*Mrs Sedley*), Cyril Raymond (*Rev. John Harris*), George Summers (*Captain Ratter*), Hay Petrie (*engineer*), Grant Sutherland (*Bob Bratt*), Robert Rendel (*Admiral*), Mary Morris (*Edwards, the chauffeuse*), Margaret Moffatt (*Kate*), Kenneth Warrington (*Cdr. Denis*),

Torin Thatcher (*submarine officer*). [Bernard Miles (*Hans, hotel receptionist*), Charles Oliver (*German officer*), Skelton Knaggs (*German orderly*), Esma Cannon, Diana Sinclair-Hall].

82 mins. *t. s* – 15 March. *UK rel* – 12 August. *UK/US dist* – Columbia. *US rel* – 7 October [77 mins]. *US title* – *U Boat 29*.

During the First World War, a German submarine officer infiltrates the British naval base at Scapa Flow, not realising that his contact has been discovered and replaced by a female British agent. Although they seem attracted to each other, Hardt remains committed to his sabotage mission, and 'Joan' to ensuring it is frustrated. Notable for its sinister atmosphere and confusing pattern of loyalties, the film's release early in the war gave it unexpected topicality – and launched Powell and Pressburger as a team.

Smith   1939

d – Michael Powell. *p. c* – D&P Productions. Embankment Fellowship Co.
p/sc – R. M. Lloyd. *ph* – Bernard Browne.

Ralph Richardson (*John Smith*), Flora Robson (*Mrs Smith*), Allan Jeayes (*Employer*), Wally Patch (*friend*) [R. M. Lloyd].

10 mins. *UK rel* – June. *UK dist* – Embankment Fellowship Centre (offered free to exhibitors to promote Embankment Fellowship Centres).

This short film was made to promote the work of a charity offering support to unemployed middle-aged men, mostly ex-servicemen. Richardson plays a man dismissed by his employer who is in despair, until a friend introduces him to the Embankment Fellowship. According to *Kinematograph Weekly*: 'The film concludes its 10 minutes' entertainment with an appeal for interest and assistance, but so deftly is the story told and the appeal made that it is in no way annoying to patrons. On the other hand, it elicits sympathy. ' (6 July 1939). Despite this recommendation, it seems to have been unshown in the months before war was declared, and was only discovered in 2004 by Mark Fuller.

The Lion Has Wings   1939

d – Michael Powell, Brian Desmond Hurst, Adrian Brunel [and Alexander Korda].
p. c – London Film Productions. *p* – Alexander Korda. *assoc. p* – Ian Dalrymple.
p. manager – David Cunynghame. [*sc* – Adrian Brunel, E. V. H. Emmett]. From a story by Ian Dalrymple. *ph* – Osmond Borradaile, Harry Stradling, Bernard Browne. *art d* – Vincent Korda.
sup. ed – William Hornbeck. *ed* – Henry Cornelius, Charles Frend. *m* – Richard Addinsell. *m. d* – Muir Mathieson. *sd rec* – A. W. Watkins. [*tech. adv* – Squadron Leader H. M. S. Wright].
narrator – E. V. M. Emmett (English version); Lowell Thomas
(US version). *extracts from* – *Fire Over England*, *The Gap*.

Ralph Richardson (*Wing Cdr. Richardson*), Merle Oberon (*Mrs Richardson*), June Duprez (*June*), Robert Douglas (*briefing officer*), Anthony Bushell (*pilot*), Derrick de Marney (*Bill*), Brian Worth (*Bobby*), Austin Trevor (*Schulemburg*), Ivan Brandt (*officer*), G. H. Mulcaster (*controller*), Herbert Lomas (*Holveg*), Milton Rosmer (*Head of Observer Corps*), Robert Rendel (*Chief of Air Staff*), Archibald Batty (*air officer*), Ronald Adam (*bomber chief*), Bernard Miles (*observer*), John Longden (*controller*), Ian Fleming, Miles Malleson, Charles Garson, Carl Jaffe, John Penrose, Frank Tickle, Torin Thatcher.

76 mins. *t. s* – 17 October. *UK rel* – 3 November. *UK/US dist* – United Artists.
US rel – 19 January 1940.

An intended morale booster, quickly devised and made under Korda's leadership in the weeks after war was declared, with Richardson as an RAF officer contemplating the struggle ahead, intercut with documentary material contrasting German regimentation and British tradition, reconstruction of early fighting, training footage and an extract from Korda's 1937 *Fire Over England*, with Flora Robson as Queen Elizabeth I facing the threat of the Armada. Although the speed of production was admired, many found it unintentionally humorous, even alarming, in what it showed of British preparedness.

The Thief of Bagdad 1940

d – Ludwig Berger, Michael Powell, Tim Whelan [also: Zoltan Korda, William Cameron Menzies, Alexander Korda]. *p. c* – Alexander Korda Films Inc. [London Films]. An Alexander Korda Presentation. *p* – Alexander Korda. *assoc. p* – Zoltan Korda, William Cameron Menzies. *p. manager* – David Cunynghame. [*p. asst* – Andre de Toth]. *assoc. d* – Geoffrey Boothby, Charles David. [*2nd asst. d* – Jack Clayton]. *sc* – Lajos Biro. *adapt/dial* – Miles Malleson. *ph* – Georges Perinal. *col* – Technicolor. *assoc. ph* – Osmond Borradaile. [*cam. op* – Robert Krasker. *cam. asst* – Denys Coop]. *sp. effect design* – Lawrence Butler. [*sp. effects* – Tom Howard, Johnny Mills]. *col. consultant* – Natalie Kalmus. *sup. ed* – William Hornbeck. *ed* – Charles Crichton. *p. designer* – Vincent Korda. *scenic backgrounds* – Percy Day. [*assoc. art d* – William Cameron Menzies, Frederick Pusey, Ferdinand Bellan]. *m* – Miklos Rozsa. *m. d* – Muir Mathieson. [*songs* – 'Since Time Began' by Nic Roger, William Kernell; 'I Want to be a Sailor' by Miklos Rozsa, R. Denham. *orchestral arr* – Albert Sandrey]. *costume* – Oliver Messel, John Armstrong, Marcel Vertes. *sd* – A. W. Watkins.

Conrad Veidt (*Jaffar*), Sabu (*Abu*), June Duprez (*Princess*), John Justin (*Ahmad*), Rex Ingram (*Djinn*), Miles Malleson (*Sultan*), Morton Selten (*the old king*), Mary Morris (*Halima*), Bruce Winston (*merchant*), Hay Petrie (*astrologer*), Adelaide Hall (*singer*), Roy Emmerton (*jailer*), Allan Jeayes (*the storyteller*). [Viscount (*the dog*), Glynis Johns, John Salew, Norman Pierce, Frederick Burtwell, Otto Wallen, Henry Hallett, Cleo Laine].

106 mins. *t. s* – 24 December. *UK/US rel* – 25 December. *UK/US dist* – United Artists. *prizes* – Academy Awards for Color Cinematography, Color Art direction, Special Effects.

A reworking of the same *Arabian Nights* material on which Fairbanks's and Walsh's classic 1924 film was based – about a beggar boy who thwarts the evil Vizier Jaffar, and with the help of the magical djinn he releases from captivity in a bottle – now with more emphasis on spectacle and exploiting the still-new appeal of colour. Impatient with Ludwig Berger's approach, Korda brought in Powell and Whelan to direct separate scenes – mainly with Sabu, Veidt and Ingram in Powell's case. After the outbreak of war, the production was moved from Denham to Hollywood, where it was finished in time for a Christmas release.

An Airman's Letter to His Mother 1941

d/sc/ph – Michael Powell. *add. ph* – Bernard Browne. *narr* – John Gielgud.

5 mins. *rel* – June. *dist* – MGM.

Inspired by and based on a inspirational letter from a young flyer published posthumously in *The Times*, this short film shows an imagined mother receiving the letter in her cottage, and reading it surrounded by reminders of her son's youth which correspond to themes in his letter.

Contraband 1940

d – Michael Powell. *p. c* – British National. *p* – John Corfield. *assoc. p* – Roland Gillett. *p. manager* – Anthony Nelson-Keys. [*asst. d* – William Reidy]. *sc* – Emeric Pressburger. *scen* – Michael Powell and Brock Williams. [Based on a story by Pressburger]. *ph* – F. A. Young. [*cam. op* – Skeets Kelly]. *ed* – John Seabourne [and Joseph Sterling]. *art d* – Alfred Junge. *m* – Richard Addinsell. 'The White Negro' cabaret *des/executed* – Hedley Briggs. *m. d* – Muir Mathieson. *sd* – A. W. Watkins, C. C. Stevens. [*stills* – Frank Buckingham].

Conrad Veidt (*Captain Andersen*), Valerie Hobson (*Mrs Sorensen*), Hay Petrie (*Axel Skold, mate of* SS Helvig/*Erik Skold, chef of 'Three Vikings'*), Joss Ambler (*Lt. Cmdr. Ashton, RNR*), Raymond Lovell (*Van Dyne*), Esmond Knight (*Mr Pidgeon*), Charles Victor (*Hendrick*), Phoebe Kershaw (*Miss Lang*), Harold Warrender (*Lt Cmdr Ellis, RN*), John Longden, Eric Maturin (*Passport officers*), Paddy Browne (*singer in 'Regency'*). [Henry Wolston, Julian Vedey, Sydney Moncton, Hamilton Keen (*Danish waiters*), Leo Genn, Stuart Latham, Peter Bull (*brothers Grimm*), Dennis Arundell (*Lieman*), Molly Hamley Clifford (*Baroness Hekla*),
Eric Berry (*Mr Abo*), Olga Edwards (*Mrs Abo*), Tony Gable (*Miss Karoly*), Desmond Jeans, Eric Hales (*the Karolys*), John Roberts (*Hanson*), Manning Whiley (*Manager of 'Mousetrap'*), Bernard Miles (*man lighting pipe*), Torin Thatcher (*sailor*), Mark Daly (*taxi driver*),
Frank Allenby, John England, Haddon Mason, Johnnie Schofield, Townsend Whitling, Ross Duncan, Albert Chevalier].

92 mins. *t. s* – 20 March. *UK rel* – May. *UK dist* – Anglo. *US rel* – 29 November. *US dist* – United Artists. *US title* – *Blackout* [80 mins].

Quickly following their success with *The Spy in Black*, Powell and Pressburger devised a topical thriller set in the early days of the war that would use many of the same personnel, although now with a more satirical tone. Veidt plays Andersen, a Danish captain, who sets out to uncover a German spy-ring in London that seems to be based in restaurants and cabarets. The progress of the chase provided many opportunities for homages to Fritz Lang's thrillers and for inventive design by Junge.

49th Parallel   1941

d/p – Michael Powell. *p. c* – Ortus Films [and Ministry of Information]. *assoc. p* – Roland Gillett, George Brown. *in charge of prod* – Harold Boxall. *assoc. d* – A. Seabourne.
[*continuity* – Betty Curtiss]. *sc* – Emeric Pressburger. Based on a story by EP. *scen* – Rodney Ackland and EP. *ph* – Frederick Young. *cam. op* – Skeets Kelly, Henty Henty-Creer. [*cam. assts* – D. Mason, C. Holden, J. Body. *2nd unit cam. asst* – D. Fox]. *ed* – David Lean.
assoc. ed – Hugh Stewart. [*original ed* – John Seabourne. *asst. ed* – Hazel Wilkinson].
art d – David Rawnsley. *assoc. art d* – Sydney S. Streeter, Frederick Pusey. *sp. backgrounds* – Osmond Borrowdaile. *m* – Ralph Vaughan Williams. *m. d* – Muir Mathieson. *sd sup* – A. W. Watkins. *sd rec* – C. C. Stevens, Walter Darling. [*sd mixer* – Gordon K. McCallum. *sd cam. op* – J. B. Aldred]. *Canadian adviser* – Nugent M. Clougher.

The U-boat crew: Richard George (*Captain Bernsdorff*), Eric Portman (*Lt. Ernst Hirth*), Raymond Lovell (*Lt. Kuhnecke*), Niall MacGinnis (*Vogel*), Peter Moore (*Kranz*), John Chandos (*Lohrmann*), Basil Appleby (*Jahner*). *The Canadians*: Laurence Olivier (*Johnnie Barras, the trapper*), Finlay Currie (*Albert, the factor*), Ley On (*Nick, the eskimo*), Anton Walbrook (*Peter*), Glynis Johns (*Anna*), Charles Victor (*Andreas*), Frederick Piper (*David*), Leslie Howard (*Philip Armstrong Scott*), Tawera Moana (*George, the Indian*), Eric Clavering (*Art*), Charles Rolfe (*Bob*), Raymond Massey (*Andy Brock*), Theodore Salt, O. W. Fonger (*US Customs officers*). [Lionel Grose].

123 mins. *t. s* – 8 October. *UK rel* – 24 November. *UK dist* – GFD. *US rel* – 15 April 1942 [104 mins]. *US dist* – Columbia. *US title* – *The Invaders*. *Prizes* – Academy Award to Pressburger for the original script.

A German U-boat is destroyed off the coast of Canada and the surviving crew members set off to reach neutral America. On their travels they meet a cross-section of Canadians, all with different ethnic backgrounds and beliefs, but all resistant to the Nazi doctrines put forward by the Germans. As the band diminishes, only the fanatical Lt. Hirth is left, and he is finally captured by a Canadian hobo on the US border. Much of the film was shot on location across Canada, with Ministry of Information support, as part of the campaign to bring America into the war.

One of Our Aircraft Is Missing   1942

d/p/sc – Michael Powell, Emeric Pressburger. *p. c* – The Archers. A British National Films
Presentation (with the co-operation of the Royal Air Force, the Air Ministry and Royal
Netherlands government, London. *assoc. p* – Stanley Haynes. *unit p. manager* – Sydney S.
Streeter. *p. secretary* – Joan Page. *assoc. d* – John Seabourne. [*asst. d* – W. Mills. *2nd asst. d* – P.
Seabourne. *3rd asst. d* – E. Coventry]. *ph* – Ronald Neame. *assoc. ph* – Robert Krasker. [*cam. op* –
Guy Green. *cam. asst* – David Mason]. *ed* – David Lean. *assoc. ed* – Thelma Myers. *art d* – David
Rawnsley. [*asst. art d* – John Elphick. *draughtsman* – H. White].
sp. effects – F. Ford, Douglas Woolsey. *sd sup* – A. W. Watkins. *sd rec* – C. C. Stevens.
[*sd cam* – J. B. Aldred. *boom op* – Gordon McCallum. *sd asst* – R. Morgan. *stills* – Fred Daniels].
tech advisers – M. Sluyser, James P. Power, RBA.

Crew of 'B for Bertie': Hugh Burden (*John Glyn Haggard*), Eric Portman (*Tom Earnshaw*), Hugh
Williams (*Frank Shelley*), Bernard Miles (*Geoff Hickman*), Emrys Jones (*Bob Ashley*), Godfrey
Tearle (*Sir George Corbett*). *People of Holland*: Googie Withers (*Jo de Vries*), Joyce Redman (*Jet van
Dieren*), Pamela Brown (*Els Meertens*), Peter Ustinov (*priest*), Alec Clunes (*organist*), Hay Petrie
(*Burgomaster, Piet van Dieren*). *And on the North Sea*: Roland Culver (*naval officer*), David Ward,
Robert Duncan (*German airmen*). [David Evans (*Len Martin*), Selma van Dias (*Burgomaster's
wife*), Arnold Marle (*Pieter Sluys*), Robert Helpmann (*Julius de Jong*), Hector Abbas (*driver*),
James Carson (*Louis*), Bill Akkerman (*Willem*), Joan Akkerman (*Maartje*), Peter Schenke
(*Hendrik*), Valerie Moon (*Jannie*), John Salew (*German sentry*), William D'arcy (*German officer*),
Robert Beatty (*Sgt. Hopkins*), Stewart Rome (*Cmdr. Reynolds*), John Longden (*man*), Gerry
Wilmott (*announcer*), Michael Powell (*despatching officer*), John Arnold, John England, James
Donald, Gordon Jackson].

103 mins. *t. s* – 18 March. *UK rel* – 27 June. *UK dist* – Anglo. *US rel* – 16 October
[86 mins]. *US dist* – United Artists.

The crew of 'B for Bertie' bales out of their damaged bomber over Holland and is hidden by the
Dutch resistance movement, despite the presence of collaborators, as they make their way to
safety. As well as an admiring portrait of the Dutch withstanding occupation, the crew offers a
cross-section of English attitudes to war; and several aspects of the film's narrative would inspire
later Archers' films, notably *Blimp* and *A Matter of Life and Death*.

The Silver Fleet   1943

d – Vernon C. Sewell, Gordon Wellesley. *p. c* – The Archers. A Michael Powell and
Emeric Pressburger Presentation (with the co-operation and advice of the Royal Netherlands
government and of the Royal Navy). [*p* – Michael Powell, Emeric Pressburger]. *assoc. p* – Ralph
Richardson. *p. manager* – George Maynard. [*asst. d* – Dennis Kavanagh. *2nd asst. d* – John
Arnold. *3rd asst. d* – W. Herlihy. *continuity* – Phyllis Ross].
sc – Vernon Sewell, Gordon Wellesley [based on a story by Pressburger, 'Remember Jan de Wit'].
ph – Erwin Hillier. *cam. op* – Cecil Cooney. [*cam. asst* – E. D. Besche].
sp. effects – Eric Humphriss. *ed* – Michael C. Chorlton. [*asst. eds* – Betty Orgar, Sidney Samuel].
p. designer – Alfred Junge. *m* – Allan Gray. *sd* – John Dennis, Desmond Dew.
[*sd cam. op* – H. Raynham. *boom op* – Stan Lambourne, D. N. Barclay]. *adviser* – M. Sluyser.

Ralph Richardson (*Jaap van Leyden*), Googie Withers (*Helene van Leyden*), Esmond Knight (*von
Schiffer*), Beresford Egan (*Krampf*), Frederick Burtwell (*Captain Muller*), Kathleen Byron
(*schoolmistress*), Willem Akkerman (*Willem van Leyden*), Dorothy Gordon (*Janni Peters*), Charles
Victor (*Bastiaan Peters*), John Longden (*Jost Meertens*), Joss Ambler (*Cornelis Smit*), Margaret
Emden (*Bertha*), George Schelderup (*Dirk*), Neville Mapp
(*Joop*), Ivor Barnard (*Admiral von Rapp*), John Carol (*Johann*), Lt Schouwenaar RNN

(*U-boat captain*), Lt. van Dapperen RNN (*U-boat lieutenant*), John Arnold (*U-boat navigator*), Philip Leaver (*Chief of Police*), Laurence O'Madden (*Captain Schneider*), Anthony Eustrel (*Lt. Wernicke*), Charles Minor (*Bohme*), Valentine Dyall (*Markgraf*), and personnel of the Royal Netherlands Navy.

88 mins. *t. s* – 24 February. *UK rel* – 15 March. *UK dist* – GFD. *US rel* – 1 July 1945 [77 mins]. *US dist* – Producers Releasing Corporation.

The Archers' first film as arm's-length producers was both a further celebration of Dutch resistance and a parable about the dilemmas faced under occupation. Van Leyden runs a shipyard and is put under pressure to work for the Germans. At first he complies, and is branded a quisling by his own people, but after realising his duty, he sacrifices himself in a trap to kill a party of leading Nazis at sea.

The Life and Death of Colonel Blimp   1943

d/p/sc – Michael Powell, Emeric Pressburger ('with acknowledgment to David Low, creator of the immortal Colonel'). *p. c* – The Archers/Independent Producers. *p. management* – Sydney S. Streeter, Alec Saville [*p. manager* – Tom White]. *asst. p* – Richard Vernon. *floor manager* – Arthur Lawson. *asst. d* – Ken Horne, Tom Payne. [*p. runner* – Roger Cherrill].
ph – Georges Perinal. *col* – Technicolor. *col. control* – Natalie Kalmus. *chief electrician* – Bill Wall. *cam. op* – Jack Cardiff, Geoffrey Unsworth, Harold Haysom. *sp. ph. effects* – W. Percy Day. *ed* – John Seabourne. *asst. ed* – Thelma Myers, Peter Seabourne. *p. designer* – Alfred Junge. *m* – Allan Gray. *m. cond* – Charles Williams. *sd* – C. C. Stevens, Desmond Dew. *costume* – Joseph Bato, Matilda Etches. *make-up* – George Blackler, Dorrie Hamilton. *military adviser* – Lt. General Sir Douglas Brownrigg. *period advisers* – E. F. E. Schoen,
Dr C. Beard.

James McKechnie (*Spud Wilson*), Neville Mapp (*Stuffy Graves*), Vincent Holman (*Club Porter, 1942*), Roger Livesey (*Clive Candy*), David Hutcheson (*Hoppy*), Spencer Trevor (*Period Blimp*), Roland Culver (*Colonel Betteridge*), James Knight (*Club Porter, 1902*), Deborah Kerr (*Edith Hunter*), Dennis Arundell (*Cafe Orchestra leader*), David Ward (*Kaunitz*), Jan van Loewen (*indignant citizen*), Valentine Dyall (*von Schonborn*), Carl Jaffe (*von Reumann*), Albert Lieven (*von Ritter*), Eric Maturin (*Colonel Goodhead*), Frith Banbury ('*Babyface' Fitzroy*), Robert Harris (*Embassy Secretary*), Arthur Wontner (*Embassy Counsellor*), Count Zichy (*Colonel Borg*), Anton Walbrook (*Theo Kretschmar-Schuldorff*), Jane Millican (*Nurse Erna*), Ursula Jeans (*Frau von Kalteneck*), Phyllis Morris (*Pebble*), Muriel Aked (*Aunt Margaret Hamilton*), John Laurie (*John Montgomery Murdoch*), Reginald Tate (*Van Zijl*), Capt. W. H. Barrett, US Army (*the Texan*), Cpl. Thomas Palmer, US Army (*sergeant*), Yvonne Andree (*Nun*), Marjorie Greasley (*Matron*), Deborah Kerr (*Barbara Wynne*), Felix Aylmer (*bishop*), Helen Debroy (*Mrs Wynne*), Norman Pierce (*Mr Wynne*), Harry Welchman (*Major John E. Davis*), A. E. Matthews (*president of tribunal*), Deborah Kerr (*Angela 'Johnny' Cannon*), Edward Cooper (*BBC official*), Joan Swinstead (*secretary*). [Diana Marshall (*Sybil*), Wally Patch (*sergeant clearing debris*), Ferdy Mayne (*Prussian student*), John Boxer (*soldier*), John Varley, Patrick Macnee].

163 mins (later cut to *c*. 131 mins). *t. s* – 8 June. *UK rel* – 26 July (charity premiere 10 June). *UK dist* – GFD. *US rel* – 4 May 1945 [148 mins]. *US dist* – United Artists. *NFA restoration* – 1985.

General Clive Candy is caught napping on the eve of a Home Guard exercise, and defends himself by recalling his exploits before and after the First World War, which led to an enduring friendship with the German officer he fought in a duel in Berlin. When the officer, Theo, marries the girl who had first invited Clive to Germany, he begins a search for his feminine ideal, only to lose his wife soon after their marriage. After long years of colonial and military service, he sees an opportunity to put his experience to use by organising the Home Guard, but discovers that even here his approach is out of step with the demands of total war. Although this war will be fought by younger people and with different tactics, Clive still stands for the values that they are defending. Churchill tried to prevent the film being made, believing it was an attack on the army's reputation, and obstructed its export; but Rank stood firm and it achieved considerable success. Later shortened and re-edited, the film was largely forgotten until its restoration in the mid-1980s.

The Volunteer   1943

d/p/sc – Michael Powell, Emeric Pressburger. *p. c* – The Archers. A Ministry of Information Film. *p. sup* – Sydney S. Streeter. *ph* – Freddie Ford. *ed* – Michael C. Chorlton [and John Seabourne]. *p. designer* – Alfred Junge. *m* – Allan Gray. *m. cond* – Walter Goehr. *sd* – Desmond Dew.

Ralph Richardson (*himself, the star*), Pat McGrath (*Alfred Davey, the dresser*). [Laurence Olivier (*man outside window at Denham Studios canteen*), Michael Powell (*man taking snapshots outside Buckingham Palace*), Anna Neagle, Herbert Wilcox (*people leaving Denham canteen*), Anthony Asquith (*film director*), Tommy Woodroofe].

24 mins. *t. s* – 5 November. *rel* – 10 January 1944. *UK dist* – Anglo.

A recruitment promotion film for the Fleet Air Arm, which capitalised on The Archers' friendship with Ralph Richardson, already serving as a pilot, and contrasted to comic – almost surreal – effect pre-war life for him as an actor, and for his dresser, with active service on an aircraft carrier.

A Canterbury Tale   1944

d/p/sc – Michael Powell, Emeric Pressburger. *p. c* – The Archers. A. Michael Powell and Emeric Pressburger Presentation. *p. manager* – George Maynard. *asst. d* – George Busby. [*2nd asst. d* – John Arnold, George Aldersley. *3rd asst. d* – Parry Jones. *continuity* – June Arnold]. *ph* – Erwin Hillier. [*cam. op* – Cecil Cooney. *focus puller* – Eric Besche. *clapper loaders* – Derek Browne, S. Shrimpton, J. Body, J. Demaine. *2nd cam. ops* – George Stretton, Desmond Dickinson. *models* – W. Percy Day. *back projection* – Charles Staffel]. *ed* – John Seabourne. [*asst eds* – David Powell, Roger Cherill]. *p. designer* – Alfred Junge. [*draughtsmen* – Elliot E. Scott, William Kellner, Harold Hurdell, H. Westbrook]. *m* – Allan Gray. *m. cond* – Walter Goehr. *sd rec* – C. C. Stevens, Desmond Dew. *sd rec exteriors* – Alan Whatley.
[*sd maintenance* – S. Hayers, J. Stirton (*interiors*); R. Day, W. Day (*exteriors*). *sd cam. op* – Winston Ryder (*ints*), S. Hayers (*exts*). *boom op* – George Paternoster (*exts*), Gordon K. McCallum (*ints*). *boom asst* – P. Lloyd. *sd asst* – Alan Thorne]. *period adviser* – Herbert Norris.

Eric Portman (*Thomas Colpeper, JP*), Sheila Sim (*Alison Smith*), Dennis Price (*Sgt. Peter Gibbs*), Sgt. John Sweet, USA (*Sgt. Bob Johnson*), Esmond Knight (*Narrator/Seven Sisters soldier/village idiot*), Charles Hawtrey (*Thomas Duckett*), Hay Petrie (*Woodcock*), George Merritt (*Ned Horton*), Edward Rigby (*Jim Horton*), Freda Jackson (*Prudence Honeywood*), Betty Jardine (*Fee Baker*), Eliot Makeham (*organist*), Harvey Golden (*Sgt. Roczinsky*), Leonard Smith (*Leslie*), James Tamsitt (*Terry Holmes*), David Todd (*David*), Beresford Egan (*PC Ovenden*), Antony Holles (*Sgt. Bassett*), Maude Lambert (*Miss Grainger*), Wally Bosco (*ARP warden*), Charles Paton (*Ernie Brooks*), Jane Millican (*Susanna Foster*), John Slater (*Sgt. Len*), Michael Golden (*Sgt. Smale*), Charles Moffatt (*Sgt. Stuffy*), Esma Cannon (*Agnes*), Mary Line (*Leslie's mother*), Winifred Swaffer (*Mrs Horton*); Michael Howard (*Archie*), Judith Furse (*Dorothy Bird*), Barbara Waring (*Polly Finn*), Jean Shepheard (*Gwladys*), Margaret Scudamore (*Mrs Colpeper*), Joss Ambler (*police inspector*), Jessie James (*waitress*), Kathleen Lucas (*passer-by*), H. F. Maltby (*Mr Portal*), Eric Maturin (*Geoffrey's father*), Parry Jones Jr (*Arthur*), [US version only: Kim Hunter (*Bob's fiancée*)]

124 mins [later cut to 95 mins]. *t. s* – 9 May. *UK rel* – *2I* August. *UK dist* – Eagle-Lion.
US rel – 21 January 1949 [93 mins]. *NFA restoration* – 1977.

Three wartime 'pilgrims', a land girl, an American sergeant on leave and a British tank officer,
find themselves in a village near Canterbury where local girls are being terrorised by a mysterious
assailant who pours glue over their hair at night. The three begin to make enquiries that lead
them to suspect the local magistrate, a staunch advocate of traditional values, who admits his
frustration at failing to find an audience for his lectures on the Pilgrim's Way. As the three
converge on Canterbury, all receive unexpected 'blessings' – news of loved ones from far away;
and a chance to play the cathedral organ – and the glueman's unmasking is forgotten amid
celebrations before troop departures on the eve of D-Day. Like *The Edge of the World* and *Blimp*,
the film was only known in a shortened and reordered version before its restoration in 1977,
which led to a major revaluation.

I Know Where I'm Going!   1945

d/p/sc – Michael Powell, Emeric Pressburger. *p. c* – The Archers. A. Michael Powell and Emeric
Pressburger Presentation. *asst. p* – George R. Busby. *asst. d* – John Tunstall. [*2nd asst. d* – Bill
Herlihy. *3rd asst. d* – Parry Jones. *continuity* – Patricia Arnold. *asst. continuity* – Ainslie L'Evine].
ph – Erwin Hillier. *cam. op* – Cecil Cooney. [*focus puller* – Eric Besche. *clapper loader* – Harold
Case] *sp. ph. effects* – Henry Harris. [*add. sp. effects* – George Blackwell. *models* – Gilleran. *back
projection* – Charles Staffel]. *ed* – John Seabourne.
[*2nd asst. ed* – Sidney Hayers, James Pople]. *p. designer* – Alfred Junge. [*asst. art d* – Warde
Richards. *draughtsmen* – Eliot E. Scott, Harry Hurdell, William Kellner, Mr Buxton].
m – Allan Gray. *m. cond.* – Walter Goehr. *songs* – sung by members of the Glasgow Orpheus
Choir. (*choir*) *principal* – Sir Hugh Roberton. *sd rec* – C. C. Stevens. [*sd cam. op* – T. Bagley. *boom
op* – Gordon McCallum. *boom asst* – Fred Ryan. *sd maintenance* – Roy Day. *dubbing crew* –
Desmond Dew, Alan Whatley. *technical adviser* – John Laurie. *Gaelic adviser* – Malcolm
MacKelloig. *stills* – Max Rosher].

George Carney (*Mr Webster*), Wendy Hiller (*Joan Webster*), Walter Hudd (*Hunter*), Capt.
Duncan MacKenzie (*Captain of 'Lochinvar'*), Ian Sadler (*Iain*), Roger Livesey (*Torquil MacNeil*),
Finlay Currie (*Ruairidh Mohr*), Murdo Morrison (*Kenny*), Margot Fitzsimmons (*Bridie*), Capt.
C. W. R Knight, FZS (*Colonel Barnstaple*), Pamela Brown (*Catriona Potts*), Donald Strachan
(*shepherd*), John Rae (*old shepherd*), Duncan MacIntyre (*old shepherd's son*), Jean Cadell
(*postmistress*), Norman Shelley (*Sir Robert Bellinger*), Ivy Milton (*Peigi*), Anthony Eustrel
(*Hooper*), Petula Clark (*Cheril*), Alec Faversham (*Martin*), Catherine Lacey (*Mrs Robinson*),
Valentine Dyall (*Mr Robinson*), Nancy Price (*Mrs Crozier*), Herbert Lomas (*Mr Campbell*), Kitty
Kirwan (*Mrs Campbell*), John Laurie (*John Campbell*), Graham Moffat (*RAF sergeant*), Boyd
Stevens, Maxwell Kennedy, Jean Houston (*singers in the ceilidh*), Arthur Chesney (*harmonica
player*), 'Mr Ramshaw' (*Torquil, the eagle*).

91 mins. *t. s* – 30 October. *UK rel* – 17 December. *UK dist* – GFD. *US rel* – 9 August 1947. *US
dist* – Universal.

Joan has always known where she wanted to go, from an early age to her impending marriage to the
head of a major industrial company. But as she travels north for the planned Scottish island wedding,
she discovers there is more to life than material success. While waiting for a storm to abate, she meets
and reluctantly falls in love with the impoverished laird of the island her fiancé has rented. After she
survives a rash attempt to reach the island during the storm, they decide to make their future together.
Written quickly to fill a gap in the production schedule, but highly complex to make with its
combination of location shooting and studio-created special effects, this continued The Archers'
'crusade against materialism' and looking forward to the values that would shape the post-war world.

A Matter of Life and Death 1946

d/p/sc – Michael Powell, Emeric Pressburger. *p. c* – A Production of The Archers. *unit manager* – Robert C. Foord. *asst. p* – George R Busby. *asst. d* – Parry Jones, Jr. [*2nd asst. d* – Paul Kelly. *3rd asst. d* – Patrick Marsden. *continuity* – Bunny Parsons. *asst. continuity* – Ainslie L'Evine]. *ph* – Jack Cardiff. *col* – Technicolor. *cam. op* – Geoffrey Unsworth.
[*2nd cam. op* – Chris Challis. *focus pullers* – Chris Challis, Eric Besche. *clapper loader* – D. R. E. Allport]. *chief electrician* – Bill Wall. *motorbike shots* – Michael Chorlton. *col. control* – Natalie Kalmus. *assoc. col. control* – Joan Bridge. *sp. ph. effects* – Douglas Woolsey, Henry Harris and Technicolor Ltd. *add. sp. effects* – W. Percy Day [and George Blackwell, Stanley Grant. *back projection* – Jack Whitehead]. *p. designer* – Alfred Junge. *asst. art d* – Arthur Lawson. [*draughtsmen* – W. Hutchinson, Don Picton, William Kellner]. *ed* – Reginald Mills. *liaison ed* – John Seabourne Jr. [*asst. ed* – Dave Powell]. *m* – Allan Gray. *m. cond* – Walter Goehr. *asst. m. cond* – W L Williamson. *sd rec* – C. C. Stevens. [*sd cam. op* – Harold Rowland. *boom op* – Dave Hildyard. *boom assts* – G. Sanders, M. G. Colomb. *sd maintenance* – Roy Day. *dubbing crew* – Desmond Dew, Alan Whatley. *pre-dubbing* – John Dennis]. *costume* – Hein Heckroth. *make-up* – George Blackler. *hair* – Ida Mills. [*table tennis trainer/adviser* – Alan Brook. *operating theatre tech. adv* – Capt. Bernard Kaplan, RAMC. *stills* – Eric Gray].

David Niven (*Peter David Carter*), Kim Hunter (*June*), Robert Coote (*Bob Trubshaw*), Kathleen Byron (*an officer angel*), Richard Attenborough (*an English pilot*), Bonar Colleano (*Flying Fortress captain*), Joan Maude (*Chief Recorder*), Marius Goring (*Conductor 71*), Roger Livesey (*Dr Frank Reeves*), Robert Atkins (*vicar*), Bob Roberts (*Dr Gaertler*), Edwin Max (*Dr McEwen*), Betty Potter (*Mrs Tucker*), Abraham Sofaer (*the judge/the surgeon*), Raymond Massey (*Abraham Farlan*). [Tommy Duggan (*American policeman*), Roger Snowden (*Irishman*), Robert Arden (*GI*), Joan Verney (*girl*), Wendy Thompson (*nurse*), Wally Patch (*ARP Warden*)].

104 mins. *t. s* – 12 November. *UK rel* – 30 December. *UK dist* – GFD. *US rel* – March 1947. *US dist* – Universal. *US title* – Stairway to Heaven.

What began as a wartime propaganda commission, to improve Anglo-American relations, became in the months after the war had ended a fantasy 'trial' of Britain, heard before a celestial jury of Americans. The case is both medical and theological, although ultimately political: Peter Carter should have died when he fell from his bomber without a parachute, but heaven failed to find him – allowing him to fall in love with June, an American WAC controller. As medical diagnosis and celestial diplomacy proceed in parallel, his doctor is killed in an accident and becomes his advocate in heaven, securing literally a new lease of life for Peter to enjoy with June. Using extensive model and matte work, The Archers set out to create the antithesis of a wartime film – 'a stratospheric joke', but one with serious and poetic themes behind its spectacular Technicolor images.

Black Narcissus 1947

d/p/sc – Michael Powell, Emeric Pressburger. *p. c* – A Production of The Archers, for Independent Producers Ltd. *asst. p* – George R Busby. *asst. d* – Sydney S. Streeter. [*2nd asst. d* – Kenneth Rick. *3rd asst. d* – L. Knight, Robert Lynn. *continuity* – Winnifred Dyer. *asst. continuity* – Joanne Busby]. *sc* – based on the novel by Rumer Godden. *ph* – Jack Cardiff. *col* – Technicolor. *col. cons* – Natalie Kalmus. *assoc. col. cons* – Joan Bridge. [*cam. op* – Chris Challis, Ted Scaife, Stan Sayer. *focus pullers* – Ian Craig, Ronald Cross. *clapper loaders* – H. Salisbury, M. Livesey. *Technicolor cam. asst* – Dick Allport. *lighting electrician* – Bill Wall]. *ed* – Reginald Mills. [*1st asst. ed* – Seymour Logie. *2nd asst. ed* – Lee Doig, Noreen Ackland]. *sp. ph. effects* – Percy Day. [*sp. effects cam* – Douglas Hague. *synthetic pictorial effects* – Syd Pearson. *foreground miniatures* – Jack Higgins]. *p. designer* – Alfred Junge. *art d* – Arthur Lawson. [*draughtsmen* – Eliot E. C.

Scott, Don Picton, William Kellner, J. Harman, G. Beattie, A. Harris. *scenic artist* – Ivor Beddoes. *set dresser* – M. A. S. Pemberton. *Indian set dresser* – E. Harvinson. *chief constuction manager* – Harold Batchelor]. *m/sd score/m. cond* – Brian Easdale. *m. perf. by* – London Symphony Orchestra. *sd rec* – Stanley Lambourne. *dubbing mixer* – George K. McCallum. [*chief production mixer* – John H. Dennis. *sd cam. op* – H. Roland. *boom op* – George Paternoster. *boom asst* – Mick Stolovich. *sd maintenance engineer* – Fred Hugheson. *dubbing crew* – J. B. Smith, Bill Daniels. *dubbing ed* – John Seabourne Jr. *m. rec* – Edward A. Drake. *asst. sd rec* – J. G. De Coninck]. *costume* – Hein Heckroth. [*dress sup* – Elizabeth Hennings. *wardrobe mistress* – Dorothy Edwards. *wardrobe master* – Bob Raynor. *make-up* – George Blackler. *asst. make-up* – Ernest Gasser. *hair* – Biddy Chrystal. *asst. hair* – June Robinson. *stills* – George Cannon (colour), Max Rosher (b/w), Fred Daniels (portrait)].

Deborah Kerr (*Sister Clodagh*), Flora Robson (*Sister Philippa*), Jenny Laird (*Sister 'Honey' Blanche*), Judith Furse (*Sister Briony*), Kathleen Byron (*Sister Ruth*), Esmond Knight (*the old General*), Sabu (*Dilip Rai, the young General*), David Farrar (*Mr Dean*), Jean Simmons (*Kanchi*), May Hallatt (*Angu Ayah*), Eddie Whaley Jr (*Joseph Anthony*), Shaun Noble (*Con*), Nancy Roberts (*Mother Dorothea*), Ley On (*Phuba*).

100 mins. *t. s* – 22 April. *UK rel* – 26 May. *UK dist* – GFD. *US rel* – December. *US dist* – Universal. *Prizes* – Academy Award to Jack Cardiff for Col Cinematography.

A group of nuns is dispatched to a remote Himalayan community, on the invitation of the local ruler, to establish a school and clinic for his people. But few of the group are prepared for the stress of isolation in this windy mountain-top palace, amid the challenges and temptations they face. Sister Ruth conceives a passion for the local ruler's English manager, Mr Dean, and when she is rebuffed tries to kill her superior, Sister Clodagh, before falling to her own death. The nuns retreat from their mission as the rains begin. Famously filmed entirely in southern England, *Black Narcissus* won Academy Awards for its design and cinematography, while its chaste yet passionate melodrama continues to fascinate.

The End of the River   1947
d – Derek Twist. *p. c* – The Archers. *p* – Michael Powell, Emeric Pressburger. *asst. p* – George R. Busby. *asst. d* – Geoffrey Lambert. *sc* – Wolfgang Wilhelm. *ph* – Christopher Challis. *ed* – Brereton Porter. *art d* – Fred Pusey. *asst. art d* – E. E. C. Scott. *m* – Lambert Williamson. *m. d* – Mulr Mathieson. *sd* – Charles Knott.

Sabu (*Manoel*), Bibi Ferriera (*Teresa*), Esmond Knight (*Dantos*), Antoinette Cellier (*Conceicao*), Robert Douglas (*Jones*), Torin Thatcher (*Lisboa*), Orlando Martins (*Harrigan*), Raymond Lovell (*Porpino*), James Hayter (*Chico*), Nicolette Bernard (*Dona Serafina*), Minto Cato (*Dona Paul*), Maurice Denham (*defending counsel*), Eva Hudson (*Maria Gonsalves*), Alan Wheatley (*Irygoyen*), Charles Hawtrey (*Raphael*), Zena Marshall (*Sante*), Dennis Arundell (*Continho*), Milton Rosmer (*judge*), Peter Illing (*ship's agent*), Nino Rossini (*Feliciano*), Basil Appleby (*ship's officer*), Milo Sperber (*Ze*), Andreas Malandrinos (*officer of the Indian Protection Society*), Arthur Goullet (*pedlar*), Russell Napier (*padre*).

83 mins. *t. s* – 23 October. *UK rel* – 1 December. *UK dist* – Rank. *US rel* – 7 July 1948 [80 mins].

A young South American peasant working in a remote forced-labour camp falls in love with a fellow-inmate and, after they escape, marries her. He later joins a revolutionary brotherhood of Maritime Workers, but this is revealed to be corrupt and he is eventually arrested for killing a man in a brawl. His defence is innocence of the forces that have used him, and he is released to return to the end of the river, reunited with his wife. The second of two films produced by The Archers, with many of their associates involved, but having no direct involvement by Powell or Pressburger.

## The Red Shoes												1948

d/p/sc – Michael Powell, Emeric Pressburger. *p. c* – A Production of the Archers. *asst. p* – George Busby. *asst. d* – Sydney S. Streeter. [*2nd asst. d* – Kenneth Rick. *3rd asst. d* – J. M. Gibson]. *continuity* – Doreen North. [*asst. continuity* – Joanne Busby. *p. asst* – Gwladys Jenks]. sc – from an original screenplay by Emeric Pressburger. Based on a story by Hans Christian Andersen. *add. dial* – Keith Winter. *ph* – Jack Cardiff. *col* – Technicolor. *col. cons* – Natalie Kalmus. *assoc. col. cons* – Joan Bridge. *cam. op* – Christopher Challis. *Technicolor composite ph* – F. George Dunn, E. Hague. [*focus puller* – George Minassian.

cam. assts – Robert Kindred, John Morgan]. *ed* – Reginald Mills. *liaison ed* – John Seabourne Jr. [*asst. ed* – Noreen Ackland. *2nd asst. ed* – Tony Haynes, Laurie Knight]. *p. designer* – Hein Heckroth. *art d* – Arthur Lawson. *painting* – Ivor Beddoes. *special [painting?]* – Joseph Natanson. *scenic artist* – Alfred Roberts. [*asst. art d* – Elven Webb. *draughtsmen* – Don Picton, V. B. Wilkins, V. Shaw, Albert Withy, G. Heavens, B. Goodwin. *masks* – Terence Morgan II]. *m/m. arr/m. cond* – Brian Easdale. *m. played by* – Royal Philharmonic Orchestra. *'Red Shoes' ballet seq cond* – Sir Thomas Beecham. *singer* – Margherita Grandi.

m. of 'Café de Paris' seq – Ted Heath's Kenny Baker Swing Group. *sd* – Charles Poulton. *m. rec* – Ted Drake. *dubbing* – Gordon McCallum. [*dubbing ed* – Len Trumm. *sd cam. op* – H. V. Clarke. *boom op* – Al Burton. *boom asst* – G. Daniels. *sd maintenance* – Richard De Glanville. *dubbing crew* – Gordon K. McCallum, J. B. Smith]. *costume* – Miss Shearer's dresses: Jacques Fath of Paris, Mattli of London. Mlle Tcherina's dresses: Carven of Paris. *wardrobe* – Dorothy Edwards. [*make-up* – Eric Carter. *sup make-up* – Ernie Gasser]. *choreo. of the ballet 'The Red Shoes'* – Robert Helpmann. Part of the Shoemaker created and danced by Leonide Massine. [*stills* – George Cannons. *asst. stills* – Alistair Phillips].

Ballet of 'The Red Shoes'
solo dancer and asst. maitre de ballet – Alan Carter. *solo dancer and asst. maitresse de ballet* – Joan Harris. *with* – Joan Sheldon, Paula Dunning, Brian Ashbridge, Denis Carey, Lynne Dorval, Helen ffrance, Robert Dorning, Eddie Gaillard, Paul Hammond, Tommy Linden, Trisha Linova, Anna Marinova, Guy Massey, John Regan, Peggy Sager, Ruth Sendler. *accompanist* – Hilda Gaunt.

Marius Goring (*Julian Craster*), Jean Short (*Terry*), Gordon Littman (*Ike*), Julia Lang (*balletomane*), Bill Shine (*balletomane's mate*), Leonide Massine (*Grischa Ljubov*), Anton Walbrook (*Boris Lermontov*), Austin Trevor (*Professor Palmer*), Esmond Knight (*Livingstone 'Livy' Montague*), Eric Berry (*Dimitri*), Irene Browne (*Lady Neston*), Moira Shearer (*Victoria Page*), Ludmilla Tcherina (*Boronskaja*), Jerry Verno (*George, stage-door keeper*), Robert Helpmann (*Ivan Boleslawsky*), Albert Basserman (*Ratov*), Derek Elphinstone (*Lord Oldham*), Madame Rambert (*herself*), Joy Rawlins (*Gladys, Vicky's friend*), Marcel Poncin (*M Boudin*), Michel Bazalgette (*M. Rideaut*), Yvonne Andre (*Vicky's dresser*), Hay Petrie (*Boisson*). [Richard George (*doorman*)].

134 mins. *t. s* – 20 July. *UK rel* – 6 September. *UK dist* – GFD. *US rel* – 1 October 1951. *US dist* – Universal.

Marrying *Trilby* to Hans Christian Andersen, Pressburger's original script about a ballet dancer was written for Korda in the late 1930s, but The Archers reclaimed it to create an allegory of art feeding off and ultimately destroying ordinary life, as Vicky Page achieves stardom under the impresario Boris Lermontov, but is then forced to choose by her composer husband, Julian, which leads to her suicide. Under the painterly control of Heckroth, décor and costume combined with dance, music and stylised acting to create a blazing manifesto for The Archers' 'total cinema' that would be widely influential, especially on the American musical.

The Small Back Room   1949

d/p/sc – Michael Powell, Emeric Pressburger. *p. c* – A Production of The Archers. A London Film Presentation. *asst. p* – George R. Busby. [*assoc. p* – Anthony Bushell. *p. asst* – Charles Orme]. *asst. d* – Sydney S. Streeter. [*2nd asst. d* – Archie Knowles. *3rd asst. d* – Jackie Green]. *continuity* – Doreen North. *sc* – based on the novel by Nigel Balchin.
ph – Christopher Challis. *cam. op* – Freddie Francis. [*focus puller* – Will Lee. *clapper loader* – John Kotze]. *ed* – Clifford Turner. *sup. ed* – Reginald Mills. [*asst. cutter* – Tom Simpson. *junior cutter* – Frankie Taylor]. *p. designer* – Hein Heckroth. *art d* – John Hoesli. [*asst. art d* – Ivor Beddoes. *set dresser* – Dario Simoni. *chief draughtsman* – Wallace Smith. *draughtsmen* – Edward Clements, Henry Pottle. *junior draughtsmen* – Pat Sladden, Peter Childs. *p. buyer* – Charles Townsend]. *m* – Brian Easdale. *nightclub m* – Ted Heath's Kenny Baker Swing Group and Fred Lewis. *sd* – Alan Allen. *dubbing* – Bill Sweeny. [*sd ed* – Cyril Swern.
sd mixer – K. Allen. *sd maintenance* – George Stevenson. *sd cam. op* – Alec Rapstone. *boom op* – Peter Butcher. *asst. boom op* – P. Myers]. *costume* – Josephine Boss. [*wardrobe master* – Jack Dalmayne. *wardrobe assts* – Arthur Skinner, May Walding. *make-up sup* – Dorrie Hamilton. *make-up asst* – Peter Evans. *hair* – Constance Pyne. *asst. hair* – Iris Tilley. *casting* – Madeleine Godar. *publicity* – Vivienne Knight. *stills* – Anthony Hopking. *technical observer* – Cmdr. George K. Mills].

Michael Gough (*Capt. Stuart*), Henry Caine (*Sgt-Major Rose*), Milton Rosmer (*Professor Mair*), Cyril Cusack (*Cpl. Taylor*), Kathleen Byron (*Susan*), Sidney James (*Knucksie*), David Farrar (*Sammy Rice*), Leslie Banks (*Col. Holland*), Sam Kydd (*Crowhurst*), Emrys Jones (*Joe*), Michael Goodliffe (*Till*), Jack Hawkins (*R. B. Waring*), Geoffrey Keen (*Pinker*), June Elvin (*Gillian*), David Hutcheson (*Norval*), Robert Morley (*the minister*), Roddy Hughes (*Welsh doctor*), Bryan Forbes (*Petersen, dying gunner*), Walter Fitzgerald (*Brine*), James Dale (*Brigadier*), Elwyn Brook-Jones (*Gladwin*), Roderick Lovell (*Don Pearson*), Anthony Bushell (*Col. Strange*), James Carney (*Sgt. Groves*), Renee Asherson (*ATS Cpl.*) [Ted Heath (*bandleader*), Patrick Mcnee (*committee member*)].

106 mins. *t. s* – 27 January. *UK rel* – 21 February. *UK dist* – British Lion. *US rel* – 23 February 1952. *US dist* – Snader Productions.

Based on Nigel Balchin's anti-heroic novel about backroom 'boffins' engaged in secret war work, the story of Sammy's obsessive quest to understand a new German bomb is intertwined with his tortured love for Susan. Low-key, shadowy interiors alternate with the bleak landscapes of bomb-disposal in a film now widely hailed as an authentic British film noir.

Gone to Earth   1950

d/p/sc – Michael Powell, Emeric Pressburger. *p. c* – London Films. The Archers (London). Vanguard Productions (Hollywood). A. Michael Powell and Emeric Pressburger Production. An Alexander Korda and David O. Selznick Presentation. *asst. p* – George Busby. *p. asst* – Charles Orme. *asst. d* – Sydney S Streeter. *2nd asst. d* – Archie Knowles. *continuity* – Doreen Francis. *asst. continuity* – Joanna G. Busby. *sc* – based on the novel by Mary Webb. *ph* – Christopher Challis. *col* – Technicolor. *cam. op* – Freddie Francis. *focus puller* – Bill Lee. *Technicolor tech* – George Minassian. *Technicolor asst* – Dick Allport. *Technicolor cons* – Joan Bridge. *process shots* – W. Percy Day. *chief elec* – Bill Wall. *p. designer* – Hein Heckroth. *art d* – Arthur Lawson. *asst. art d* – Ivor Beddoes. *set dresser* – Bernard Sarron. *draughtsman* – Maurice Fowler. *ed* – Reginald Mills. *m* – Brian Easdale. Played by the Boyd Neel Orchestra. *sd rec* – Charles Poulton, John Cox. *boom op* – Peter Butcher.
sd cam. op – Charles Earl. *sd maintenance* – P. R. Stephenson. *costume* – Julia Squires. *dress supervision* – Ivy Baker. *wardrobe mistress* [*sic*] – Bill Smith. *wardrobe master* –

Michael Hart. *wardrobe assts* – Dick Richards, May Walding. *make-up* – Jimmy Vining. *make-up asst* – Connie Reeves. *hair* – Betty Cross. *asst. hair* – Eileen Bates. *animals* – Capt. C. W. R. Knight, FZS. *animal trainer* – Jean Knight. *puppeteer* – Alec Mozeley. *publicity* – Vivienne Knight. *stills* – Bert Cann.

Jennifer Jones (*Hazel Woodus*), David Farrar (*Jack Reddin*), Cyril Cusack (*Edward Marston*), Sybil Thorndyke (*Mrs Marston*), Edward Chapman (*Mr James*), Esmond Knight (*Abel Woodus*), Hugh Griffith (*Andrew Vessons*), George Cole (*Albert*), Beatrice Varley (*Aunt Prowde*), Frances Clare (*Amelia Comber*), Raymond Rollett (*landlord/elder*), Gerald Lawson (*roadmender/ elder*), Bartlett Mullins, Arthur Reynolds (*chapel elders*), Ann Tetheradge (*Miss James*), Peter Dunlop (*cornet player*), Louis Phillip (*policeman*), Valentine Dunn (*Martha*), Richmond Nairne (*Mathias Brooker, Martha's brother*), Owen Holder (*Brother minister*).
[*US version only*: Joseph Cotten (*narrator*)].

110 mins. *t. s* – 19 September. *UK rel* – 6 November. *UK dist* – British Lion. *US rel* – July 1952 [82 mins. *add. d* – Rouben Mamoulian.]. *US title* – The Wild Heart. *US dist* – RKO Radio.

Hazel is a child of nature, living on the Shropshire borders at the turn of the century, the daughter of a blind harpist and coffin-maker, and haunted by her dead mother's superstitions. Although she is drawn to the sadistic squire, Jack Reddin, she agrees to marry the meek Reverend Marston, but the conflict between these two is too great and she eventually plunges to her death, while being hunted trying to save her beloved fox.

The Elusive Pimpernel   1950

d/p/sc – Michael Powell, Emeric Pressburger. *p. c* – London Film Productions [and The Archers]. A. Michael Powell and Emeric Pressburger Production. A London Films Presentation. *asst. p* – George R. Busby. [*p. asst* – Charles Orme. *p. secretaries* – Gwladys Jenks, Marjorie Mein. *accountant* – P. Corbishley]. *asst. d* – Sydney S. Streeter. [*2nd asst. d* – Archie Knowles. *3rd asst. d* – David Tomblin. *French asst. d* – Paul Pantaleon. *asst. to Mr Powell* – Bill Paton. *French unit man* – M. Charlot]. *continuity* – Doreen North. [*asst. continuity* – Joanna Busby.] *sc* – based on the romance by Baroness Orczy. *ph* – Christopher Challis. *col* – Technicolor. *cam. op* – Freddie Francis. [*focus puller* – Bill Lee. *cam. asst* – Gerry Anstiss. *Technicolor tech* – George Minassian. *Technicolor asst* – Dennis Bartlett]. *process shots* – W. Percy Day. *chief elec* – Bill Wall. *Technicolor color d* – Natalie Kalmus. *p. designer* – Hein Heckroth. *asst. des* – Ivor Beddoes. *art d* – Arthur Lawson. *location art d* – Joseph Bato. *set dresser* – Scott Slimon. *sup. scenic artist* – W. S. Robinson. [*asst. art d* – Elven Webb. *chief draughtsman* – Maurice Fowler. *draughtsman* – John Peters. *jnr draughtsman* – Patricia Sladen]. *ed* – Reginald Mills. [*assembly ed* – Noreen Ackland. *asst. ed* – Derek Armstrong. *2nd asst. ed* – Francis Taylor, S. Rowson]. *m/m. cond* – Brian Easdale. Played by the Philharmonia Orchestra. [*m. asst* – Fred Lewis]. *sd* – Charles Poulton, Red Law. [*sd mixer* – George Adams. *sd cam. op* – Bernard Hesketh. *boom op* – Peter Butcher. *boom asst* – Brian Coates. *sd maintenance* – Norman Bolland, George Barrett. *dubbing crew* – Bob Jones. *costume* – Ivy Baker. *asst. costume* – Bernard Sarron. *jnr costume* – Nandi Heckroth. *wardrobe master* – Jack Dalmayne. *wardrobe mistress* – Ethel Smith. *French costume* – M. Decrais]. *make-up* – Jimmy Vining. [*studio make-up* – Harold Fletcher]. *hair* – Betty Cross. [*master of horse* – A. G. Parry Jones. *nautical tech adviser* – Lt. Cmdr. G. E. Mills. *publicity* – Vivienne Knight. *stills* – Richard Cantouris].

David Niven (*Sir Percy Blakeney*), Margaret Leighton (*Lady Marguerite Blakeney*), Cyril Cusack (*Chauvelin*), Jack Hawkins (*Prince of Wales*), Arlette Marchal (*Comtesse de Tournai*), Gerard Nery (*Philippe de Tournai*), Danielle Godet (*Suzanne de Tournai*), Edmond Audran (*Armand St Juste*), Charles Victor (*Colonel Winterbottom*), Eugene Deckers (*Captain Merieres*), David Oxley (*Captain Duroc*), Raymond Rollet (*Bibot*), Philip Stainton (*Jellyband*), John Longden (*Abbot*),

Robert Griffiths (*Trubshaw*), George de Warfaz (*Baron*), Arthur Wontner (*Lord Grenville*), Jane Gil Davies (*Lady Grenville*), Richard George (*Sir John Coke*), Cherry Cottrell (*Lady Coke*).

The Gentlemen of the League: David Hutcheson (*Lord Anthony Dewhurst*), Robert Coote (*Sir Andrew ffoulkes*), John Fitzgerald (*Sir Michael Travers*), Patrick Macnee (*Hon. John Bristow*), Terence Alexander (*Duke of Dorset*), Tommy Duggan (*Earl of Sligo*), John Fitchen (*Nigel Seymour*), John Hewitt (*Major Pretty*), Hugh Kelly (*Mr Fitzdrummond*), Richmond Nairne (*Beau Pepys*). [Peter Copley (*tailor*), Howard Vernon (*Comte de Tournai*), Peter Gawthorne (*Chauvelin's servant*), Archie Duncan, James Lomas (*men in bath*), Sally Newland].

109 mins. *t. s* – 9 November. *UK rel* – 1 January 1951. *UK dist* – British Lion. *US rel* – 1955. *US dist* – Caroll Pictures. *US title* – *The Fighting Pimpernel*.

Sir Percy Blakeney poses as a fop in the entourage of the Prince of Wales, but secretly helps smuggle refugees from the Revolutionary Terror out of France, pitting his wits against the sinister Chauvelin. Originally conceived as a musical, but finally made as a jokey period drama, the film tried to revive the understated heroism of the original Leslie Howard *Scarlet Pimpernel*, building on Niven's engaging persona. But if the tone is sometimes uncertain, the extensive use of French locations, including Mont St Michel for its climax, is an unqualified success.

The Tales of Hoffmann   1951

d/p/sc – Michael Powell, Emeric Pressburger. *p. c* – British Lion Film Corporation [with Vega Productions and The Archers]. A Michael Powell and Emeric Pressburger Production. A London Films Presentation. *asst. p* – George Busby. [*p. asst* – Charles Orme. *p. asst. and sec* – Gwladys Jenks]. *asst. d* – Sydney Streeter. [*2nd asst. d* – Leslie Hughes. *3rd asst. d* – Fred Slark. *dial. coach* – Molly Terrain]. *continuity* – Pamela Davies. *sc* – from Dennis Arundell's adaptation of the French text by Jules Barbier. *ph* – Christopher Challis. *col* – Technicolor. *cam. op* – Fred Francis. *composite ph* – E Hague. *chief elec* – W. Wall. [*Technicolor asst* – John Kotze]. *p. designer* – Hein Heckroth. *art d* – Arthur Lawson. *asst. des* – Ivor Beddoes, Terence Morgan II. *scenic artist* – E. Lindegaard. [*draughtsmen* – Maurice Fowler, Don Picton, Kenneth McCallum Tait, Peter Moll. *set dresser* – Bernard Sarron. *property buyer* – George Durrant]. *ed* – Reginald Mills. [*assembly ed* – Noreen Ackland. *2nd asst. d* – Andreas Michailidis]. *m* – Jacques Offenbach. *m. cond* – Sir Thomas Beecham, conducting The Royal Philharmonic Orchestra. *asst. m. d* – Frederick Lewis. *sd rec* – Ted Drake. *rec. sup* – John Cox. *costume* – Josephine Boss (Miss Shearer and Miss Ayars). *wardrobe* – Ivy Baker. [*dress liaison* – Terence Morgan II. *wardrobe master* – Michael Hart. *wardrobe mistress* – Bill Smith. *wardrobe assts* – Fred Cook, Mrs Attride]. *make-up* – Constance Reeve. [*asst. make-up* – Tom Smith]. *hair* – Joseph Shear. [*asst. hair* – Eileen Bates]. *marionettes* – John Wright. *choreo* – Frederick Ashton. *asst. choreo* – Alan Carter, Joan Harris. [*publicity* – Vivienne Knight. *stills* – Bert Cann].

Prologue and Epilogue: Robert Rounseville (*E. T. A. Hoffmann, a poet*), Pamela Brown (*Nicklaus, his faithful friend and companion [sung by Monica Sinclair]*), Robert Helpmann (*Councillor Lindore, sinister opponent of Hoffmann throughout his life*), Moira Shearer (*Stella, prima ballerina, loved by Hoffmann, desired by Lindore*), Philip Leaver (*Andreas, Stella's servant, a rogue*), Frederick Ashton (*Kleinzach*), Moira Shearer (*his lady-love*), Meinhart Maur (*Luther, of 'Luther's Tavern' [sung by Fisher Morgan]*). [Edmond Audran (*dancer*), John Ford (*Nathaniel [sung by Rene Soames]*), Richard Golding (*Hermann [sung by Owen Brannigan]*)].

The Tale of Olympia: Moira Shearer (*Olympia, the doll [sung by Dorothy Bond]*), Robert Rounseville (*Hoffmann as a young student*), Robert Helpmann (*Coppelius, maker of magic spectacles [sung by Bruce*

Dargavel]), Leonide Massine (*Spalanzani, a fashionable creator of puppets and automatons [sung by Grahame Clifford]*), Frederick Ashton (*Coshenille, half-human, half-puppet [sung by Murray Dickie]*).

The Tale of Giulietta: Ludmilla Tcherina (*Giulietta, a courtesan [sung by Margherita Grandi]*), Robert Helpmann (*Dapertutto, her satanic master, collector of souls [sung by Dargavel]*), Robert Rounseville (*Hoffmann, now a man of the world, travelling through Venice*), Leonide Massine (*Schlemil, who has lost his shadow and his soul for Giulietta [sung by Brannigan]*), Lionel Harris (*Pitichinaccio, a hunchback [sung by Dickie]*).

The Tale of Antonia: Ann Ayars (*Antonia, a young opera singer fatally ill with consumption*), Mogens Wieth (*Crespel, her father, a great conductor now living on his memories [sung by Brannigan]*), Robert Rounseville (*Hoffmann, now a famous poet*), Leonide Massine (*Franz, a deaf servant [sung by Clifford]*), Robert Helpmann (*Dr Miracle, demonic physician who fans the flames of ambition that destroy Antonia [sung by Dargavel]*). [*mother's voice sung by Joan Alexander*].

[Sir Thomas Beecham (*himself*)] *singers*: Robert Rounseville, Owen Brannigan, Monica Sinclair, Rene Soames, Bruce Daravgel, Dorothy Bond, Margherita Grandi, Grahame Clifford, Joan Alexander, Murray Dickie, Fisher Morgan, Sadler's Wells Chorus.

138 mins [reduced to 112 mins before release]. *t. s* – 17 May. *UK rel* – 26 November. *UK dist* – British Lion. *US rel* – 13 June 1952. *US dist* – United Artists. *Prizes* – Special Jury Prize; Prize of the Commission Supérieure Technique, Cannes Festival 1951.

Offenbach's last opera, based on eerie stories by the master of the supernatural tale, E. T. A. Hoffmann, who features as a hapless poet, eternally deceived in love – first by the inventor of a mechanical doll with which he falls in love; then by a Venetian courtesan manipulated by her protector; and finally by a dying singer under the influence of the sinister Dr Miracle. The opera was conducted by Beecham, who suggested it as a subject, then filmed to playback using a dazzling array of scenic and camera effects.

Arctic Fury (Aila, pohjolan tytär) 1951

d – Jack Witikka. *p* – Erik Blomberg, Michael Powell, Jack Witikka. *sc* – Erik Blomberg, Jack Witikka, John Seabourne. *ph* – Erik Blomberg, Auvo Mustonen. *ed* – John Seabourne. *art d* – Jack Witikka. *m* – selections from Sibelius (*The Tempest*, *The Bard*, *En Saga* etc). *narr* – Matti Oravisto. *sd* – Harald Koivikko.

Mirjami Kuosmanen (*Aila*), Tapio Rautavaara (*Reino*), Hilda Pihjalamäki (*Morokka's mother*), Anton Soini (*Morokka, Aila's father*), Jalmari Parikka (*Shopkeeper*), Tauno Rova (*Sami*), Ale Porkka (*the younger Sami*), Mogens Wieth (*Harm, an American writer*).

77 mins. *Finnish dist* – Suomi Filmi.

An American-born writer of Finnish extraction tells the story of his return to his parents' country, and of a tragedy that he sees unfold during the annual reindeer round-up north of the Arctic Circle. The clandestine relationship between Reino, a hunter and also reindeer thief, and Aila, who is the daughter of a big herder, leads to the death of her father at Reino's hands and to the two lovers killing each other. The *Finnish National Filmography* notes: 'Due to the participation of Englishman Michael Powell in the production of the film and its intended foreign distribution, *Aila, pohjolan tytär* attracted much attention and expectations.' Much of the comment seems to have been critical of Witikka's direction (and of Seabourne's contribution to the project), while praising the photography. According to the critic of the *Helsingin Sanomat*, '*Aila* is significant for its stunning photography… The film had the potential to become an event which would have interested a wider audience, even in Finland, had the narrative had more pace, better tempo and had the story itself been developed. '

Oh ... Rosalinda!!   1955

d/p/sc – Michael Powell, Emeric Pressburger. *p. c* – An Associated British Picture Corporation Presentation. A Michael Powell and Emeric Pressburger Presentation. *assoc. p* – Sydney Streeter. *p. manager* – Charles Orme. *asst. d* – John Pellatt. [*2nd asst. d* – Alec Gibb. *3rd asst. d* – David Mycroft. *continuity* – June Faithfull]. *sc* – based on Johann Strauss' operetta *Die Fledermaus. ph* – Christopher Challis (CinemaScope). *col* – Technicolor. *cam. op* – Norman Warwick. [*focus puller* – Kelvin Pike. *clapper loader* – Peter Hendry. *2nd cam. op* – J Stilwell]. *ed* – Reginald Mills. [*asembly cutter* – Alan Tyrer. *asst. ed* – Nick Gurney. *2nd asst. ed* – Henrietta Gordon]. *p. designer* – Hein Heckroth. *asst. designer* – Terence Morgan II. *assoc. art d* – Arthur Lawson. [*2nd asst. art d* – Bernard Sarron. *draughtsman* – Peter Pendrey]. *m* – Johann Strauss. *lyrics* – Dennis Arundell. *m. d* – Frederick Lewis. *m. perf by* – Wiener Symphoniker Orchestra. *m. cond* – Alois Melichar. *sd rec* – Leslie Hammond, Herbert Janeczka. *dubbing ed* – Noreen Ackland. [*sd cam. op* – Bud Abbott. *boom op* – Dennis Whitlock. *boom asst* – Hugh Strain. *dubbing crew* – Len Shilton, Len Abbott, H. Blackmore, M. Bradbury]. *Ludmilla Tcherina's clothes created by* – Jean Desses of Paris. *make-up* – Constance Reeve. *hair* – A. G. Scott. *choreo* – Alfred Rodrigues. [*stills* – Ronnie Pilgrim, Bert Cann].

Anthony Quayle (*General Orlovsky*), Anton Walbrook (*Dr Falke, the Fledermaus [singing dubbed by Walter Berry]*), Richard Marner (*Colonel Lebotov*), Ludmilla Tcherina (*Rosalinda [singing dubbed by Sari Barabas]*), Michael Redgrave (*Colonel Eisenstein*), Mel Ferrer (*Captain Alfred Westerman [singing dubbed by Alexander Young]*), Nicholas Bruce (*hotel receptionist*), Anneliese Rothenberger (*Adele*), Dennis Price (*Major Frank [singing dubbed by Dennis Dowling]*), Oskar Sima (*Frosh*).

The ladies: Barbara Ash, Hildy Christian, Caryl Gunn, Griselda Hervey, Jill Ireland, Olga Lowe, Ingrid Marshall, Alicia Massey-Beresford, Eileen Sands, Herta Seydel, Anna Steele, Dorothy Whitney.

The dancers: Betty Ash, Yvonne Barnes, Pamela Foster, Patricia Garnett, Annette Gibson, Eileen Gourla, Prudence Hyman, Maya Koumani, Sara Luzita, Jennifer Warmsley, Igor Barczinsky, Cecil Bates, Denis Carey, Peter Darrell, David Gilbert, Robert Harrold, Jan Lawski, William Martin, Kenneth Melville, Morris Metliss, Kenneth Smith.

The gentlemen: Michael Anthony, Richard Bennett, Nicholas Bruce, Ray Buckingham, Rolf Carston, Terence Cooper, Robert Crewdson, Edmund Forsyth, Roger Gage, Raymond Lloyd, Orest Orloff, Robert Ross, Frederick Schiller, John Schlesinger, Frederick Schrecker. [Arthur Mullard (*Russian guard*), Roy Kinnear].

101 mins. *t. s* – 15 November. *UK rel* – 2 January 1956. *UK dist* – Associated British-Pathe.

Strauss's popular operetta, updated to a post-war Vienna, misruled by the four Occupying Powers – USA, USSR, France and Britain – whose pleasure-seeking representatives are easy prey for a Viennese fixer, Dr Falke, 'the Bat'. Most of the cast were dubbed for their singing (as in *Hoffmann*), but Redgrave bravely both sings and dances. Using the still-new CinemaScope process, Vienna was designed by Heckroth as a chocolate-box confection sparkling amid the drabness of post-war Europe.

The Sorcerer's Apprentice (GB/W. Germany)   1956

d – Michael Powell. *p. c* – 20th Century-Fox Film Corporation/Norddeutscher Rundfunk. *p. manager* – Harald Voller. *sc* – based on a story by Goethe. *Eng. text* – Dennis Arundell. *ph* – Christopher Challis (CinemaScope, Technicolor). *cam. op* – Freddie Francis. *ed* – Reginald Mills. *p. devised/designed* – Hein Heckroth. *set constr* – K. H. Joksch. *m. perf* – Hamburg State Opera Orchestra. *choreo* – Helga Swedlund. *cast* – Sonia Arova (*solo dancer*).

13 mins [cut from *c.* 30 mins]. *UK rel* – 14 July. *dist* – 20th Century-Fox.

A ballet created in Stuttgart, where Heckroth now worked, based on the story by Goethe that had inspired Paul Dukas's *Scherzo*, which in turn accompanies Disney's version of the story, with Mickey Mouse, in *Fantasia* – although Heckroth's and Powell's film owes nothing to this.

The Battle of the River Plate   1956

d/p/sc – Michael Powell, Emeric Pressburger. *p. c* – Arcturus Productions. A Michael Powell and Emeric Pressburger Production. *assoc. p* – Sydney Streeter. *exec. p* – Earl St. John. *p. controller* – Arthur Alcott. *p. manager* – John Brabourne. *asst. d* – Charles Orme. *ph* – Christopher Challis (VistaVision). *col* – Technicolor. *cam. op* – Austin Dempster. *sp. effects* – Bill Warrington, James Snow. *ed* – Reginald Mills. *p. designer* – Arthur Lawson. *asst. art d* – Donald Picton. *artistic adviser* – Hein Heckroth. *m* – Brian Easdale. *m. d* – Frederick Lewis. *sd ed* – Arthur Stevens. *sd rec* – C. C. Stevens, Gordon K. McCallum. *make-up* – Geoffrey Rodway. *naval adviser* – Capt. F. S. Bell, CB, RN Ret. *technical adviser on prison sequences* (Graf Spee) – Capt. Patrick Dove of the *Africa Shell*.

John Gregson (*Captain F. S. Bell, HMS Exeter*), Anthony Quayle (*Commodore Henry Harwood, HMS Ajax*), Ian Hunter (*Captain Woodhouse, HMS Ajax*), Jack Gwillim (*Captain Parry, HMNZS . Achilles*), Bernard Lee (*Captain Patrick Dove, MS Africa Shell*). HMS Sheffield (*HMS Ajax*), HMS Delhi (formerly Achilles) (*HMNZS Achilles*), HMS Jamaica (*HMS Exeter*), HMS Cumberland (*HMS Cumberland*), US heavy cruiser Salem (*the German pocket battleship Admiral Graf Spee*), Lionel Murton (*Mike Fowler*), Anthony Bushell (*Mr Millington-Drake, British Minister in Montevideo*), Peter Illing (*Dr Guani, Foreign Minister, Uruguay*), Michael Goodliffe (*Captain McCall, British naval attaché, Buenos Aires*), Patrick Macnee (*Lt. Cmdr. Medley, RN*), John Chandos (*Dr Langmann, German Minister, Montevideo*), Douglas Wilmer (*M. Desmoulins, French Minister, Montevideo*), William Squire (*Ray Martin*), Roger Delgado (*Captain Varela, Uruguayan Navy*), Andrew Cruickshank (*Captain Stubs, Doric Star*), Christopher Lee (*Manolo*), Edward Atienza (*Pop*), April Olrich (*Dolores*), Peter Finch (*Captain Hans Langsdorff, Admiral, Graf Spee*), [Maria Mercedes (*Madame X*), John Schlesinger (*German officer*), John Le Mesurier (*Padre*), Anthony Newley, Nigel Stock (*British officers aboard* Graf Spee), Richard Beale (*Captain Pottinger, Ashlea*), Brian Worth, Ronald Clarke].

119 mins. *t. s* – 29 October. *UK rel* – 24 December. *UK dist* – JARFlD (Rank). *US rel* – November 1957 [106 mins]. *US title* – *Pursuit of the Graf Spee*. Selected for the Royal Film Performance, 1956.

The hunt for the German 'pocket battleship', which had been attacking merchant ships in the Atlantic early in the Second World War, leads a squadron of British cruisers into a fierce battle, before the *Graf Spee* takes refuge in the neutral port of Montevideo, Uruguay. The script was partly based on Captain Dove's account of being captured by the *Graf Spee*, whose captain is portrayed (by Peter Finch) with quiet dignity, leading up to his decision to scuttle the damaged ship, rather than run the risk of capture or internment. The naval battle scenes were filmed mainly in the Mediterranean, with British Navy co-operation and the *USS Salem* playing the *Graf Spee*.

Ill Met by Moonlight   1957

d/p/sc – Michael Powell, Emeric Pressburger. *p. c* – A Michael Powell and Emeric Pressburger Production for The Rank Organisatlon Film Productions [and Vega Productions]. *exec. p* – Earl St John. *assoc. p* – Sydney S. Streeter. *p. controller* – Arthur Alcott. *p. manager* – Jack Swinburne. *asst. d* – Charles Orme. [*2nd asst. d* – Harold Orton. *3rd asst. d* – David Tringham]. *sc* – based on the book of the same title by W. Stanley Moss. *ph* – Christopher Challis (VistaVision). *cam. op* – Austin Dempster. [*focus puller* – Steve Claydon. *cam. asst* – Ronald Anscombe]. *sp. ph. effects* – Bill

Warrington [and F. George, H. Marshall, Cliff Culley, D. Hume]. *ed* – Arthur Stevens. [*assembly cutter* – Noreen Ackland. *1st asst. ed* – Jack Gardner, A. Godfrey. *2nd asst. ed* – Norman Wanstall]. *art d* – Alex Vetchinsky. [*asst. art d* – Maurice Pelling. *draughtsmen* – Lionel Couch, Harry Pottle, Bruce Grimes]. *m* – Mikis Theodorakis. *m. d* – Frederick Lewis. [*m. rec* – Ted Drake]. *sd ed* – Archie Ludski. *sd rec* – Charles Knott, Gordon K. McCallum. [*sd ed. asst* – D. Lancaster. *sd cam. op* – Martin McClean. *boom op* – Basil Rootes. *boom asst* – Ken Reynolds. *dubbing crew* – Gordon K. McCallum, W. Daniels, C. Le Messurier]. *costume* – Nandi Routh. *make-up* – Paul Rabiger. [*stills* – Harry Grimes]. *technical advisers* – Micky Akoumianakis of Knossos, Crete; Major Xan Fielding, DSO.

Dirk Bogarde (*Major Patrick Leigh-Fermor, DSO, OBE*), Marius Goring (*Major General Karl Kreipe*), David Oxley (*Captain William 'Billy' Stanley Moss*), Demitri Andreas (*Niko*), Cyril Cusack (*Sandy*), Laurence Payne (*Manoli*), Wolfe Morris (*George*), Michael Gough (*Andoni Zoidakis*), John Cairney (*Elias*), Brian Worth (*Stratis Saviolkis*), Roland Bartrop (*Micky Akoumianakis*), George Eugeniou (*Charis Zographakis*), Paul Stassino (*Yanni Katsias*), Adeeb Assaly (*Zahari*), Theo Moreas (*village priest*), Takis Frangofinos (*Michali*), Christopher Lee (*German officer at dentist*), Peter Augustine, John Houseman, Phyllia Houseman. [Andreas Malandrinos, Christopher Rhodes, David McCallum].

104 mins. *t. s* – 29 Jan 1957. *UK rel* – 4 March 1957. *UK dist* – Rank. *US rel* – July 1958 [93 mins]. *US title* – Night Ambush.

Like *The Battle of the River Plate*, a Second World War episode that pitted British against German qualities. Two adventurers enlisted as British officers, the writer Leigh-Fermor and Moss (on whose book it is based), plot to capture the German general in charge of occupied Crete and take him to Cairo. With the help of the local Resistance movement, they succeed – although to Powell's disappointment, the tense politics of the eastern Mediterranean made shooting the film on location impossible and it was relocated to the South of France.

Luna de miel [*Honeymoon*] Spain/GB   1959
d/p – Michael Powell. *p. c* – A Michael Powell Production for Suevia Films-Cesario Gonsalez (Spain)/Everdene (GB). *director general of p* – Jaime Prades *assoc. p* – Sydney S Streeter, Judith Coxhead, William J. Paton. *p. sec* – Samuel Menkes. *asst. d* – Ricardo Blasco. *sc* – Michael Powell, Luis Escobar. *ph* – Georges Perinal (Technirama). *col* – Technicolor. *assoc. ph* – Gerry Turpin. *Technicolor tech* – George Minassian, Ronald Cross. *chief electrician* – William Wall. *ed* – Peter Taylor. *assembly ed* – John V. Smith. *art d/costume* – Ivor Beddoes. *asst. art d* – Eduardo Torre de la Fuente, Roberto Carpio, Judy Jordan. *m* – Mikis Theodorakis. *m. cond* – Sir Thomas Beecham. Antonio's 'Zapateado' by Sarasate, arr. Leonard Salzedo; 'Honeymoon Song', arr. Wally Stott, sung by Marino Marini and his Quartet. *sd* – Fernando Bernaldes. *sd ed* – Janet Davidson. *sd sup* – John Cox.

Ballets
El Amor Brujo: *sc* – Gregorio Martinez Sierra. *m* – Manuel de Falla. *sets* – Rafael Durancamps. *choreo* – Antonio. *soloist* – Maria Clara Alcala, Pastora Ruiz (*sorceror*).

Los Amantes de Teruel: *m* – Mikis Theodorakis. *cond* – Sir Thomas Beecham. *choreo* – Leonide Massine.

Anthony Steel (*Kit Kelly*), Ludmilla Tcherina (*Anna*), Antonio (*himself*), Leonide Massine ('*Der Geist*'), Rosita Segovia (*Rosita Candelas*), Carmen Rojas (*Lucia*), Antonio's Spanish Ballet Troupe (*themselves*), [Juan Carmona (*Pepe Nieto*), Maria Gamez, Diego Hurtado, Michael Powell (*voice of guide describing* The Lovers of Teruel)].

109 mins. *France* – 18 March 1961. *UK t. s* – 31 January 1962 [90 mins]. *UK rel* – 8 February
1962. *UK dist* – BLC. *Prize* – Special Prize of Commission Supérieure Technique, Cannes
Festival 1959.

Kit and his new wife, a ballerina who has promised to give up her career on marriage, tour Spain
on their honeymoon. They meet the dancer Antonio and his troupe – then a potent force in
popularising Spanish dance – and Anna is tempted to return to dancing, while her conflict over
giving up her career gives rise to a dream, inspired by a local legend. A fraught co-production
hampered Powell's efforts to reunite many of his former music and dance collaborators, and
revive the dream-ballet genre of *The Red Shoes* and *The Tales of Hoffmann*.

Peeping Tom   1960

d/p – Michael Powell. *p. c* – Michael Powell (Theatre) Ltd. A Michael Powell Production. [*assoc.
p* – Albert Fennell]. *p. manager* – Al Marcus. *p. assts* – Judith Coxhead, William J. Paton. *asst. d* –
Ted Sturgis. [*2nd asst. d* – Dennis Johnson. *3rd asst. d* – Carl Mannon]. *continuity* – Rita Davison.
[*asst. continuity* – Diane Vaughan]. *sc* – Leo Marks, from his own story. *ph* – Otto Heller. *col* –
Eastman Color. *cam. op* – Gerry Turpin. *chief elec* – Victor E. Smith. [*focus puller* – Derek Browne.
clapper loader – Jimmy Hopewell]. *ed* – Noreen Ackland. [*asst. ed* – Alma Godfrey. *2nd asst. ed* –
John Rushton]. *art d* – Arthur Lawson. *asst. art d* – Ivor Beddoes. *set dresser* – Don Picton. *constr.
manager* – Ronald Udell. [*draughtsman* – Maurice Pelling. *prop buyer* – Harry Hanney]. *m /m. d* –
Brian Easdale. *percussion number* – Wally Stott. *solo piano* – Gordon Watson. *sd rec* – C. C.
Stevens, Gordon McCallum. *sd ed* – Malcolm Cooke. [*sd cam. op* – Simon Kay. *boom op* – Gus
Lloyd. *sd maintenance* – J. Johnson]. *costume* – Miss Massey's dresses: Polly Peck; Miss Shearer's
dress: John Tullis of Horrockses. *wardrobe* – Dickie Richardson. [*wardrobe asst* – Vi Ganham].
make-up – W. J. Partleton. *hair* – Pearl Orton. *hats* – The Millinery Guild.
[*pub. director* – William Burnside. *unit pub* – Lillana Wilkie. *stills* – Norman Gryspeerdt].

Carl Boehm (*Mark Lewis*), Moira Shearer (*Vivian*), Anna Massey (*Helen Stephens*), Maxine
Audley (*Mrs Stephens*), Brenda Bruce (*Dora*), Miles Malleson (*elderly gentleman*), Esmond Knight
(*Arthur Baden*), Martin Miller (*Dr Rosan*), Michael Goodliffe (*Don Jarvis*), Jack Watson
(*Inspector Gregg*), Shirley Anne Field (*Diane Ashley*), Pamela Green (*Milly*). [Bartlett Mullins
(*Mr Peters*), Nigel Davenport (*Sg.t Miller*), Brian Wallace (*Tony*), Susan Travers (*Lorraine*),
Maurice Durant (*publicity chief*), Brian Worth (*assistant director*), Veronica Hurst (*Miss Simpson*),
Alan Rolfe (*store detective*), John Dunbar (*police doctor*), Guy Kingsley-Poynter (*P. Tate, the
cameraman*), Keith Baxter (*Baxter, the detective*), Peggy Thorpe-Bates (*Mrs Partridge*), John
Barrard (*small man*), Roland Curram (*young man extra*), John Chappell (*clapper boy*), Paddy
Edwardes (*girl extra*), Frank Sanguineau (*first electrician*), Margaret Neal (*stepmother*), Michael
Powell (*A. N. Lewis, Mark's father*), Columba Powell (*Mark as a child*)].

109 mins. *t. s* – 31 March. *UK rel* – 16 May. *UK dist* – Anglo Amalgamated. *US rel* – 15 May
1962 [86 mins]. *US dist* – Astor. *US reissue* – 1980 [Corinth Films, 'presented by Martin
Scorsese', 109 mins].

Mark, a studio camera assistant and amateur film-maker, has grown up in the shadow of his
father's psychological experiments, practised on him as a child. While he now experiments on
others by filming his murder of them, he forms a tentative relationship with Helen, who lives
with her blind mother in the lower part of Mark's house, and wants him to illustrate her
children's book about a magic camera. But Mark cannot resist his murderous compulsion and
finally photographs his own death. Critics' outrage at *Peeping Tom* blighted Powell's subsequent
career, although the film had achieved cult status by the 1970s.

The Queen's Guards   1961

d/p – Michael Powell. *p. c* – Imperial. A Michael Powell Production. *assoc. p* – Simon Harcourt-Smith. *p. sup/assoc. d* – Sydney Streeter. *p. manager* – John Wilcox. *sc* – Roger Milner, from an idea by Simon Harcourt-Smith. *ph* – Gerald Turpin. *col* – Technicolor. *cam. op* – Derek Browne, Austin Dempster, Skeets Kelly, Robert Walker, James Bawden, Robert Huke, Dudley Lovell, Norman Warwick. *ed* – Noreen Ackland. *art d* – Wilfred Shingleton. *m/m. d* – Brian Easdale. *sd rec* – Red Law. *sd ed* – James Shields. *costume* – Bridget Sellers. *wardrobe master* – McPhee. *ladies costume* – Mattli. *make-up* – James Hines. *hair* – Anne Box.

Daniel Massey (*John Fellowes*), Raymond Massey (*Capt. Fellowes*), Robert Stephens (*Henry Wynne-Walton*), Jack Watson (*Sgt. Johnson*), Peter Myers (*Gordon Davidson*), Ursula Jeans (*Mrs Fellowes*), Frank Lawton (*Cmdr. Hewson*), Anthony Bushell (*Major Cole*), Jess Conrad (*Dankworth*), Cornel Lucas (*photographer*), Ian Hunter (*Mr Dobbie*), Elizabeth Shepherd (*Susan*), Judith Stott (*Ruth*), Duncan Lamont (*Wilkes*), Jack Allen (*Brig. Cummings*), Laurence Payne (*Farinda*), Eileen Peel (*Mrs Wynne-Walton*), William Fox (*Mr Walters*), Patrick Connor (*Brewer*), William Young (*Williams*), Roland Curram, Nigel Green (*Abu Sibdar*), Anthony Selby (*Kishu*), John Chappell (*P. Walsh*). [Jack Watling (*Capt. Shergold*), Andrew Crawlord (*Biggs*), René Cutforth (*commentator*)].

110 mins. *t. s* – 9 October. *rel* – 23 October. *dist* – 20th Century-Fox.

During the annual Trooping of the Colour ceremony in central London, a young guards officer recalls in flashback his training at Sandhurst and a Middle East airlift operation, in which he tried to live up to the expecations of his father, now crippled but still living in a military dream-world, fighting battles with model soldiers and grieving for another son lost in action. The father finally acknowledges his living son's achievements, listening to the ceremony in Horseguards Parade. The two parts were played by real-life father and son, Raymond and Daniel Massey, echoing Powell's own appearance with his son in *Peeping Tom*, but the film met with little commercial or critical success.

Never Turn Your Back on a Friend   1963
[TV film for the *Espionage* series]

d – Michael Powell. *p. c* – Herbert Brodkin Ltd. *exec. p* – Herbert Hirschman. *p* – George Justin. *assoc. p* – John Pellatt. *p. manager* – Tom Sachs. *asst. d* – Bruce Sherman. *sc* – Mel Davenport. Series based on an idea by Charles H. Hill. *ph* – Ken Hodges. *cam. op* – Herbert Smith. *ed* – John Victor Smith. *p. designer* – Wilfred Shingleton. *art d* – Tony Woollard. *m/m. cond* – Malcolm Arnold. *sd rec* – David Bowen. *sd ed* – Dennis Rogers. *costume* – Kim Ziegler. *make-up* – Alex Garfath. *hair* – Daphne Martin. *titles* – Maurice Binder. *casting* – Rose Tobias Shaw.

George Voskovek (*Professor Kuhn*), Donald Madden (*Anaconda*), Mark Eden (*Wicket*), Julian Glover (*Tovarich*), Pamela Brown (*Miss Jensen*).

54 mins. tx – 1 January 1964.

Thirteenth film in a television series that ran for only one season, devoted to stories of espionage across the ages, from the American Revolution to the contemporary Cold War. Other directors contributing included Seth Holt, Ken Hughes, Ted Kotcheff and Stuart Rosenberg, along with newcomer David Greene, whose *Sebastian* Powell would co-produce.

A Free Agent   1964
[TV film for the *Espionage* series]

d – Michael Powell. *p. c* – Herbert Brodkin Ltd. *exec. p* – Herbert Hirschman. *p* – George Justin. *assoc. p* – John Pellatt. *p. manager* – Tom Sachs. *asst. d* – Jake Wright. *continuity* – Joy Mercer. *sc* –

Leo Marks. *ph* – Geoffrey Faithfull. *cam. op* – Alan McCabe. *ed* – John Victor Smith. *p. designer* – Wilfred Shingleton. *art d* – Anthony Woollard. *m/m. cond* – Benjamin Frankel. *title m* – Malcolm Arnold. *sd rec* – Cyril Smith. *sd ed* – Dennis Rogers. *wardrobe* – Jackie Cummins. *make-up* – Alex Garfath. *hair* – Alice Holmes. *titles* – Maurice Binder. *casting* – Rose Tobias Shaw.

Anthony Quayle (*Phillip*), Siân Phillips (*Anna*), Norman Foster (*Max*), George Mikell (*Peter*), John Wood (*Douglas*), John Abineri (*town clerk*), Ernst Walder (*watch factory mechanic*), Gertan Klauber (*innkeeper*), Vivienne Drummond (*Miss Weiss*), Jan Conrad (*chief mechanic*).

52 mins. *tx* – 21 March.

A Soviet agent falls in love with a woman on the other side, and so comes under the scrutiny of both his allies and his enemies. The twenty-fourth and final episode in the series.

Herzog Blaubarts Burg [*Bluebeard's Castle*] (W. Germany)   1964
d – Michael Powell. *p. c* – Suddeutscher Rundfunk. Eine Norman Foster Produktion.
p – Norman Foster. *p. manager* – W. Tjader. *libretto* – Béla Balázs. *ph* – Hannes Staudinger. *col* – Technicolor. *ed* – Paula Dvorak. *p. designer* – Hein Heckroth. *art d* – Gerd Krauss.
m – Bela Bartók's opera *Herzog Blaubarts Burg* (1911). *cond* – Milan Horvath.

Norman Foster (*Bluebeard*), Anna Raquel Sartre (*Judit*).

60 mins. *UK premiere* – 9 November 1978.

Bartók's only opera, not staged until 1918, was based on a Symbolist libretto written in 1910 by the future film theorist Béla Balázs, based on Perrault's fairy tale. The Duke reluctantly opens the seven doors in his castle to show his eighth wife the bloody secrets that lie behind them, before she joins the ghostly wives as darkness falls. In later life, Powell hoped to film Bartók's pantomime-ballet *The Miraculous Mandarin* and make a documentary to complete a trilogy on the composer, but was unable to get backing for this project.

The Sworn Twelve   1965
[TV film for *The Defenders* series]

d – Michael Powell. *sc* – Edward DeBlasio. *cast* – E. G. Marshall, Murry Hamilton, King Donovan, Ruby Dee, Jerry Orbach. 50 mins.

A 39846   1965
[TV film for *The Nurses* series]

d – Michael Powell. *sc* – George Bellak. *cast* – Michael Tolan, Shirl Conway, Joseph Campanella, Jean-Pierre Aumont, Kermit Murdock. 50 mins.

They're a Weird Mob (Australia/UK)   1966
d/p – Michael Powell. *p. c* – Williamson (Australia)/Powell (GB). A Michael Powell Production.
assoc. p – John Pellatt. *unit manager* – Bruce Bennett. *p. sup* – Lee Robinson. *location manager* – Jefferson Jackson. *asst. d* – Claude Watson. *2nd asst. d* – David Crocker. *continuity* – Doreen Soan. *sc* – Richard Imrie [pseud. Emeric Pressburger]. based on the novel by Nino Culotta [pseud. John O'Grady]. *ph* – Arthur Grant. *col* – Eastmancolor.
cam. op – Keith Loone, Graham Lind, Dennis Hill. *ed* – G Turney-Smith. *art d* – Dennis Gentle. *m* – Laurence Leonard, Alan Boustead. *m. d* – Laurence Leonard. *songs* – 'Big Country', 'In this Man's Country' by Reen Devereaux; 'I Kiss You. You Kiss Me' by Walter Chiari. Cretan dance from *Ill Met by Moonlight* by Mikis Theodorakis. *sd* – David Copping. *sd rec* – Alan Allen. *sd re-rec* – Ted

Karnon. *sd ed* – Don Saunders, Bill Creed. *costume* – Chris Jacovides. *wardrobe mistress* – Barbara Turnbull. *make-up* – Joan Adelsteine, Barbara Still. *hair* – Leon Daunais. *casting* – Gloria Payten.

Walter Chiari (*Nino Culotta*), Clare Dunne (*Kay Kelly*), Chips Rafferty (*Harry Kelly*), Alida Chelli (*Giuliana*), Ed Devereaux (*Joe*), Slim DeGrey (*Pat*), John Meillon (*Dennis*), Charles Little (*Jimmy*), Anne Haddy (*barmaid*), Jack Allen (*fat man in bar*), Red Moore (*texture man*), Ray Hartley (*newsboy*), Tony Bonner (*lifesaver*), Alan Lander (*Charlie*), Keith Petersen (*drunk man on ferry*), Muriel Steinbeck (*Mrs Kelly*), Gloria Dawn (*Mrs Chapman*), Jeanne Dryman (*Betty*), Gita Rivera (*Maria, sister of Giuliana*), Judith Arthy (*Dixie*), Doreen Warburton (*Edie*), Barry Creyton, Noel Brophy, Graham Kennedy.

112 mins. *t. s* – 7 October. *UK rel* – 13 October. *UK dist* – Rank.

A young Italian journalist comes to Sydney to work on his cousin's Italian-language newspaper, only to find that the cousin has fled to Canada, leaving nothing but debts. Nino starts to pay them off and to learn English, discovering Australia and its customs in the process.

Sebastian   1968

d – David Greene. *p. c* – Maccius. *p* – Herbert Brodkin, Michael Powell. *sc* – Gerald Vaughan-Hughes, based on a story by Leo Marks. *ph* – Gerald Fisher. *ed* – Brian Smedly-Aston. *p. designer* – Wilfred Shingleton. *m* – Jerry Goldsmith.

Dirk Bogarde (*Sebastian*), Susannah York (*Becky Howard*), Lilli Palmer (*Elsa Shahn*), John Gielgud (*Head of Intelligence*).

100m mins. *dist* – Paramount.

Tongue-in-cheek espionage thriller in high 1960s Cold War style, co-produced by Powell and drawn from Leo Marks' own experience in wartime Intelligence, with Bogarde as a professor surrounded by glamorous women and much play on cryptographic clues.

Age of Consent (Australia)   1969

d – Michael Powell. *p. c* – Nautilus Productions (Australia). *p* – James Mason, Michael Powell. *assoc. p* – Michael Pate. *p. sup* – Brian Chirlian. *p. manager* – Kevin Powell. *asst. d* – David Crocker. *sc* – Peter Yeldham, based on a novel by Norman Lindsay. *ph* – Hannes Staudinger. *col* – Eastmancolor. *cam. op* – John McLean, Graham Lind. *underwater ph* – Ron Taylor. *chief elec* – Tony Tegg. *ed* – Anthony Buckley. *art d* – Dennis Gentle. *m/m. cond* – Stanley Myers. *sd ed* – Tim Wellburn. *sd rec* – Paul Ennis, Lloyd Colman. *boom op* – Alfred Higgins. *costume* – Anne Senior. *make-up* – Peggy Carter. *hair* – Robert Hynard. *casting* – Gloria Payten. *New York paintings* – Paul Delprat. *'Lonsdale' trained by* – Scotty Denholm.

James Mason (*Bradley Morahan*), Helen Mirren (*Cora*), Jack MacGowran (*Nat Kelly*), Neva Carr-Glyn (*Ma Ryan*), Antonia Katsaros (*Isabel Marley*), Michael Boddy (*Hendricks*), Harold Hopkins (*Ted Farrell*), Slim DeGrey (*Cooley*), Max Meldrum (*TV interviewer*), Frank Thring (*Godfrey*), Clarissa Kaye (*Meg*), Judy McGrath (*Grace*), Lenore Caton (*Edna*), Diane Strachan (*Susie*), Roberta Grant (*Ivy*), Lonsdale (*Godfrey, the dog*), Prince Nial (*Jasper*). [Dora Hing (*receptionist*), Hudson Frausset (*New Yorker*), Peggy Cass (*New Yorker's wife*), Eric Reiman (*art lover*), Tommy Hanlon Jr (*Levi-Strauss*), Geoff Cartwright (*newsboy*)].

103 mins [UK/US 98 mins]. *UK rel* – 15 November. *US rel* – 14 May. *dist* – Columbia.

A jaded expatriate Australian artist returns to the scene of his first inspiration on the Brisbane coast and discovers the innocently seductive Cora, who poses for him in the nude. Despite trouble from Cora's drunken grandmother and an unwelcome visit from an old mate on the scrounge, Brad and Cora find each other in the end.

The Boy Who Turned Yellow   1972

d – Michael Powell. *p. c* – Roger Cherrill Ltd for the Children's Film Foundation. A CFF Production. *asst. p* – Drummond Challis. *p. manager* – Gus Angus. *asst. d* – Neil Vine-Miller. *sc* – Emeric Pressburger. *ph* – Christopher Challis. *col* – Eastmancolor. *ed* – Peter Boita. *art d* – Bernard Sarron. *electronic m* – Patrick Gowers, David Vorhaus, *sd* – Roger Harrison. *sd rec* – Bob Jones, Ken Barker.

Mark Dightam (*John Saunders*), Robert Eddison (*Nick*), Helen Weir (*Mrs Saunders*), Brian Worth (*Mr Saunders*), Esmond Knight (*doctor*), Laurence Carter (*schoolteacher*), Patrick McAlinney (*Supreme Beefeater*), Lem Kitaj (*Munro*).

55 mins. *UK rel* – 16 September. *dist* – Children's Film Foundation. *Prize* – Children's Film Foundation award, 'Chiffy', 1978.

A London schoolboy suddenly turns yellow while travelling on the Underground and is later visited by an alien, Nick ('short for "electronic"'), who emerges from the family television and takes him on a tour of the Tower of London. Caught by the Beefeaters and accused of treason, he is about to be beheaded when he manages to get home with Nick's help, and return to his original colour.

Que la fête commence (France)   1974

d – Bertrand Tavernier. *p. c* – Fildebroc. Productions de la Guéville. Universal Pictures France. *sc* – Jean Aurenche, Bertrand Tavernier. *p* – Michelle de Broca, Yves Robert.
ph – Pierre William Glenn. *ed* – Armand Psenny. *art d* – Pierre Guffroy.

Philippe Noiret (*Philippe d'Orléans, le Regent*), Jean Rochefort (*L'abbé Dubois*), Jean-Pierre Marielle (*Marquis de Pontcallec*), Christine Pascal (*Emilie*), etc. Powell appeared in a cameo role as an Englishman, which was cut from the final release version.

117 mins. *rel* – 1975. *prizes* – French Critics' prize as best French film of the year; various César awards.

Four years after the death of Louis XIV, in 1719, the debauched Regent presides over a scheming court, in which the corrupt Abbé Dubois pursues his ambitions while most around him pursue their pleasures. A remarkable panorama of pre-revolutionary France realized in great historical detail.

Return to the Edge of the World   1978

d/sc – Michael Powell. *p. c* – Poseidon Films/BBC Television. exec. p – Frixos Constantine. *p* – Michael Powell, Sydney Streeter. *ph* – Brian Mitchison. *ed* – Peter Mayhew. *m/m. cond* – Brian Easdale. *sd* – David Hahn.

85 mins. *UK premiere* – 3 October 1978.

A return visit to the island of Foula with members of the cast and crew of *Edge of the World*, including Powell, Sydney Streeter, John Laurie, Grant Sutherland and Frankie Reidy. In the form of a prelude and epilogue to the 1940 version of *Edge of the World* (62 mins).

Pavlova – A Woman for All Time (USSR/GB)   1983

d/sc – Emil Lotianou. *p. c* – Mosfilm/Poseidon. *p* – Frixos Constantine, Seraphim Karalexis, Erik Waisberg. *ph* – Evgeny Guslinsky. *ed* – Jim Connock, Elena Galkina, Irina Kolotikova [Michael Powell, Thelma Schoonmaker]. *art d* – Boris Blank.

Galina Baliaeva (*Pavlova*), James Fox (*Victor d'Andre*), Sergei Shakourov (*Mikhail Fokine*), Vsevolod Larionov (*Sergei Diaghilev*), Lina Boultakova (*Pavlova as a child*), Martin Scorsese (*Gatti-Cassaza*), Bruce Forsyth (*Alfred Batt*), Roy Kinnear (*gardener*), etc.

155 mins [133 mins in UK]. *rel* – UK premiere 10 March 1985.

Anna Pavlova (1881–1931) was the most famous and probably wealthiest ballet dancer of all time. After establishing herself in St Petersburg, she began to tour internationally in 1908, sometimes with Diaghilev's Ballets Russes, before settling in London with her husband Victor d'Andre in 1912 and establishing a dance school. The film's origins lay in a project on the life of Pavlova that Erwin Hillier had brought to Powell. His then partner Frixos Constantine initiated a Russian-based international co-production, which was eventually written and directed by Emil Lotianou, with Powell credited only as Western Version Supervisor.

Index

Notes: Films listed by title are by Powell, or Powell and Pressburger, unless otherwise stated. Page numbers in **bold** indicate detailed analysis; those in *italic* refer to illustrations or extensively illustrated sections. *n* = endnote.